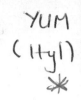

Writing and

Censorship affects us all. It is not a new issue: it has been a constant, if neglected, condition of writing for centuries. But what do we mean by freedom of speech? And who exercises the controls and constraints?

Writing and Censorship in Britain explores an issue of vital contemporary importance, from a range of cultural and literary perspectives, from the Tudor period to the present.

Written by some of the leading experts in the field, this major new collection charts struggles for artistic expression, reveals how censorship is appropriated as a legitimate tactic in the defence of oppressed and marginalised groups, and analyses the struggles writers have employed in the face of its complex dynamics.

Here variously defined, defended and deplored, censorship emerges as both an unstable and a potent concept. Through it we define ourselves: as readers, as writers and as citizens.

The editors: Paul Hyland and Neil Sammells are, respectively, Head of History and Senior Lecturer in English at Bath College of Higher Education.

Writing and Censorship in Britain

Edited by
Paul Hyland
and Neil Sammells

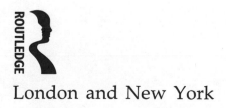

London and New York

First published 1992
by Routledge
11 New Fetter Lane, London EC4P 4EE

Simultaneously published in the USA and Canada
by Routledge
a division of Routledge, Chapman and Hall, Inc.
29 West 35th Street, New York, NY 10001

This collection © 1992 Routledge;
individual contributions © 1992 individual contributors

Typeset in 10 on 12 point Palatino by
Intype, London
Printed and bound in Great Britain by
T J Press (Padstow) Ltd, Padstow, Cornwall

British Library Cataloguing in Publication Data
Writing and Censorship in Britain
I. Hyland, Paul II. Sammells, Neil
363.3

Library of Congress Cataloging in Publication Data
Writing and censorship in Britain/edited by Paul Hyland
  and Neil Sammells.
     p. cm.
  Includes bibliographical references and index.
  1. Censorship—Great Britain—History. 2. English literature—
  Censorship—History. I. Hyland, Paul. II. Sammells, Neil.
Z658.G7W75 1992
025.2'13'0941—dc20   91–48118

ISBN 0–415–07332–4
     0–415–08353–2 (pbk)

Contents

Notes on the contributors   vii

Acknowledgements   ix

1 Writing and censorship: an introduction
Neil Sammells   1

Chronology   15

Part I: Tudors and Stuarts: castration and control

2 Censorship and the 1587 'Holinshed's' Chronicles
Annabel Patterson   23

3 'Those who else would turn all upside-down': censorship
and the assize sermon, 1660–1720
Barbara White   36

4 'All run now into Politicks': theatre censorship during
the Exclusion crisis, 1679–81
Janet Clare   46

Part II: The eighteenth century: liberty and licence

5 Richard Steele: scandal and sedition
Paul Hyland   59

6 John Gay: censoring the censors
Calhoun Winton   81

7 'An old tragedy on a disgusting subject': Horace Walpole
and *The Mysterious Mother*
Peter Sabor   91

8 'The memory of the liberty of the press': the suppression of radical writing in the 1790s
Alan Booth 107

Part III: The Victorian period: responsibility and repression

9 A land of relative freedom: censorship of the press and the arts in the nineteenth century (1815–1914)
Robert Justin Goldstein 125

10 Blasphemy, obscenity and the courts: contours of tolerance in nineteenth-century England
M. J. D. Roberts 141

11 Victorian obscenity law: negative censorship or positive administration?
David Saunders 154

12 'The physiological facts': Thomas Hardy, censorship and narrative breakdown
Richard Kerridge 171

Part IV: The twentieth century: radicals and readers

13 Censorship and the Great War: the first test of new statesmanship
Adrian Smith 185

14 D. H. Lawrence: a suitable case for censorship
Damian Grant 200

15 The treatment of homosexuality and *The Well of Loneliness*
Katrina Rolley 219

16 Censorship and children's literature: some post-war trends
Peter Barry 232

17 Joyce, postculture and censorship
Richard Brown 243

Select bibliography 259
Index 262

Notes on the contributors

PETER BARRY is Principal Lecturer in English at La Sainte Union College of Higher Education, Southampton. He writes on children's literature and is editor of the journal *English*.

ALAN BOOTH is Lecturer in History at the University of Nottingham. He has published widely on Britain in the 1790s and is currently working on a study of eighteenth-century politics and propaganda.

RICHARD BROWN is Lecturer in English at the University of Leeds, where he heads the Joyce research group. Among his publications is *James Joyce and Sexuality*.

JANET CLARE is Lecturer in English at Bath College of Higher Education. She is the author of *'Art Made Tongue-tied by Authority': Elizabethan and Jacobean Dramatic Censorship*.

ROBERT JUSTIN GOLDSTEIN is Professor of Political Science at Oakland University, Michigan. Among his books are *Political Repression in 19th Century Europe* and *Political Censorship of the Arts and the Press in Nineteenth-Century Europe*.

DAMIAN GRANT is Senior Lecturer in English at the University of Manchester. He is the author of *Tobias Smollett* and *Realism*. He is currently working on a study of D. H. Lawrence.

PAUL HYLAND is Head of History at Bath College of Higher Education. He has produced a modern-language edition of Ned Ward's *London Spy* and is co-editor, with Neil Sammells, of *Irish Writing: Exile and Subversion*. He is joint-editor (with Neil Sammells) of *Irish Studies Review*.

RICHARD KERRIDGE is a postgraduate student at the University of Cambridge. He has published on nineteenth-century fiction, and has twice won the British Broadcasting Corporation's prize for nature writing.

ANNABEL PATTERSON is Professor of English at Duke University, North Carolina. Her many publications include *Censorship and Interpretation: the Conditions of Writing and Reading in Early Modern England*.

M. J. D. ROBERTS is Senior Lecturer in Modern History at Macquarie University, Sydney. He is the author of articles on nineteenth-century moral reform and is completing a book on volunteer movements for the reform of morals and manners in England 1787–1886.

KATRINA ROLLEY is a dress historian and teaches at Middlesex Polytechnic. She has published on lesbian dress and identity and is the joint author of a forthcoming book on fashion from 1900 to 1920.

PETER SABOR is Professor of English at Queen's University, Ontario. In addition to his books on Horace Walpole, he has recently co-edited *Samuel Richardson: Tercentenary Essays* and Frances Burney's *Cecilia* and *The Wanderer*.

NEIL SAMMELLS is Senior Lecturer in English at Bath College of Higher Education. He is the author of *Tom Stoppard: the Artist as Critic* and co-editor, with Paul Hyland, of *Irish Writing: Exile and Subversion*. He is joint-General Editor (also with Paul Hyland) of *Crosscurrents*, published by Longman.

DAVID SAUNDERS teaches in Humanities at Griffith University, Brisbane. He is co-author of *On Pornography: Literature, Sexuality and Obscenity Law* and author of *Authorship and Copyright*.

ADRIAN SMITH is Principal Lecturer in History at La Sainte Union College of Higher Education, Southampton. He is currently working on a history of the Ministry of Defence since 1945.

BARBARA WHITE is Senior Tutor for Advanced Studies in England, having previously taught at the Open University. She is currently preparing a modern-language edition of the memoirs of a seventeenth-century criminal, Mary Carleton.

CALHOUN WINTON is Professor of English at the University of Maryland. He is the author of many articles in eighteenth-century studies, a two-volume biography of Richard Steele and a forthcoming book on *John Gay and his Theatre*.

Acknowledgements

We wish to thank the contributors to this book for their commitment and enthusiasm, and for responding with patience and good humour to our cavils and queries. Thanks are also due to colleagues at Bath College of Higher Education for their interest and support.

P.H.
N.S.

Chapter 1

Writing and censorship: an introduction

Neil Sammells

'Censorship,' claims Jolyon Jenkins, 'never really goes away: it just changes its form.' He cites as evidence the abolition of stage-censorship in 1967 and the creation, twenty-one years later, of the Broadcasting Standards Council: 'We get rid of the Lord Chamberlain, and get Lord Rees-Mogg instead.' For Jenkins, the aristocratic nomenclature is both significant and symptomatic. Censorship, he insists, is 'rarely if ever determined by any democratic process, but by the interests of powerful elites.'[1] This assessment is typical of a dominant modern tradition in writing about censorship in Britain. Censorship is thus defined as the repressive intervention of authority, its presence traced most clearly in the operations of law. Jenkins also adopts a characteristic tone: the subject is tackled with indignation, modulated by a sense of almost mournful resignation.

The best-known surveys in this tradition are those by Donald Thomas and David Tribe.[2] Significant books with a narrower focus include those by F. S. Siebert and John Sutherland.[3] Richard Davenport-Hines's account of attitudes to sex in Britain has a broader target, but he has much to say about the treatment of writers and writing.[4] All contend, like Jenkins, that the history of censorship in Britain is not a history of progress. None shares the simple optimism of the Victorian historian H. T. Buckle, who proclaimed in his *History of Civilisation in England* (1857–61) that the disappearance of pre-publication censorship, with the lapsing of the Licensing Act in 1695, laid the foundations 'of that great Public Press, which, more than any other single cause, has diffused among the people a knowledge of their power and has thus, to an almost incredible extent, aided the progress of English civilisation'.[5] For Thomas, the processes of censorship are self-replicating. There is, he argues, little real difference, for instance, between the 1857 Obscene Publications Act ('Lord Campbell's Act') and its 1959 successor, despite the latter's attempt to protect literature by distinguishing it from pornography. Both Acts, he insists, 'accept the hypothesis that literature may deprave and corrupt its readers, though the later Act with a Victorian regard for Great Books, specifies literary merit as an extenuating circumstance'.[6]

Thomas is typical, also, in writing about censorship out of a sense of crisis. He sees in the technology of the later twentieth century a means of 'silencing men' which, though bloodless, 'might have been the envy of the Tudors and the Stuarts'.[7] Siebert's treatment of press freedom is predicated on his Cold-War assumptions about communism.[8] David Tribe writes as a member of the Executive Committee of the National Council for Civil Liberties, wary of the threat to individual freedoms from ever-more sophisticated information-gathering by the state.[9] In this respect, John Sutherland's case is, perhaps, the most complex. He presents us with a troubled teleology. He claims that 'liberalisation was fought every inch, but its tide in the 1960s was irresistible'. However, his attitude to the fruits of this decensorship is far from unambivalent; indeed, his response to the loosening of controls on pornography is a powerful evocation of the liberal's dilemma: 'It is possible to browse with equanimity through Foyles [bookshop] and congratulate one's country on the degree of literary freedom it tolerates. Walk a hundred yards west, through Soho, and I, for one, feel a Kurtzian exterminatory rage.'[10] The crisis that confronts Sutherland is one created by the debate about censorship itself, as its parameters are redrawn – most clearly by feminism. Davenport-Hines, however, presents his readers with a less abstract crisis: the physical threat of AIDS, as 'a Copernican event in the history of sexuality'. Attitudes to AIDS replicate earlier attitudes to syphilis and syphilitics, he claims; we take refuge in ignorance and silence. Of the Government's suppression of a report by the Aids Advisory Committee on drug-use and sexual intercourse in jails, Davenport-Hines notes: 'The only immorality is to facilitate the spread of HIV by the suppression or denial of truth.'[11] Censorship doesn't go away, it just changes its form, and it can kill.

That censorship might kill would come as no surprise, of course, to Salman Rushdie. The publication of his *The Satanic Verses* in September 1988, and the response of the Muslim world – including the Ayatollah Khomeini's proclamation of a *fatwa*, or death-sentence, against Rushdie in 1989 – has intensified the sense of crisis so characteristic of current debate. For many, the Rushdie affair has simply reconfirmed the terms of the argument: censorship is about the power of collective interests over individual interests; it is an attempt to silence the dissenting voice. Rushdie's initial tactics in the face of such potentially lethal opposition were an attempt to define his dilemma in precisely this way. 'One of the reasons for writing,' he claimed on television in January 1989, 'is to slightly increase the sum of what it's possible to think.' 'Let us never believe,' he insisted, 'that the way in which people in power tell us to look at the world is the only way we can look.' To do so would be 'a kind of appalling self-censorship'. *The Satanic Verses*, he pointed out, was born of his fascination with the very notion of censorship and with the conflict between 'the sacred text and the profane text, between revealed literature and imagined literature'.[12]

For his supporters, such as Michael Foot, Rushdie's defence of the free creative spirit, and its incarnation in imaginative literature, placed him alongside such heroic opponents of religious intolerance as Montaigne, Swift and Voltaire. For others, like Anthony Burgess, Rushdie's predicament prompted a call to the barricades; the *fatwa* was tantamount to a *jihad*, or 'a declaration of war on citizens of a free country and as such it is a political act. It has to be countered by an equally forthright, if less murderous, declaration of defiance.'[13] Such militancy was eschewed by the editors of *The Rushdie File*, a collection of documents outlining the events and arguments of this contemporary *cause célèbre*. Instead, they evinced a touching faith in the healing properties of education, information and reason: 'We hope that the File will help people to think through the affair; hope, too, that somehow we learn to live with our differences in a spirit of toleration.'[14] Unfortunately for many of Rushdie's defenders, the iconic status afforded him in the mythology of western liberal humanism has been tarnished somewhat by his announcement of his conversion to Islam.

A further dimension to the debate over *The Satanic Verses* has been its implications for what John Sutherland calls 'The censorship of enlightenment'. Sutherland is chiefly concerned with militant developments in the late 1970s and early 1980s which altered perspectives on censorship. The obscenity trial of the editors of the magazine *OZ* in 1971 had, for 'progressive opinion', posed a simple choice: between an enlightened sexual and political radicalism, and the repressive hypocrisy of the old guard. By the end of the decade, however, the situation was more complicated. In some 'leftist' quarters, censorship had come to be regarded as a legitimate tactic in the defence of oppressed or marginalised groups: a significant movement away from an overriding emphasis on the plight of the individual. In this respect, the most important contribution came from feminists such as Susan Brownmiller and Andrea Dworkin – the latter's *Pornography: Men Possessing Women* (1981) redefined the obscene and the pornographic as that containing or condoning violence against women. The logic of such an argument could, as Sutherland notes, be extended to cover other threatened or vilified groups, such as gays and blacks.[15] In the present book, Peter Barry charts the activities of such 'censorship of enlightenment' in writing for children: the attempts to ensure its ideological soundness by purging it of any traces of racism or sexism.

Under this kind of radical pressure, the editors of a journal such as the *New Statesman* could find themselves, according to Sutherland, 'strongly in favour of censorship of the doctrinaire kind that would have made them indignant some years earlier'.[16] These realignments in attitudes to censorship have created uncomfortable and inelegant alliances, particularly between some feminists and conservative anti-pornography campaigners anxious to protect 'the family' against a host of demons, including feminism. The Rushdie affair has, in this respect, produced some equally curious spectacles. Perhaps none was stranger than that, in 1989, of left-wing Labour MPs, such as Bernie Grant and Brian Sedgemoor, joining Conservatives in supporting an unsuccessful Early Day Motion in the House of Commons to extend the law of blasphemy to religions other than Christianity.

However manifold and pointed its ironies, the 'censorship of enlightenment' is clear in its challenging of liberal assumptions about the primacy of the individual, and the central function of freedom of expression in guaranteeing political freedoms. Such assumptions have deep roots. The classic texts in establishing this tradition are Milton's *Areopagitica* (1644), Locke's *Letters Concerning Toleration* (1689–92) and Mill's *On Liberty* (1859). Milton's attack on censorship, in the name of Protestantism, is premised on the notion, according to Christopher Hill, that 'given freedom of debate, the reason which is common to all men is likely to lead them to recognize the same truths'. To censor a book is, then, to stifle debate and to kill reason, the image of God in man. Milton defines censorship as popish: it is a familiar and oft-repeated tactic, one which insists that censorship is something which happens elsewhere and is foreign to the British way of life. Similarly foreign and pernicious is Plato's *The Republic*. Milton dismisses Plato's contention that the first step towards guaranteeing the health of the body politic is to establish a censorship of the writers of fiction, allowing only such tales as inculcate right-doing. These tolerationist considerations do not, however, prevent Milton from drawing the line at Roman Catholicism, which he regards as mere 'priestly despotism'.[17]

Mill follows Milton in identifying censorship as an index of despotism, and assumes his premises to be unanswerable: 'The time, it is to be hoped, is gone by, when any defence would be necessary of the "liberty of the press" as one of the securities against corrupt or tyrannical government.'[18] For Marxists, however, this is far from self-evident. Herbert Marcuse's 1965 essay, 'Repressive tolerance', for instance, is a determined dismantling of what he calls Mill's 'liberalist theory'. Milton had claimed of censorship that it guaranteed only a dull conformity; Marcuse says the same of freedom of expression. The term is rendered meaningless when, in practice, 'toleration is administered to manipulated and indoctrinated individuals who parrot, as their

own, the opinion of their masters'. For Marcuse, tolerance is an instrument for the continuation of servitude; firmly established liberal
societies such as Britain and the United States granted freedom of
speech and assembly to their enemies 'provided they did not make
the transition from word to deed, from speech to action'.[19] No genuine
grasp of alternatives, no real chance of liberation, is possible until
'false consciousness' is destroyed. This can only be done by 'stopping
the words and images which feed this consciousness'. Paradoxically,
freedom is to be found only in censorship. Marcuse is explicit in what
he advocates: 'To be sure, this is censorship, even precensorship,
but openly directed against the more or less hidden censorship that
permeates the free media.'[20]

Marcuse identifies freedom of expression as an ideological construct
with specific functions in western democratic societies and cultures.
In his view, it can only be effectively countered by a censorship which
is not repressive, but creative. His 'problematisation' of such apparently easy terms as repression, tolerance and censorship anticipates
the recent work of the French social scientist Michel Foucault. Foucault, though, is not just anti-liberal, he is anti-Marxist too: 'the search
for a general theory of history is not on his agenda'. What he offers
instead 'is a constant pluralizing and decapitalizing of all the great
concepts, first principles, and fundamental grounds that our [western]
tradition has produced'.[21] Central to this deconstructive strategy is
Foucault's analysis of the different ways in which we, as human beings
operating within a given culture, are made subjects; that is to say,
'subject to someone else by control and dependence' and tied to our
identities 'by a conscience or self-knowledge'.[22] Foucault maintains that
sexuality is fundamental to these processes of self-formulation and
self-subjugation. However, Foucault counsels us against regarding
sexuality as a 'natural given' which must be kept in check by power.
In his narrative of sexuality as a historical construct, censorship plays
a more subtle and paradoxical role than might be expected by those
who regard it simply as an agent of prohibition.

Foucault's analysis of censorship is focused on his redefinition of
Victorianism. In Volume 1 of *The History of Sexuality* (1976) he sums
up what he refers to as 'the repressive hypothesis': our 'restrained,
mute, and hypocritical society' is, to this day, dominated by a prudery
inherited from the nineteenth century in which, on matters of sex,
silence became the rule and 'the legitimate and procreative couple laid
down the law' (pp. 292–3). Untrammelled sex could only be practised
– and spoken about – in the dangerous margins: the brothel and the
mental hospital. Foucault turns this notion of Victorianism and its
legacy upside down. Far from being characterised by prohibition and
silence, the Victorian period was, he argues, dedicated to incitement

– to the creation of new ways of talking about sex, to the proliferation of discourses about sex, particularly the medical and the legal. Seen from this angle, the anonymous author of *My Secret Life* is not a courageous fugitive from Victorianism; his detailed narrative of a life dedicated to libertinism makes him, instead, the embodiment of the true spirit of his age, 'the most naive representative of a plurisecular injunction to talk about sex' (p. 305). Such incitement operated not only at the level of discourse, but at the level of practice too. Foucault claims that the Victorian Age was characterised by 'a dispersion of sexualities, a strengthening of their disparate forms, a multiple implantation of "perversions" ' (p. 317). This multiplication of sexual possibilities and pleasures was not a threat to authority, but an aspect of power itself – and an opportunity to exercise it. Sex now became something that needed to be administered and managed, rather than simply judged: 'the end of good government is the correct disposition of things – even when these things have to be invented so as to be well-governed.'[23]

According to Foucault, censorship operates as a paradoxical tactic within this general strategy of incitement. This is most obviously the case in the peculiar allure of the censored. There is gratification to be found in defining the relationship between sex and power in terms of repression; the defiance of taboos seems an act of self-assertion, a declaration of individuality, and a form of political statement. As Foucault puts it:

> If sex is repressed, that is, condemned to prohibition, nonexistence, and silence, then the mere fact that one is speaking about it has the appearance of a deliberate transgression. A person who holds forth in such language places himself to a certain extent outside the reach of power; he upsets established law; he somehow anticipates the coming freedom.
>
> (p. 295)

Foucault here finds himself in the same camp as Quentin Crisp, who dismisses this individualist fantasy of repression and defiance with characteristic insouciance. He claims that, considering censorship in general terms, he has never felt those vague feelings of frustration that most men (but no women) have expressed to him at one time or another. He also recalls that when he has demanded of the aggrieved in what wild excesses they would indulge if nothing prevented them, their answers have been puerile:

> They don't really know what they would do or say if all taboos were removed but they feel a very real anger. Of this we have evidence when they are drunk. Then they climb up lamp-posts,

insult strangers, sing loudly in the street or embark on some other pointless folly.[24]

Crisp and Foucault are united in recognising that power and pleasure are indivisible, that they are bound together in excitation and incitement. The same is true of the relationship between expression and censorship. In chapter 7, for instance, Peter Sabor examines the extraordinary self-censorship imposed by Horace Walpole on his incest-tragedy *The Mysterious Mother*; Walpole's prolonged and elaborate strategy ensured that the work acquired a distinctive and potent glamour, the *frisson* of the forbidden. The text's suppression became not a barrier but a means to its articulation.

Foucault is not the first to recognise that censorship can incite rather than prohibit. In 1625 Francis Bacon claimed that the suppression of seditious publications could simply turn them into 'a wonder long-lived'.[25] One of the main planks of Milton's tolerationist argument in *Areopagitica* was a similar belief that suppressing sects and texts could only help them to spread.[26] In the 1920s, Bertrand Russell questioned the wisdom of censoring pornography; he thought nine-tenths of its appeal was due to its 'secrecy and stealth' and the 'indecent feelings concerning sex which moralists inculcate in the young'.[27] This anti-censorship argument finds proof positive in the history of Lawrence's *Lady Chatterley's Lover*; its publishers having been prosecuted in 1960 under the Obscene Publications Act of 1959, the novel sold six million copies in Britain alone over the next twenty years. The case of Howard Brenton's *The Romans in Britain* (1980) is similar. In 1982, Mary Whitehouse brought a private prosecution, under the Sexual Offences Act of 1956, against Michael Bogdanov, the director of the National Theatre production, for procuring an act of gross indecency between two actors. (Brenton's play presented buggery as a metaphorical and literal representation of imperialism, pointing the finger at Britain's presence in Ireland. This confirms Quentin Crisp's observation that the two main subjects to which a censor might object are sex and politics, and that it must be hard to decide which is the more filthy.) Norman St John Stevas claimed in the House of Commons that 'attacks on this play at the National have had one effect – to fill the theatre'.[28] The point is made forcibly by Jolyon Jenkins; the spiritual heirs of John Stuart Mill can take heart from one fact, he assures us: 'as every attempt at suppression shows, from *Lady Chatterley*, to *Inside Linda Lovelace*, to *Spycatcher*, censorship doesn't work.'[29] The 'counter-effects' of censorship can thus be seen as testimony to the resilience and fertility of the individual voice, and to the self-defeating obduracy of authority. To Foucault, they are nothing of the sort: censorship always works – not as prohibition, but as power.

David Saunders's chapter in this book is an application of Foucauldian analysis to the techniques of power in Victorian society. He restates Foucault's denial of the repressive hypothesis and claims that Victorian censorship in relation to pornography was an attempt to exercise good government by paying specific attention to the differing capacities of possible readerships. The specific danger of cheap editions of 'pornographic' literature was that they might fall into the hands of the vulnerable; Saunders argues that this amounts to the enlightened sensitivity which we might recognise in contemporary reception theory. The potency of cheap editions has been a recurring theme in debates about censorship in Britain, and in its application to specific cases. Donald Thomas points out, for instance, that while William Pitt, as Prime Minister, approved of the prosecution of Tom Paine in 1792 for his publication of *The Rights of Man* at a price the working man, and woman, could afford, he made no attempt to suppress William Godwin's radical *Enquiry Concerning Political Justice* (1793) because it cost three guineas a copy.[30] The same concerns can be seen at work in the *Lady Chatterley's Lover* trial. In his opening address, Counsel for the Prosecution, Mervyn Griffith-Jones, asked the jurors whether they would approve of their young sons and young daughters – 'because girls can read as well as boys' – reading the novel. 'Is it a book,' he continued, with a rhetorical flourish, 'that you would leave lying around in your own house? Is it a book that you would even wish your wife or your servants to read?'[31] As with the prosecution of the Mayflower edition of John Cleland's *Fanny Hill* in 1964 – this time successful – it is difficult to assuage the suspicion that these three-and-sixpenny paperbacks were on trial as much for their price as for their content: they could now be purchased and read by anyone, not just by the expert witnesses produced to testify to their literary worth. Richard Davenport-Hines points to similar attitudes when *Mein Kampf* was issued in English paperback translation in 1972. He also draws attention to another oddity produced by the Rushdie affair: Roy Hattersley, the Deputy Leader of the Labour Party, opposing, in 1989, a paperback edition of *The Satanic Verses* for reasons Griffith-Jones might not have found incomprehensible. For Davenport-Hines the Foucauldian conclusions of David Saunders would, no doubt, smack less of sophistication than of sophistry. Davenport-Hines declares of the endemic fear of cheap editions that 'this patronizing censorship based on class discrimination remains at the heart of British public life'.[32]

Foucault's notion of sexuality, and its relationship to authority and power, runs directly counter to the central tenets of Freudianism – as outlined most clearly in *The Interpretation of Dreams* (1900) and *Three Essays on the Theory of Sexuality* (1905). Freud argues that the personality is a site for conflicting forces. The *id*, the *ego* and the *superego* play their antagonistic roles in the psycho-sexual melodrama which each of us acts out in our growth to maturity. The Reality Principle eventually triumphs: the father threatens the male child's Oedipal desire for the mother with the punishment of castration. Sexual desire is thus repressed and the male child is able to identify with the place and function of the father. This amounts to the development of the *super-ego*, and the child's acceptance of morality, law and religion – in effect, the whole panoply of patriarchal constraint. However, repressed desire does not simply disappear: it sinks back into the unconscious. Dreams testify to these energies at work in the personality. They are the result of the attempts of the 'split subject' to manage the yearnings of the unconscious. Freudian psychoanalysis is, then, a therapeutic process in which unconscious desires are placed and acknowledged.

Freud assumes the relationship between pleasure and power to be conflictual, rather than – as Foucault argues – complicitous. It is not, therefore, surprising to discover that Freudianism informs, in many cases, those definitions of censorship which deplore it as the agency of external constraint and repressive authority, and as a denial of the deep, creative drives of the individual personality. Donald Tribe, for instance, declares a clear and unproblematic link between sex and liberty: those who call for sexual freedom usually demand religious, social and political freedoms as well. Writing in 1973, Tribe would have had in mind the sort of claim made by Germaine Greer in 1971, when trumpeting the cause of sexual liberation: 'censorship is the outward and continuing expression of the distortion of the human erotic faculty. It is the one public point at which we can join battle with what enslaves us.'[33] Greer's 'counter-culture' sentiments were shared by the editors of *OZ* who in the same year were imprisoned for joining the battle and suggesting, among other incendiary matter, that Rupert Bear was equipped with outsize reproductive organs. Tribe compounds his point with an identification which, in the wake of the AIDS epidemic, looks positively prelapsarian; describing ours as an age that calls for participatory democracy, he names sex as 'the most direct and personal form of participation'.[34] In *Sex, Death and Punishment*, Davenport-Hines is more inclined to associate sex with the isolation-ward than the ballot-box. Nevertheless, he shares Tribe's Freudian premises. Society's ever-present need to vilify homo- or bisexuality, and to censor that which might contribute to its contagion, is explained for him by the psychoanalytic notion of projection 'whereby emotions, vices and qualities which an individual either rejects or refuses to recognize in himself are expelled from the self and relocated in another person or persons'.[35] Such transference might also involve, as Richard Webster believes, exporting the very need to censor:

> Hating in the figure of the censor what we cannot acknowledge in ourselves, we imagine that we are opposed not to another human being, but to a kind of devil incarnate – an agent of absolute purity and cruel repressiveness to whom we attribute quite unrealistic powers.[36]

Censorship thus acquires a demonology of its own, in which special status is accorded to such as Sir William Joynson-Hicks, the Home Secretary loathed by, among many others, D. H. Lawrence (as Damian Grant tells us in chapter 14) and, in our own day, to Mary Whitehouse and the Muslim burners of *The Satanic Verses*.

Freudian approaches to censorship tend to see it as both immutable and implacable: rooted deep in the human psyche, yet fundamentally antagonistic to the desires and needs of individuals. However, seen from another angle, Freud and Foucault stand closer than this suggests. In a sense, Freud acknowledges that censorship can be creative; in Foucauldian terms, it has the power to *produce* as it polices. This is clearly the case in our dream-processes: the images and narratives we construct are the result of a censoring of the unconscious, of its turbulent and 'seditious' demands. The unconscious is not reduced to silence, but impelled to strange articulacy. These insights shape a branch of contemporary literary theory which sees in psychoanalysis a model for the relationship between the reader and a text. Like a therapist, the reader must attend to the unspoken, unconscious meanings beneath the surface of a given text: to what it cannot say, and to the ways it finds of not saying it. Imaginative writing is defined by absences and indirections. For psychoanalytic literary theory, what we understand by 'literature' is not threatened by censorship – it is produced by censorship.

Annabel Patterson's *Censorship and Interpretation: the Conditions of Writing and Reading in Early Modern England* (1984) is a significant non-Freudian variation on the idea that literature is the result – rather than simply the target – of censorship-pressures. 'It is to censorship,' she argues, 'that we in part owe our very concept of "literature", as a kind of discourse with rules of its own.'[37] From the middle of the sixteenth century, she points out, writers developed codes of communication in order to say what they had to publicly, without directly confronting or provoking the authorities. In other words, ambiguity became a social and cultural force of considerable consequence. We might say that writers and censors colluded rather than collided. Both sides entered into a 'cultural bargain', the terms of which were fully intelligible to each. This bargain meant that any writer was aware of how far he or she could go in addressing contentious issues, how to encode their opinions so that nobody would be *required* to make an example of them. Less scholarly, but more stylish, is Quentin Crisp's comparable definition of literature in terms of its ubiquitous obliquity: a consideration which allows him to come out on the side of censorship. When censorship laws were more strict, he says, meanings had to be implied rather than stated; this evoked in writers a delicacy and finesse 'which in turn quickened the imagination of a reader or moviegoer'. He feels it probable that his own work has never given offence because 'even at school I never formed the habit of using the shortest words for the longest things'. Of the furore over attempts in America to ban Robert Mapplethorpe's explicit photographs celebrating the pyrotechnics of gay sex, Crisp is impatient: the aesthetes behaved like precocious children who, as soon as anything is forbidden, want it. Art should be made so difficult that only the most dedicated practitioners would persist: 'if censorship were more strict, artists in whatever medium might work more carefully and, with luck, produce less.'[38]

The desire to characterise literature in terms of its slipperiness – its obliquity, ambivalence and ambiguity – is shared by John Sutherland. He contends that Parliament, and still more courts, are 'bad places in which to evaluate literature'. The critic, he tells us, respects complexity and undertone. In the witness-box, called as an 'expert' to testify to literary worth (under the auspices of the 1959 Obscene Publications Act), he or she is called upon to 'talk down, to oversimplify, to lie'.[39] This approach, then, rests on a relatively unproblematic definition of literature as privileged discourse. Literature distances itself from other kinds of writing, which can, indeed should, be evaluated by blunter and cruder criteria; in this respect, Sutherland's position is typically liberal-humanist. Such emphasis on literary value can, however, produce curious alliances. Despite his subversion of 'bourgeois' notions of toleration and repression, for instance, Herbert Marcuse also actively promotes a vision of art and literature as occupying a special space (what he calls the 'aesthetic dimension'), and displaying special virtues. Indeed, for Marcuse, literature acquires a force that is almost redemptive. He cites Baudelaire on the 'destructive tolerance' of art by capitalism; the radical impact of art, its inevitable protest 'against established reality', is allowed to spend itself in the marketplace. In other words, literature is defined by the challenge it presents to established order, an order all-too-skilled in absorbing it and putting a price upon it. 'The authentic *oeuvre*,' says Marcuse, 'is not and cannot be a prop of oppression, and pseudo-art (which can be such a prop) is not art.'[40] In other words, the censorship – 'even precensorship' – which Marcuse calls for can be founded in a clear distinction between types of discourse: the privileged and the non-privileged. This clarity allows Marcuse to declare that censorship of art and literature is always regressive. In the Marcusean future there will be no censorship of writing that is art because there will be no need for it; any writing which needed to be censored could not have been art. Marcuse would, presumably, also share Sutherland's scepticism about the usefulness of literary critics as expert witnesses to these qualitative differences.

As we have seen in Salman Rushdie's distinction between the profane text and the sacred text, considerations of 'literariness' and its definition in terms of censorship have been central to the debate over *The Satanic Verses*. Carlos Fuentes, for example, draws upon Bakhtin in his defence of Rushdie and the 'dialogic novel'. For the Ayatollahs, maintains Fuentes, reality is 'dogmatically defined once and for all in a sacred text. But a sacred text is, by definition, a completed and exclusive text. You can add nothing to it. It does not converse with anyone.' The sacred text sets up a monologue; the profane text, by which Fuentes principally means the novel in the western tradition, sets up a dialogue. The novel 'is the privileged arena where languages in conflict can meet'. This is no gratuitous exercise, it reveals 'that, in dialogue, no one is absolutely right; neither speaker holds an absolute truth, or, indeed, has an absolute hold over history'.[41] Western democracy is synonymous with the willingness to listen; totalitarianism announces itself with a single voice, and is dedicated to the silencing of others. It is a familiar formulation, and one which lends itself to dramatic representation, as in Tom Stoppard's plays about the eastern bloc, such as *Every Good Boy Deserves Favour* (1977), *Professional Foul* (1978) and *Squaring the Circle* (1984), and in those extolling life in democratic Britain, such as *The Real Thing* (1982).[42] (There are similar preoccupations in Harold Pinter's recent 'dramaticules' – such as *One for the Road* (1984) – presenting nightmarish interrogations.) Fuentes ends with another familiar declaration, that censorship doesn't work: 'by making the imagination so dangerous that it deserves Capital punishment, the sectarians have made people everywhere wonder what it is that literature can say that can be so powerful and, indeed, so dangerous.'[43] In effect, Fuentes, no less than Sutherland, Marcuse and others, is attempting to confirm not just differences between discourses, but a hierarchy of discourses – with the 'literary' at the top.

This collection accepts no such sharp and ready distinctions between types of writing. It avoids a narrow concern with literature to the exclusion of other kinds of writing, and with literary criticism to the exclusion of other kinds of analysis. Essays on famous writers (such as Hardy, Lawrence or Joyce) and specific texts (for instance, Shakespeare's *Richard II*, John Gay's *The Beggar's Opera*, Radclyffe Hall's *The*

Well of Loneliness) are placed alongside those dealing with material which is decidedly non-literary, even 'ephemeral': sermons, journalism, political pamphlets, writing for children. This breadth of focus is matched by the diversity of approaches. Censorship and its effects are variously defined, described, defended and deplored. Despite the chronology which follows, we offer no neat narrative; censorship is an unstable concept which cannot support such historical certainty. For me, two reflections arise most insistently from these contributions. First, censorship never goes away, and it *always* works – inscribing itself even in those texts which seek and seem to elude it. Second, censorship is a notion of extraordinary potency. Through it we define ourselves as readers, as writers, and as citizens.

NOTES

1 J. Jenkins, 'The public interest', in D. Jones and S. Platt (eds), *Banned*, London, Channel 4 Television, 1991, p. 4.
2 D. Thomas, *A Long Time Burning: the History of Literary Censorship in Britain*, London, Routledge & Kegan Paul, 1969. D. Tribe, *Questions of Censorship*, London, Allen & Unwin, 1973.
3 F. S. Siebert, *Freedom of the Press in England, 1476–1776*, Urbana, University of Illinois Press, 1965. J. Sutherland, *Offensive Literature: Decensorship in Britain, 1960–1982*, London, Junction Books, 1982.
4 R. Davenport-Hines, *Sex, Death and Punishment: Attitudes to Sex and Sexuality in Britain since the Renaissance*, London, Fontana, 1991.
5 Quoted in Thomas, *A Long Time Burning*, p. 6.
6 ibid., p. 292.
7 ibid., p. 318.
8 Siebert, *Freedom of the Press in England*, p. 13.
9 Tribe, *Questions of Censorship*, p. 17.
10 Sutherland, *Offensive Literature*, pp. 2, 9.
11 Davenport-Hines, *Sex, Death and Punishment*, pp. 1, 362.
12 In L. Appignanesi and S. Maitland (eds), *The Rushdie File*, London, Fourth Estate, 1989, pp. 29–30.
13 ibid., p. 102.
14 ibid., p. vii.
15 Sutherland, *Offensive Literature*, p. 193.
16 ibid. Sutherland also claims that David Caute, the literary editor, resigned in 1981 in protest at the journal's 'book-burning' campaign against children's literature. For a discussion of the *New Statesman*'s stand *against* censorship in an earlier era, see A. Smith's chapter in this volume.
17 C. Hill, *Milton and the English Revolution*, London, Faber, 1977, pp. 150, 154.
18 J. S. Mill, 'On Liberty', cited in E. Widmer (ed.), *Freedom and Culture: Literary Censorship in the 1970s*, Belmont, Calif., Wadsworth, 1970, p. 11.
19 H. Marcuse, 'Repressive tolerance', cited in Widmer (ed.), *Freedom and Culture*, pp. 29–30.
20 ibid., p. 36.

21 P. Rabinow (ed.), *The Foucault Reader*, Harmondsworth, Penguin, 1984, pp. 12, 14.
22 M. Foucault, in *The Foucault Reader*, p. 21. All subsequent references to Foucault's writings are to this edition and are included parenthetically in the text.
23 P. Rabinow, in *The Foucault Reader*, p. 21.
24 Q. Crisp, 'Arts diary', *Guardian*, 11 April 1991, p. 22.
25 Quoted in A. Patterson, *Censorship and Interpretation: the Conditions of Writing and Reading in Early Modern England*, Madison, University of Wisconsin Press, 1984, p. 14.
26 See Hill, *Milton and the English Revolution*, p. 153. Hill gives an ironic example of what Milton meant: the Protestant Thomas James, Bodley's first Librarian, used the Roman Catholic list of banned texts and writers – the *Index Librorum Prohibitorum* of 1559 – to order books for his library.
27 Quoted in G. Robertson, *Obscenity: an Account of Censorship Laws and their Enforcement in England and Wales*, London, Weidenfeld & Nicolson, 1979, p. 38.
28 Quoted in Sutherland, *Offensive Literature*, p. 183.
29 Jenkins, 'The Public Interest', p. 4.
30 See Thomas, *A Long Time Burning*, p. 3.
31 Quoted in Sutherland, *Offensive Literature*, p. 23.
32 Davenport-Hines, *Sex, Death and Punishment*, pp. 226–7.
33 Quoted by R. Webster, 'Stealing the Goose', in Jones and Platt (eds), *Banned*, p. 25.
34 Tribe, *Questions of Censorship*, p. 12.
35 Davenport-Hines, *Sex, Death and Punishment*, p. 3.
36 Webster, 'Stealing the Goose', in Jones and Platt (eds), *Banned*, p. 25.
37 Patterson, *Censorship and Interpretation*, p. 4.
38 Crisp, 'Arts Diary', p. 22.
39 Sutherland, *Offensive Literature*, p. 9.
40 Marcuse, 'Repressive tolerance', p. 30.
41 C. Fuentes, in Appignanesi and Maitland (eds), *The Rushdie File*, p. 245.
42 See N. Sammells, *Tom Stoppard: the Artist as Critic*, London, Macmillan, 1988.
43 Fuentes, in Appignanesi and Maitland (eds), *The Rushdie File*, p. 246.

Chronology

1534 Henry VIII's parliament makes it possible to commit treason 'by words or writing'.

1538 Henry VIII replaces the Church with the Privy Council as the licensing authority for printed publications. The Star Chamber (which could impose mutilation, hanging and disembowelment) and the Court of High Commission exercise jurisdiction over offences against the licensing laws. This licensing system, in a variety of forms, is the basis for pre-publication censorship until 1695.

1545 The Master of the King's Revels is appointed official stage-censor.

1559 A list of banned books is issued by the Roman Catholic Church: the first *Index Librorum Prohibitorum*. The *Index* will later proscribe specific books, like Samuel Richardson's *Pamela* (1741), as well as all the works of such writers as Hume, Zola, Maeterlinck, Sartre, Moravia, Gide.

1579 Elizabeth I attempts to have an author, Stubbe, hanged for felonious writings, but the grand jury refuses to indict. Instead, Stubbe is convicted under one of the statutes of *Scandalum Magnatum*, which date from 1275 and which make it illegal to invent or spread 'false news' about the monarchy or magnates of the realm. Stubbe saves his neck but loses a hand.

1633 William Prynne, having deviously obtained a licence for his book, is tried for seditious libel by Star Chamber for publishing *Histriomastix* ('Women Actors notorious Whores') a few weeks before the Queen acts in a pastoral. Prynne is fined £5,000, imprisoned for life and has both his ears cut off in the pillory. He continues to write on behalf of the Puritan cause from the Tower of London, for which, in 1637, he loses the stumps of his ears and is branded on both sides of his face.

1641 Parliament abolishes the prerogative courts of Star Chamber and the High Commission, which had enforced the licensing laws. The press enjoys a brief period of freedom from pre-publication censorship, at the beginning of the Civil War.

1642 The Lord Chamberlain takes over as official stage-censor.

1643 Parliament reintroduces a licensing system; offenders now face the House of Commons or its Committee on Examinations, rather than the prerogative courts.

1644 Publication of Milton's attack on censorship, *Areopagitica*: 'Who kills a man kills a reasonable creature, God's image; but he who destroys a good book, kills reason itself, kills the image of God.'

1648 After the defeat of Charles I, plays are banned.

1649 Parliament makes it treasonable to produce subversive books.

1651 Publication of Thomas Hobbes's *Leviathan*, which contains a justification of censorship.

1662 After the Restoration of Charles II, the new government attempts to control publication by a series of licensing acts requiring renewal by successive parliaments.

1663 Sir Charles Sedley is convicted for 'shewing himself naked on a balcony, and throwing down bottles pist in *vi et armis* among the people in Covent Garden, *contra pacem* and to the scandal of the Government'.

1679 Parliament refuses to re-enact the Licensing Statute, as a response to the government's refusal to license anti-Catholic pamphlets during the Exclusion Crisis (the attempt to exclude Charles II's Catholic brother, James, from the line of succession). The licensing system is not renewed until 1685.

1688 Under prosecution for seditious libel, 'the Seven Bishops' are acquitted.

1695 The House of Commons allows the Licensing Act to lapse, thereby ending pre-publication censorship. John Locke is an influential campaigner against the renewal of the Act.

1698 The Blasphemy Act outlaws printed and other forms of blasphemy.

1712 The Stamp Act, amended in 1725, 1743 and 1757, imposes taxes on the publication of newspapers, periodicals and pamphlets.

1719 John Matthews, printer of *Vox Populi, Vox Dei*, is hanged for high treason under the Regency Act of 1706.

1727 Edmund Curl is convicted of obscenity for publishing *Venus in the Cloister, or the Nun in her Smock*. This is an important legal development: obscene libel is now established as an offence at common law. Obscenity is no longer linked to conduct, as in Sedley's case (1663).

1737 The Stage Licensing Act is passed. Robert Walpole introduces parliamentary sanction for the role of the Lord Chamberlain, in response to Henry Fielding's stage-attacks on the government.

1749 John Cleland's *Memoirs of a Woman of Pleasure* (*Fanny Hill*) is outlawed.

1763 John Wilkes is found guilty of seditious libel for criticising the King's speech in *The North Briton*; he is also found guilty of obscene libel for the publication of Pego Borewell's *Essay on Woman*. The poem's title-page boasts an erect penis measured against a ten-inch scale. Wilkes is outlawed for both offences.

1768 Wilkes returns, is fined and imprisoned. The 'Wilkes and Liberty' riots express his popular support.

1792 Thomas Paine is convicted of seditious libel for publishing *The Rights of Man*.

Fox's Libel Act empowers juries to determine the criminality of seditious libels.

1843 A new Stage Licensing Act is passed empowering the Lord Chamberlain to forbid any play 'whenever he shall be of opinion that it is fitting for the preservation of good manners, decorum, or the public peace so to do.'

1857 The Obscene Publications Act ('Lord Campbell's Act') is passed.

1859 The publication of John Stuart Mill's *On Liberty*, an influential attack on censorship: 'The peculiar evil of silencing the expression of an opinion is, that it is robbing the human race.'

1868 The 'Hicklin' judgement, under the 1857 Act, establishes the definition of the obscene as that tending to deprave and corrupt.

1877 Charles Bradlaugh and Annie Besant are prosecuted for publishing an American contraceptive-manual, Charles Knowlton's *The Fruits of Philosophy*.

1889 The passing of the Official Secrets Act, Section 2. This allows for a 'public interest defence' by civil servants, which is dropped in the 1989 reforms.

Henry Vizetelly is convicted for publishing Zola in English translation.

1893 Oscar Wilde's *Salome* is banned by the Lord Chamberlain for depicting Biblical characters on stage. Wilde threatens to take up French citizenship in protest.

1898 George Bedborough is convicted for publishing the first volume of *Studies in the Psychology of Sex* by Havelock Ellis.

1928 Radclyffe Hall's *The Well of Loneliness* is banned under the 1857 Act. Thomas Inskip, the Attorney General, describes the novel as lesbian propaganda.

1932 Count Geoffrey de Montalk, self-styled uncrowned King of Poland, is convicted of obscenity for the publication of *Here Lies John Penis*. The judge tells him: 'A man may not say he is a poet and be filthy. He has to obey the law just the same as ordinary citizens.' De Montalk asks for several years' imprisonment in Buckingham Palace. He gets six months in Wormwood Scrubs.

1954 Prosecutions for obscenity are launched against a series of novels: Margot Bland's *Julia*, Stanley Kaufman's *The Philanderer*, Walter Baxter's *The Image and the Search*, and Hugh MacGraw's *The Man in Control*. In response to this spate of prosecutions, the Society of Authors sets up the Herbert Committee.

1959 A new Obscene Publications Act is passed, formed on the basis of the Herbert Committee's report. The Act attempts to establish a distinction between 'literature' and 'pornography'. Though a book might be 'such as to deprave and corrupt persons likely to read it', there can be no conviction if it has been published 'for the public good'.

1960 The first prosecution under the 1959 Act – of Penguin's paperback edition of Lawrence's *Lady Chatterley's Lover*. The jury (five of whom have difficulty reading the oath) accept the testimony of thirty-five expert witnesses to the novel's literary worth and its having been published for the public good. During the next twenty years, Penguin sell six million copies of the book.

1964 Mayflower's 'three-and-six-penny' edition of Cleland's *Fanny Hill* is banned under the 1959 Act. Cleland's novel had, in 1821, been the first book to be prosecuted as obscene in the United States.

1965 The Race Relations Act makes publication of racist literature a criminal offence.

1966 Kenneth Tynan becomes the first person to say 'Fuck' on British television.

1967 Theatre censorship ends with the abolition of the Lord Chamberlain, parliament having been alerted by the threatened prosecution of Edward Bond's play, *Saved*. Hugh Selby's *Last Exit to Brooklyn* is prosecuted under the 1959 Act. The jury ignores the experts and finds the novel obscene. This verdict is reversed in the Court of Appeal.

1970 Richard Branson, in pre-Virgin guise, is prosecuted under the 1918 Venereal Diseases Act for displaying posters offering students help on sex-matters.

1971 'Counter-culture' magazines, *IT*, *Little Red Schoolbook*, *OZ*, *The Mouth* are tried for obscenity.

1976 *Inside Linda Lovelace* is tried for obscenity.

1977 Mary Whitehouse brings a successful prosecution for blasphemous libel against *Gay News* for publishing James Kirkup's poem 'The Love that dares to speak its name'. The verdict is upheld by the House of Lords, which prompts Viscount Dilhorne's observation: 'I am unable to reach the conclusion that the ingredients of the offence of publishing a blasphemous libel have changed since 1792. Indeed, it would, I think, be surprising if they had.'

1982 The Old Bailey trial of Michael Bogdanov, director of Howard Brenton's *The Romans in Britain* (the *Spectator*: 'What a fucking play'). Mary Whitehouse brings a private prosecution under the 1956 Sexual Offences Act. The prosecution is abandoned, but the judge accepts the 'admissability' of the case.

1984 Civil servant Clive Ponting is acquitted after being prosecuted under the Official Secrets Act for leaking documents about the sinking of the *Belgrano* during the Falklands War.

1985 Under pressure from the government, the BBC Board of Governors decides not to allow the broadcast of a *Real Lives* documentary about Ulster.

1986 Winston Churchill MP fails to introduce new obscenity laws for television after the broadcasting of Derek Jarman's *Sebastiane*.

1988 'Gay's the Word' Bookshop in Bloomsbury is prosecuted under

Customs and Excise legislation dating from 1876. (Offending items include medical books on HIV as well as works by Kate Millett and Oscar Wilde.)

An Amended Local Authorities Bill is passed by the House of Commons; Clause 28 bans material promoting homosexuality.

Home Secretary Douglas Hurd announces a ban on the broadcasting of direct statements by representatives of Sinn Féin and the Ulster Defence Association.

The Broadcasting Standards Council is established under Lord Rees-Mogg.

Salman Rushdie's *The Satanic Verses* is published by Viking/Penguin.

A new Official Secrets Act is passed, partly as a response to the Law Lords' finding against the government in its attempts to ban Peter Wright's *Spycatcher*. The new Act dispenses with the 'public interest' defence.

1989 Ayatollah Khomeini announces a death sentence against Salman Rushdie. The *Sunday Sport* offers a one million pound reward for anyone directly responsible for bringing the Ayatollah to trial in Britain.

1990 Rushdie drops plans for a paperback edition of *The Satanic Verses*.

1991 During the Gulf War BBC radio draws up a proscribed list of records, including 'Walk like an Egyptian' by The Bangles, 'Midnight at the Oasis' by Maria Muldaur and 'Billy don't be a Hero' by Paper Lace.

The Japanese translator of *The Satanic Verses* is stabbed to death.

Part I

Tudors and Stuarts: castration and control

Chapter 2

Censorship and the 1587 'Holinshed's' Chronicles

Annabel Patterson

In 1968, Stephen Booth, discussing the censorship of the 1587 edition of 'Holinshed' from the perspective of literary criticism, delivered a verdict which it is now time to dispute: 'we care about *Holinshed's Chronicles* because Shakespeare read them.'[1] In the 1990s, thanks to the rise of cultural history, there are other evaluative possibilities. Rather than be dismissed as a somewhat baggy collection of raw material for genius, which even historians have tended to regard as primitive and undisciplined in its historiographical method, the 1587 'Holinshed' can now be read in its own right as an independent witness to the Elizabethan cultural scene. This massive production (three volumes in 1587, six in the early nineteenth-century edition[2]) contains vast amounts of useful information about sixteenth-century culture, both high and popular. For example, the texts of Court and civic entertainments, such as Sidney's *Four Foster Children of Desire* performed before the Queen in 1581 (6: pp. 453–5), or the elaborate welcome designed for the Earl of Leicester in the Netherlands in 1585 (6: pp. 649–60); descriptions of working conditions, workmen's songs and industrial time-keeping rituals during the rebuilding of the port of Dover (6: pp. 862–6);[3] and crowd behaviour at times of festival or disaster. And beyond its potential use as an underinvestigated archive of social practices, the 1587 *Chronicles* is the most striking exhibit we possess of early modern censorship, how it worked and what were its consequences for writers of all kinds.

We know that Tudor and Stuart governments regarded English historical materials as subject to their control. Official scrutiny of history-writing included restricted access to public records, the recruitment of historians to serve the ideological needs of particular monarchs, a licensing system that singled out histories as one of the genres that required special supervision, and censorship after the event. When the Bishops' Order of 1599 reiterated the injunction that 'noe English historyes be printed excepte they bee allowed by some of her maiesties privie Counsell',[4] it reminded all publishers and booksellers of half a century of surveillance. In Mary's reign (1553–8) the *Mirror for Magistrates* was 'hyndred by the lord Chauncellor' and only printed in 1559.[5] Comparable hindrances under Elizabeth included the deletion of dangerous scenes from the play of *Sir Thomas More*[6] and both quartos of Shakespeare's *Richard II*, and the calling-in of Sir John Hayward's *History of Henry IV* in 1599, with serious consequences for its author.[7] But none of these episodes matches for revelatory force the censorship of the 1587 *Chronicles*, which had taken the daring step of continuing the story of Elizabeth's reign literally up to the moment of publication. In this 'Continuation' the last section deals with the events of 1586, concluding with the trial of Mary, Queen of Scots. When the *Chronicles* appeared at the booksellers in January 1587, and the Privy Council became aware of its contents, there was an immediate governmental intervention. On 1 February Whitgift, as Archbishop of Canterbury, was ordered to recall and reform the work.[8] Unsold copies were collected from the booksellers; but instead of merely suppressing them, a committee was appointed to *revise* (the original term was *castrate*) the text, according to certain principles of which there is no remaining record.[9] On the basis of the few copies that survived uncastrated, a nineteenth-century edition replaced what had been deleted, permitting us to speculate about the censors' reasoning.[10] From the fact of revision alone, we must infer first that the authorities approved of the project in principle, and second that they took a highly *textualised* interest in the representation of recent history. It was not merely a question of what facts or events could be recounted, but the manner of their recounting that mattered.

Like the *Mirror for Magistrates*, the 1587 *Chronicles* was a group project. Despite our continuing to call it 'Holinshed', the second edition was not in fact prepared by Raphael Holinshed, who died in 1580. The first edition had chronicled Elizabeth's reign up to the year 1572, and Holinshed himself had subsequently continued the story through 1578; but when he died the work was taken over by a team of antiquaries, William Harrison, John Hooker, Abraham Fleming, Francis Boteville, otherwise known as Francis Thynne, and John Stow.[11] There is disagreement as to who was the principal compiler and editor. Stephen Booth supported the claim of Abraham Fleming, who certainly signed the preface to the 'Continuation';[12] while Elizabeth Story Donno argued, partly on the basis of the title-page, that the major figure was John Stow, who had provided Holinshed with material for the first edition. Stow's own *Chronicle* had been published in 1580 and his qualifications as a historian were greatly superior to those of Fleming.[13] In earlier parts of Holinshed's account, for example of the reign of Mary Tudor, there are many interesting additions, for which Fleming seems to have been responsible, though he often marks his supplementary material as having been taken from Stow, presumably with Stow's collaboration. In addition, a substantial chunk of material on the life and death of the Sidneys, father and son, was contributed by Edmund Molineux, who had been Sir Henry Sidney's secretary in Ireland. When the edition was called in, Thynne's monumental catalogues of ecclesiastical office-holders and genealogical inserts simply disappeared, and sections of his continuation of the history of Scotland were rewritten. The material on the Sidneys was severely truncated; among the casualties were the elegies for Philip Sidney and the description of the composition of his *Arcadia*. Also much condensed was John Stow's account of Leicester's visit to the Netherlands; and, most to our purpose here, the detailed description of the Babington Plot and its consequences, whose authorship was attributed in a marginal note to Abraham Fleming, was replaced by a very much briefer and less colourful version of those events. But *nothing* was altered in those sections of the history that had been covered in the first edition, despite the fact that they had been considerably amplified in the interim. Presumably the government was no longer interested in the texture of the *Chronicles* for the reign of Mary Tudor.

What did the authorities think they saw in the text that required its 'castration'? And why did the 1587 chroniclers introduce material that was vulnerable to censorship? Stephen Booth stated in 1968 that the 1587 censorship was unintelligible to modern readers. More precisely, he said: 'There are no common denominators among the materials removed and there is nothing in any of the excised pages that looks obviously dangerous to governmental policy.'[14] I disagree. Different hypotheses have been adduced to explain *why* the material on the Sidney family or Leicester's visit to the Netherlands was not just deleted but carefully condensed;[15] it seems self-evident that the long description of the Babington Plot and its consequences required similar treatment. Not only was this material 'hot', in the sense that the events it described had not yet reached their political climax in the execution of Mary, Queen of Scots; but a careful (or suspicious) reading of this section of the text suggests that it was too ambiguously written to satisfy the government's need to keep a tight control on public opinion. Within the space of a chapter, this segment of the problem must stand metonymically for a complete analysis of the censorship of the *Chronicles*; but it is also more directly germane, even than the material on the Sidney family, to our understanding of the category of 'literature' and its evolution in the early modern period.

The cultural control of public opinion requires all authorised texts to speak in a single voice, to express (or at least to claim to express) the voice of society speaking unanimously. We have already seen that the 1587 *Chronicles* was in no sense a monograph, but a collaborative venture, a phenomenon increased by its internal procedures of compilation and documentation. Holinshed himself had initiated what might well have been recognised (had his audience known the Bakhtinian term) as heteroglossia, when, for example, he incorporated into his account of Wyatt's rebellion at the beginning of Mary's reign a very long and dramatic account of the trial for treason of Sir Nicholas Throckmorton. Though implicated in the rebellion, Throckmorton was saved by the jurors, who, at considerable risk to themselves, refused to vote him guilty. Holinshed had described this insert as 'expressed in a dialog for the better understanding of every man's part', and invited his readers to engage in an act of interpretation:

> I have thought it not impertinent to insert the same: not wishing that it should be offensive to anie, sith it is in every mans libertie to weie his words uttered in his own defense, and likewise the dooings of the quest [jury] in quitting him, as maie seeme good to their discretions, sith I have delivered the same as I have found it, without prejudicing anie mans opinon, to thinke thereof otherwise than as the cause maie move him.

(6: p. 31)

The voice of Sir Nicholas himself is consistently heard throughout this long 'dialog', which is typographically presented as if it were a stage-play, challenging the prosecution's interpretation of the law, insisting on the legal distinction between words and deeds ('overt act') and, in the process, reminding his audience that law, as it changes with each new regime, is entirely contingent on historical and political circumstance. Many pages later, Holinshed had carefully recorded some information he had found in John Foxe's *Actes and Monumentes* (1563), as to the fate of eight of 'those honest men that had beene of Throckmortons quest', who refused, though imprisoned, to admit their verdict was wrong, and who were called to appear in the Court of Star Chamber, where the 'lords taking their words in marvellous evill part, judged them worthie to paie excessive fines' (6: p. 64).

When Abraham Fleming augmented this section of the text, he did so from the perspective of an ardent Protestant who, writing from the safety of Elizabeth's reign, felt free to indicate how much popular resistance there had been to Mary's succession, to that complete but temporary reversal of England's religious and hence political direction. In reproducing Throckmorton's trial and its sequel, Fleming added not one but three marginal notes drawing attention to the jury's intimidation: 'Eight of maister Throckmorton's jurie appeere in the star-chamber'; 'The hard judgement of the lords against those eight honest men'; and 'Further extremitie against Throckmorton's quest' (6: p. 64).

None of his readers in 1587 could have failed to note the significance of the episode.

Wyatt's rebellion, the cause of Throckmorton's difficulties, stood in the *Chronicles* as a major expression of aristocratic resistance to the Queen's marriage to Philip II of Spain, but Fleming made sure that popular protest was also well represented. To this end he followed Holinshed's example by transplanting material from John Foxe's *Actes and Monumentes*. For example, in retailing the story of how Bishop Edmund Bonner set up a rood to welcome the new and unpopular king to London, Fleming added (quoting verbatim from Foxe):

> Not long after this, a merrie fellow came into [St] Paules, and spied the rood with Marie and John new set up, wherto (among a great sort of people) he made low curtsie and said [to the crucifix]: Sir, your maistership is welcome to towne. I had thought to have talked further with your maistership, but that ye be heere clothed in the queenes colours. I hope ye be but a summers bird, for that ye be dressed in white and greene.

> (6: p. 63)

The insult transposed from the Catholic king to his symbol was light-heartedly, indeed poetically, transgressive. Less comedic, however, was another symbolic protest against the marriage. For 8 April 1554, there appears this entry, attributed to John Stow: 'a cat with her head shorne, and the likeness of a vestment cast over hir, with hir fore feet tied togither, and a round peece of paper like a singing cake betwixt them, was hanged on a gallows in Cheape, neere to the crosse' (6: p. 28). At least in terms of the now discredited regime of Mary Tudor, therefore, the documentary and analytical protocols of the *Chronicles* were established. Far from simply inveighing against sedition or rebellion, and in the guise of neutral reporting of any noteworthy incident, the chroniclers represented public opinion as unavoidably as seriously divided.

It is usually said of the Elizabethan chroniclers that their chief objective was to serve the state and to argue in favour of obedience and national unity. This view, which has been promoted both by historians and literary critics, results in part from taking at face value editorial comments which were clearly prudential or sycophantic. Yet the most striking fact about the Elizabethan chronicles is that the moral they claim to draw is emphatically contradicted by the story they tell;[16] and in particular the 'Continuation' of Holinshed, far from being an upbeat hegemonic statement, is a calendar of woes. It foregrounds natural disasters; local crimes and their punishment; instances of treason and their punishment, leading for their climax to the Babington Plot, a

Roman Catholic conspiracy of young aristocrats led by Anthony Babington.

The complicity of Mary Stuart in this plot against Elizabeth's life, the chronicler makes clear, leads to *her* trial and condemnation. The plot was discovered by Walsingham's agents in July 1586, and the conspirators were duly executed with the fullest degree of cruelty permitted by the law. Needless to say, the 1587 *Chronicles* formally adopted the position that the conspiracy was diabolical, and that the rigours of the law were acceptable. But the entire project had, as we have seen, acquired certain habits of multivocality. Like Holinshed, who so carefully represented both the case of Sir Nicholas Throckmorton and that of his 'honest' jurors, the 1587 chronicler offered (before the censorship occurred) a dialogic approach to the Babington Plot. He too recorded the voices of alienated aristocrats, for the text includes the 'literary' responses of the Babington conspirators in the Tower, who, he wrote, 'occupied their wits in dolorous devises, bemoning their miseries, of the like stampe to this here annexed, savouring more of prophane poetrie than christianitie, of fansie than religion'. There follows the poem we now know as 'Tichborne's Elegie', identified in the margin as 'written with his owne hand in the Tower before his execution, printed by John Wolfe 1586':

> My prime of youth is but a frost of cares,
> My feast of joie is but a dish of paine:
> My crop of corne is but a field of tares,
> And all my good is but vaine hope of gaine:
>   The daie is past, and yet I saw no sun,
>   And now I live, and now my life is doone.
>
> My tale was heard, and yet it was not told,
> My fruit is falne, and yet my leaves are greene:
> My youth is spent, and yet I am not old,
> I saw the world, and yet I was not seene:
>   My thread is cut, and yet it is not spun,
>   And now I live, and now my life is doone.

(6: p. 911)

This poem, of which I quote two of the three stanzas, has been celebrated as one of the most moving of the era's meditations on death,[17] not least because of its formal rigidities as an expression of the ultimate personal crisis. The short story of the young man whose life is about to be taken rings out with clear pathos, despite the fact that, as he tells us in the only unconventional line in the poem, his 'tale was heard, and yet it was not told'. Not told, that is, as he would have told it.

The poem's appearance in the national archive was, therefore, surely peculiar, as was the specification of the elegy's previous printing by John Wolfe. For Wolfe himself had a history of protest – against the licensing system in which, as a printer, he was forced to operate. Wolfe apparently had large ideas, conflating a theory of the Reformation as a liberation both of the spirit and the press with civil libertarianism and anti-monopoly fervour. He became the leader of a group of piratical printers agitating against the Stationers' Company monopoly over printing, but whose agenda had larger political dimensions. They 'stood upon this point that they were freemen, and might print all lawfull bokes notwithstanding any comaundement of the Quene, and that the Quenes comaundementes in this case were no lawe, nor warranted by lawe'. 'Tush,' Wolfe was reported to have said, 'Luther was but one man, and reformed all the world for religion, and I am that one man, that must and will reforme the governement of this trade.'[18] Wolfe was, therefore, an *agent provocateur* in a larger political context. When the authorities tried to tame him by throwing him into prison, he petitioned Burghley and Walsingham, and encouraged his colleagues to organise more widely. They retained lawyers, and set up a distribution system for the sale of their pirated books outside of London. And they 'incensed *the meaner sort of people* throughout the City . . . [so] that it became a common talk in Alehouses, tavernes and such like places, whereupon issued dangerous and undutifull speaches of her Majesties most gracious government'. According to S. L. Goldberg, whose account of Wolfe I follow, 'it took a second imprisonment and a raid on his secret presses to make Wolfe willing to be bought out by the Company in 1583'.[19] But if Wolfe was bought out of piracy, he was not necessarily tamed. In 1599 he would reappear as the publisher of Sir John Hayward's notorious *History of Henry IV*, in circumstances that suggest he was not motivated merely by financial gain – or rather, that the very certainty of financial gain from such a project implied a prior assessment of its potential for political provocation.[20]

Ostensibly, Wolfe had published Tichborne's elegy in order to reject it, in a pamphlet dutifully entitled *Verses of Prayse and Joye, Written upon her Maiesties preservation. Whereunto is annexed Tychborne's lamentation, written in the Towre with his owne hand, and an aunswere to the same* (1586); but the effect of such a strategy (an answer to the poem requires the publication of that which is to be refuted) was itself formally dialogic. For the 1587 *Chronicles* to enter Wolfe's name, recently notorious as a campaigner for a freer press, in the public record, and to associate him with the Babington conspirators' desire for self-expression was, to say the least, to introduce voices in counterpoint to the official view.

But there is more. Babington himself, so the chronicler tells us, managed to distribute to friends outside the Tower certain poems, which were apparently printed illegally: 'the copies are common (yet never authorised for the print).' His objective might have been to appeal for royal clemency on account of his rank; but it was surely also, as the act of publication implies, an appeal for *popular* sympathy. The 1587 *Chronicles* proceeded, before the censorship, to describe one of these illegal documents:

> to procure the speedier commiseration (in his fansie) he falleth into a familiar tale of a certaine man, that having a great flocke of sheepe, mooved either with a sheepish unruliness, or for his better commoditie, threatened everie daie by one and one to dispatch them all: which he dailie performed according to his promise, untill such time as the terror of his accustomed butcherie strake the whole flocke into such a fear, as whensoever he came and held up his knife, advising at that instant but the slaughter of one, the whole number of them would quake, fearing each one his particular chance. Which tale he applieth to himself, being one of the brutish herde (as he confesseth) that for their disordinat behaviour the law justlie condemneth, and threatneth to dispatch one after another.
>
> (6: p. 912)

This extraordinary insert was marked out for readerly interest, indeed, *literary* attention, by the marginal gloss 'A fable or tale which Babington applieth to his present case of wretchednesse.' Whatever the chronicler's intention in so permitting the forbidden material a second circulation, the effect would surely have been to permit precisely that 'commiseration' the fable was intended to promote.

Traditionally, one of the functions of the fable was to encode unequal relations of political or socioeconomic power by transferring such problems to stories from the animal kingdom. The chronicler noted that this was 'a familiar tale'. In fact, it was a remarkable adaptation of the Aesopian fable of *The Sheep and the Butcher* which appeared in the ubiquitous editions descended from Steinhowel's (and hence also in Caxton's fifteenth-century English translation) with a woodcut showing the butcher cutting the throat of one sheep while the rest of the flock look on. The moral of the original fable was that personal safety depends on group solidarity, and of the tragedy that results when, like sheep, men fail to unite in resistance to a seemingly irresistible power. Babington, through the voice of the chronicler, intelligently rewrote the old fable so as to add to its ancient message of sympathy for the too-passive sheep an unmistakable indictment of the psychology of repression. His brilliant conception of how the shepherd terrifies his flock into submission by a daily, ritual execution of one of their number was a genuine insight into the Elizabethan theory of public executions as, literally, exemplary ritual; a theory to which the 1587 *Chronicles* did not subscribe unproblematically. Fleming was careful to explain the huge crowds at the executions as *not* being drawn by any dangerous sympathy for the conspirators: 'although the assemblie were woonderfull great, and the traitors all goodlie personages, clothed in silkes, &c: and everie waie furnished to moove pitie . . . yet . . . there appeared no sadnesse or alteration among the people, at the mangling and quartering of their bodies' (6: p. 916). Yet it is extremely hard to believe that this careful representation of Babington's fable would have served to *alienate* natural sympathy. Despite the editorial comment, the story transmits its own message. A sheepish 'unrulinesse' (which is only one of the two motives offered, the other being 'better commoditie') scarcely justifies such 'accustomed butcherie' as indeed, common sense asserts, must surely work *against* the economy of sheep-farming; while the plot of the fable must have punched a large hole through the ideal of a peaceful pastoral world, with the Queen at its centre, that courtier or would-be courtier poets had already established as typically 'Elizabethan'.

A few pages later, marking the spot with another marginal gloss ('A prettie apolog allusorie to the present case of malcontents') the chronicler proceeded himself to rewrite for the occasion the ancient Aesopian fable of *The Frogs desiring a King*:

> God make prince and people of one mind, and plant in all subjects a reverend regard of obedience and contentment of present estate, supported with justice and religion: least longing after novelties, it fare with them as with the frogs, who living at libertie in lakes and ponds, would needs (as misliking their present intercommunitie of life) with one consent sue to Jupiter for a king, and so did.
>
> (6: p. 922)

Again, he delivered the official position editorially. At the end of the all-too-familiar story, when the too-passive log has been replaced by the too-active stork or heron, the frogs, 'seeing their new king so ravenouslie gobling up their fellowes, lamentablie weeping besought Jupiter to deliver them from the throte of that dragon and tyrant. But he . . . made them a flat answer, that (will they nill they) the herne should rule over them.' 'Whereby we are taught,' the chronicler concluded, 'to be content when we are well and to make much of good queene Elizabeth, by whom we enjoie life and libertie' (6: p. 922).

The Frogs desiring a King has had a long political history of its own, perhaps precisely because its venerable plot has always been too complicated for unambiguous application.[21] On the one hand it appears to argue for a divinely sanctioned monarchy, and the required obedience of subjects no matter how harsh the rule; on the other it implies a contractual relationship, whereby the frogs freely brought monarchy upon themselves. In fact, the chronicler has made matters worse than in simpler versions of the fable, by emphasising the earlier, republican state of the frogs, 'living at libertie in lakes and ponds' or 'intercommunitie' (a word here used for the first time in the vernacular) and moving to petition 'with one consent'. All of this jars with the 'libertie' that is finally said to derive from Elizabeth's rule; and even more striking is the way in which the second fable would have resonated with the central premise – sequential execution of the powerless – of *The Sheep and the Butcher*.

Today's reader can therefore speculate on the complexities of a cultural process that produces such a text. Was the chronicler, as is commonly argued in circles where a neo-Marxist theory of literature converges with deconstructive strategies of reading, merely the unwitting vehicle of the political unconscious, of the way the documents of hegemony reveal to the more knowing minds of a later day the cracks and contradictions in any ruling ideology? Or, was he *consciously* struggling with conflicting imperatives and sympathies? The second hypothesis seems to accord best with the dialogic nature of this text, and with its determination to let voices alternative to those of the regime be heard, even when they are not raised in harmonious consensus; the uncut text apparently intended, without for a moment questioning the fact of the conspiracy, to let the conspirators speak for themselves. The final proof of intention must surely be what happened to these remarkable materials. All dissident voices were silenced. In place of the long account of the Babington Plot the censored text offered only a brief summary of events, now disproportionately dominated by the dutiful 'oration of maister James Dalton one of the councillors of the citie of London'. Tichborne's elegy disappeared, as did Babington's version of *The Sheep and the Butcher*; but *The Frogs desiring a King*, no longer dangerously reverberating with echoes of the earlier fable, was carefully retained.

Finally, we can be fairly certain that the compilers of the 1587 *Chronicles* knew precisely what was expected of them. The text recorded how:

> a preacher at Pauls crosse was *commanded from authoritie*, to deliver some notice to the assemblie . . . namelie, that diverse of the traitors were apprehended, and without anie torture or torment confessed their treasonable *intentions*; which were, to murther hir maiestie, and procure meanes for the arrivall of forren powers, whereby the land might be overrun, heaven and earth confounded, and all things turned topsie turvie.
>
> (6: p. 909; italics added)

The chronicler's own intentions cannot, I have suggested, have been identical to those of the preacher, or of the government which 'commanded' him to interpret the conspiracy as an attack on cosmic order. Rather, he emitted awareness of the fictionality of his task – that is to say, the production of univocality, or political consensus. Describing the conspirators' arrest, he engaged in social ventriloquism:

> people thronged together to see the unnaturall beasts that were attached, . . . which how damnable it was, the whisperings, communications, and lowd speeches of the multitude, pointing at them with the finger of infamie as traitors of singular note some saieng, Looke, looke, yonder go the errant traitors that would have killed our queene, yonder goe the wretches that would have burnt our citie, that would have alienated the state of the land, that would have laid all open unto bloudshed, slaughter, desolation, and sporte: yonder they go whome heaven above dooth abhore, the earth below detest, the sun, moone, and starres be ashamed of, all creatures doo cursse and count unworthie of breath and life . . . whom none can pitie without suspicion of impietie, none lament but with lacke of loialtie, none favorablie speak of but with great note of ingratitude and privie trecherie? To this effect tended the interchangable speeches of the people, all with one voice disclosing the conceipts of their mind against these eminent traitors.
>
> (6: p. 898)

One can hear the voice of consensus here, but not without hearing also the way it has been constructed. Leaving aside the question of whether the 'people' (a problem of political and socioeconomic definition) 'really' responded in this way (a problem of historical verifiability), the rhetorical strategy of the passage gradually undermines its apparent complaisance with official ideology. The cosmic claims ('yonder they go whome . . . the sun, moone, and starres be ashamed of') rapidly give place to the unrealistic assertion that the speeches of 'the people' were 'interchangable', 'all *with one voice* disclosing the conceipts of their mind'. It appears, too, that unanimity is *required*, since 'none can pitie' the conspirators 'without suspicion of impietie . . . none favorablie speak' of them 'without great note of ingratitude and privie trecherie'. If, in the tradition that Holinshed had established, the Babington conspirators stand where Sir Nicholas Throckmorton stood (surveying the shifts in official ideology, as a Roman Catholic monarch succeeded a Protestant, and was then herself succeeded by another Protestant), the committee who continued Holinshed's work had something in common with the jurors at Throckmorton's trial, giving the verdict demanded by the government, but registering also a minority opinion.

Eventually, of course, like one-third of the jurors, the chroniclers partially succumbed, in the sense that Fleming himself apparently carried out the revisions required by the Privy Council. Yet there is a strong irony in the fact that it was *only* the most recent history of Scotland and England that attracted the authorities' attention. They left untouched the text that Holinshed had established, and that Fleming had augmented in the same historiographical tradition – a tradition of open enquiry that at moments verged on open resistance. Thanks to this oversight we can now determine at least part of the meaning of this most significant case of early modern censorship; and we can see how 'literature' functioned, not always as the medium of courtly compliment, but sometimes as the site of ambiguity in political interpretation.

NOTES

1 S. Booth, *The Book called Holinshed's Chronicles*, San Francisco, Book Club of California, 1968, p. 72.
2 *Holinshed's Chronicles of England, Scotland and Ireland*, 6 vols, London, 1808; reprinted New York, AMS Press, 1965. I shall cite the modern reprint by volume and page number in the text.
3 See A. Patterson, *Shakespeare and the Popular Voice*, Oxford, Basil Blackwell, 1989, pp. 101–2.
4 The terms of the Order are recorded in the Stationers' Register for 4 June 1599.
5 L. B. Campbell (ed.), *The Mirror for Magistrates*, Cambridge, Cambridge University Press, 1938; reprinted New York, Barnes & Noble, 1960, p. 8.
6 See W. W. Greg (ed.), *The Book of Sir Thomas More*, Oxford, Oxford University Press, 1911, pp. xiii–xv.
7 See M. Dowling, 'Sir John Hayward's troubles over his life of Henry IV', *The Library*, 4th series, vol. 11, 1930–1, pp. 212–24; and Patterson, *Shakespeare and the Popular Voice*, pp. 80–5.
8 See J. R. Dasent (ed.), *Acts of the Privy Council, 1586–87*, London, HMSO, 1901, pp. 311–12.
9 For a description of the so-called Fleming papers, which included Fleming's personal account 'de Modo Castrandi, Reformandique Chronica', advertised but never published by Francis Peck in 1732, and now presumed lost, see A. Castanien, 'Censorship and historiography in Elizabethan England: the expurgation of Holinshed's *Chronicles*', unpublished Ph.D. dissertation, University of California, Davis, pp. 26–7.
10 In addition to Booth's study, the two most important attempts to describe and analyse the revisions hitherto are Castanien's painstaking thesis, and E. S. Donno, 'Some aspects of Shakespeare's Holinshed', *Huntington Library Quarterly*, vol. 50, 1987, pp. 229–47.
11 Publication had been expected since 1584, when it was twice entered in the *Stationers' Register*, on 6 October and 30 December. It is evident, though, that the revision kept being expanded to give it up-to-the-minute topicality.
12 Booth, *The Book called Holinshed's Chronicles*, pp. 61–71. He based his assessment on the arguments of S. C. Dodson, 'Abraham Fleming, writer and

editor', *University of Texas Studies in English*, vol. 34, 1955, pp. 51–66; and W. E. Miller, 'Abraham Fleming: editor of Shakespeare's *Holinshed*', *Texas Studies in Language and Literature*, vol. 1, 1959–60, pp. 89–100.

13 Donno, 'Some aspects of Shakespeare's Holinshed', p. 231.

14 Booth, *The Book called Holinshed's Chronicles*, p. 60.

15 Donno, 'Some aspects of Shakespeare's Holinshed', pp. 242–4, assumed that those relating to the Sidneys were dictated by the queen's hostility to Sir Philip, stemming from his activities in the Low Countries. Castanien, on the contrary, stated that these, 'with one possible exception, seem to have been made to make the text more lucid, remove repetitions and to save space rather than because of official disapproval or a desire to lessen the honors paid to the dead' (p. 279). She also assumed that those relating to Leicester's activities were revised in response to the earl's own complaints, and that their objective was to reduce the emphasis on entertainment and to make him seem more efficient and responsible as a military commander (pp. 271–2).

16 This point was made long ago by L. F. Dean, 'Tudor theories of history writing', *Modern Philology*, vol. 1, 1941, pp. 1–24.

17 A. Stein, *The House of Death*, Baltimore, Johns Hopkins University Press, 1987, pp. 76–83.

18 S. L. Goldberg, 'A note on John Wolfe, Elizabethan printer', *Historical Studies, Australia & New Zealand*, vol. 7, 1955, pp. 55–6. See also H. R. Hoppe, 'John Wolfe, printer and publisher, 1579–1601', *The Library*, 4th series, vol. 14, 1933; J. Loewenstein, 'For a history of literary property: John Wolfe's Reformation', *English Literary Renaissance*, vol. 18, 1988, pp. 389–412; and C. C. Huffman, *Elizabethan Impressions: John Wolfe and his Press*, New York, AMS Press, 1986.

19 Goldberg, 'A note on John Wolfe', p. 56. See also Loewenstein, 'For a history of literary property', p. 405, who concludes from the appointment of Wolfe as beadle of the Stationers' Company in 1587 that he had turned his coat: 'No longer identifying his interests with those of the least powerful, we find him instead *policing* the company, securing the rights of capital, rights that he had now arrogated to himself.'

20 From a literary perspective, the most tantalising aspect of Wolfe's career is as printer of the second edition of Spenser's *Shepheardes Calender* in 1586, the year of the Babington Plot; to be followed by his printing, in 1590, of the first instalment of Spenser's *Faerie Queene*.

21 See A. Patterson, *Fables of Power*, Durham, NC, Duke University Press, 1991.

Chapter 3

'Those who else would turn all upside-down': censorship and the assize sermon, 1660–1720

Barbara White

Twice a year during the seventeenth century a political-cultural spectacle was witnessed: two judges of the common-law benches at Westminster attended by a formidable company of officials, barristers and servants, set forth from Temple Bar on a punishing schedule of assizes in the major towns in one of the six circuits they had elected to ride. The High Sheriff of each county was responsible for orchestrating a sumptuous and precisely executed ritual aimed at portraying and honouring the judges as the most eminent and awe-inspiring representation of national authority that was likely to be seen in the provinces. This ritual focused on the grandiose progress of the judges, from the borders of each county to an assize town. They were escorted en route by the High Sheriff, at least a dozen newly armed and liveried javelin men, and a large proportion of the wealthiest local gentry, some of whom would simply send their carriages in a show of power that was literally, if not metaphorically, empty. Once comfortably lodged and formally introduced to important members of county society, the judges changed their robes and were escorted either to a cathedral or a church to listen to a sermon. At its conclusion the judges solemnly proceeded to court to open the assize.[1]

The ritual, with its attention to the most minute detail of ceremony, was an integral part of a procedure and ideology of law which focused on the circuit judge as a personification of justice, religious orthodoxy and state power.[2] The pomp and splendour of the assizes, in theory at least, instilled fear and awe into the hearts of onlookers; specifically those disaffected to institutions of authority. The ritual was believed by Church and State to be a powerful weapon of coercion; the magisterial presence being used to frighten subjects into good behaviour demonstrated by loyalty to the king, faithfulness to the 'True Religion' (the Church of England) and obedience to the law. Whether the ritual was always successful in promoting this ideology lies beyond the scope of this chapter; however, instances of judges being stabbed and poor turnouts of local dignitaries to welcome judges, for example, suggest something of a discrepancy between the intention and the effect of the ceremonial.[3] The central function of the sermon within this ritual was to promote an understanding of society and social obligation based on a religious theory of kingship. In this respect, and by dint of preaching a doctrine of loyalty and obedience, the sermons were overwhelmingly conformist. The political climate might change, yet the preachers remained constant in promulgating the belief that the duty of subjects was to obey – whether the monarch be a Roman Catholic or a foreigner. They remained tacit, for instance, on the problems of allegiance created by the events of the Glorious Revolution of 1688.[4]

Such conformity was largely ensured by an array of censorship controls governing the selection of preachers, the content of their sermons and the sermons' publication. An estimated 12,000 sermons were delivered at the assizes in England between 1660 and 1720: a period of distinct difficulty for the clergy in attempting to preach loyalty and obedience at a time of revolutionary change. Approximately three hundred of these sermons are extant in printed form. That so few have survived is not a measure of any subversive activity on the part of preachers. It reflects, instead, the success of the assize authorities (in particular the High Sheriff, judges and their retinues, the Gentlemen of the Grand Jury and the bishop) in regulating the genre. Only three printed sermons resulted in court action,[5] and no more than a dozen abused conventions to any serious degree.[6] Of these, five were preached by the notorious polemicists Henry Sacheverell and Benjamin Hoadly.[7] Apart from such exceptions, the clergy conformed to the genre by observing its conventions of form and function, and avoiding embroilment in polemic or controversy. Annabel Patterson's discussion of 'systems of oblique communication' has little relevance here, if only because so few flouted assize-sermon conventions.[8] Some of the preachers who found themselves at odds with the authorities published their sermons themselves in order to put an end to alleged misrepresentations of their views, but they do not appear to have developed, for their own protection, 'codes of communication' within the printed text. Rather, as in Samuel Bolde's call for moderation towards Dissenters or, conversely, Henry Sacheverell's savage condemnation of nonconformity they put their case in a direct and vehement manner which courted judicial reaction.

Censorship began with the handpicking of preachers who were to officiate at the assizes: their main duties being to attend the Sheriff during the assize, to preach a sermon and to say 'Amen' at the conclusion of the death sentence. Long before the High Sheriff extended a formal invitation to preach, the minister in question had already undergone a careful pre-selection process. This process could be carefully controlled because of the strong personal relationships which frequently existed between the assize preachers and High Sheriffs. Often the preacher was a vicar in the parish where the High Sheriff lived, and was well known to the sheriff and his family. Hence William Burrell's desire in 1711 to make public his obligation to Henry Collins, High Sheriff of Sussex, and Thomas Tanner's fawning description in 1677 of the Right Honourable Sir Courtenay Pole.[9]

There is clear evidence that in extending invitations to preach, High Sheriffs followed directives dating at least from 1632: a letter from the Archbishop of York to the Bishop of Chester stated that they should be 'chosen of the gravest and most discreet and learned ministers in the counties' and that they were to have 'sufficiency' and 'experience'.[10] Thus, even lowly ministers, like Jonathan Bernard, vicar of Ospringe in Kent from 1679 to 1714, who quietly fulfilled his parochial duty in 'obscure concealment', satisfied these requirements. Indeed, it is significant that the majority of those being asked to publish had either no record of previous publications other than one or two assize sermons, or had distinguished themselves as scholars, finding a modest celebrity in popular devotional works, biblical criticism and ecclesiastical histories, as well as in non-ecclesiastical subjects such as poetry, mathematics, gardening and botany. The directives further stressed that ministers were to 'handle only such points as are seasonable and fit for such assemblies, and that they forbear to meddle with the persons of men, or anything prejudicial to the laws or present government or anything else not befitting their calling'. As a result, what these ministers held in common was that they gave no 'scandal and offence, which is of dangerous consequence'.[11] Rather, they confined themselves to preaching standard doctrines of obedience and uniformity.

The High Sheriff, or other assize official, was given a further opportunity to act as censor when he visited or wrote to the minister inviting him to preach. As can be seen in the case of Daniel Kenrick, vicar of Kempsey in Worcestershire, a poet and physician, the High Sheriff was in a position to offer polite guidance on what would be appropriate for the sermon. Behind the grateful platitudes expressed in Kenrick's Dedication to Sir Walter Kirkham Blount of Soddington for his 'kind and upright conversation', lies a larger and typical example of gentlemanly pressure masking clear censorship control. Blount, a Roman Catholic, had invited Kenrick to preach on Romans 13.1, 'Let every soul be subject to the Higher Powers', in the particularly sensitive year of 1688. It was with probable pressure from Blount that Kenrick promoted, against the teachings of his church, the notion of obedience to the King's desire for the toleration of Catholics. Paradoxically, by conforming to the genre's insistence on loyalty and obedience, and attempting to vindicate James II's religious policies, Kenrick found himself at the centre of controversy with predictable outcome:

> I must confess, such has been the Rude Insolence ev'n of my Brethren, and those of my own Communion, towards me, upon my Preaching of this Sermon, that I may be judg'd by some to want rather a Regiment, than a private Person for my Patron.[12]

On hand were other equally powerful forms of indirect censorship; notably, the formalised nature of the sermons themselves and the expectations of the audiences, which played an active part in the ritual. Preachers operated within a set of powerful and universally understood conventions governing the form and function of a proper assize sermon, observed by a public which was fully cognisant with what constituted a good sermon. Individual detractors, for example, condemned preachers first and foremost for their failure to comply with the true purpose of assize sermons. Thus, Richard Skingle's anonymous critic, writing in 1699, felt that 'another preacher would have chosen a more suitable text for an *Assize-Sermon*'.[13] Similarly, an anonymous 'hearty Lover of the Church and present Constitution' noted in a letter of advice in 1710 that Samuel Peploe's address was 'quite contrary to the Form and Method of Assize Sermons'.[14] From this letter we learn that Peploe's congregation boycotted him for appearing to justify Absolom's rebellion against the Royal father, and thereby appears to condone resistance to the Crown in times of extreme national crisis: 'several of your own Hearers, who duely frequented divine Service, and were well inclin'd to our excellent Church, are very indifferent whether or no they any more be present at your Sermons.'[15] Similar pressure affected the publication of Laurence Echard's sermon on Proverbs 11.1: 'A false balance is an abomination to the Lord but a just weight is his delight.' Echard used the text to suggest malpractice amongst the local tradesmen and lawyers.[16] Incensed by this, they pressurised the High Sheriff to withdraw his invitation to Echard on the grounds of Echard's disrespect to his superiors. This informal censorship by an assize public regulated the form of the assize sermon and communicated clearly to preachers what was required of them. Overwhelmingly, therefore, they constrained themselves to preaching according to a formula laid down within the ceremonial. David Llewelin, for example, preaching in 1677, understood 'the proper work of a divine upon the present occasion' as convincing the congregation that they were 'obliged by the Christian religion to observe the laws which they [the magistrates] come to dispense, and to be affected with reverence and gratitude to persons, that are employed in an office so weighty in itself, and so beneficial to our country'.[17] For Ralph Skerret, in the wake of the 1715 Jacobite Rebellion, his duties simply meant

> to preach up Loyalty and Obedience to our Governors, is not meddling with the Affairs of State but of the Gospel; and therefore may, and ought always to be inculcated as Occasion requires. And never sure was there more Occasion for enforcing these necessary Christian Virtues than at Present; when these Admirable Preservatives against Sedition and Riots, are by Artful Pretences made the Support and Encouragement to the most Licentious Proceedings.[18]

It was standard form, therefore, for ministers to compliment God's representatives (i.e. magistrates and kings) for their personal godliness, to encourage them in their duties, and to urge all subjects to honour and obey them. The process invariably paid great attention to exposing malign spirits threatening the peace and stability of the realm. If the High Sheriff, Grand Jury and occasionally the judges and bishop had exerted their influence successfully, then the sermon would receive immediate approbation. Formal thanks, and possibly a visit and a dinner invitation, would follow, with a request that the sermon be made public for the instruction of all. The preacher would dutifully oblige. His Dedication would offer obedience to the High Sheriff's commands and requests for his protection and patronage, as well as compliments on his person. This would be qualified by platitudes on the preacher's own unworthiness, his aversion to publication, the sermon's unpolished and hasty preparation and a predictable homily on the seditions and turbulence of the age.

On the rare occasions that these practices failed to prevent 'meddling' sermons, censorship became more overt, and even violent. An incident recounted by Thomas, Earl of Ailesbury, illustrates this point. When Thomas Pomfrett preached before Judge Jeffreys in 1685:

> [The] text was on the subject of 'Shadrach, Meshach, and Abednego, that would not bow their knee to an idol at the command of the King'. Either the choice of the text and the suggestion conveyed therein, or the opening of the sermon, so irritated the Chief Justice that he rose up in a passion, and but for the expostulation of his brother judge, was like to have 'plucked the preacher out of the pulpit'. However, Pomfrett, 'flying from his text and uttering all loyalty and obedience', the judge was equally 'impatient, as he had been fiery at first, to embrace the preacher coming down the steps, thanked him for his loyal and good sermon, ordered him to print it and to dedicate it to him.'[19]

More common than physical abuse was a refusal by the High Sheriff and Grand Jury to give the customary invitation to publish. Thus,

Alan Chamber, writing to James Lowther from Kendal in 1719, gives evidence of two sermons preached in Newcastle and Appleby protesting at high taxes on malt and land.[20] There is no evidence, however, of either being printed. Moreover, publication could be made contingent upon alterations. It was common practice to omit sections of sermons that had given offence, or to substantially emend them to meet with approval. Thus, Henry Constantine, preaching in 1683, deleted prefatory remarks 'which had given some disgust'.[21] Similarly, Thomas Willis in the same year used the invitation to publish to print his sermon in its entirety and to include certain passages which he had omitted when the sermon was originally given.[22] This was not seized as an opportunity for subversion but, rather, to reinforce his conformity by writing at length on the duty of judges and the beauty of justice.

In extreme cases, offensive sermons resulted in the presentment of a minister before the very assize at which he had preached. In 1714, for example, Robert Bull was brought before Justice Baron Price by the Grand Jury for the county of Gloucester within three days of delivering an address which tended 'to Sedition, and to the Disturbance of Her Majesty's Subjects'. Bull's campaign of vindication centred on his allegation that the Clerk of Assize had tampered with the Grand Jurors in order to get this presentment, that they had not actually heard the sermon but had presented Bull on false information obtained by the Clerk. Bull published his sermon himself 'just as it was Preach'd, without adding to, or expunging out of it, one Line, Word or Syllable'.[23]

Rather than a ploy to avoid censorship and get unacceptable ideas into print, Bull's interest seems to have been much more to do with proving his conformity. If the printed sermon accurately reflects its spoken counterpart, then Bull was probably justified in his complaint of 'gross Misrepresentations'. The sermon itself may have been a little passive in its defence of religion, but in its attacks on the legitimate target of Roman Catholicism and in its loyal utterances to Queen Anne, it is a model of conformity. In the printed version, Bull included letters from the Grand Jury of the City of Gloucester, and the Mayor and Council, requesting publication – to lend support to his insistence on the conformist nature of his sermon. The case of Samuel Bolde, the noted defender of nonconformity, is also worthy of attention. In 1682, he preached a sermon against the persecution of Dissenters. As a consequence, Bolde was prosecuted in both the ecclesiastical courts and at the assize for a scandalous libel against the Church of England. As punishment, Bolde was sentenced to preach three recanting sermons approved by a council of clergymen at Dorchester, Blandford and Shaftesbury, and was threatened with the loss of the office and benefice of his parochial church and rectory at Steeple, as well as further proceedings against him if he failed to comply.[24] A similar punishment awaited Thomas Bradley preaching in March 1663 at the York assize.[25] His attempts to blame the government for the maladministration of the excise resulted in a personal warning from Charles II about meddling in matters of state, and in his being forced to make a public retraction in a sermon at the next assize.

Control ranged, therefore, from urbane counsel and polite instruction to concerted local pressure, physical intimidation and judicial action. A set of powerful and repressive deterrents was available should more 'civilised', though equally coercive and manipulative, forms of regulation fail. What we see then is an organised network of censorship and not simply the censorship of the written word. It was fast – as in the case of Robert Bull – and effective, growing out of the very ritual the sermon was expected to complement. Rarely were the most repressive measures required, for the real force of censorship lay in the power of tradition. Cockburn dismisses assize sermons because of what he calls ministers' preparedness to mask 'their feelings with well worn platitudes and inoffensive generalisations on tolerance, suffering and the peace of God'. Since assize sermons critical of the Stuart regime were rarely printed, he feels that they were an 'inadequate reflection of the attitudes of the Stuart clergy in general'.[26] However, the evidence provides, instead, a powerful statement of the relationship between ritual and censorship. Whilst the ceremonial was taken seriously by participants and observers alike, the mechanism for indirect and self-censorship functioned effectively – ensuring the inoffensive and conformist nature of the genre. It is telling then, that Thomas Hearne was outraged by a minor deviation in the ritual for the 1729 Oxford assizes. He complained that the assizes had been robbed of a proper sermon by moving it from Assize Monday to Sunday, thereby preventing some of the participants in the ritual, the Gentlemen of the Grand Jury, from hearing it.[27]

The control of assize sermons usually lapsed only when the High Sheriff and members of his retinue failed to discharge their duties, authorised the publication of unsuitable sermons and hindered the publication of proper ones, as in the case of Charles Jones.[28] Jones's sermon of 1705 was the victim of some sort of rift, probably political, between members of the Grand Jury. An advertisement placed in the *Post Man* by a member of the Grand Jury, John Piggott, declared that the body of the Grand Jury had rejected and burned a request for publication.[29] But the same paper also carried a refutation by Harry Bridges, who also served on the Grand Jury, and who claimed that the majority of the Grand Jury had in fact requested the sermon's publication. Lapses in duty were rare, if only because negligence of any aspect of the assize ritual reflected on the loyalty of the High

Sheriff. Nepotism may have been a factor in the selection process; it seems likely that George Sacheverell, High Sheriff of Derby, who invited Henry Sacheverell to preach his contentious sermon in 1709, was a relative and shared his politics. The extent of political influence in general is more difficult to gauge, mainly because of the problems in ascertaining the politics of the lesser-known ministers that made up the bulk of the assize sermon clergy. It is probable, for example, that Benjamin Hoadly's invitation to preach in Hertford in March and July 1708 came from a High Sheriff of similar political views, since this was an election year and the Whigs were in power. Yet such party alignments were rare, and ministers rose above party divisions to find common ground in praising monarchical government, non-resistance, and the Church of England.

Censorship of assize sermons was couched in, and grew out of, the very ritual they perpetuated. The extent of this censorship can be seen in its ability to control not just the occasional wayward preacher, but the genre as a whole – amounting to an estimated 12,000 sermons during the period 1660–1720. Assize sermons are not to be regarded as insignificant or merely platitudinous; they were taken seriously by the authorities, becoming the focal point for a whole system of censorship throughout the land and were designed to promote an ideology of obedience among the literate and the illiterate, the governing and the governed. A mark of the success of this censorship is the conformity of the genre, with ministers like Henry Pigott, preaching in 1675, demonstrating a self-conscious determination to uphold and dignify the status of the assize sermon:

> The design why you begin *assizes* with a *sermon*, and why we *preach*, is that *all* may know that 'tis from *God*, that you exercise a *coercive* power [. . .] to keep Church and State in honour and safety, and to *compel* to good morality those who *else* would turn all upside-down, whilst yet they clamour upon *us* or *you*.[30]

NOTES

1 For discussion of the assize ritual, see T. G. Barnes (ed.), *Somerset Assize Orders, 1629–40*, Somerset Record Office, vol. 65, Frome, Butler & Tanner, 1959, pp. xii–xxx, and J. S. Cockburn, *A History of English Assizes, 1558–1714*, Cambridge, Cambridge University Press, 1972.

2 For this aspect of ritual, see D. Hay, 'Property, authority and criminal law', in D. Hay, P. Linebaugh and E. P. Thompson (eds), *Albion's Fatal Tree: Crime and Society in Eighteenth Century England*, Harmondsworth, Penguin, 1975, and E. P. Thompson, *Whigs and Hunters: the Origin of the Black Act*, Harmondsworth, Penguin, 1975.

3 See Cockburn, *History of English Assizes*, pp. 53, 54, 66.

4 Of the nineteen sermons located which were published within five years

of the Glorious Revolution, only two were directly concerned with problems of allegiance. These were Francis Carswell's *England's Restoration Paralleled in Judah's* 'or, the Primitive Judge and Counsellor, in a sermon before the Honourable Judge at Abington Assizes for the County of Berks, August 6th 1689' (1689), and W. Wilson's *A Sermon* 'preached before the Judge at the Assizes held at Nottingham, July 19th 1689' (1689).

5 S. Bolde, *A Sermon against Persecution*, 'preached March 26th 1682, when the brief for the persecuted Protestants in France was read in the Parish Church of Shapwicke in Dorsetshire. Then published, to put a stop to false reports. And now republished; with a brief relation of the prosecutions against the author in the ecclesiastical court and at the assizes for the said sermon and for his Plea for Moderation towards Dissenters' (1720); R. Bull, *A Sermon* 'preached in the Cathedral of Gloucester, on Sunday, July 18th 1714, at the Assizes held by Mr. Baron Price' (1714); H. Sacheverell, *The Communication of Sin*, 'A sermon preached at the Assizes held at Derby, August 15th 1709' (1709).

6 Notably, E. Fowler, *A Sermon* 'preached before the Judges in the time of the Assizes in the Cathedral Church of Gloucester on Sunday, August 7th 1681. Published to put a stop to false and injurious representations' (1681); J. Savage, *Security of the Established Religion, the Wisdom of the Nation*, 'A sermon preached at the Assizes held at Hertford, August 7th, 1704, before the Right Honourable the Lord Chief Justice Holt and Mr. Justice Gould' (Cambridge, 1704); T. Walker, *A Sermon* 'preached at Great St. Mary's Church in Cambridge before the Right Honourable Lord Chief Justice Holt at the Assizes held there, August 1st 1693' (Cambridge, 1693).

7 Sacheverell was involved in a famous trial before the House of Lords for two sermons in which he attacked nonconformists and the Revolution Settlement of 1689: see G. Holmes, *The Trial of Doctor Sacheverell*, Methuen, 1973. Hoadly was an aggressive Latitudinarian who received important promotions in the reigns of George I and George II for his championship of Whig principles, receiving the Bishopric of Bangor in 1715 and the rich see of Winchester in 1734. He supported the civil claims of the Dissenters, opposed sacerdotal privilege and upheld Revolution principles against the champions of hereditary right and passive obedience. No other assize-sermon preacher insisted so vehemently on the supremacy of law. See N. Sykes, 'Benjamin Hoadly, Bishop of Bangor' in F. J. C. Hearnshaw, *The Social and Political Ideas of some English Thinkers of the Augustan Age, 1650–1750*, London, Harrap, 1928.

8 A. Patterson, *Censorship and Interpretation: the Conditions of Writing and Reading in Early Modern England*, Madison, University of Wisconsin Press, 1984, p. 44.

9 W. Burrell, *A Sermon* 'preached at the Assizes at East Grinsted in Sussex, March 18th 1711' (1712). T. Tanner, *Wisdom and Prudence* 'exhibited in a sermon before the Right Honourable the Lord Chief Justice Rainsford and the Lord Chief Justice North, in their late western circuit' (1677).

10 Historical Manuscripts Commission (HMC), 14th Report, App. 4, p. 49.

11 ibid.

12 D. Kenrick, *A Sermon* 'preached in the Cathedral Church of Worcester at the Lent Assize, April 7th 1688' (1688), the Dedication. It is not absolutely clear that Blount was Sheriff, but he was obviously a man of influence. It is noticeable that the title page does not bear the normal 'Published at the

request of the High Sheriff and Gentlemen of the Grand Jury' but rather, 'Allowed to be Published'.

13 *The Church Defended against Mr. Skingle's assize sermon at Hertford*, 'In a letter to a friend by a true lover of the orthodox clergy' (1699), p. 2. Skingle is accused of making 'a Conventicle of his Church', p. 16.

14 *Remarks on Mr. Peploe's Sermon* 'preached at the Assizes held at Lancaster, April 7th 1710, in a Letter of Advice by a Hearty Lover of the Church and Present Constitution' (1710), p. 3.

15 ibid.

16 L. Echard, *The Hainousness of Injustice Done under the Pretence of Equity*, 'in a sermon preached in the Cathedral Church of Lincoln before Baron Turton at the Assizes held for that County, on Monday, August 8th 1698' (1698).

17 D. Llewelin, *A Sermon*, 'preached at the Assizes at Northampton, August 13th 1677' (1678), p. 3.

18 R. Skerret, *A Sincere Zeal for the Protestant Interest and our Happy Constitution in Church and State*, 'recommended in a sermon preached at the Summer Assizes, held at Chelmsford in Essex, July 18th 1716, before the Right Honourable the Lord Chief Justice Parker and the Honourable Mr. Justice Powys' (1716), the Dedication.

19 Quoted in H. Cobbe, *Luton Church: Historical and Descriptive*, London, G. Bell & Sons, 1899, pp. 227–8. See also W. E. Buckley (ed.), *Memoirs of Thomas, Earl of Ailesbury Written by Himself*, 2 vols, London, Nichols & Sons, 1890, vol. 1, pp. 159–60.

20 HMC, 13th Report. App. 7, p. 122.

21 H. Constantine, *A Sermon* 'preached at the Assizes held at York, July 23rd 1683, not long after the discovery of the late horrid conspiracy against His Majesty's person and government' (1683), the Dedication.

22 T. Willis, *God's Court Wherein the Dignity and Duty of Judges and Magistrates is shown* 'in a sermon preached at the Assizes held at Kingston-Upon-Thames, July 26th 1683' (1683), the Dedication.

23 R. Bull, *A Sermon* 'preached in the Cathedral at Gloucester, July 18th 1714', the Dedication.

24 S. Bolde, *A Plea for Moderation towards Dissenters*, 'occasioned by the Grand Jury's presenting the sermon Against Persecution at the last Assizes held at Sherburn in Dorsetshire. To which is added an answer to the objections commonly made against that sermon' (1682).

25 T. Bradley, *A Sermon* 'preached in the Minster at York at the Assizes held there, March 13th 1663' (York, 1663), and *Caesar's Due and the Subjects Duty* 'or, a Present for Caesar in a sermon preached in the Minster at York, at the Assizes there held, August 3rd 1663, by way of recantation of some passages in a former sermon preached in the same place and pulpit at the last assizes immediately before it' (York, 1663).

26 Cockburn, *History of English Assizes*, p. 66.

27 C. E. Doble (ed.), *Hearne's Remarks and Collections*, Oxford, Clarendon Press, 1915, p. 249.

28 C. Jones, *Against Indifference in Religion*, 'A sermon preached in the Cathedral Church of Wells, before the Right Honourable the Lord Chief Baron Ward and the Honourable Mr. Baron Price at the Assizes held there, August 15th 1705' (1705).

29 See the *Daily Courant*, 10 December 1705.

30 H. Pigott, *A Sermon* 'preached at the Assizes at Lancaster on Sunday, March 19th 1675/76' (1676), p. 29.

Chapter 4

'All run now into Politicks': theatre censorship during the Exclusion crisis, 1679–81

Janet Clare

The general view of the Restoration stage as closely affiliated to the Court has been little disputed. Dramatists such as Sir Robert Howard, the Earl of Orrery, Sir George Etherege, Sir Charles Sedley, William Wycherley and John Dryden, who furnished the repertoires of the theatres after 1660, were courtiers and friends of the king.[1] Their heroic plays and comedies of manners were geared to the cosmopolitan tastes of royal and royalist former exiles. Charles II and his brother James, Duke of York, were the patrons of the only two licensed acting companies. As had been the case since the days of Elizabeth, plays were perused prior to performance and censored by the Master of the Revels; the interests of the government and theatre management were, for the most part, entwined at the time when the Office of the Revels was occupied by Thomas Killigrew (1673–7) and then, for nearly half a century, by his son Charles (1677–1725). Thomas Killigrew, actor and manager of the King's Company based at Drury Lane, had shared the king's exile while William Davenant, who presided over the Duke's Company had remained on the fringes of royalist circles.[2] These associations exemplify Annabel Patterson's model of censorship: an implicit social code, a conscious and collusive arrangement governing relationships between authors and authorities which was intelligible to all parties.[3] In the Restoration period, however, such interrelationships were fundamentally restrictive, in that Court sponsorship of the theatre precluded the development of any real oppositional drama.

When the tacit understanding between the state and the theatrical profession broke down, the deployment of censorship became more pervasive, the immediate resort of a government anxious to shore up its defences. This was the case during the period 1679–81, which saw the emergence of the Whig Party and its attempt to pass an Exclusion Bill in order to remove the rights of succession of the Catholic Duke of York. Anti-Catholic feeling ran high following the allegations by Titus Oates of a Popish plot in the summer of 1678. The formation of Whig and Tory parties at this time, combined with fears of Catholic

plotting at home and abroad and of an anti-Catholic uprising, brought
drama clearly into the political arena. Some playwrights protested
that they were driven into political engagement by financial necessity.
Audiences were dwindling. John Crowne, in the Prologue of his adaptation from Shakespeare's *2 and 3 Henry VI*, *Henry the Sixth, the first
part*, performed in 1681, wrote that he had reworked the play 'when
very few wou'd come to see the *Show/* Play-houses like forsaken Barns
are grown'.[4] Thomas Shadwell, in his address to the reader of *The
Lancashire Witches* (1682), wrote that 'the Poet must have a relish of
the present time'; the old comedy of manners, of 'vanities and knave-
ries', will no longer suffice, for 'all run now into Politicks, and you
must needs, if you touch upon any humour of this time, offend
one of the Parties'.[5] However, the defensive note struck by Shadwell
underplays the active part the dramatists took in promoting alignments
with a specific faction or patron.

The Exclusion crisis brought Whig dramatists to the fore. Elkanah
Settle's anti-Catholic tragedy, *The Female Prelate Being the History of the
Life and Death of Pope Joan* (1680), discloses its partisanship in its dedi-
cation to the Whig peer and chief advocate of Exclusion, the Earl of
Shaftesbury.[6] The play describes the legendary duplicity of Joanna
Anglica, sometime lover of the Duke of Saxony, who, adopting the
guise of his confessor, poisons the Duke in revenge for her rejection.
Incongruously, she is then elected Cardinal of Rheims, and then Pope.
In its representation of popularist notions of Catholic dogma and
chicanery, the play fuels native anti-papalism. Before the Consistory,
and in the presence of Saxony's heir, Joan, as Cardinal, seeks to excuse
her murder of the Duke with cynical sophistry: "'Tis the intention of
the mind, and not / The deed that makes the crime.'[7] She then attacks
Saxony for being a 'Traitor to *Rome*, to *Rome's* Supremacy, to *Rome's*
Religion, and *Rome's* God a Traitor', and, to praise from her fellow
cardinals, produces fake evidence of Saxony's heresy. The iniquities
of papal supremacy are articulated by the young Duke in familiar
militant Protestant terms:

> Farewel, ye Scarlet Blood-hounds:
> Are these the Lords that yoke the necks of Kings!
> How sensless is that dull Imperial Head
> That makes his Scepter to the Crosier bow

(p. 19)

The passage is a barely concealed attack on the heir to the English
throne.

Anti-Catholic propaganda knits together the play's episodic structure. The cruelty of the Inquisition is exposed in a prison scene depicting the torture of heretics. Several scenes present Joan's sexual liaison

with her servant Lorenzo. In the final Act, she announces a 'Holyday', to be commemorated with a papal procession. Two citizens declare that they will spend their holiday 'down-right drunk' in a tavern, for they know no 'other use of a Holy day but first to go to Church, and then be drunk' (p. 65). The stage direction 'Enter Pope, Cardinals, Priests and other Officers, as in the form of a Procession' (p. 69) suggests a mock ritual reminiscent of the London pageants of November 1679 (allegedly designed by Settle under Shaftesbury's patronage), in which effigies of the Pope were burnt. The final comic-grotesque touch is the announcement that the Pope has miscarried during the procession. To prevent any further scandals, the cardinals decree that popes-elect will henceforth be examined by 'a reverend Matrons hand'.

The Female Prelate is quite blatantly Whig propaganda, and as serious political drama it has nothing to commend it. It panders to a century of anti-papalism, now whipped up to new levels of paranoia by the fabrications of the supposed Popish plot. What is of interest here is that the play was performed at the Theatre Royal by the King's Company in 1680, presumably with the sanction of the Master of the Revels. Settle, backed by Shaftesbury, had grasped the opportunity to stage a play designed to appeal to the supporters of Exclusion when opposition from all classes to Charles's defence of his brother's rights was at its height. Settle, in the Dedication, acknowledges that the decline in popularity of the theatre facilitated performance of The Female Prelate: 'Or if at last the Theatre had e'er revived again, this prophane Heretical Play must never have dared to have looked Light i' th' face' (sig. A3v). With the outcome of the Exclusion debate uncertain, and conscious of the need to attract an audience, Killigrew, as manager of the Theatre Royal, presumably took the risk of licensing an oppositional play.

Killigrew must also have approved Nathaniel Lee's Lucius Junius Brutus, which was acted by the rival Duke's Company at the playhouse in Dorset Gardens in December 1680.[8] In its representation of the expulsion of the last Roman king, the tyrannical Tarquin, and in the triumphant founding of the Republic by Brutus, the play is boldly anti-monarchical. As he had done earlier in his anti-Catholic tragedy Caesar Borgia (1679), Lee included allusions to the licentiousness and luxury of the Court, which audiences might construe as they chose. Moreover, Lee must have been aware that the king had been libelled as 'young Tarquin' by republican propagandists during his exile.[9] Lee could argue that both the play's constitutionalism and its presentation of a decadent court could be found in his dramatic source, Livy's Ab Urbe Condita. But this begs the questions as to why he quarried the work of the most celebrated classical historian whose republican allegiances were manifest, and why he chose to dramatise a revolution at such a critical moment. Certainly, at no other time during Charles II's reign would a playwright have dared to write a republican play.[10] Classical republican ideas, identified with men such as James Harrington and Henry Neville, were in circulation and influential immediately before the Restoration, but the Sedition Act of 1661 made it treasonable to publish or discuss views which were calculated 'to deprive or depose' Charles 'from the stile, honour, or kingly name of the imperial crown of this realm'.[11] Harrington might argue that Aristotle, Livy and Machiavelli had been allowed to express republican sentiments whilst living under other forms of government, but his plea went unheeded. Late in 1680, with the Whigs and their demands for Exclusion dominating the October Parliament, Lee was, however, evidently prepared to take the risk of using the stage, and the metaphor of the classical conflict, to challenge the main political ideology.

That censorship was being practised irregularly is evidenced by the direct intervention of the Lord Chamberlain, the Earl of Arlington, to whom the Master of the Revels was subordinate. Arlington intervened to suppress *Lucius Junius Brutus* after three performances, on the grounds that it contained 'scandalous expressions and reflections upon the government'.[12] Charles Gildon in his early eighteenth-century adaptation, was more specific; in his Preface, he records that Lee's *Lucius Junius Brutus* had been formerly prohibited by Arlington 'as an Antimonarchical Play', and written 'when the Nation was in a Ferment of Whig and Tory as a complement to the Former'.[13] Gildon had hoped to circumvent the interdiction placed on Lee's play by giving it the anodyne title of *The Patriot* and by removing 'Reflections on monarchy'. But the play carried its pre-history with it, and the Master of the Revels, despite Gildon's expedient alterations, refused to license it. Not until Gildon resorted to the time-honoured device for evading censorship, the transposition of dramatic location, in this instance from Rome to Florence, was the play licensed for performance. This post-history of a censored Restoration political tragedy is significant also because it illuminates another case of censorship. When Nahum Tate presented his adaptation of Shakespeare's *Richard II* in December 1680, shortly after the suppression of Lee's play, it was refused a licence. The play's pre-history as a subversive text, and its intransigent ideology, had marked it out for the attention of the censor.[14]

With Tate's adaptation of Shakespeare's *Richard II*, it was not the political loyalties of the playwright which were suspect, for Tate's royalist credentials were known, but the subject-matter.[15] The Master of the Revels suppressed the play without even the customary reading. Tate recorded his grievance in his dedicatory letter to a friend, George Raynsford; he had expected that his play would have found Protection from whence it received Prohibition, and so questionless it would, could I have obtained my Petition to have it perused and dealt with according as the contents Deserv'd, but a positive Doom of suppression without Examination was all that I could procure.[16]

Tate evidently thought that the changes from the source would ensure his play's licensing. In contrast to Shakespeare's richly ambivalent treatment of the deposition of an anointed king, Tate's design is clear. He states in the Dedication that his purpose was 'to engage the pitty of the Audience for him [Richard] in his Distress', which he could not have done, had he not 'shewn him a Wise, Active and Just Prince' (sig. A2r). Thus, he omits the malevolent lines which Richard addresses to his dying uncle John of Gaunt, together with the reports of Richard's tyranny. Moreover, Tate adds material which modifies the centrality, in the original, of Richard's deposition by Bolingbroke, supported by nobles and commons. In Tate's version, Richard resigns his crown altruistically in order to avert civil war:

My gen'rous Friends, let Crowns and Scepters go
Before I swim to 'em in Subjects' blood.
The King in pity to his subjects quits
His Right, that have no pity for their King.

(p. 39)

Since Richard is here no tyrant, the ideological contest (present in Shakespeare's play) between resistance and passive obedience to a tyrannical ruler, does not become an issue. Self-evidently, Tate's adaptation is much less politically provocative than Shakespeare's but, in spite of this, it was suppressed. Tate subsequently resorted to the usual strategy for circumventing censorship by transferring the dramatic location, in this instance to Sicily, and the play was put on as *The Sicilian Usurper*. This was, he asserted in his Epistle dedicatory, a great disadvantage, since

many things were by this means render'd obscure and incoherent that in the native dress had appeared not only proper but gracefull. I call'd my Persons Sicilians, but might as well have made them Inhabitants of the Isle of Pines, or World in the Moon, for whom an Audience are like to have small Concern.

(sigs A2v–A3)

Even so distanced from Shakespeare's play and from British political history, *The Sicilian Usurper* was suppressed after three performances.

This prohibition was caused by the reputation of *Richard II* as a play accommodating rebellion. As such, Tate's adaptation had a pre-history of censorship. The censorship of the deposition scene by the Master of the Revels in 1595 meant that for well over a decade the play was not performed in its entirety.[17] The Earl of Essex had commissioned a performance before his abortive rebellion in 1601, and one of the actors was interrogated at Essex's trial. The text was evidently perceived as tendentious, and Tate discloses a political naivety in his conviction that even the substantial changes he had made to the dialogue could evoke a more favourable response from the censor to a potentially inflammatory play at a time of such political instability.

As with the other 'political' plays censored during the Exclusion crisis, Tate's *Richard II* was published without interference from the censor, largely because of the breakdown of press censorship.[18] However, in his Dedication, Tate offers another explanation for the discrepancy between the implementation of stage and press censorship. It was to be expected that the work would be 'buried in Oblivion', and 'so it might have happened had it drawn its being from me alone, but it still retains the Immortal Spirit of its first-Father' (sig. A). The assumption here is interesting, since it betrays a somewhat paradoxical response to Shakespeare. The play's Shakespearian origins facilitated publication; but performance of Tate's play could only have been censored without the customary perusal of the stage licenser because Shakespeare's drama carried the taint of subversion.

The Lord Chamberlain's direct intervention to suppress Lee's constitutionalist *Lucius Junius Brutus* and Tate's rendition of royal deposition, coincided with Charles's assertions to Parliament that Exclusion would reduce England to an elective monarchy and raise the danger of civil war. With the failure of the Exclusion Bill, the dissolution of Parliament in January 1681 and its subsequent recall at Oxford in March, the Tories had regained the initiative. Some of those who had acted as witnesses to the alleged Popish plot came forward to give evidence that they had been suborned to give false information. In July, Shaftesbury was arrested, imprisoned in the Tower and accused of high treason. For the next five months, politicians were engaged in campaigns to bring about either the Earl's condemnation or his acquittal. In November, Dryden produced the crypto-historical *Absalom and Achitophel*, with its satirical attack on Shaftesbury as Achitophel. But the Whigs still remained powerful in London, and this may have contributed to the keener surveillance of the stage by the Master of the Revels and the Lord Chamberlain. As well as a work by the Whig playwright Shadwell, another by Tory playwright John Crowne was censored in 1681.

Crowne's first adaptation from Shakespeare's *Henry VI* plays, *The Miseries of Civil War* (1680), had been performed without any official interference. In this rewriting of Shakespeare's epic dynastic contest,

Crowne's propagandist objectives are obvious. To point up the warning, he introduces scenes of soldiers ransacking villages, extorting money from simple countrymen and preparing to ravish their daughters. In the Epilogue his purpose becomes explicit: the nation must learn a lesson from the Wars of the Roses and put down the Catholics and dissenters in order to prevent further strife. Crowne's Toryism did not exclude pronounced anti-Catholic sentiments, which are prevalent in his next Shakespearian adaptation, that of *Henry the Sixth, the First Part* (1681). In the Prologue, Crowne promises 'a little Vinegar against the Pope' (sig. A2r) and, in his Dedication to Sir Charles Sedley, he claims that his play is 'no indifferent Satyre upon the most pompous, fortunate and potent Folly, that ever reigned over the minds of men, called Popery' (sig. A1r). To this end, there is the usual mockery of Holy days, Latin prayers, and Catholic casuistry. Further, he enlarges the role of Cardinal Beaufort, who is responsible for plotting the murder of the Protector, the Duke of Gloucester. Beaufort suborns three murderers – 'soft Church Tools' – to kill Gloucester, telling them ''tis a charity to the whole Church . . . stopping of a Hereticks windpipe,/ Is stopping a wide leak sprung in the Church' (pp. 50–1). Despite their different party allegiances, there is no distinction of purpose between Crowne's religious satire and that of Settle's *The Female Prelate*.

Nearly a decade later, Crowne revealed the fate of *Henry the Sixth, the first part* in his dedication to *The English Friar* (1690), where he records that his play had 'pleased the best men of England but displeased the worst, . . . for ere it liv'd long, it was stifled by command'.[19] We can only speculate that again the Lord Chamberlain, whose Catholic leanings were to lead to a deathbed conversion to Rome, had intervened to suppress the play.[20] In the Dedication, Crowne asserted that Sedley's name had supported the play's publication, as had Shakespeare's the production. Yet, as Nahum Tate had discovered, Shakespeare's name could not guarantee a play's immunity from censorship. Crowne's adaptation also had a pre-history. In the 1590s, the two latter plays of the *Henry VI* trilogy had suffered from censorship because of their representation of rebellion, dynastic struggle and usurpation.[21] In reviving these early political histories, Crowne had chosen to present potentially inflammatory events. Whatever additions, and asseverations of loyalty, he might make, there was a certain intransigence in the subject of a monarch beset by faction and forced to abdicate – which could not easily be moulded to a position of royalist orthodoxy.

Later in 1681, with no conclusive evidence against Shaftesbury, the Whigs rallied. Their renewed strength may have facilitated the performance in November at the Duke's Theatre of Thomas Shadwell's

Whig satire *The Lancashire Witches*, but not before it had been subjected
to censorship. In his address to the reader in the published text of
1682, Shadwell expatiates on the political conditions in which the play
was written and the controversy it generated. The Tories, he claimed,
had expediently couched their true objections to anti-Catholic satire in
other, spurious terms: 'great opposition was design'd against the Play
(a month before it was acted) by a Party, who (being to[o] ashamed
to say it was for the sake of the Irish priest) pretended that I had
written a satyr upon the Church of England.'[22] Significantly, Shadwell
articulates the tensions present not only in the Tory position but also
in the application of censorship throughout the Exclusion crisis. Most
Tories were no great champions of Catholicism; but the need to distance themselves from the Whig opposition to the Catholic successor
ensured the suspension of doctrinal scruples. Yet, the Tories knew
that any express predilections towards Catholicism would lose them
popular support: hence they faced the problem of censoring a Whig
play which demonstrated its allegiance exclusively through religious
satire.

The lapsing in 1679 of the Press Licensing Act meant that Shadwell
was able to publish parts of *The Lancashire Witches* which had been
prohibited in performance. He was quick to draw attention to this in
his Preface:

> How strict a scrutiny was made upon the Play you may easily see,
> for I have in my own vindication Printed it just as I first writ it;
> and all that was expunged is Printed in the Italick Letter. . . . The
> Master of the Revels (who I must confess used me civilly enough)
> Licens'd it at first with little alteration: But there came such an
> Alarm to him, and a Report that it was full of dangerous reflections,
> that upon a Review, he expunged all that you see differently
> printed, except about a dozen lines which he struck out at the first
> reading.
>
> (p. 99)

Here we have the fullest account from any Restoration dramatist of
the almost casual, but none the less effective operation of stage censorship under Charles II. Significantly, Shadwell was later to write, in the
Prologue to *Bury Fair* (1689), that his Whig sympathies had effectively
silenced him as a playwright; that is, until the Revolution of 1688.[23]

From the typography of the 1682 text of *The Lancashire Witches*, we
can appreciate some of the issues which were deemed censorable
during the crisis of 1681. Predictably, the Master of the Revels has
removed passages in which the Irish priest, Tegue O'Divelly, reveals
himself as the charlatan he is, and also those in which Sir Edward's
chaplain, Smerk, is exposed as ignorantly complicit with Tegue's

doctrine and politics. The censor took exception to Smerk's pro-Catholic declarations: 'For my part, though I differ in some things, yet I honour the Church of Rome as a true Church', and 'For my part, I think the Papists are honest, loyal men, and the Jesuits dyed innocent' (p. 143). Toryism becomes suspect when the rascally Smerk articulates its extremes: 'Parliaments? tell me of Parliaments? with my Bible in my hand, I'le dispute with the whole House of Commons; Sir, I hate Parliaments, none but Phanaticks, Hobbists, and Atheists, believe the Plot' (p. 144). The Epilogue of the play – a dialogue between the actress Mrs Barry and Tegue – sets out to play down the satire. Tegue fears that what has gone before 'will offend a Party in de Naation', an anxiety treated dismissively by Mrs Barry: 'For all Religions laugh at foolish Priests' (p. 189). But Shadwell's disingenuous argument evidently did not hoodwink the Master of the Revels, who perceived the dual targets of Shadwell's satire: Catholicism and Tory Anglicanism.

Late Restoration dramatic censorship, with its alternate displays of leniency and repression, was symptomatic of a society on the brink of civil war. Censorship did not invariably follow party lines. *The Lancashire Witches* may have been read off by the Master of the Revels against Shadwell's known Whigism, but it was the pre-history of Tate's *Richard II* as a subversive text, and its intransigent ideology, which marked it out for the attention of the censor. Those playwrights who were alert to the disarray of institutionalised censorship seized the opportunity to write political drama and for the first time since 1660 some oppositional drama reached the stage and circulated in print. That few of these plays were more than propaganda signifies another mode of control, that of the inhibiting relationship of playwright and patron determined by intense party politics.

NOTES

1 See E. Boswell, *The Restoration Court Stage*, Cambridge, Mass., Harvard University Press, 1932; A. B. Nicholl, *A History of Restoration Drama*, 4th edn, Cambridge, Cambridge University Press, 1952; M. Foss, *The Age of Patronage: the Arts in Society 1660–1750*, London, Hamish Hamilton, 1971, pp. 19–50; J. Loftis, R. Southern, M. Jones and A. H. Scouten (eds), *The Revels History of Drama in English*, vol. V, 1660–1750, London, Methuen, 1976, pp. 3–40; J. M. Armistead, *Four Restoration Playwrights*, Boston, Mass., G. K. Hall, 1984; and R. W. Bevis, *English Drama: Restoration and Eighteenth Century, 1600–1789*, London, Longman, 1988, pp. 25–36.
2 For an illuminating discussion of William Davenant's conception of the function of drama from the perspective of government, see A. Patterson, *Shakespeare and the Popular Voice*, Oxford, Basil Blackwell, 1989, pp. 23–4.
3 A. Patterson, *Censorship and Interpretation: the Conditions of Writing and Reading in Early Modern England*, Madison, University of Wisconsin Press, 1984, pp. 15–20.

4 *Henry the Sixth, the first part,* 1681, sig. A2r. Quotations, signature and page references are from the facsimile, Cornmarket Press, 1969. The play is not included in *The Dramatic Works of John Crowne,* 4 vols, London, H. Southeran & Co., 1873.

5 'The Lancashire Witches', in *The Complete Works of Thomas Shadwell,* 5 vols, ed. M. Summers, London, Fortune Press, 1927, vol. IV, p. 99.

6 For a detailed account of Shaftesbury's part in the Exclusion debate, see K. H. D. Haley's *The First Earl of Shaftesbury,* Oxford, Oxford University Press, 1968.

7 Elkanah Settle, *The Female Prelate,* Act II. ii (p. 13). There is no modern edition. Quotations, page and signature references are from the 1680 quarto.

8 See *Lucius Junius Brutus,* ed. J. Loftis, Lincoln, University of Nebraska Press, 1967, pp. xi–xiii.

9 See the Commonwealth journal, *Mercurius Politicus,* no. 66, 4–11 September 1651.

10 For details of the reception of classical republican ideas, see Z. Fink, *The Classical Republicans: an Essay in the Recovery of a Pattern of Thought in Seventeenth Century England,* Evanston, Ill., Northwestern University Press, 1945.

11 13 Charles 2, statute 1, ch. 1.

12 See *Lucius Junius Brutus,* ed. Loftis, p. xii.

13 See 'The Patriot or the Italian Conspiracy' in *The Plays of Charles Gildon,* ed. P. R. Backscheider, New York, Garland, 1979, no pagination, sig. A3r.

14 I use the terms 'pre-history' and 'post-history' after the manner of Günter Grass in 'The prehistory and posthistory of the tragedy of *Coriolanus* from Livy and Plutarch via Shakespeare down to Brecht and myself' in *The Plebeians Rehearse the Uprising: a German Tragedy,* London, Secker & Warburg, 1966.

15 See C. Spenser, *Nahum Tate,* New York, Twayne, 1972. Tate praises James II in his sequel to Dryden's *Absalom and Achitophel.*

16 *The History of King Richard the Second,* 1681, sig. A2r. There is no modern edition. Quotations, signature and page references are from this quarto.

17 See J. Clare, 'The censorship of the deposition scene in *Richard II',* *Review of English Studies,* vol. XLI, 1990, pp. 89–94.

18 For press censorship during the period, see J. Walker, 'The censorship of the press during the reign of Charles II', *History,* vol. 35, 1950, pp. 219–38, and T. Grist, 'Government control of the press after the expiration of the Printing Act in 1679', *Publishing History,* vol. 5, 1979, pp. 49–77. In the context of opposition pamphlets and satires, Grist comments: 'Only after publications reached the streets could the government act to punish the offending stationers, both printers and booksellers. But by then the propaganda value had probably been achieved' (p. 53).

19 'The English Friar', in *The Dramatic Works of John Crowne,* vol. IV, p. 19.

20 See Haley, *Shaftesbury,* p. 162.

21 See J. Clare, *'Art Made Tongue-tied by Authority':* *Elizabethan and Jacobean Dramatic Censorship,* Manchester, Manchester University Press, 1990, pp. 39–43.

22 To the Reader, 'The Lancashire Witches', in *The Works of Thomas Shadwell,* vol. IV, p. 99.

23 'Bury Fair', *The Works of Thomas Shadwell,* vol. IV. Shadwell claimed:

> 'Twas Loyalty that was thought fit
> T'attone for want of Honesty and Wit.

No wonder Common Sence was all cry'd down,
And Noise and Nonsence swagger'd thro the Town.
Our author then opprest, would have you know it
Was silenc'd for a Non-conformist Poet.

(p. 296)

Part II

The eighteenth century: liberty and licence

Chapter 5

Richard Steele: scandal and sedition

Paul Hyland

When, in her speech to Parliament on 9 April 1713, Queen Anne announced that her government had secured a general peace with France after twenty years of war, there was no prospect that the cessation of 'so long and burthensome a war' would produce any 'calming of men's minds at home'.[1] Throughout her reign the nation had been beset by arguments between the Whigs and Tories not only over the aims and conduct of the war but over religious and political problems that had divided society at least since the Revolution of 1689. Unwittingly, due to her failing health and inability to produce an heir, Anne herself had aggravated what she called these 'groundless jealousies' of faction. And, although she attempted to calm her subjects by assuring them of 'the perfect friendship there is between me and the House of Hanover', her designated heirs since 1701, few, if any, would have been convinced. The well-known hostility of the Hanoverians towards her Tory ministry's peace proposals, and the barely concealed delight of those subjects who continued to support the hereditary right of her half-brother the Pretender (still living under French protection) were obvious causes for alarm. Thus, for all her insistence on 'What I have done for securing the Protestant Succession', the suspicion that her Tory ministers, with or without her knowledge, were now secretly preparing for a Jacobite restoration which would destroy all the laws and liberties of the post-Revolution constitution, would not be allayed by royal rhetoric. It was a common observation in the spring of 1713 that 'the nearer we draw to Peace Abroad, the farther we seem to drive from Peace at Home'.[2]

Amidst these fears of treason, civil war and French invasion over the succession, few would have been surprised to hear the Queen 'expressly mention' her 'displeasure' with the press. From the beginning of her reign, Anne had drawn attention to its 'pernicious practices' in the hope of countering the unprecedented growth of printed matter that had been unleashed since the lapsing of the Licensing Act in 1695.[3] Pre-publication censorship had been fraught with problems, but its expiration threatened to undermine the rights and duties of governments to curb the flood of information, criticism and abuse which it was widely believed would otherwise submerge the state. To this end, Anne's ministers had resorted to the ancient law of libel which, particularly under Lord Chief Justice Holt's pronouncements, was amended and extended to become the chief means of policing the production and distribution of the printed word.[4] Yet, despite the extensive powers of arrest and harassment which governments could exercise over anyone associated with a libel, the threat of fine, imprisonment and pillory, such as Defoe experienced in 1703, had not put an effective muzzle on the press.

On the contrary, by adopting a range of esoteric strategies (such as irony, allegory and innuendo) and simple subterfuges (such as counterfeited copy, anonymity and false colophon), polemicists and publishers had so successfully encased their texts in cryptics that it was often difficult for anyone to unlock their codes, let alone for the crown to put an unanswerable case before a judge and jury. This steganography – combined with the loopholes of a law that was originally devised for other purposes, the determination of leading lawyers and politicians to defend their party's propagandists, the inevitable costs and publicity associated with court action, and the risks of failure to attain both a conviction and a stringent sentence – did not fully protect the press from prosecution. Even in February 1713 one of the most notorious and best-defended Whig journalists, George Ridpath, had been convicted for insinuating that the Queen was 'in concert' with her half-brother – though he escaped punishment with the help of Lord Chief Justice Thomas Parker. However, the fact that it was primarily the intent and meaning of a writing which had now become the subject of most legal proceedings (rather than whether or not the licensing laws had been broken, irrespective of the content of the composition) did nothing to secure the confidence or secrets of the state.

In 1713, few would have doubted Anne's 'displeasure at the unparalleled licentiousness in publishing seditious and scandalous libels', or disputed her contention that 'the impunity such practices have met with, has encouraged the blaspheming everything sacred, and the propagating opinions tending to the overthrow of all religion and government'. Due to a variety of practical and principled objections, however, several attempts to enact new regulations (such as the compulsory registration of all publications) had failed throughout her reign. By a rather specious process of taxation, the introduction of the Stamp Act in 1712 had enabled Robert Harley, the Lord Treasurer, to monitor the production of opposition propaganda; but this new measure and the extensive network of loyal writers, publishers and informers that he had cultivated over many years could not determine the sort of subjects that might be raised or debated by the press. Thus for all his success in manipulating public opinion over the peace negotiations, most notably through his surreptitious sponsoring and prompting of Defoe and Swift, in 1713 Harley still proposed to launch a system of compulsory registration to facilitate the detection and prosecution of those who propagated unruly opinions. For this reason, in drafting the Queen's Speech, with Swift's assistance, he repeated the specific warning that 'some new law' would be required 'to put a stop to this growing evil' of the press. However, not only was the bill lost after its second reading in a bitterly divided House of Commons but, two days after Anne's opening of the session, Harley was confronted with a wholly unexpected problem.

The arrest of Defoe on 11 April, due to a private suit proposed by Ridpath and two other writers under prosecution, was an act of extraordinary defiance. It began with the acquisition of manuscripts which were presented to Thomas Parker as evidence of Defoe's authorship of three anonymous pamphlets, including *Reasons against the Succession of the House of Hanover* published in February 1713. Seizing the opportunity afforded by a literal reading of what were widely recognised as ironical productions, the Whig Lord Chief Justice then mischievously suggested that since 'The very Titles of two of them are libellous and seditious, and neare Treason; And the third sawcy', the Attorney General ought to take over the prosecution 'for the Honour of her Maty and the Ministry'. As Defoe beggingly told Harley, this meant either that the ministry would have to sacrifice its author to Parker's 'Partiallity and Favour' or, 'if your Ldpp *Did* protect me', the Whigs would have proof 'That I Was Secretly Entertaind and Employd by your Ldpp'. Critically, in either case, failure to adopt Parker's recommendation would allow the Whigs to proclaim the ministry's unwillingness to defend the Hanoverian succession. On reflection, Defoe proposed a 'Seeming prosecution' which would allow him to 'Complain Loudly of the Oppression' and petition 'to be brought to Tryall'. But while Harley, with the assistance of the Treasury Solicitor, successfully duped Parker into releasing Defoe from prison, to Defoe's distress the case continued for seven months until Harley was able to secure a royal pardon for his client's 'Ironicall Writing'.[5]

Although Defoe's arrest was in part an act of vengeance, for he and Swift had often called for Ridpath's prosecution, it signalled a new determination by the Whigs both to resist Harley's furtive manipulation of the press, and to expose the ministry's alleged equivocation over the succession.[6] Initially, in the spring of 1713, the celebrated moralist, essayist and dramatist Richard Steele lent only occasional support to these objectives; issuing a pseudonymous little tract protesting that Harley was prepared to subvert the constitution in order to secure Parliament's approval of the peace treaty, and writing several papers in his *Guardian* attacking Swift and the *Examiner*, the ministry's most forceful paper. However, by the end of the summer, having resigned his posts in government and won a seat in Parliament as MP for Stockbridge, it was clear that Steele was willing 'to ripen the Question of the Succession upon my own Head', as he put it, using his unique prestige and popularity to alarm the public of the dangers it was facing. Before the end of the year, not only had his signature sold five editions of *The Importance of Dunkirk Consider'd* (22 September 1713), a long essay implying Anglo-French collusion, and made his outspoken *Englishman*, 'intended to raize in this divided Nation that lost Thing called Publick Spirit', the highest-selling journal, but it had elevated him to iconic or demonic status as the champion of the opposition.

During the winter of 1713 Steele sent a letter to his wife telling her that he had 'resolved to go to the [Hanover] Club and ask for a subscription' to support the lengthy discourse upon which, 'by labouring in the common Cause', he hoped to champion the Hanoverian succession.[7] The work upon which he had been toiling was *The Crisis*; designed as 'an Antidote against the treasonable Insinuations which are licentiously handed about the Town'[8] and, in particular, two anonymous and learned tracts which had been published in October, *The Hereditary Right* and *Seasonable Queries*, both advocating James Stuart's rights to the succession. In Hanover, the Electress Sophia was also asked to subsidise Steele's treatise, though neither her response nor the subscription lists 'for divulging The Crisis all over the Kingdom' have been discovered. Even so, when the work finally appeared on 19 January 1714, it was soon rumoured that Steele's signature, extensive advertising, and the fear that Anne was dying, would raise £2,000 from the sale of 40,000 copies.[9]

In so far as it reflected contemporary anxieties, *The Crisis* could not have been more aptly named. It consisted largely of a recital of the laws which determined and safeguarded the Hanoverian succession, each followed by a little explication. This amounted to an impressive testimony, especially as the furious debates and private deals associated with the legislation were not even mentioned. Yet as soon as Steele had reached 'the happy Conclusion' that 'all Notions of Hereditary Right . . . are at an end', he proceeded with a series of horrific stories and scenarios predicting national 'Slaughter and Confusion'. Despite these dangers, Swift and others 'dared to drop Insinuations about altering the Succession', and reports were being circulated of the Pretender's conversion to the Church of England. According to Steele, only 'soft Fools' would credit this dissimulation, for 'A Popish

Prince will never think himself obliged by the most Solemn, even the Coronation Oath, to his Protestant Subjects', as potted histories of Catholic atrocities in England, France and Ireland bore witness. Even 'the Life of her Majesty' was 'in most imminent Danger' from the 'bloody Zealots' of Catholicism. With all this and no doubt more in mind, Steele finally reiterated his conviction that 'The only preservation against these Terrours are the Laws' that he had listed.[10]

Since Steele had insisted upon the security *and* the vulnerability of the succession, the Tory press had no difficulty in finding *The Crisis* thoroughly confusing.

> There is one natural Observation which many People have made upon the Book, that one part of it plainly contradicts the other. For in some places he endeavours to prove it impossible that a Popish Successor should ever attain his End in these Nations, and in others that it is not only probable, but very feasible for him to do it.[11]

Nor was this the only problem. The Dedication to the Clergy warning them not to inflame the nation, and the Preface justifying the Revolution, were reckoned presumptuous and seditious; offences that were not mitigated by Steele's subsequent efforts 'to explain himself in a New Edition of the Crisis'.[12] However, the response to 'two and twenty Pages spent in reciting Acts of Parliament' was withering:

> Thou pompously wilt let us know
> What all the World knew long ago,
>
> . . .
>
> That we a German Prince must own
> When A..N for Heav'n resigns her Throne.[13]

Having raised the public's hopes by a barrage of advertisements, it was argued that 'the Mountain' had brought forth 'a poor insignificant Mouse'. Instead of 'a scene of indigested Matter', it was felt that 'a Gentleman of Mr Steele's Delicacy should have treated his Guests to something New', for 'the whole Subject of the Book is only an Account of what was known before by every Man of Sense'.[14] Thus deflated, Steele saw his work appropriated to support the government's own contention that the succession was secure. In a letter to Sophia, the Earl of Strafford even argued 'I need no better proofs, than that famous book of Steel's, called, The Crisis, which the Whigs cry up so much, and which I think is demonstration to your Royal Highness, that you have nothing to fear from the Tories.'[15] Apart from Swift's aspersions on the Act of Union (1707), only a few Jacobites like Charles Lesley and Henry Cheap objected publicly and illegally to the laws that Steele had cited, 'because no Act of Parliament can be compleat or perfect without the [exiled] King's Assent'.[16] But such a rare reaction only emphasised the general disappointment and derision.

Fortunately for Steele, the Tory response to his 'Seasonable Remarks on the Danger of a Popish Successor' pulled no punches. These pages were represented as 'the foulest Insinuations that ever was cast upon the Ministry', exciting the people to 'Civil Dissensions', and were 'Criminal to the last Degree'.[17] From Lymington it was reported that a 'Jacobite Mob there, at the instigation of a certain Justice of the Peace' burned *The Crisis* 'in a publick bonfire', and that another magistrate 'had like to have been murder'd, for endeavouring to prevent it'.[18] Thus the violence of the response to Steele's 'Remarks' had saved his reputation. In public, the Whigs claimed that *The Crisis* was written 'with the greatest Advantages of Stile and Argument'; that it was read 'by all Ranks, Sexes, and Ages', if only because 'the Name of a Great Man is prefix'd to it'; that all Steele's critics were 'against the Revolution and the Protestant Succession'; and that 'a better Plan could not have been laid, for opening the Eyes of a stypify'd insensible Nation'.[19] In private, however, they too had reservations. A week after its appearance, one observer noted: 'The Crisis is own'd by the very Whigs to be a dull rapsody ill patch'd together, and despis'd by All.'[20] Nor was this just wishful thinking. Four days earlier one of Steele's supporters, John Toland, commented, 'I think it a very good Book, but it does not answer the expectation of many others, who are good friends to him and the Cause.'[21] Whatever the verdict on *The Crisis* as a work of propaganda, nobody doubted that its author would be punished.

Faced with the problem of what action to take against Steele's persistent and blatant insinuations that the succession was in danger, the ministry had several options. First, it could continue to do nothing. This would be interpreted by the Whigs as an unqualified admission of the veracity of Steele's assertions: spurring a host of other propagandists to repeat and extend his allegations; demoralising Tory politicians and pamphleteers who had been calling for his prosecution; and allowing Steele to carry his inflammatory language into Parliament. The consequential loss of ministerial authority and credibility did not bear contemplation. Second, the government could order a prosecution for seditious libel, which was precisely what Steele wanted. Any test of the legality of his writings in a court of law would lead to a major drama in which the ministry's commitment to the succession would be put on trial. Moreover, with Parker on the bench leaning towards the defence, almost anything could happen.[22] Judging by the precedents there could be little doubt about Steele's guilt; but a very heavy sentence would be essential in his case. Yet, if he were imprisoned and thus kept out of Parliament, he would be martyred. Nobody had forgotten that the present Tory ministry had arisen in 1710 on the back of Sacheverell's impeachment by the Whigs. Third, the government could wait for the Committee of Elections to expel Steele from the Commons in accordance with a petition lodged against him for electoral bribery and corruption.[23] This had been frequently predicted by the press but, as Defoe and others realised, the Whigs would soon have Steele returned in a by-election. Moreover, as expulsion by Committee would cast no reflection on Steele's propaganda, it would look a feeble gesture. Alternatively, the government could ask the Commons to consider the offensive and seditious nature of Steele's writings, and vote for his expulsion. 'The most Insolent Pamphlet writer that ever was permitted to go Unpunishd' would thus be censored, and precluded from re-entering parliament, without the ministry risking a prosecution. According to Defoe, this would 'Suppress and Discourage' the opposition 'and break all Their New Measures', for 'The New Champion of the Party' intended 'to Trye and Experimt Upon the Ministry and shall Set up to make Speeches in The house and Print them That the Mallice of the Party may be Gratifyed and The Ministry be Bullyed in as Publick a Manner as possible'.[24] However, there was one nagging problem associated with this option. The Whigs would obviously oppose the motion, but the extent to which they might succeed in splitting the Tories by turning the debate into a test of the Hanoverian succession remained in question.

Although the return of about 350 Tories in the general election of 1713 represented an outstanding triumph for the peacemakers, the scale of their electoral success did not augur well for party unity. The natural propensity of the party to form factions could only be accelerated by the sense of security that such a seemingly unassailable majority provided. Moreover, the divisions among the leading ministers would be widened as Secretary of State Bolingbroke demanded and Harley resisted the adoption of more radical policies; each in accordance with their own perceptions of the opportunities and dangers created by the force of Tory numbers. Above all, in Parliament and government the party was undecided and divided over the succession. For the majority of Tory members the choice between the Pretender and the House of Hanover depended as much upon circumstantial factors as upon fundamental principles: whether the Queen would leave a will, as the *The Hereditary Right* suggested, bequeathing her kingdoms to her half-brother; whether the Church of England would be better protected by a Lutheran prince or by a newly converted Stuart; whether the House of Hanover's hostility towards the peace party, and its collusion with the Whigs, were irreversible.[25] Behind these considerations lay a much deeper struggle over the legitimacy and meaning of the Revolution. However, in the newly elected

House of Commons only about fifty Tories were committed Jacobites, and about the same number were fully committed Hanoverians. In any debate over Steele's expulsion, it was to this small but influential group of 'Whimsicals', led by Sir Thomas Hanmer and the Earl of Anglesey, that the opposition needed to appeal.

The groundwork for an alliance between the Whigs and the Hanoverian Tories had been laid during the autumn of 1713. The Whigs, in collaboration with the House of Hanover, had invited Hanmer, Anglesey and others to join with them in opposition to the Court. Suspicious of Whig policies and motives, and uncertain of the extent of Jacobitism within the ministry, Hanmer and Anglesey could not be persuaded to oppose the ministry at every turn. Even so, their commitment to the Hanoverian succession seemed strong enough for the Whigs to hope that the Whimsicals would cause a stir on their own account in Parliament, and so show the nation that fears for the succession were not being raised for party ends. To prevent a Whig–Whimsical alliance, Harley had invited Hanmer to accept the Speakership when Parliament assembled on 16 February 1714, a date fixed at the beginning of the year. There was no prospect, however, of this averting a confrontation over Steele's expulsion. On 15 February, Steele closed the *Englishman* with another signed assault upon the ministry; its 'Profession of Zeal for the Church'; its alleged failure to stop 'great Numbers of young lusty Fellows, all Irish Papists' enlisting for the Pretender; and its support of the *Examiner*, the *Post Boy*, and other 'Oracles of Policy'. *The Crisis* had received a mixed reception, but there could be no doubt about the nature of the provocation offered in the final *Englishman*. Having crushed *The Crisis* with magisterial contempt, Swift appended a few thoughts to his *Publick Spirit of the Whigs* (23 February 1714) noting that the final *Englishman* was 'of so insolent and seditious a Strain, that I care not to touch it'.[26]

On 16 February the Queen was evidently too ill to open Parliament, but the Commons duly assembled and elected Hanmer as its Speaker. Since this was to be expected, Steele's decision to make his maiden speech during the proceedings became the focus of attention. However, by flattering himself while praising Hanmer, his words were partially obscured by Tory hecklers crying 'The Tatler, the Tatler' at the 'Fresh Water Member'.[27] The speech was swiftly published and later amended and defended in *Mr Steele's Apology*, published after Anne's death in July 1714. Even so, it was felt among the Tories that Steele had 'made so ill a beginning that he wou'd for ever after be the standing jest of the house whenever he rise up to speak'.[28]

In the fortnight before Parliament reassembled on 2 March, Harley drafted the Queen's Speech. To his original jottings, reworked by Swift, on 25 February he added the lines that would prepare the

Commons for an examination of Steele's writings.[29] Since the Tory press was unanimous in its belief that Steele had personally insulted the Queen, it was no surprise when she announced:

> I wish that effectual care had been taken, as I have often desired, to suppress those Seditious Papers and factious rumours, by which designing men have been able to sink credit, and the innocent have suffered. There are some who are arrived to that height of malice, as to insinuate that the Protestant Succession in the House of Hanover is in danger under my government. Those who go about thus to distract the minds of men with imaginary dangers can only mean to disturb the present tranquility, and bring real mischief upon us.[30]

Both Houses agreed with her in their Addresses, even though the Whigs thought her reference to the Hanoverian Succession sounded cold and unfriendly. However, as soon as Anne had left the chamber, the Earl of Wharton tried to turn the tables.

Accidentally producing a revised version of *The Publick Spirit of the Whigs* (in which Swift's offensive remarks about the Scots had been deleted), Wharton proceeded, having been handed a copy of the first edition, to draw attention to Swift's criticism of the Act of Union and his derision of Scottish nobles, especially Argyle. Since 'the sixteen Scotch Peers, who sate in the House . . . were the Principal support of those at the Helm',[31] the best the ministry could do was to amend Wharton's contention that the pamphlet was 'a false scandalous and factious libel' on the Scottish peers, a charge that constituted 'scandalum magnatum', so that in the resolution adopted it was deemed only 'a false, malicious, and factious libel, highly dishonourable and scandalous to the Scotch Nation'.[32] Not to be outwitted, Harley joined with the Whigs in calling for John Morphew to be taken into Black Rod's custody. Although Harley also professed no knowledge of the libel, the next day he posted Swift a hundred pounds to make a quick escape from London. On 4 March, Morphew admitted that he had received the printed copies from John Barber, and it was agreed that both persons should be examined on the following day. Morphew then confessed that he was publisher as well as seller of the pamphlets, but Barber refused to answer anything that would be self-incriminating.

In their efforts to 'discover' the pamphlet's author, the Lords examined Morphew and Barber several times, together with their employees. However, the information that the Whigs were looking for was not forthcoming. To block any further investigations the Earl of Mar, Secretary for Scotland, informed the Lords that he had already ordered Barber's prosecution. This he had done before the Earl of Wharton had drawn attention to the matter. The Whigs were therefore forced to pursue a different strategy and, after a three-day adjournment, on 9 March they proposed to ask the Queen to issue a proclamation offering a reward for the discovery of the author. The all-party committee chosen to draw up the petition submitted its proposals to the House on 11 March, whereupon the Whimsical Finch family called for an embarrassing insertion. The amendment, tabled by Lord Guernsey but formulated by his brother the Earl of Nottingham, stated that 'the Author of the said seditious Libel pretends to know the Secrets of Your Majesty's Administration'.[33] After a long debate the amendment was rejected by 53 to 35 votes, but the Address was agreed upon without contest, for the Tories 'were too wise to divide the house in a matter where we were sure to have the scotch to a man against us'.[34] In their address the Lords protested:

> that nothing may be wanting on our parts, towards the discovering and punishing so great a criminal, as we take the Author of the said libel to be, we most humbly beseech your majesty, that your majesty will be graciously pleased to issue your royal proclamation, with a promise therein of such reward as your majesty shall, in your royal wisdom, think fit.[35]

The Queen's reply was more succinct and pointed: 'My Lords; I thank you for the concern you shew for suppressing all seditious Libels. And have given orders for a Proclamation according as desired.'[36]

Although the Whigs and Finchs could do no more to bring their *bête noire*, and Steele's greatest adversary, to justice, their efforts had not been wasted. They had forced the ministry publicly to disown its *chef de propagande* and to prosecute John Barber. The royal proclamation offering three hundred pounds for discovery of the 'Author or Authors' of the pamphlet was prepared by Edward Northey, the Attorney General, and issued on 15 March at a meeting of the Privy Council. In the eyes of Northey and the Scottish Secretary, the evidence against Barber was barely sufficient to merit prosecution; but this could not have been expected to bother the Lord Chief Justice. Nor, in June, did it deter Harley from giving fifty pounds to Barber for his lover, the author Mary Manley: Steele's former mistress and now bitter critic.

Thus, the ministry had been put on the defensive as soon as Parliament had opened. Swift too was clearly shaken. A month later it was reported 'his Pannick is almost over and he begins to revive, his drooping spirits are rais'd, and John Barber can look upon a gibbet with chearfulness rather than betray his friend'.[37] But, like Defoe, Swift's confidence in the ministry's ability to protect him had been shattered. Seeking reassurance he petitioned the Queen in mid-April for the post of Historiographer Royal but, considering just his recent

record, it was a useless gesture. In the critical last months of the
Tory ministry he was virtually paralysed as an effective propagandist.
Having retired to Letcombe Bassett he wrote *Some Free Thoughts upon
the Present State of Affairs* (1741), and on 1 July very cautiously sent the
manuscripts to Charles Ford for perusal and publication. Although the
work was in many respects a perceptive commentary, it was also as
much a critique of the Tory Party and its leaders as an attack upon
the opposition. When Bolingbroke was shown the papers he kept
them for several vital weeks 'in order to make some Alterations'; no
doubt to some of the reflections on his own behaviour. Had he
believed that publication 'might have done any Service', he would
surely not have taken quite so long over his deliberations.

The first move to expel Steele from the Commons was made shortly
after Defoe had provided Harley with a long and detailed 'Collection
of Scandal' from Steele's writings, and the Lords had shown that they
intended to pursue their search for Swift by petitioning the Queen.[38]
On Thursday 11 March, John Hungerford, a staunch Tory lawyer and
office-holder, asked the House 'to take into consideration that part of
the Queen's Speech, which related to the suppressing Seditious Libels;
and complained in particular, of several scandalous papers lately published under the name of Richard Steele'. He was seconded by Thomas
Foley, the Lord Treasurer's cousin by marriage, who told the House
that it was necessary to protect members of the administration 'from
malicious and scandalous libels'. These complaints were supported by
William Wyndham, Chancellor of the Exchequer, who added that
'some of Mr Steele's writings contained insolent reflections on the
queen herself, and were dictated by the spirit of rebellion'. Since Steele
was absent, Arthur Moore, a close friend of Bolingbroke's, suggested
that it would be improper to continue, so 'it was resolved to put off
the Consideration of that Matter till the Saturday'. However on Friday,
Foley, acting largely upon Defoe's 'Collection of Scandal', made a
formal complaint 'against certain paragraphs' in the *Englishman* nos 46
and 57, and *The Crisis*, 'Which pamphlets being brought up to the
Table, it was order'd that Richard Steele Esq . . . attend in his Place
the next Morning'.[39]

Steele had been kept out of 'the first attack' on the instructions of
Lord Halifax, for it was hoped that, by delaying the proceedings,
leading Whigs, such as James Stanhope (who had still to be elected),
would have time to get to London. On Saturday, Steele, 'follow'd to
the House by great Numbers of Persons that crowded the Lobby and
Court of Requests', took his seat as ordered, and listened to the two
Auditors of the Imprest, Foley and Edward Harley, the Lord Treasurer's brother, 'and some other members, severely animadvert upon the
rancour and seditious spirit' of his writings.[40] Thereafter, James

Craggs, a member of the Hanover Club, rose to Steele's defence, but it was ruled that Steele should be heard instead. When asked whether he were author of the selected paragraphs, he answered that 'he had caused several books to be printed and that he knew not but the errors of the printer might be construed as his'.[41] He therefore asked for a week to consult the texts and to prepare, if need be, a defence. When Edward Harley objected in favour of a hearing on the Monday, Steele retorted that he was sure that a man who had led such an 'Exemplary and Sanctimonious Life' as a Dissenter, would not wish 'to force any one to incur the Pains of eternal Damnation by breaking the Sabbath-Day, which he must do, if held up to such Terms'. Amused and offended, 'after sevll Debates' the House gave Steele till Thursday.[42]

On returning home to Bloomsbury Steele was in good spirits, feeling that the House had been 'in very good inclination to me'. On Monday he embarrassed the ministry by calling for its papers pertaining to the demolition of Dunkirk to be laid before the House. Although his proposal was rejected, a subsequent motion by Richard Lumley, another member of the Hanover Club, to ask the Queen what steps had been taken to remove the Pretender from Lorraine, was passed without division. On the same day, the Queen had issued her proclamation for the discovery of the 'Author or Authors' of *The Publick Spirit of the Whigs*, and two days earlier Stanhope had been elected at Wendover. Nor were these the only hopeful signs before the hearing. When Sir John Percival arrived from Dublin on Sunday 14 March, he noted:

> I found the nation in a much greater ferment than we could imagine in Ireland. The fear of an Intention in the Ministry to bring in the Pretender possess'd the minds of severall who till now were esteem'd very high Torys. Some whisper'd their Jealousies, others clap'd their fingers on their Mouths, as not knowing what to think, while the Whiggs made no Scruple in all places to say the Pretender was comeing.[43]

There could not have been a better time for Steele to state his case.

By midday on Thursday 18 March the House was packed. According to the press, the French Ambassador's cheesemonger had already laid a bet of one hundred pounds to a shilling 'That the Commons would send Mr Steele to the Tower', and the next day's *Examiner* had already been printed with 'an insulting Account' of the verdict to be passed.[44] Even so, Percival, Baron Schutz (the Hanoverian envoy) and others, 'some of them Great Quality', had filled the galleries and Speaker's chamber to hear the case. It was opened by Foley who asked if Steele would acknowledge authorship of the marked passages brought before the House. Steele replied that having consulted his manuscripts he could now own the passages 'with the same Unreservedness' with which he had abjured the Pretender. Foley then proposed that Steele should withdraw, 'but after several Speeches it was carried, That he should stay in order to make his Defence'. Having won this point, Steele asked the House to consider each of the twelve marked passages separately so that he could 'hear what was urged against him to each, and thereupon answer'. Walpole and Stanhope supported this suggestion, arguing that as 'they could find nothing' that 'required to be explained', 'the burden of proving the evil' rested firmly with the government. Unwilling to divide the House on this matter of procedure, the Whigs finally agreed that Steele should make his defence 'generally'.[45] It was now 3 o'clock.

Before Steele opened his defence, the orders against strangers were read, the back doors locked, and 'Several Gentlemen who had plac'd themselves in the Galleries, and the Speaker's Chamber, refusing to withdraw, were by Order of the House taken into Custody of the Serjeant at Arms'.[46] According to Schutz, 'the heat in the chamber had become so terrible that it was almost unbearable', so he and most other observers, including Percival, withdrew without protest.[47] To support his case Steele had illegally printed a compilation of all the marked passages complained of in his writings, a copy of which was given to every member; and it was to this document that 'he sometimes spoke, but chiefly read'.[48] He began by saying that he was tired, that he had not had time to revise his speech, that he had intended to defend his writings 'paragraph by paragraph', and that he had been 'forced to rack his brains to discover in his writings the very things which he had taken such care not to put there'.[49] With Walpole and Stanhope on either side of him, and Addison prompting, he proceeded to talk 'for near Three Hours'.

Although it had been agreed that Steele should make his defence 'generally', he answered 'paragraph by paragraph', reading each of the offending passages and frequently citing his own works to justify his claims. First, he insisted that 'no Man had ever receiv'd greater Provocations' from 'Those Writers who declared themselves the professed Advocates of the Ministry, and give themselves the Air of being in the Secrets of the Administration'. They were the 'first Aggressors' and it was in answer to one in particular, Swift, that he had initially employed his pen. Surely it was better to be 'affrighted with imaginary Danger' of the Pretender than to be 'lulled into imaginary Security'. He could see no reason why he should be accused of speaking disrespectfully of the universities for he had always held them 'in the greatest Honour and Esteem'. Similarly, it had not been his intention to imply that the clergy were against the Protestant succession for he was a sincere 'Churchman' and had consistently advanced virtue and religion, 'even in so trifling a thing as a Comedy'. He had praised Swift's *Project for the Advancement of Learning* in 1709, and had even written papers in support of Tory clerics, so his impartiality in these matters was above reproach. In speaking of 'the Enemies of our Constitution' he had meant 'Popish Emissaries, Jacobites and Non-jurors'; only his accusers had thought that he referred to ministers of state. In the 'Seasonable Remarks' of *The Crisis* he had praised the Duke of Marlborough, insisted upon the demolition of Dunkirk according to the peace treaty, and expressed pity for the Catalonians. Whatever the 'Warmth and Spirit' of these pages, he had 'declared again and again . . . a due Observance to the Laws of the Land'. By wishing that 'his Electoral Highness [at Hanover] would be so grateful as to signifie to all the World, the perfect good Understanding he has with the Court of England', he had not meant to reflect upon the Queen but, on the contrary, to 'quieten the Minds of all of her Majesty's Subjects'. If his writings contained 'distant Implications and far-fetch'd Innuendoes' he should be prosecuted in a court of law. Finally, he appealed to the House to honour its traditions by protecting him from the executive, and then, 'with a very awkward and unwilling Air', withdrew.[50] Whether his speech 'gave entire Satisfaction to all not inveterately prepossess'd against him', or whether it was 'so weak and so frivalous as made his friends ashamed of him', was a matter of opinion.[51] Unquestionably, however, Steele had conceded nothing.

Having sat patiently through this marathon, half of which had consisted of quotations, it was expected that Harley's men would reply in kind. But after candles had been brought in, Foley merely noted that 'it was plain to everybody, that the Writings complained of, were seditious and scandalous', and then sat down again.[52] According to Steele, 'The Accuser arraigned a Man for Sedition, with the same Indolence as another Man pares his Nails', for Foley 'might have blown his Nose, and put the Question'.[53] The Tories clearly did not want a long debate, but the Whigs could not be stopped. Seizing his first great opportunity to address the House since his own expulsion in 1712 for peculation, Walpole spoke for an hour and a half, 'every sentence raking the ministry with his volleys, which were as witty as they were powerful'.[54] Like Steele, he insisted that to fall upon a member who had offended the executive was a serious and unprecedented misuse of Parliament, for if Steele's writings were illegal then they should be prosecuted in the courts. Everything that Steele had written was on behalf of the Hanoverian succession, and this was the true reason for his persecution. The ministry's commitment to that succession could be adjudged by its decision to allow the Pretender's messenger access to the inner chambers of the Court. The peace treaty had been broken in several instances, and the Lord Treasurer had even permitted his own famous library to be searched for manuscripts that were later published in *The Hereditary Right*. From an examination of Steele's writings, Walpole had thus steered the debate into a discussion of the ministry's record with regard to the succession, and it was to this issue that others largely spoke.[55]

Although the two Auditors, the Chancellor of the Exchequer, and the Attorney General responded to the Whig assault, the backbenchers of the Tory Party sat in silence through the whole debate. At 11 o'clock the question was put as to whether *The Crisis* and the last number of the *Englishman* were

> scandalous and seditious Libels, containing many Expressions highly reflecting upon Her Majesty, and upon the Nobility, Gentry, Clergy, and Universities of this Kingdom, maliciously insinuating, that the Protestant Succession in the House of Hanover is in Danger under Her Majesty's Administration, and tending to alienate the Affections of Her Majesty's good Subjects, and to create Jealousies and Divisions among them.[56]

The House divided and found Steele guilty by 245 to 152 votes, and on the strength of this it was agreed without further division that he should be expelled. To seal the victory some Tories called for the author to be committed, but Charles Caesar, Treasurer to the Navy, and Edward Harley amused the weary members by noting that Steele's creditors would now take care of that.

Although the ministry would not have been displeased with a majority of ninety-three, particularly considering its poor performance in the first fortnight of the session, the list of members who had voted in Steele's favour was not reassuring.[57] All of the Hanover Club's MPs had voted in Steele's favour.[58] Moreover, without any lead from Hanmer, the Whigs had enlisted twenty-three MPs whose support could not have been anticipated. However, more serious was the ministry's failure to answer the disclosures which the Whigs had made in the course of the debate. These revelations would be hurled at the ministry in Parliament and the press in the weeks to come, for if Percival is correct, 'very many honest Torys' left the House 'in discontent' at what had been alleged.

Among the most damaging of the disclosures were those concerning the Lord Treasurer's alleged protection and patronage of Jacobite pamphleteers. Swift had already been condemned in the Lords for undermining the succession by casting aspersions upon the Act of Union. Now in the Commons the writings of Defoe were also turned to Steele's defence. It is worth recalling Percival's report:

I know of several Torys who went away surprized at things wch fell in ye Debate; one thing particularly mentioned there set the house in a flame, wch was concerning ye author of a Pamphlet called reasons agt ye Hanoverian Succession. It was produced in ye House & very vile paragraphs were quoted out of it, wch were directed at ye succession, and after this was done, it was affirmed that my Ld Treasurer had procured a Noli Prosequi for ye author.[59]

Harley had secured a royal pardon for Defoe in order to protect him from Lord Parker. But it could not have been expected that this would serve as an excuse for a Whig to read the pamphlet in the Commons without any hint of the ironic intonation that Defoe had obviously intended. This was probably Walpole at his most censorious, for it was in his speech that further evidence of Harley's complicity with Jacobite propagandists was presented. According to Walpole, the Lord Treasurer had not only allowed the author of *The Hereditary Right* free access to his library but, through the Secretary to the Treasury, William Lowndes, had actually ordered and financed a search for the will and testament of Henry VIII, a copy of which had been appended to the famous treatise. The charge was exceptionally damning in that *The Hereditary Right*, a massive scholarly work published on 12 October 1713, had suggested that Anne should settle the succession by following Henry VIII's example. Understandably, the Whigs were horrified at the proposal and throughout the winter their propagandists had answered *The Hereditary Right* from every angle. But in the Commons, the Secretary to the Treasury 'seemed not to deny' Walpole's accusation, for 'He only said, that Will was not so rare a piece, since it was to be seen in a place he named, in Westminster Abbey'.[60] To the Whigs this was as good as a confession, and firm proof of the fact that *The Crisis* had been attacked primarily because it was the most popular answer to a Jacobite book that the Lord Treasurer had sponsored. But not all the evidence had been cited.

Although Harley undoubtedly allowed his library to be used for many purposes, the first reaction to *The Hereditary Right* had come not from the Whigs but from the government. Within a fortnight of its appearance a publisher, Richard Smith, and the person from whom he had received the manuscript, Hilkiah Bedford, a private schoolmaster and non-juring chaplain, had been arrested.[61] Harley certainly knew that Bedford was not the author, for a week later he received a letter from the deprived Dean of Worcester, George Hickes, imploring him not to prosecute a man 'for skreening a writer, wch your Lordp, if you have read the book, must acknowledge hath no ordinary pen'.[62] Even so, the Duke of Marlborough wrote to Hanover on 19 November claiming that the work had been written 'by direction or conivence' of the Lord Treasurer, and citing all of the evidence that Walpole later submitted to the House of Commons.[63] Marlborough also noted that the printer had been arrested 'for form's sake', but this is unlikely considering the reception that a Jacobite could be expected to receive from the Lord Chief Justice. On 15 February 1714 Bedford was convicted and committed to Marshalsea, even though it was generally agreed that he was not the author.[64] Swift's assessment of the verdict, written in response to Steele's contention that Jacobite writers enjoyed immunity, was by no means extraordinary:

> as for the poor Non-juring Clergyman, who was trusted with committing to the Press a late Book on the Subject of Hereditary Right, by a Strain of the 'Summum Jus', he is now, as I am told, with half a Score Children, starving and rotting among Thieves and Pickpockets, in the common Room of a stinking Jail.[65]

Thus Bedford was in prison when Walpole made his discreetly edited disclosures and it was rumoured that Parker would be 'turned out by addresses from both Houses, and ye Handle is that he fined a person who was convicted of cursing ye Queen, but 20 marks'.[66] However, Parker was less lenient in his treatment of non-jurors. On 4 May Bedford was sentenced to a fine of one thousand marks and three years' imprisonment; a punishment that was severe even by the later standards of the Whigs. Moreover, he was also ordered 'to be carried to the several Courts in Westminster with Paper upon his hat notifying his Crime and Judgement'. Bedford appealed against this aspect of the sentence, and 'in consideration of his being a clergyman of the Church of England the ignominious part of his punishment' was remitted in a warrant signed by Secretary Bromley two days later.[67] Immediately the Whigs took this as 'the greatest affront which her Majesty could offer to the Electoral family',[68] and although Defoe and others explained that Bedford 'fell into the Hands of Justice', that he was not the author, and that clemency had been shown to him because he was a clergyman, the Whigs made the most of what they pretended was a general pardon.

The Crisis had also been designed to answer another Jacobite tract published in October 1713, *Seasonable Queries relating to the Birth and Birthright of a Certain Person*. As the Tory press soon pointed out, when the work was printed as part of a larger treatise twelve years earlier, the Whig ministry at that time had not ordered its prosecution.[69] In October 1713 however, the bookseller John Stone was arrested as the publisher and printer, and on 5 June 1714 he was sentenced to a fine of twenty nobles, six months' imprisonment and two visits to the pillory.[70] All this was hardly evidence of the Jacobite impunity that Steele and Walpole had alleged. Yet, on 18 March in the House of

Commons it well emphasised Steele's own determination to be a *cause célèbre*. Having cited part of the Lord Chancellor, Sir Simon Harcourt's remarkable defence of Sacheverell's sermon in 1710,[71] Steele closed his own defence insisting, 'I think that I have taken no more Liberty than what is consistent with the Laws of the Land. If I have, let me be tried by those Laws.'[72] Moreover, he was serious. The following day he wrote to the Speaker:

> My reputation which is dearer to Me than my life, is wounded by this Vote and I know no way to heal it, but by appealing to the laws of my Countrey that they may have their due effect in the protection of Innocence.
>
> I therefore Humbly desire proper Questions may be put to bring about resolutions of this kind to wit.
>
> That Mr. Steele who is Expelled this House for_____may be prosequuted at law for His said offence, & that no non pros. or noli prosequi may be admitted in His case.
>
> That Mr Steele is *or is not* capable of being reelected into this present Parliament.[73]

Only after further consideration, and a polite but unambiguous reply from Hanmer, did Steele withdraw this extraordinary request.

Having been denied a platform in the Commons and the courts, Steele soon vented his anger in the press. Furious at the 'extraordinary Method' by which the ministry had chosen to disgrace him, and in particular at the Lord Treasurer's raising of 'a Posse' to expel him, on 20 March he launched a series of vicious satires on the Harley family in his hitherto light-hearted *Lover*. These bitter personal assaults were typical of the paper wars which had raged since Steele's decision 'to ripen the Question of the Succession', and which, by mid-1714, had produced over sixty pamphlets and a host of newspaper and periodical reports on every aspect of his life and works. As a form of writing, such *ad hominem* abuse was largely alien to Steele's manner, and on 22 April he returned to more trusted methods in a political periodical, the *Reader*. On the same day, however, another tri-weekly, the *Monitor*, appeared. This journal, ostensibly the work of 'a Plurality' but 'generally suppos'd' to be written by Defoe,[74] was designed to shadow Steele and his secretary, the editor of the *Patriot*, throughout the parliamentary session. But, not content to chew over bones of political contention, such as Hilkiah Bedford's pardon, on 11 May Defoe accused his adversary of pornographic writing. The *Lover* had published a letter from a man who had fallen in love with a young lady when she had fallen from her horse and landed 'Topsie Turvey'. To Defoe's question 'Is this suffered in a Christian Country?', Steele retorted 'Yes it is', for 'We who follow *Plato* . . . can see a Lady's

Ankle with as much Indifference as her Wrist.'[75] But Defoe was not convinced: 'It was not the Lady's Ankle . . . that fired this Man's Soul, and raised his Love; but her mere naked Posterior Beauty raised his Grosser Affections; and this the Platonick Philosopher would have us call LOVE.'[76]

Contradicted in every quarter, Steele continued to goad the ministry until its collapse at Anne's death on 31 July 1714. In the previous year he had staked his reputation upon signed political writings, for which he hoped and expected to be prosecuted in the courts. Swift had responded for the government but, due to a few ill-chosen words, had found himself outlawed by royal proclamation. Defoe, under royal pardon, had also countered Steele at every turn, and had even answered Swift's 'infamous libel' on the Scottish nation. Among lesser figures, Ridpath had fled to Holland, Toland had gone into hiding, and Bedford had been wrongfully imprisoned. All, except Bedford, were supporters of the Hanoverian succession, but none had advocated freedom of expression. Each called for the suppression of those writings which had inspired and defined his own position. Moreover, in the name of liberty and justice, Parliament, the press and the law had all been used to silence opposition.

Perhaps, at a time of political crisis, as in 1714, this is to be expected. If so, perhaps this critical year in British history may be excepted from 'the growth of toleration after 1695' that so many scholars have detected. A year after George I's accession, Defoe had been recruited by Parker as an undercover writer for the new regime. Swift had fled to Ireland, Bolingbroke to France, and Harley had been committed to the Tower. Steele was rewarded with a royal bounty, a knighthood, a subsidy for political writings, a safe seat in Parliament, and a patent to reform the theatre at Drury Lane from 'Offensive and Scandalous Passages and Expressions' – which he didn't.

NOTES

1 W. Cobbett (ed.), *Parliamentary History of England*, 36 vols, London, 1806–20, vol. VI, cols 1171–3.

2 *Britain*, no. 22, 21 March 1713.

3 See L. Hanson, *Government and the Press 1695–1763*, Oxford, Oxford University Press, 1936; F. S. Siebert, *Freedom of the Press in England 1476–1776*, Urbana, University of Illinois Press, 1952; R. Astbury, 'The renewal of the Licensing Act in 1693 and its lapse in 1695', *The Library*, 5th series, 1978, vol. XXXIII, pp. 296–322; A. Downie, 'The growth of government tolerance of the press to 1790', in R. Myers and M. Harris (eds), *Development of the English Book Trade 1700–1899*, Oxford, Oxford Polytechnic Press, 1981, pp. 36–65; G. C. Gibbs, 'Government and the English press, 1695 to the middle of the eighteenth century', in A. C. Duke and C. A. Tamse (eds),

Too Mighty to be Free: Censorship and the Press in Britain and the Netherlands, Zutphen, De Walburg Pers, 1987, pp. 87–106.

4 P. Hamburger, 'The development of the law of seditious libel and the control of the press', *Stanford Law Review,* 1985, vol. 37, pp. 661–765.

5 G. H. Healey (ed.), *The Letters of Daniel Defoe,* Oxford, Clarendon Press, 1955, pp. 403–25. See also P. R. Backscheider, *Daniel Defoe,* Baltimore, Johns Hopkins University Press, 1989, pp. 322–8.

6 P. B. J. Hyland, 'Liberty and libel: government and the press during the succession crisis in Britain, 1712–1716', *English Historical Review,* 1986, vol. 101, pp. 863–88.

7 R. Blanchard (ed.), *The Correspondence of Richard Steele,* Oxford, Clarendon Press, 1968, p. 292.

8 Advertisement in the *Englishman,* no. 8, 22 October 1713.

9 *Jack the Courtier's Answer,* 20 February 1714, p. 4. At least seven editions of *The Crisis* were published in 1714. See also the *Examiner,* vol. V, no. 30, 12 March 1714.

10 R. Blanchard (ed.), *Tracts and Pamphlets by Richard Steele,* London, Frank Cass, 1967, pp. 127–81.

11 *Remarks Upon Mr. Steele's Crisis,* 23 January 1714, pp. 15–16.

12 C. Lesley, *A Letter from Mr. Lesly to a Member of Parliament, post* 23 April 1714, pp. 6–7.

13 *The First Ode of the Second Book of Horace,* 6 January 1714, ll. 7–8, 11–12.

14 *Remarks on Mr. Steele's Crisis, etc.,* 26 January 1714, pp. 4, 14; *Remarks Upon Mr. Steele's Crisis,* p. 5.

15 Strafford to Sophia, 12 February 1714: J. Macpherson, *Original Papers containing the secret history of Great Britain,* 2 vols, 1776, vol. II, pp. 567–8.

16 *A Letter to Richard Steele Esq., post* 17 April 1714, p. 29.

17 *Remarks Upon Mr. Steele's Crisis,* p. 12; *Remarks on Mr. Steele's Crisis, etc.,* pp. 22–3.

18 *Flying Post,* no. 3460, 6 March 1714.

19 *Flying Post,* no. 3454, 20 February 1714; *A Defence of Mr. Steele, post* 25 March 1714, p. 3; *A Defence of the Crisis,* 18 March 1714, p. 3.

20 W. Bishop to A. Charlett, 26 January 1714: Bodleian Library, Ballard MSS XXXI, fol. 124.

21 P. Desmaizeaux (ed.), *The Miscellaneous Works of Mr. John Toland,* 2 vols, London, 1747, vol. II, pp. 431–3. Toland was lying low for fear that his pamphlet, *The Art of Restoring,* would be prosecuted when it appeared on 26 January.

22 In a letter to Thomas Parker six years later, Steele recalled, 'That you were Lord Chief Justice was a Consideration which gave me much Resolution in the last Reign': *Correspondence of Richard Steele,* p. 150.

23 *Journals of the House of Commons,* 1803, vol. XVII, p. 480. See also *Another Letter from a Country-Whig,* 17 November 1713, pp. 5–7; *John Tutchin's Ghost to Richard St . . . le,* 8 December 1713, advert.; E. Harley to R. Harley, 9 November 1713: British Library, Loan 29/143, unfolioed.

24 Defoe to R. Harley, 19 February and 2 March 1714: *Letters of Daniel Defoe,* pp. 430–2.

25 This nagging fear was well expressed by Swift in an insertion (later deleted) to the first draft of *An Enquiry into the Behaviour of the Queen's last Ministry,* 1765: H. Davis (ed.), *The Prose Writings of Jonathan Swift,* 14 vols, Oxford, Basil Blackwell, 1939–63, vol. VIII, p. 218.

26 *Prose Writings,* vol. VIII, p. 68.

27 *Post Boy*, nos 2931 and 2932, 20 and 23 February 1714; *A Speech suppos'd to be spoke by R . . . St . . . l*, 25 February 1714.

28 P. Wentworth to Strafford, 2 March 1714: British Library, Add. MSS 31144, fols 436–7.

29 British Library, Loan 29/7/11.

30 *Parliamentary History*, vol. VI, col. 1257.

31 *The History of the First and Second Session, post* 18 October 1714, p. 23.

32 *Journals of the House of Lords*, vol. XIX, p. 628.

33 M. F. Bond (ed.), *Manuscripts of the House of Lords*, HMC, 1953, vol. X, p. 229.

34 P. Wentworth to Strafford, 12 March 1714: British Library, Add. MSS 31144, fols 440–1. In this debate, Lord Halifax told the ministry that 'He believed if they would recommend the Crisis to her Maties Perusall she would think quite otherwise of the book than they do': *Correspondence of Richard Steele*, p. 294.

35 *Parliamentary History*, vol. VI, col. 1264.

36 ibid., col. 1265. For further discussion see M. J. Quinlan, 'The prosecution of Swift's *Public Spirit of the Whigs*', *Texas Studies in Literature and Language*, 1967, vol. 9, pp. 167–84; J. Harris, 'Swift's *The Publick Spirit of the Whigs*: a partly censored state of the Scottish paragraphs', *Papers of the Bibliographical Society of America*, 1978, vol. 72, pp. 92–4; J. I. Fischer, 'The legal response to Swift's *The Public Spirit of the Whigs*', in J. I. Fischer, H. J. Real and J. Wooley (eds), *Swift and His Contexts*, New York, AMS Press, 1989, pp. 21–38. Most of the important documents are cited by Fischer who argues that Mar 'chose to prosecute' Swift's pamphlet.

37 E. Lewis to T. Harley, 14 April 1714: British Library, Add. MSS 40621, fols 191–2.

38 For the association of events see, especially, W. Berkeley to Strafford, 16 March 1714: British Library, Add. MSS 22220, fols 103–5; R. Harley to T. Harley, 14 March 1714: British Library, Add. MSS 40621, fols 175–80. Defoe wrote *The Scots Nation and Union Vindicated* (1714) in answer to Swift's 'infamous libel'.

39 *Parliamentary History*, vol. VI, col. 1266; A. Boyer, *Political State*, 1714, vol. VII, pp. 240–1; *History of the First and Second Session*, pp. 28–9.

40 *History of the First and Second Session*, p. 29.

41 Sir Edward Knatchbull's diary: A. N. Newman, 'Proceedings in the House of Commons, March–June 1714', *Bulletin of the Institute of Historical Research*, 1961, vol. XXXIV, pp. 211–12.

42 *Parliamentary History*, vol. VI, col. 1267; Dyer's 'Newsletter', 13 March 1714.

43 Percival's diary: British Library, Add. MSS 47087, fol. 61.

44 *Flying Post*, no. 3468, 27 March 1714; *The Case of Richard Steele*, 24 March 1714, p. 11.

45 *Parliamentary History*, vol. VI, col. 1268; *History of the First and Second Session*, p. 33; *Tracts and Pamphlets by Richard Steele*, p. 298.

46 *The Case of Richard Steele*, p. 10.

47 Schutz to Bothmer, 19 March 1714: British Library, Stowe MSS 226, fols 306–8.

48 *Extracts of Remarkable Passages out of Mr. Steele's Writings*, no colophon, 12–18 March 1714. The pamphlet ran to eighteen pages without an introduction or editorial notes. The passages coincide with those reprinted in *Mr. Steele's Apology*. With the exception of passages 1, 3 and 4, the extracts were based upon Defoe's 'Collection of Scandal'.

49 Schutz to Bothmer: Stowe MSS 226, fols 306–8.
50 *Tracts and Pamphlets by Richard Steele*, pp. 298–337.
51 *Political State*, vol. VII, p. 246; Dyer's 'Newsletter', 20 March 1714.
52 *Parliamentary History*, vol. VI, 1269.
53 *Tracts and Pamphlets by Richard Steele*, p. 290.
54 Schutz to Bothmer: Stowe MSS 226, fol. 308.
55 For Walpole's 'eminent Part in this affair', see especially his notes: Cambridge University Library, Cholmondeley MSS 65/86/1–4.
56 *Tracts and Pamphlets by Richard Steele*, p. 290.
57 Lists were published in *Mr. Steele's Apology; The Miscarriages of Whig-Ministry*, 1714; *A Collection of White and Black Lists*, 1715. Each contains 153 names. Steele noted that Lord Finch was shut out of the division. When the *Apology* was reprinted in his *Political Writings*, 1715, Steele added two more members who allegedly voted in his favour.
58 J. Oldmixon provides a list of members of the club 'as it stood November, 4, 1713': *The History of England*, London, 1735, p. 509.
59 Percival's diary: British Library, Add. MSS 47087, fol. 63.
60 *Parliamentary History*, vol. VI, col. 1270.
61 They were granted bail at £100 and £500, on 24 and 26 October 1713: Public Record Office (PRO), S.P. 44/77/144–5.
62 Hickes to Harley, 31 October 1713: British Library, Loan 29/201, unfolioed. The principal author appears to have been George Harbin: see British Library, Add. MSS 5853, fols 105, 146. However, Hickes may well have lent a hand: see, *The Last Will and Testament of the Reverend Dr. George Hickes*, 1716, pp. 14, 17; and the letters of Harbin and Hickes: British Library, Loan 29/65, and 146/8.
63 Marlborough to Robethon, 19 November 1713: *Original Papers*, vol. II, pp. 515–16.
64 *Post Boy*, no. 2929, 16 February 1714; *A Help to History*, vol. III, February 1714.
65 *Prose Writings*, vol. VIII, pp. 64–5.
66 Percival to Dering, 23 March 1714: British Library, Add. MSS 47027, fols 162–6.
67 PRO, S.P. 44/357/389–90. Bromley made it very clear that he was not remitting any other part of the sentence. Bedford's prosecution cost the government over £233: PRO, T. 54/23/1–4.
68 Letter to Bothmer, 14 May 1714: *Original Papers*, vol. II, p. 619.
69 *Post Boy*, no. 2877, 17 October 1713; *Examiner*, vol. IV, no. 49, 23 November 1713.
70 *Post Boy*, no. 2978, 10 June 1714; *A Help to History*, vol. II, June 1714. John Lawrence was also arrested in October 1713: PRO, S.P. 44/77/145.
71 'A Subject of England is not be made Criminal by a labour'd Construction of doubtful Words; or, when that cannot serve, by departing from his Words, and resorting to his Meaning': *The Tryall of Doctor Henry Sacheverell*, 1710, p. 181.
72 *Tracts and Pamphlets by Richard Steele*, pp. 336–7.
73 *Correspondence of Richard Steele*, p. 90.
74 I hope to discuss Defoe's authorship of the *Monitor* in a future essay.
75 *Lover*, no. 34, 13 May 1714.
76 *Monitor*, no. 13, 20 May 1714.

Chapter 6

John Gay: censoring the censors

Calhoun Winton

'Something there is that doesn't love a wall', Robert Frost has written ('Mending Wall', 1914). The act of separation which Frost deplores could be extended, without distorting the sense, to dramatic authors and their feelings: something there is among playwrights that doesn't love a censor, who separates them from their intended audiences. Certainly, John Gay's enthusiasm for censors was minimal, in an age and society which on the whole approved of and applauded dramatic censorship.[1] After earlier brushes with the authorities, Gay managed in the case of his ballad opera *Polly* (published 1729) to outmanoeuvre the censors, to cast them in the public eye as knaves and fools, and to pull in a very substantial sum of money from the printed version – though at the expense of seeing his opera banned. It is an amusing and instructive episode in the annals of literary censorship; the principal lesson is the obvious one: that it is much easier to censor play-productions than printed texts. That is why playwrights don't love censors.

John Gay seems to have had his earliest encounter with censoring forces in 1712, during the aborted production of his first play, the farce afterpiece *The Mohocks*. What appears to have happened is that the theatre managers exercised self-censorship and turned down Gay's play because they thought it might offend some tender political sensibilities.[2] His mainpiece farce *Three Hours After Marriage* was similarly nipped in 1717 *during* production: on its way to a successful run *Three Hours* was silenced by the theatre managers after seven performances at Drury Lane.

Three Hours, a version of the December and May theme, presents Dr Fossile, ageing physician and antiquary, who has just married Mrs Towneley but has not yet consummated the marriage. The play consists of Fossile's bungling attempts to prove her infidelities and Mrs T's machinations to prevent the proof. Anyone *au courant* would have recognised that Fossile represented Dr Joseph Woodward, a physician and antiquary who was a favourite butt of Scriblerian foolery.[3] He was also the friend and confidant of Sir Richard Steele, governor of Drury Lane. The play's sexual innuendoes offended some, the personal satire some others, including presumably Steele, who may have simply ordered the play off the boards.

Gay, with important connections in the entourage of the Prince and Princess of Wales, was well aware by the early 1720s of the establishment's power: in February 1720 the Lord Chamberlain, the Duke of Newcastle, himself directed the Drury Lane Company to produce 'Mr. Gays Pastoral Tragedy' *Dione*, no doubt at the urging of some Person of Quality.[4] The theatre company ignored or evaded the order – Newcastle's political strength was uncertain at the time – but the managers knew well enough that the Lord Chamberlain had the authority to darken the theatre if he wanted to do so, under one pretext or another.[5]

Gay hoped for substantial preferment when the Prince of Wales acceded to the throne in the autumn of 1727. Sir Robert Walpole immediately consolidated his influence with the new king and kept the reins of government in his hands.[6] He owed Gay nothing, and Gay was disappointed at the minor appointment offered him: Gentleman Usher to the Princess Louisa, who was just 2 years old. Some of that disappointment no doubt made its way into the text of *The Beggar's Opera*, which Gay was writing in the summer of 1727, with his friends Pope and Swift looking over his shoulder. The *Opera* opened to immense popular acclaim in January 1728, but it was not immediately seized on as a party document, an instrument of propaganda against the Walpole ministry.

That was the reading given by 'Phil. Harmonicus' in a letter to the editor of the leading opposition journal, *The Craftsman*, on 17 February – almost four weeks into the *Opera*'s record-breaking run. Harmonicus identifies Gay's work as 'the most venemous *allegorical Libel* against the G[overnment]t that hath appeared for many Years past'. Harmonicus goes on to explain that Macheath represents Walpole, and that Peachum and Lockit *also* represent Walpole and his brother Horatio. He demonstrates how to read the *Opera* for innuendo, of which he finds plenty.[7] In Ireland Swift reinforced the attack on Walpole, in his own way, with an essay published in the Dublin *Intelligencer* in May 1728, where he solemnly avers that 'an Opinion obtains, that in the *Beggar's Opera* there appears to be some Reflections upon *Courtiers* and *Statesmen*, whereof I am by no Means a Judge'.[8] Judge or no, however, he proceeds to interpret these reflections in his best backhanded manner.

By the late spring of 1728, then, the *Opera* had been enlisted in the cause of opposition propaganda, and Gay's satiric touches had been converted by *The Craftsman* and Swift into slashing personal attacks on Walpole and his government. Scholars have recently cast doubt on Gay's own witting role in this, and on the *Opera*'s efficacy as partisan propaganda. Bertrand Goldgar has written that these efforts by *The Craftsman* and Swift 'helped make Gay's opera a political touchstone to an extent he doubtless had not intended'.[9] Robert D. Hume judges that the *Opera* 'caused a flap, but did Walpole little harm'.[10] At the least, however, the flap ensured that Gay's *next* play would be looked at very carefully by the government.

Whatever Gay's feelings might have been in the preceding year, by the summer of 1728 he was forced to recognise himself as a member of the opposition to Walpole. Swift continued his drumfire of pamphlets against the ministry's representatives in Ireland, which had begun with *The Drapier's Letters* (1724–5). Pope published in May 1728 the first of many versions of *The Dunciad*; all London would have noticed that, as Goldgar observes, 'an astonishing number of the Dunces turn out to be government hacks or minor office-holders under Walpole'.[11] Gay was working on a sequel to *The Beggar's Opera* that summer, and Walpole had every reason to believe that it would contain at least as much political satire as the *Opera*, if not more.

Just how seriously Gay took the threat of censorship for *Polly* it is impossible to say. My guess is that he hoped his new ballad opera would be produced but that in the back of his mind he had contingency plans in case the government intervened to stop the show. John Rich, manager of the theatre at Lincoln's Inn Fields, who had produced the *Opera* there, accepted it for production. Gay had *Polly* ready for rehearsal by the end of November 1728. In the Preface to the first printed edition of the opera Gay sets forth his view, or at least his *public* view, of what happened then:

> AFTER Mr. *Rich* and I were agreed upon terms and conditions for bringing this Piece on the stage, and that every thing was ready for a Rehearsal; The Lord Chamberlain [the Duke of Grafton] sent an order from the country to prohibit Mr. *Rich* to suffer any Play to be rehears'd upon the stage till it had been first of all supervis'd by his Grace. As soon as Mr. *Rich* came from his Grace's secretary (who had sent for him to receive the before-mentioned order) he came to my lodgings, and acquainted me with the orders he had received.[12]

The office of the Lord Chamberlain, as noted earlier, in theory enjoyed powers to regulate the theatre companies which operated under the royal patent, but in practice exercised those powers sparingly. Gay must have known that there was trouble ahead. He wrote to Swift on 2 December, telling of Grafton's order to Rich and adding:

what will become of it I know not, but I am sure I have written nothing that can be legally supprest, unless the setting vices in general in an odious light, and virtue in an amiable one may give offence.[13]

In the context of Gay and Swift's friendship, this remark amounts to a knowing wink. With the tutelage of *The Craftsman* and the rest of the opposition press, the British public over the preceding two years had learned how to read 'vices in particular' into presentations of 'vices in general', and how to make the application to specific politicians. Gay goes on to relate in the Preface that he waited on the Lord Chamberlain on 7 December, asking permission to read 'a faithful and genuine copy' of the play to him. He was told to leave the manuscript with Grafton.

Precisely what happened next has never been ascertained. Did Walpole himself order the suppression or did the Lord Chamberlain act on his own initiative after taking a look at what Gay had written? Lord Hervey recalled in his *Memoirs* that Walpole 'resolved, rather than suffer himself to be produced for thirty nights together upon the stage in the person of a highwayman, to make use of his friend the Duke of Grafton's authority as Lord Chamberlain to put a stop to the representation of it'.[14] This has been accepted as definitive, but Lord Hervey was living in Italy from July 1728 until October 1729, and thus necessarily received his information at second hand. Nothing exists to corroborate his account and no scrap of documentary evidence has ever been found. Politicians dislike committing their threats and promises to writing if they do not have to do so, and it may well be that Grafton's secretary simply materialised at Lincoln's Inn Fields and told Rich the eighteenth-century equivalent of 'The Boss says don't do it.'

On the following Thursday, 12 December, Gay received his manuscript back from Grafton 'with this answer; that it was not allow'd to be acted, but commanded to be supprest. This was told me in general without any reason assign'd, or any charge against me of my having given any particular offence.' At this point, I would argue, Gay realised that the play would not be produced in the near future and that the ministry had painted itself into a corner.

The opposition press joyfully picked up the suppression as a stick with which to beat their arch-foe, Walpole: the Great Man himself. On 14 December, two days after Gay received his notice, *The Craftsman* reported that 'the Sequel to the Beggar's Opera, which was going into Rehearsal at the Theatre in Lincoln's-Inn-Fields, is suppressed by *Authority*, without any particular Reason being alleged'. The similarity of *The Craftsman*'s phrasing to that of Gay's is interesting. Who was echoing whom? The opposition astutely took the line that the government was over-reacting, in paranoid fashion. Innocent poets had to be cautious because the censor was watching and reading everything with an ear for innuendo. This reverses the strategy employed with *The Beggar's Opera*, by which opposition writers such as Swift demonstrated how political innuendo was present everywhere in that work. Now, they warned writers: be careful. In *The Craftsman* of 28 December a song entitled 'A Bob for the Court' cautioned against the use of the very name 'Macheath':

> If *Macheath* you should name in the midst of his *Gang, fa la*.
> They'll say 'tis an Hint you would *Somebody* hang: *fa la*.
> For *Macheath* is a Word of such evil Report, *fa la*.
> *Application* cries out, *That's* a Bob *for the C– – –t, fa la*.[15]

In the midst of the brouhaha, some of it probably his own creation, Gay realised that he stood to profit handsomely from the sales of the printed play. Everyone would now have to read for themselves what infamous libel the ministry had detected in the play-script. Gay elected to retain the copyright, and contracted for a very large printing – 10,500 copies, perhaps ten times the usual press-run – which he himself paid for and proof-read.

> While I am writing this [to Swift], I am [in] the room next to our dining room with sheets all-round it, and two people from the Binder folding sheets. I print the Book at my own expence in Quarto, which is to be sold for six shillings with the Musick.[16]

He also launched a subscription drive among his friends, with the suggested subscription price a guinea, though Gay reported to Swift that Henrietta, Duchess of Marlborough 'hath given me a hundred pound for one Copy'.[17]

The subscription-drive itself was part of Gay's attack on the censors. Subscribing to *Polly*, could be interpreted as a vote of protest against Court and ministry policies. That is the way the King saw it when Gay's good friend the Duchess of Queensberry approached other members of the Court, soliciting subscriptions. Lord Hervey reported in his somewhat acid fashion what he had heard; though he was still in Italy when it happened. 'Her solicitations were so universal and so pressing that she came even into the Queen's apartment, went round the drawing-room, and made even the King's servants contribute to the printing of a thing which the King had forbid being recited.'[18] The Duchess was extruded from Court and her husband resigned his royal appointment as a gesture of support for her and for Gay. She also sent a letter to the King of quite remarkable sauciness, asserting that she 'is surprised and well-pleas'd that the King hath given her so agreeable a Command as to stay away from Court, where she never came for Diversion but to bestow a great Civility upon the King and Queen', adding, in a postscript, that she had given the Vice Chamberlain 'this answer in writing to read to His Majesty', with the implication that German George had difficulty reading his own letters in English.[19]

Polly was brought forth on 5 April 1729 in a sumptuous quarto, printed on excellent paper, with a rubricated title page like that of the Book of Common Prayer. Gay was associating his play with quality. Within a week he felt the unwelcome flattery of imitation: pirate publishers had editions on the street and Gay was forced to defend his copyright in court. By June some twenty-one booksellers and printers had been enjoined from publishing unauthorised editions.[20]

In the Preface to his play, Gay mentioned aspersions which had been cast upon him:

> I think my-self call'd upon to declare my principles; and I do with the strictest truth affirm, that I am as loyal a subject and as firmly attach'd to the present happy establishment as any of those who have the greatest places or pensions.[21]

The implication, of course, is that those having the greatest places or pensions were not so firmly attached after all; the King had better look around himself carefully. If he had scrutinised his first minister, Walpole, and had read *Polly*, he might have noticed striking resemblances between life and art.

Polly presents Macheath in the British West Indies as 'Morano', a fugitive in blackface, and leader of a pirate band, with Jenny Diver from the *Opera* as his paramour. Mrs Trapes is also in the Indies, acting as a supplier of females to the colonists. When Polly arrives, seeking Macheath, Mrs Trapes undertakes to supply her to the settler Ducat, over the objections of Ducat's shrewish wife. Mrs Ducat is happy enough to connive with Polly and get her out of the house, disguised as a young man. Polly, in her breeches, encounters the pirates and Jenny Diver makes a pass at the supposed young man – or do her quick eyes penetrate the disguise? The pirates under Morano's leadership are preparing to attack the settlement. Ducat and the settlers make common cause in defence with the Native Americans, a group of most-noble noble savages, and the attack fails. Morano is captured, revealed to be Macheath in blackface, and executed. At the curtain, Polly is left to marry the Indian prince Cawwakee when her grief subsides.

By displacing the action to the West Indies, Gay has given up the wealth of local references with which *The Beggar's Opera* is enriched. On the other hand, particular references would have been highlighted for London audiences by the displacement; what Gay loses in comedy he makes up in satire. In the first scene, for example, Mrs Trapes is encouraging the colonial Ducat to live up to British customs: 'You are wealthy, very wealthy Mr. *Ducat*; and I grant you the more you have, the taste of getting more should grow stronger upon you.' What he needs is a kept mistress, which she can supply.

> *Ducat:* Madam, in most of my expences I run into the polite taste. I have a fine library of books that I never read; I build, I buy plate, jewels, pictures, or any thing that is valuable and curious, as your great men do, merely out of ostentation. But indeed I must own, I do still cohabit with my wife; and she is very uneasy and vexatious upon accounts of my visits to you.
>
> *Trapes*: Indeed, indeed, Mr. *Ducat*, you shou'd break through all this usurpation at once, and keep . . .[22]

As Goldgar has argued,

> Gay can hardly have been ignorant of the similarity between this self-portrait and the ridicule by the opposition press of Walpole's display of rich vulgarity at Houghton. [Moreover] Ducat's attempts to be unfaithful to his wife would have added one more detail to the similarity.[23]

Gay continues his attack on politicians (for politician read Walpole) a few scenes later in Trapes's soliloquy and song. There is an echo of the *Opera*'s transposition of values here: politicians are like me, a pimp, Trapes declares; only their situation is different: 'Were they in my circumstances they would act like me; were I in theirs, I should be rewarded as a most profound penetrating politician.' She sings:

> In pimps and politicians
>   The genius is the same;
> Both raise their own conditions
>   On others guilt and shame:
> With a tongue well-tipt with lyes
> Each the want of parts supplies,
> And with a heart that's all disguise
> Keeps his schemes unknown.[24]

Robert Walpole's greed, secretiveness and mendacity are displayed with a guiding fingerpost. This is strong stuff, much stronger than *The Beggar's Opera*. The ministers' instincts had been correct.

Their judgement, however, was bound to be wrong, whatever course of action they chose. If they undertook to deny the particular satire, they would simply underscore its importance and, in effect, confirm its accuracy. On the other hand, if they decided to stonewall, as they did, then they stood convicted in public opinion as, at the very least, bumbling bureaucrats and at worst, philistine tyrants. On the whole, the latter has been the judgement of literary history: Walpole and his associates have been seen as losers, and malicious losers at that. Goldgar entitles his chapter on this period 'The triumphs of wit' and adds that 'indeed, the banning of *Polly* was more useful to the opposition than its performance on stage would have been'.[25]

Gay the opposition writer, then, contrived to censor the censors and make a great deal of money from his printed edition – though just how much is uncertain. He apparently netted £1,200 from his subscription campaign, and Swift, writing to Pope in August 1729, expressed the hope that 'Mr. Gay will keep his 3,000£ and live on the interest without decreasing the principal one penny'.[26] A total of three thousand pounds from the printing, though high, is not impossible. Colley Cibber, writing years afterwards, reported that some persons believed Gay 'had been a greater Gainer, by Subscriptions to his Copy, than he could have been by a bare Theatrical Presentation'.[27] This may well be so, but the sad fact remains that Gay the playwright, as distinct from Gay the opposition writer, did not live to see his new ballad opera performed. Although *Polly* has dramaturgical problems – Macheath the hero/villain of the *Opera* is here pure villain – it also embodies some of his most imaginative musical effects. He knew what the company at Lincoln's Inn Fields could do, and he crafted *Polly* to let them do it. Perhaps surprisingly, *Polly* has more music than *The Beggar's Opera* if one counts the number of airs: seventy-one to sixty-nine. As in his earlier work, Gay borrowed his music from whatever sources interested him: British ballad tunes, popular street music, theatre music. He was still much attuned to contemporary opera, borrowing the Dead March from Attilio Ariosti's *Coriolanus* (1723). The March from Handel's *Scipione* (1726), which is familiar today as the slow march of the Grenadier Guards, he converted into an amusing quartet in Act I (Air 17). The other two borrowings from Handel, Roger Fiske has demonstrated, are 'based on minuets in *The Water Music* which had not then been published except in inaccurate song-arrangements'.[28] Gay's musical taste was both catholic and current.

Unfortunately, neither he nor his fellow Scriblerians Pope and Swift lived to see and hear *Polly*. Perhaps theatre managers continued to be wary about the Lord Chamberlain's order. The prohibition stuck. Not until June 1777 was it produced, with considerable alterations, by George Colman the Elder. It played for only seven nights but, appropriately, Catherine Hyde, Duchess of Queensberry, who had led the subscription campaign on Gay's behalf, was at the Little Haymarket for an early performance and loved it. This play, a diarist friend wrote, 'cost the Duchess her death. She went constantly to See it, & would not be prevented by a very bad cold'.[29] One of Gay's circle of friends, at any rate, lived to beat the censors and see his controversial play on the stage half a century after he wrote it.

NOTES

1 See C. Winton, 'Dramatic censorship', in R. D. Hume (ed.), *The London Theatre World, 1660–1800*, Carbondale, Southern Illinois University Press, 1980, pp. 286–308.
2 For an extended treatment of the episode, see my forthcoming book *John Gay and his Theatre*.
3 See J. M. Levine, *Dr. Woodward's Shield*, Berkeley and Los Angeles, University of California Press, 1977, pp. 9, 324.
4 Public Record Office, LC 5/157, fol. 148 verso.
5 The specific legal authority of the Lord Chamberlain was not clear in the early eighteenth century, in large part because the legal standing of the theatre companies themselves was murky. See J. Milhous, 'Company management', and C. Winton, 'Dramatic censorship', in R. D. Hume (ed.), *The London Theatre World*, pp. 1–34 and 286–308.
6 See J. H. Plumb, *Sir Robert Walpole. The King's Minister*, London, Cresset, 1960, pp. 157–76.
7 Harmonicus' letter was re-published in the middle of March 1728, appended to the 'second edition' of Christopher Bullock's *Woman's Revenge*, as *A Compleat Key to the Beggar's Opera*.
8 J. Swift, *Irish Tracts 1728–1733*, ed. H. Davis, Oxford, Basil Blackwell, 1955, p. 34.
9 B. Goldgar, *Walpole and the Wits*, Lincoln, University of Nebraska Press, 1976, p. 70.
10 R. D. Hume, *Henry Fielding and the London Theatre 1728–1737*, Oxford, Clarendon Press, 1988, p. 78.
11 Goldgar, *Walpole and the Wits*, p. 75.
12 J. Gay, *Dramatic Works*, 2 vols, ed. J. Fuller, Oxford, Clarendon Press, 1983, vol. II, p. 968. Italics reversed.
13 C. F. Burgess (ed.), *The Letters of John Gay*, Oxford, Clarendon Press, 1966, p. 78.
14 R. Sedgwick (ed.), John, Lord Hervey, *Some Materials Towards Memoirs of the Reign of King George II*, London, Eyre & Spottiswoode, 1931, p. 98.
15 Quoted in Goldgar, *Walpole and the Wits*, p. 83.
16 *Letters of John Gay*, p. 80, 18 March 1729.
17 ibid., pp. 79–80.
18 Hervey, *Memoirs*, p. 99.
19 Letter quoted in C. F. Burgess, 'John Gay and *Polly* and a letter to the King', *Philological Quarterly*, vol. 47, 1968, pp. 596–8. Burgess makes the plausible suggestion that Gay may have assisted the Duchess in composing the letter.
20 See J. Sutherland, ' "Polly" among the Pirates', *Modern Language Review*, vol. 37, 1942, pp. 291–303.
21 Gay, *Dramatic Works*, vol. II, p. 70.
22 ibid., vol. II, p. 77.
23 Goldgar, *Walpole and the Wits*, p. 82.
24 Gay, *Dramatic Works*, vol. II, p. 81. Original in italics.

25 Goldgar, *Walpole and the Wits*, p. 84.
26 G. Sherburn (ed.), *The Correspondence of Alexander Pope*, Oxford, Clarendon Press, 1956, vol. III, p. 43.
27 B. R. S. Fone (ed.), *An Apology for the Life of Colley Cibber*, Ann Arbor, University of Michigan Press, 1968, p. 136.
28 R. Fiske, *English Theatre Music in the Eighteenth Century*, 2nd edn, Oxford, Oxford University Press, 1986, p. 111.
29 A. M. Larpent quoted in L. W. Conolly, 'Anna Margaretta Larpent, the Duchess of Queensberry and Gay's *Polly* in 1777', *Philological Quarterly*, vol. 51, 1972, pp. 955–7.

Chapter 7

'An old tragedy on a disgusting subject': Horace Walpole and *The Mysterious Mother*

Peter Sabor

To publish or not to publish was the question for Horace Walpole: from 1736, when he first appeared in print with a Latin poem contributed anonymously to a Cambridge University collection, to 1786, when he issued *Postscript to the Royal and Noble Authors* in an edition of only forty copies from his private press.[1] His memoirs, a compilation of some three million words, were written for publication, but Walpole ensured that they would not appear until long after his death. His letters, similarly, were written with posterity in view, but were not to be printed during his lifetime.[2] Most of his writings appeared anonymously, and his most famous work, *The Castle of Otranto* (1765), was published in the guise of a translation by William Marshal from an Italian romance by 'Onuphrio Muralto', supposedly published in Naples in 1529. Only after thus testing the waters, and protecting his identity with a double pseudonym, did Walpole put his name to the second edition of the novel.

Far from suffering from the censorship of external agents, Walpole was his own efficient, if ambivalent, censor. In 1757 he opened a private press at his country house at Strawberry Hill, on which fourteen of his own works were to be printed. He could thus, to a considerable extent, control the response to his writings, determining the number of copies to be printed in each case, the precise date of issue and the individuals who would, or would not, be given copies. *Hieroglyphic Tales* (1785), for example, a collection of five short uncanny stories, was printed in an edition of only six copies, and even these remained in Walpole's possession until his death. Here the censorship was absolute: no one could read these psychologically revealing fantasies, since Walpole retained every copy.

Walpole began writing *The Mysterious Mother*, a blank-verse, double-incest tragedy in five acts, at Christmas 1766, completing it, after laying it aside for several months, on 15 March 1768. It was printed at Strawberry Hill between June and August of that year in an edition of fifty copies. In 1773 he wrote a one-act farce, *Nature Will Prevail*, which had a run of seven performances at the Haymarket in 1778, but he never again attempted to write a tragedy. Unlike *Nature Will Prevail*, *The Mysterious Mother* was not performed in Walpole's lifetime. Indeed, it seems never to have been staged.[3] Walpole did, however, consider the possibility of performance as soon as the play was completed, and before it had been printed. On 15 April 1768, he wrote to his friend George Montagu:

> I have finished my tragedy, but as you would not bear the subject, I will say no more of it. . . . I am not yet intoxicated enough with it, to think it would do for the stage, though I wish to see it acted: but as Mrs Pritchard leaves the stage next month, I know nobody could play the Countess; nor am I disposed to expose myself to the impertinences of that jackanapes Garrick.[4]

Characteristically, Walpole expresses his views and intentions here through a series of contradictions. He does not believe the play is stageable, yet he wishes to see it staged. It has a part that only Hannah Pritchard could play, yet Pritchard is about to end her acting career. He has, he continues, written an epilogue for his old friend the comic actress Kitty Clive, yet she may not wish to speak it.

To appreciate the importance of the Countess's part in *The Mysterious Mother* and to understand why Walpole believed that Montagu would not 'bear the subject', one must know something of the plot of this now all-but-forgotten play.[5] The period is just before the Reformation. Sixteen years before the action begins, the Countess of Narbonne's husband had been killed by a stag, just as he was returning to his wife after a long separation. On the same night, her son, Count Edmund, had arranged an assignation with his mother's maidservant. The distraught Countess took the maidservant's place, unbeknown to Edmund. From this union she bore a child, Adeliza, who was raised in a convent while Edmund was banished from the Court of Narbonne. When the play opens, Edmund has just returned, as a soldier, from his long exile. He soon meets the beautiful young Adeliza and promptly falls in love. The Countess's sinister confessor, Father Benedict, who wishes to gain control of Narbonne, suspects that Adeliza is the Countess's daughter and marries the girl to Edmund. The Countess now confesses to Edmund that a double incest has taken place, and that she is the 'mother of thy daughter, sister, wife'.[6] In a spectacular final scene, the Countess kills herself, Adeliza is banished to a convent, and Edmund returns to the wars, hoping to meet death in combat.

Walpole was never to find an actress to play the part of the Countess, nor did he approach 'that jackanapes Garrick' about a possible production of *The Mysterious Mother*. According to George Steevens, moreover, Walpole left 'strict injunctions' with his friends that the play 'should never be shown to Mr. *Garrick'*, to whose judgement he could 'by no means stoop'.[7] While avoiding Garrick's management at the Drury Lane Theatre, Walpole could also have taken his play to George Colman, manager of the rival patent theatre at Covent Garden. In 1772, the poet and dramatist William Mason urged Walpole to 'make Mr Colman a present of your *Mysterious Mother'*, further advising him to stipulate for Mary Ann Yates as Countess (*Corr*. XXVIII: pp. 55–6). Mason's promptings, however, were in vain. In 1781, when he again suggested to Walpole that 'very few plays I believe would act finer, could actors be found equal to it, and if the guilt were softened', Walpole rebuffed him once more: 'As to the *Mysterious Mother* being acted I am perfectly secure, at least while Lord Hertford is Lord Chamberlain, nay, whoever should succeed him I think would not license it without my consent' (*Corr*. XXIX: pp. 142, 144).

For other eighteenth-century dramatists, the Lord Chamberlain embodied the oppressive powers of censorship; without his consent, their plays could not be licensed for performance. For Walpole, in contrast, the Lord Chamberlain's office, held by his cousin Lord Hertford from 1766 to 1782 and in 1783, offered an assurance that no theatre manager would stage his play against his own wishes. Walpole did not reveal to Mason that during his term of office, Hertford had on several occasions turned to Walpole himself for advice on questions of censorship. Far from seeking greater liberty for dramatists, Walpole was determined to uphold the censor's role.[8]

None the less, Walpole dwelt on the possibility of producing *The Mysterious Mother*, and according to Laetitia-Matilda Hawkins, some pressure was put on him not to proceed with a performance of his play. In her *Anecdotes, Biographical Sketches and Memoirs* (1822), Hawkins denounces *The Mysterious Mother* as a work of 'enormous indecency'. She also claims that Walpole 'once threatened to produce' *The Mysterious Mother*, and that her father, the musicologist John Hawkins, was instrumental in stopping the production by appealing to the Bishop of London, Robert Lowth. There is no supporting evidence for this undated anecdote, which A. T. Hazen assigns to 1778, but Hawkins is unlikely to have fabricated it.[9]

In addition to withholding his play from the stage, for many years Walpole exercised strict control over its readership. Few among even his close friends were given copies of the 1768 edition; Walpole seems, initially at least, to have retained most copies of the impression himself.[10] Madame du Deffand, for example, one of Walpole's most important correspondents, first enquired about the play in March 1768, asking him to translate a few scenes from *The Mysterious Mother* and send them to her. In his reply, Walpole tantalised her with comments on the play, without sending her the requested translation. The tragedy, he wrote:

> ne vous plairait pas assurément; il n'y a pas de beaux sentiments. Il n'y a que des passions sans enveloppe, des crimes, des repentirs, et des horreurs . . . depuis le premier acte jusqu'à la dernière scène l'intérêt languit au lieu d'augmenter; peut-il [y] avoir un plus grand défaut?

Undeterred, du Deffand reminded Walpole that she still expected some scenes in translation from him; no such translation, however, was forthcoming. Four years later she tried a new strategy, offering to have the play translated herself if Walpole would send her a copy (*Corr.* IV: pp. 32, 40, 84; V, 267). Still Walpole prevaricated; two weeks later she asked for the play again, and then reminded Walpole that he had failed to send it to her. After the book at last arrived at the end of 1772, she kept Walpole informed of her attempts to find a translator while assuring him that no one would be permitted to read the translation except herself (*Corr.* V: pp. 270, 293, 299). Someone as close to Walpole as Madame du Deffand could thus obtain a copy of the elusive book, but only after repeated entreaties and reminders.

George Montagu, however, received *The Mysterious Mother* without recourse to such requests. In September 1769, he told Walpole that a party of young visitors had found his copy of the play, 'and boys as they are the[y] had no patience till they finished it and we read the acts amongst us. . . . They would have got it by heart. However, a few similes they have retained, and cap with one another some of the lines that struck them most' (*Corr.* X: p. 297). Walpole, of course, was alarmed by the remark that these visitors had memorised parts of the play: Montagu's copy was supposed to be for his own exclusive use, not the source of fragmentary reconstructions by others.[11] In his reply, Walpole wrote: 'I am sorry those boys got at my tragedy. I beg you would keep it under lock and key; it is not at all food for the public' (*Corr.* X: p. 298). Like the most precious items that Walpole collected at Strawberry Hill, *The Mysterious Mother* was to be kept 'under lock and key': not withheld entirely from sight, but seen only by the chosen few to whom Walpole had granted access.

Since *The Mysterious Mother* was not to be performed on stage, private readings afforded the only means of hearing the play's pseudo-Shakespearian blank verse declaimed. Some of these readings were given by Walpole himself. Lady Mary Coke recounts that in 1768 Walpole had repeated part of *The Mysterious Mother* 'in the Coach coming from Ld Cadogan's; it pleased me very much'. In April 1769 he also presented her with a copy.[12] Other readings, such as the one at Montagu's house, were carried out without Walpole's consent, and were therefore potentially damaging. Mary Hamilton writes in 1784 of having heard a reading of the play by the Irish playwright Edward Tighe, with no apparent ill consequences (*Corr*. XXXI: p. 216). Another dramatic reading, however, described by Frances Burney in 1786, was more eventful. Burney, who had recently gone into service at Windsor Castle, had borrowed a copy of the Strawberry Hill edition from Queen Charlotte: a copy borrowed, in turn, by the Queen from Lord Harcourt. After hearing the play declaimed by two readers, Leonard Smelt and Charles de Guiffardière, Burney recorded her impressions:

> Dreadful was the whole! truly dreadful! a story of so much horror, from attrocious & voluntary guilt, never did I hear! Mrs. Smelt & myself heartily regretted that it had come in our way, & mutually agreed that we felt ourselves *ill-used* in having heard it. . . . For myself, I felt a sort of indignant aversion rise fast & warm in my mind against the wilful Author of a story so horrible.[13]

Walpole seems never to have heard about this reading, which would have confirmed his worst fears about the dangers of letting his play reach an unsympathetic audience.

Walpole experienced different kinds of difficulties with his friend William Mason, who received a presentation copy of the play in 1769. Unlike such obliging friends as du Deffand and Montagu, who expressed only gratitude for similar gifts, Mason proved to be a most demanding reader. In a letter of 8 May, he informed Walpole:

> I have read your tragedy three or four times over with a good deal of attention, and as the *costume*, the characters and many of the sentiments, etc., please me highly, I cannot help wishing that capital defect in the *dénouement* was amended according to the scheme I proposed to you.

Enclosed with the letter were several pages of proposed alterations, mainly to the last two acts of the play, which have the effect of making the Countess's incestuous encounter with Edmund accidental rather than voluntary, motivated by jealousy of her husband instead of lust for her son (*Corr*. XXVIII: pp. 10–16).

Walpole's response to these proposals was twofold. To Mason he expressed delighted approval, adding that should *The Mysterious Mother* ever be performed after his death, it would owe its presentation to the alterations. While flattering Mason in this manner, Walpole recorded his genuine opinion of the proposals, in notes on Mason's letter. They would, he thought, have destroyed his object by changing the characterisation of the Countess. Jealousy would reduce her 'to a very hacked character, instead of being one quite new on the stage' (*Corr*. XXVIII: p. 9). What emerges in this private memorandum is

Walpole's enduring belief in the importance and originality of *The Mysterious Mother*, a belief that he strove to conceal from others by ceaselessly disparaging the play. Mason, however, would not let the matter rest. In several of his letters over the next ten years, he chastised Walpole for not adopting alterations that would, he believed, make *The Mysterious Mother* fit for the stage. In one of his replies, Walpole again purported to admire the changes, which he had always thought 'magic, to be effected by so few words', but nothing could induce him 'to venture it on the stage, not from superabundant modesty, but from the abusive spirit of the times. I have no notion of presenting one's self coolly to a savage mob to be torn to pieces' (*Corr.* XXVIII: p. 371).

So long as *The Mysterious Mother* remained unpublished, Walpole could maintain this pose: affecting admiration for Mason's changes, while insisting that the play would never be made public. In May 1781, however, Walpole wrote to Mason about an impending pirated edition:

> Do you know that I am in great distress? my *Mysterious Mother* has wandered into the hands of booksellers, and has been advertised with my name without my knowledge; like a legislator I have held out both rewards and punishments to prevent its appearance, but at last have been forced to advertise it myself – but unless the spurious edition appears, I shall keep it back till everybody is gone out of town, and then it will be forgotten by the winter. I intend too to abuse it myself in a short advertisement prefixed.
>
> (*Corr.* XXIX: p. 139)

The identity of the booksellers remains unknown, and the advertisements for an unauthorised edition have not been found. Walpole may have fabricated the piracy story. He had an obvious motive for doing so: by 1781 his stock of copies was exhausted. An impending piracy would give him the necessary justification for having a new edition printed; the work would thus become available without Walpole's being responsible.

Whether the threat of a pirated edition was real or not, Walpole did arrange for the play to be printed by a commercial publisher, James Dodsley, who advertised it in the *Public Advertiser* for 30 April 1781 as forthcoming, 'to prevent spurious editions which have been advertised without [Walpole's] consent' (*Corr.* XXIX: p. 139). The text was furnished, as Walpole had promised Mason, with a prefatory note, telling readers:

> The author of the following Tragedy is so far from thinking it worthy of being offered to the Public, that he has done every thing

in his power to suppress the publication – in vain. It is solely to avoid its being rendered still worse by a surreptitious edition, that he is reduced to give it from his own copy. He is sensible that the subject is disgusting, and by no means compensated by the execution. . . . He respects the judgment of the Public too much to offer to them voluntarily what he does not think deserves their approbation.[14]

The 'Public' to whom the Preface was addressed, however, was never to gain access to this edition of the play. In a letter to Mason in May 1781 and in a subsequent letter to Henry Seymour Conway, Walpole announced his intention of having the edition published in the quiet summer months, when polite society was out of town. To Conway he added that he would 'let it steal out in the midst of the first event that engrosses the public; and . . . it will be still-born, if it is twin with any babe that squalls and makes much noise' (*Corr.* XXXIX: p. 373). In the event, however, Walpole did more than arrange for a still-born publication; he withheld the entire stock for his own disposal, making the printing no publication at all.

Since the first edition had been privately printed, *The Mysterious Mother* had thus still not been published thirteen years after its completion. The *Morning Herald* for 1 June 1781 remarked that Walpole's 'friends wonder at the author's coyness of publication, all with reason agreeing with the good character of the work, that it is rather unequal, but on the whole it is to be pronounced good' (*Corr.* XXXIX: pp. 372–3). This showed considerable insight into Walpole, whose 'coyness of publication' was a lifelong characteristic, not merely one associated with this play.

As well as informing Mason about the new printing, Walpole had to justify his failure to adopt his friend's proposed emendations. In his letter of May 1781, Walpole tells Mason disingenuously: 'at first I had a mind to add your magic alterations, which in the compass of ten lines makes it excusable – but then I thought it would look like wishing to have it brought on the stage as it might be' (*Corr.* XXIX: p. 140). This justification for not accepting Mason's revisions, which would make *The Mysterious Mother* stageable and thus in danger of being produced against the author's wishes, is a brilliant rhetorical touch. In his reply, Mason counters Walpole's argument by suggesting that without his alterations, the play will be 'not only criticized but censured'; he was, however, unaware that Walpole would strive to ensure that it could be neither criticised nor censured. A week later, Walpole responded with a new gambit; he would not correct the play, he declared, because 'that would show predilection and partiality to it; partiality I have, but it is to your corrections, and it shall have none other' (*Corr*. XXIX: p. 144). Mason alone would thus receive credit for his inspired emendations, which 'shall stand by themselves in your name'.

While arranging for the new printing of *The Mysterious Mother* and fending off Mason's attempts to alter the text, Walpole also had to deal with a third problem: an impending essay on the play. In April 1781, the actor John Henderson, 'the Bath Roscius', spent a week with Walpole at Strawberry Hill. He was invited because of his close involvement with Robert Jephson's *The Count of Narbonne*, a dramatic adaptation of Walpole's *The Castle of Otranto*, which would have its première in November, and in which Henderson would play. During his visit, Henderson informed Walpole that an excerpt from *The Mysterious Mother* would appear in a new edition of David Erskine Baker's *Biographia Dramatica*, a two-volume reference work on British dramatists, with summaries of their plays, being prepared by Isaac Reed. In a letter, Walpole expressed his dismay and his desire to 'prevent that publication, as it will occasion discourse about the play, which is disgusting from the subject, and absurd from being totally unfit for the stage'. After asking Henderson whether he thought the offending passage 'could be stopped', and offering to 'pay for my folly', Walpole denounced his own play once again for its 'many defects in the execution as well as in the subject'. Henderson showed the letter to Reed, who made a copy of it and acted on Walpole's request (*Corr*. XLI: pp. 427–8). The article on *The Mysterious Mother* in the *Biographia Dramatica*, published in January 1782, concludes: 'We intended to have given the reader a specimen of it; but having learnt that the sensibility of the author (to whom every respect is due) would be wounded by such an exhibition, we deem ourselves bound to suppress it, however reluctantly.'[15]

Reed did more for Walpole, however, than refrain from quoting the play. He also cancelled the original essay, by George Steevens, and wrote a new and more flattering contribution in its place, declaring that although 'the production of such a tragedy as the present, on the modern stage, would be extremely hazardous', it was 'equal if not superior, to any play of the present century'.[16] In March 1782, Walpole thanked Henderson for 'saving my scenes from the *Biographia Dramatica*' (*Corr*. XLII: p. 5). Meanwhile, a new problem had arisen. In November 1781, the *St James's Chronicle* had printed George Steevens's cancelled article, complete with a lengthy excerpt from the play, the first occasion on which any part of it had been published.[17] In drawing attention to the principal criticism made by Mason, that 'the moment to which the guilt of our heroine is confined, was of all others such as could not fail to have unfitted her for the commission of the fact from whence her succeeding miseries were derived', Steevens's essay did exactly what Walpole wished to prevent: initiate public discussion of the psychological and sexual motivation of his heroine. The essay was, moreover, reprinted in the *Public Advertiser* for 21 November 1781, in the *European Magazine* for September 1787, in Sir Samuel Egerton Brydges's *Censura Literaria* (1809), and, with some revisions, restored to a new edition of *Biographia Dramatica* edited by Stephen Jones in 1812. Since Steevens's article thus eventually gained a wider readership than the one by Reed that had originally replaced it, Walpole's attempts at suppression were, in this case, only partly successful.

Perhaps emboldened by the example of the *St James's Chronicle*, the *Public Advertiser* printed further excerpts from *The Mysterious Mother* on 8 November 1783. Walpole took immediate action. He complained to Lady Ossory that:

> this morning at breakfast I was saluted with the first scene of my old tragedy, all sugared over with comfits like a Twelfth-cake. I have been writing to Mr Woodfall, to beg to buy myself out of his claws, and to lecture him for his gross compliments.
>
> (*Corr.* XXXIII: p. 429)

Walpole requested Henry Woodfall, printer of the *Public Advertiser*, to 'print no more of the *Mysterious Mother*, which it is a little hard on the author to see retailed without his consent'. As usual he disparaged the play, 'an old tragedy on a disgusting subject', which he was attempting to suppress and which he 'would not suffer to be represented on the stage, if any manager was injudicious enough to think of it'. Walpole particularly disliked the effusive compliments to himself that preceded the excerpt, and offered to pay to have any further instalments stopped (*Corr.* XLII: pp. 85–6). On this occasion, his request was successful; no more excerpts appeared in the *Public Advertiser*.

While striving to prevent public access to his play, Walpole was not averse to giving copies to certain close friends or distinguished acquaintances. In May 1779, for example, he received a request from a friend of long standing, Horace Mann, the English representative in Tuscany. Mann reveals the rivalry among members of Walpole's circle vying for possession of copies: 'I would never contradict those who said to me, "To be sure, you have seen it." Nor would I ask Sir William Hamilton for it, not to give him room to triumph over me on this occasion.' Walpole sent Mann a copy of the Strawberry Hill edition, disparaging the play as usual: 'I doubt it will shock more than please you, for nothing can be more disgusting than the subject' (*Corr.* XXIV: pp. 470, 481). Mann, however, responded with unrestrained delight:

The inimitable tragedy, too, I have read with exquisite feeling and admiration. . . . The subject may be too horrid for the stage, but the judicious management of it by preparing the reader for the catastrophe, the sublime ideas and expressions so admirably adapted to the personages, make it a delicious entertainment for the closet. How could you, my dear Sir, conceal it from me for so long! My nephew and I continually talk of it with ecstasy. He had almost got it by heart on his journey. . . . I shall soon be as perfect in it as he is.

(*Corr*. XXIV: p. 517)[18]

A year previously, in 1778, Walpole had received a request for the play from another friend, Lady Harcourt. The Harcourts had already received a presentation copy. Walpole, none the less, complied, sending the Harcourts a second copy of the Strawberry Hill edition and, later, presented them with a copy of Dodsley's edition of 1781.[19] Social standing, of course, had a bearing on Walpole's willingness to part with copies: the Earl and Countess Harcourt, among the loftiest of Walpole's correspondents, were favoured partly as a signal of his respect for their aristocratic rank.

Title alone, however, was not sufficient. In 1770, Walpole had offered to show the play to the Earl of Charlemont on his next visit from Ireland, but refused to send him a copy, explaining that it 'never thinks of producing itself', although it has 'peeped out of its lurking corner once or twice' (*Corr*. XLI: p. 191). (Walpole later, however, made amends by promising Lord Charlemont a copy of Dodsley's edition in 1785, while reminding him that 'this edition has not the merit of the first impression, I mean, of being printed here, and of being a rarity' (*Corr*. XLII: p. 155).) In 1773 Walpole agreed to send the play to the Earl of Hardwicke, 'as soon as ever he is able to go to Strawberry Hill'; but it is not known whether this promise was ever fulfilled (*Corr*. XLI: pp. 240–1). He did send a copy of the Strawberry Hill edition to the collector Richard Bull in 1780, but with an accompanying note, informing Bull that since this was his last remaining copy, he 'begs to have it returned as soon as [Bull] has read it, and that he will not let it go out of his hands'. In the copy itself, Bull noted: '*Mysterious Mother returned*, and afterwards sent back again to me' (*Corr*. XLI: pp. 414, 415). Walpole presumably returned the play after Dodsley's printing in 1781 made further copies available to him again.

While Walpole took every opportunity to disparage *The Mysterious Mother*, using such condemnations as a justification for withholding it, he displayed a quite different attitude to a set of drawings illustrating the text, executed in soot-water by his friend Lady Diana Beauclerk. Walpole first mentioned these drawings to Lady Ossory in December 1775, declaring that the three then completed, 'if the subject were a quarter as good as the drawings, would make me a greater genius than Shakespear, as she is superior to Guido and Salvator Rosa. Such figures! such dignity! such simplicity!' (*Corr.* XXXII: p. 289). Lady Diana made seven drawings in all, which Walpole housed in a room built especially for the purpose at Strawberry Hill. In this hexagonal room, named the Beauclerk closet, hung with Indian blue damask, Walpole placed the drawings in an ebony cabinet, also constructed for the occasion. A copy of the play itself, bound in blue leather and gilt, was kept in the Beauclerk closet, contained in a special writing-table.[20] The room thus became a shrine to *The Mysterious Mother*, to which particularly favoured visitors might be granted access.

The advantage of the drawings, as Walpole wrote to Mann in 1779, was that 'they do not shock and disgust like their original, the tragedy' (*Corr.* XXIV: p. 524). In an Appendix added to his *Description of Strawberry-Hill* (1774), he emphasised the 'beauty and grace of the figures'. In one of the drawings, Walpole admired the 'tenderness, despair, and resolution of the countess in the last scene; in which is a new stroke of double passion in Edmund, whose right hand is clenched and ready to strike with anger, the left hand relents'.[21] Lady Diana, that is, had altered the scene for her own purpose, making it more palatable and less menacing. Far from objecting to this act of bowdlerisation, Walpole applauded it. The friends to whom he showed the treasured drawings shared his opinion of them. In 1782, Lady Mary Coke declared that they were 'finer than anything of the sort I ever saw; she is certainly the greatest genius in that way that has appeared for some ages' (*Corr.* XXXI: p. 297). Mary Hamilton noted in 1784 that Walpole had shown her the Beauclerk closet for a second time, although he opened the room only 'for his most particular friends'. The play, she stated, 'is the most horrible to be conceived, but these drawings, though they recall to mind the horrid subject, are most affectingly interesting' (*Corr.* XXXI: p. 216). Another visitor to Strawberry Hill, Joseph Farington, wrote in his diary for 1793: 'We saw the small room in which are Lady Di Beauclerk's designs for Lord Orford's play of *The Mysterious Mother* . . . which are shown but seldom' (*Corr.* XV: pp. 317–18). By concealing the drawings in a cabinet in a closed room of his house, Walpole had given them the same special status as exotic rarities that he had already given to his play through suppressing the printed editions.

For a period in the 1780s, then, Walpole's self-censorship of *The Mysterious Mother* worked effectively. The fifty copies of the play printed at Strawberry Hill, having all been distributed to friends, were now unavailable. The putative pirated edition of 1781 had been quashed, and the edition printed by Dodsley in 1781 was in Walpole's possession and could be presented to especially favoured enquirers, or withheld. In 1787, Walpole promised the Dodsley edition to Lady Ossory, while emphasising that he had no copies left of the original printing (*Corr.* XXXIII: p. 579). In 1789, in a letter to the Irish antiquary Joseph Walker, Walpole declared that he would continue to suppress the play as far as it was in his power (*Corr.* XLII: p. 255). And in 1790, Walpole sent a copy of the Dodsley edition to the poet William Parsons, insisting, as usual, that he was 'unwilling to part with a copy without protesting against his own want of judgment in selecting so disgusting a subject' (*Corr.* XLII: p. 276).

This state of tranquillity, in which selected visitors to Strawberry Hill could admire Beauclerk's anodyne illustrations while an occasional copy of the play itself was bequeathed to the chosen few, was not to last. In a letter of late 1790, Walker informed Walpole that a Dublin bookseller was about to reprint *The Mysterious Mother* and offered to superintend the work, so that at least the text would be accurate. Walpole urged him not to do so: 'if the bookseller will print it, I had rather he printed it faultily, than that you should take the pains to correct the press' (*Corr.* XLII: pp. 301–2, 305). Walker did, however, read the proofs of the edition, of which he sent a copy to Walpole in March 1791. Walpole found the text 'surprisingly correct', with the exception of a few 'immaterial errors' that he noted, but he objected strongly to the flattery contained in the publisher's advertisement: vulgar compliments on his 'high rank, excellent character and eminence in literature' were more than he could bear (*Corr.* XLII: pp. 318–19, 324–5).

Walpole could have prevented publication of the Dublin edition had he been willing to pay fifty pounds in compensation to the publishers. His reasons for refusing to do so are given in a letter to Lord Charlemont of February 1791, in which he declares that the play 'must take its fate'. After twenty-three years of suppressing his play, Walpole had at last relinquished the task. He could, he wrote to Charlemont, 'indemnify the present operator', but he would then be 'persecuted by similar exactions' from others. What makes this letter of particular interest is that, for once, Walpole acknowledges some fondness for the play:

> I have not existed to past seventy-three without having discovered the futility and triflingness of my own talents – and at the same time it would be impertinent to pretend to think that there is no merit in the execution of a tragedy, on which I have been so much flattered.

In a revealing metaphor, Walpole characterises Lord Charlemont as 'both my Lord Chamberlain and Licenser', who should now withdraw his prohibition of the play and thus allow it to be published. While he still writes of the 'egregious absurdity of selecting a subject so improper for the stage', Walpole's depiction of Lord Charlemont as Lord Chamberlain suggests that his original scheme for a production had never been wholly relinquished (*Corr.* XLII: pp. 308–10).

No such production materialised, but during the 1790s *The Mysterious Mother* became public property at last. The Dublin edition of 1791 was reprinted in London in the same year, apparently without Walpole's knowledge or consent, and another London edition appeared in 1796, a year before his death.[22] This edition elicited a letter in the *Monthly Magazine* discussing the date of the source for the play, and a substantial review by William Taylor in the *Monthly Review*, some months after Walpole's death. German critics also discussed the play in reviews of 1797 and 1798. Far from being the preserve of a handful of Walpole's friends, *The Mysterious Mother* had now made its way to European, as well as English, readers and reviewers.[23]

Walpole's dual attraction to and repulsion from his tragedy resembles his ambiguous attitude towards publishing his collected works. In 1768, he began printing his own writings in a quarto edition at Strawberry Hill, finishing volume one, containing *The Mysterious Mother*, in 1770. Parts of volume two were printed in the 1770s, but Walpole neither completed nor published the edition. On the one hand he took the pains to organise the material, began printing it in a sumptuous format, using a fresh supply of Caslon type bought especially for the occasion, and later arranged with Mary Berry for its completion and publication after his death. On the other hand he left the edition in a fragmentary state, and printed only a handful of copies of the one completed volume. In a letter of 1792 to the publisher George Nicol, Walpole rejected a proposal for a collected edition of his works: 'I would no more hear of a splendid and ornamental edition of my trifling writings, than I would dress my old, emaciated, infirm person in rich and gaudy clothes.' To justify his own printing of his works, Walpole explained that a 'little printer' had been planning an unauthorised edition to be published on his death; the Strawberry Hill edition was begun, he claimed, to discourage any such attempt (*Corr.* XLII: pp. 371–3).

The story, of course, is familiar. An anonymous publisher had, according to Walpole, planned an edition of *The Mysterious Mother* in 1781; hence Walpole's justification for Dodsley's edition of the same year. Now we hear that another anonymous publisher had planned an edition of his collected works before 1768; hence Walpole's justification for beginning to print them himself. While Walpole recoiled from public discussion of his play, he could never be satisfied if his works remained unknown; as well as censoring, he could not refrain from advertising it. Wilmarth Lewis notes that in arranging his works for posthumous publication, Walpole 'printed his "Epitaph on Lady Walpole," with its praise of her sensibility, charity, and unbigoted piety, immediately after *The Mysterious Mother*'.[24] Martin Kallich, similarly, suggests that 'it is possible to read *The Mysterious Mother*, like *The Castle of Otranto*, as a disturbing nightmarish fantasy – what Freud calls a punishment dream – and as a typical Oedipal family romance with a highly personal, although unconscious, meaning for the writer'.[25] There is, however, no need to invoke Freudian psychology to explain Walpole's love–hate relationship with *The Mysterious Mother*: his simultaneous desire to censor and promulgate the play. This is, after all, what he did with most of his writings.

For all his concealed pride in *The Mysterious Mother* and his long-cherished thoughts of having it performed on stage, Walpole's 'coyness of publication' ensured that the play would remain a closet drama. His own Lord Chamberlain, he had effectively censored the tragedy by withholding it from the common readers and theatre audiences whose judgement measures a play's success. In his Prologue to the play, Walpole contrasts the bloodlessness of contemporary drama, governed by 'timid laws' of decorum, with the 'magic' of Shakespeare's stage. Mocking those who would restrict the scope of drama, he enquires:

> Can crimes be punish'd by a bard enchain'd?
> Shall the bold censor back be sent to school,
> And told, This is not nice; That is not rule?[26]

This assault on the censor, however, was itself censored by Walpole, who permitted the Prologue to be printed for the first time only in the posthumous edition of his collected works, and not in its proper place but removed to a section of 'Miscellaneous Verses' in a different volume. Other dramatists of the age may have been enslaved by 'timid laws', but they, at least, published their plays, permitted reviews, and exposed their compositions to the hazards of the stage.

NOTES

1 Information on the publication of Walpole's writings is taken from A. T. Hazen, *A Bibliography of Horace Walpole*, New Haven, Conn., Yale University Press, 1948, and *A Bibliography of the Strawberry Hill Press*, rev. edn, New York, Barnes & Noble, 1973.
2 See P. Sabor, *Horace Walpole: a Reference Guide*, Boston, Mass., G. K. Hall, 1984, p. xv.
3 In Sir Samuel Egerton Brydges's *Censura Literaria*, 1805–9, vol. IX, p. 189, Joseph Haslewood claims that *The Mysterious Mother* was 'publicly rep-

resented' in Ireland; no records of an Irish production, however, have been found.

4 *The Yale Edition of Horace Walpole's Correspondence*, ed. W. S. Lewis *et al.*, 48 vols, New Haven, Conn., Yale University Press, 1937–83, vol. X, p. 259. All subsequent references are to this edition and are included parenthetically in the text by volume and page number.

5 No edition is currently in print. The play appeared, together with *The Castle of Otranto*, in an inaccurate edition edited by M. Summers, Constable, 1924. J. Dolan's doctoral dissertation, 'Horace Walpole's *The Mysterious Mother*: a critical edition', University of Arizona, 1970, has not been published.

6 *The Works of Horatio Walpole*, ed. M. Berry, 5 vols, London, 1798, vol. I, p. 120.

7 G. Steevens, 'The Mysterious Mother', *European Magazine*, vol. 12, September 1787, p. 191.

8 See L. W. Conolly, 'Horace Walpole, unofficial play censor', *English Language Notes*, vol. 9, 1971, pp. 42–6; and Conolly, *The Censorship of English Drama 1737–1824*, San Marino, Calif., Huntington Library, 1976, pp. 26–7.

9 L. M. Hawkins, 'Anecdotes', in *Horace Walpole: the Critical Heritage*, ed. P. Sabor, London, Routledge & Kegan Paul, 1987, p. 303; Hazen, *Strawberry Hill*, p. 79.

10 Hazen states that he found records of only six presentation copies: *Strawberry Hill*, p. 79. Other presentation copies, however, have since come to light, and more are known through references in Walpole's correspondence. The conjecture that Walpole may have 'destroyed a sizable proportion of the edition' (*Corr.* vol. XXXIII, p. 579), seems unwarranted.

11 Hazen, however, notes that Walpole's 'reluctance to give copies away . . . tended to encourage people to make MS copies of it; at least seven are extant': *Strawberry Hill*, p. 81.

12 Lady Mary Coke, *Letters and Journals*, ed. J. A. Home, 4 vols, Edinburgh, David Douglas, 1889–96, vol. II, p. 314, vol. III, p. 64.

13 Sabor (ed.), *Critical Heritage*, p. 141.

14 ibid., p. 136.

15 ibid., p. 139.

16 ibid., pp. 138, 139; R. H. Perkinson, 'Walpole and the *Biographia Dramatica*', *Review of English Studies*, vol. 15, 1939, pp. 204–6.

17 *St James's Chronicle*, 8–10, 15–17 November 1781; see *Corr.* vol. XXXIII, p. 429.

18 Hazen errs in stating that while Walpole 'finally allowed Sir Horace Mann to see a copy, he required Mann to send it back': *Strawberry Hill*, pp. 79–81. What Mann returned was a packet of Walpole's letters to him; see *Corr.* vol. XXIV, p. 522.

19 *Corr.* vol. XXXV, p. 493. The usually authoritative notes to the edition err in stating that the request for a second copy is 'somewhat mysterious'. A probable explanation is that the Harcourts had already lent their copy of the play to Queen Charlotte, who had it in her possession in 1786 when it was borrowed by Frances Burney; see Sabor (ed.), *Critical Heritage*, p. 140.

20 See W. S. Lewis, *Rescuing Horace Walpole*, New Haven, Conn., Yale University Press, 1978, pp. 107–15.

21 Berry, *Works of Horatio Walpole*, vol. II, p. 503.

22 See R. H. Perkinson, 'Walpole and a Dublin pirate', *Philological Quarterly*, vol. 15, 1936, pp. 391–400.

23 See Sabor, *Horace Walpole: a Reference Guide*, pp. 17–19.
24 W. Lewis, *Horace Walpole*, London, Rupert Hart-Davis, 1961, p. 163.
25 M. Kallich, *Horace Walpole*, New York, Twayne, 1971, p. 112.
26 Berry, *Works of Horatio Walpole*, vol. IV, p. 396.

Chapter 8

'The memory of the liberty of the press': the suppression of radical writing in the 1790s

Alan Booth

As he penned the dedication to his *Life of Samuel Johnson*, James Boswell reflected upon the difference between the Walpole era and the year 1790:

> Parliament then kept the press in a kind of mysterious awe. . . . In our time it has acquired an unrestrained freedom, so that the people in all parts of the kingdom have a fair, open, and exact report of the actual proceedings of their representatives and legislators, which in our constitution is highly to be valued.[1]

The rise of parliamentary reporting was seen as a good example of the progress of press freedom in the last decades of the century.[2] Despite some misgivings at the apparent increase in the libelling of public figures, it was commonly held that the press was the most visible testament to the country's much vaunted liberty; a liberty which guaranteed national prosperity and separated Britons from the enslaved masses of continental despotisms. Such assumptions were testimony to the self-confidence of the propertied classes, those who considered themselves 'the people', the political public. Yet in the 1790s the rhetoric of English freedom was to be severely tested as events in France stimulated a fundamental rethinking of political axioms. The emergence of new types of political discourse, new channels of communication and, above all, a mass political public, shook the confidence of the governing classes. In a divided society those who seemed, however obliquely, to criticise the government were branded 'jacobins', and publicly reviled in an effort to prevent political ideas from reaching or influencing a mass audience.

In the late eighteenth century, liberal and humanitarian sentiments flourished among the propertied classes. A wide range of writing reflected the demands of this growing public of 'enlightened' sensibilities. In many provincial towns, circulating and subscription libraries, book clubs and reading societies had spread rapidly during the second half of the century. Coffee-houses and the more select literary and philosophical societies provided a forum for discussion of topical issues. The press flourished: the 90 newspapers and journals published in 1750 had expanded to 264 by 1800.[3] The book trade grew commensurately, provincial printing increased, and the number of novels printed per annum rose from about twenty between 1740 and 1770 to forty between 1770 and 1800. This was an integral part of what has been termed a cultural revolution, fed by a burgeoning consumerism.[4] As the reading public grew, so did the numbers of those informed about political issues and wishing to have a voice in the political life of the country.

This was the identification of reading public and political public made by Boswell. However, the 'desire for reading' was not exclusive to the propertied classes; it had long been a feature of popular culture. Few households were without some reading-matter. Many ordinary families owned a Bible and one or two of the ballads and chapbooks which were the stock of eighteenth-century popular literature. Possession does not necessarily signify the habit of reading, nor desire the ability to read, and the obstacles to both were great. None the less, even at the lower levels of plebeian society perhaps 40 per cent could read, and among the artisans and tradesmen who formed the backbone of the industrial workforce, the figure was far higher.[5] Moreover, although wages varied enormously, a wide range of literature, including pamphlets and books such as *Gulliver's Travels*, was within reach of the pockets of most artisans and even many labourers. But purchase was only one means of acquisition and there were many other ways of obtaining reading-matter. Some reading clubs and libraries were accessible to the labouring classes. One near Stockport had a subscription of a penny a month in the 1780s, while a Bury St Edmunds library in 1783 allowed the borrowing of individual books at a penny a night for a single volume.[6] Francis Place recalled how, in the mid-1780s as a young London apprentice, he 'used to borrow books from a man in Maiden Lane, Covent Garden, leaving a small sum deposit, and paying a trifle for reading them, having only one at a time'.[7] Hiring newspapers was also common. Friendly societies bought papers for their members; families, friends and workmates clubbed together to read the latest news, the literate reading aloud to the less skilled. 'Without newspapers,' declared one observer in 1790, 'our coffee houses, ale houses and barbers' shops would undergo a change next to depopulation; and our country cottagers, the curate, the exciseman and the blacksmith would lose the satisfaction of being as wise as William Pitt.'[8] Of course, much of what was read was not directly political but, it has been claimed, a print culture is by its very nature more critical than an oral culture: reading encourages analysis, independent thought and, ultimately, stimulates political consciousness.[9]

Although the thirst for news is not proof of political sophistication, it reveals an interest in current affairs which almost certainly prepared the ground for the popular politics of the 1790s. Interest in the issues of the day was widespread, and not only in desultory tap-room talk or barber-shop chat. In debating societies in London, Birmingham, Norwich, Liverpool, Manchester, and even smaller northern towns such as Stockport, Rochdale and Oldham, audiences of small traders and artisans could entertain and improve themselves on a varied diet of topical subjects.

In 1791–2 the depth and significance of this mass-reading and politically interested public was dramatically revealed. Tom Paine's *Rights of Man* was a landmark in popular political journalism. Paine's critique of monarchic and aristocratic rule was not new, but his prose cut through the niceties of eighteenth-century literary discourse, speaking to working men in a language they could understand and highlighting the political significance of literacy. It was politics for people to read aloud, full of memorable and quotable phrases. If Part One (1791) broke through the boundaries of contemporary political discourse, Part Two (1792) redrew them. Onto a restatement of the case against monarchy and aristocracy, Paine grafted an imaginative vision of a democratic republican society, a society of equal opportunity providing comprehensive welfare benefits for all its citizens. Part Two was a publishing sensation: Paine issued the work in a cheap sixpenny edition, at the same time reissuing Part One in a similar format. This clinched its success and by the end of 1793, 200,000 copies had been sold: a feat hitherto unparalleled in the history of British publishing.[10] It seemed, in a matter of months, to be ubiquitous:

> If you walked the streets, *The Rights of Man* stared you in the face upon every wall; turned into a shop, *The Rights of Man* lay upon the counter. Did a lady make a purchase of linen, *The Rights of Man* wrapt it round when sent home. No paper was ever found of such general use: whether to line a box, bottom a pie, light a pipe, or any inferior purpose, it was always at hand.[11]

The *Rights of Man* marked a watershed in the history of mass political literacy. The confidence which it inspired encouraged working men throughout the country to translate their interest in politics and current affairs into political action. In January 1792 the London Corresponding Society (LCS) was formed, and during the spring and summer many similar bodies followed in the provinces. These men, numbering only hundreds of activists at most, and sometimes no more than a handful, made political education their priority in the campaign for universal manhood suffrage and annual parliaments.[12] Their meetings were dominated by political readings followed by discussion. The LCS dealt with a flood of requests from the provinces for instructional material, and dispensed rules and regulations, addresses, pamphlets, songs and ballads in their thousands, as did larger provincial societies.[13] Radical booksellers emerged in most of the larger towns, together with half a dozen radical newspapers, such as the *Manchester Herald*, *Cambridge Intelligencer* and *Sheffield Register*. A few intrepid spirits, mostly in the capital, began to publish cheap radical periodicals. Daniel Isaac Eaton's *Politics for the People* (1793–5) and Thomas Spence's *Pig's Meat* (1793–5), constitute the beginning of a tradition of serious political periodicals for the common people. The outpouring of radical writing, from pamphlets to wall chalkings, was remarkable.[14] It is difficult to recapture this feeling of a people on the threshold of mass political literacy but print intoxicated them with possibility.

By mid-1792 it was clear that something had to be done to 'protect' the lower orders from this Paineite poison. Those in authority could no longer be as complacent as in the previous year. Such writing was 'fuel for the passions' of labouring men, ruled by their emotions.[15] The Royal Proclamation of May 1792, timed to correspond with Paine's indictment for publishing the *Rights of Man*, has been described as 'a virtual declaration of war against the radical press'.[16] It was an unambiguous attempt to rouse the propertied classes into action. In a testimony to the impact of radical propaganda, it railed against 'divers wicked and seditious writings . . . printed, published and industriously dispersed, tending to excite tumult and disorder, by endeavouring to raise groundless jealousies in the minds of our faithful and loving subjects'. Loyal subjects were urged to 'avoid and discourage all proceedings tending to produce riots and tumults', and magistrates to hunt out the authors, printers and distributors of seditious writings and submit reports to the government.[17] As a rallying cry for a general reaction, this was a definite success: 315 towns and cities sent 'loyal addresses' to the Home Office and, as the year wore on, the need for a more systematic alliance of the propertied seemed increasingly evident. Newspaper editors turned the spotlight on France where events were growing more alarming, whilst at home industrial unrest seemed symptomatic of a groundswell of popular discontent. The press fuelled a panic, and reports of a planned insurrection in London no longer seemed far-fetched.[18]

By the winter of 1792, the mobilisation of loyalism was already well under way. On 20 November an Association for the Preservation of Liberty and Property was formed at the Crown and Anchor tavern in London by John Reeves. The evidence suggests that his close friendship with Evan Nepean, an under-secretary at the Home Office, probably alerted him to government intentions to promote the formation of associations to stem the tide of radical doctrines. With or without official sanction, Reeves acted promptly, secure in the knowledge that he could count on the blessing of senior ministers. Within a month, loyal associations were springing up across the country. Between November 1792 and February 1793 well over 1,500 were established. Together they formed a national grid of repression. The printed declaration of the inhabitants of Brigg in Lincolnshire was typical. Its first resolution stated that

> Urged by loyalty to our King, attachment to our glorious constitution and a just regard to our own happiness, we will use every legal means in our power to detect, and bring to justice all persons holding seditious discourses, or circulating any pamphlets or papers tending to excite tumults, or to alienate the affections of the people from the present wise constitution of this country.[19]

Of course some societies were more active than others. The most industrious, as in London and Manchester, even had Committees of Papers to deal specifically with radical writing, and Reeves himself was said to be compiling an 'Index Expurgatorious of all dangerous and seditious books', rumoured to exceed forty volumes.[20] All societies, however, had the suppression of 'seditious' literature as a central part of their mission. On 1 December 1792 a second Royal Proclamation urged the loyal to even greater efforts against seditious writings. At the same time, the Treasury Solicitor sent detailed instructions to provincial magistrates on how to proceed against seditious publications and requested help from local solicitors in prosecuting offenders. He identified Pigott's *The Jockey Club* (1792) and any work by Paine as particularly offensive; any other suspicious works were to be sent to him for advice on whether to prosecute.[21] The counter-offensive had begun.

Prosecution was selective. The authorities generally took little notice of reformist or intellectual publications, focusing their attentions on cheap material promoting fundamental constitutional reform to a mass audience. The works proscribed in the Royal Proclamation of December 1792 provided the safest, and therefore most common, grounds for prosecution. In Birmingham, Stafford, Chester, Manchester, Sheffield, Newark and Liverpool these works formed the basis of legal action. Activists were at particular risk, especially those publishers and booksellers involved in the radical societies. The bookshop of Richard Phillips of Leicester was raided in December 1792 for the *Rights of Man*, though several other booksellers in the town were also selling it. 'Phillips,' remarked a local magistrate, 'is the printer of a violently republican newspaper here, called the *Herald*, and is at the head of a society of Paineites.'[22] Matthew Faulkner and Samuel Birch, the Manchester booksellers and publishers of the *Manchester Herald*, were indicted in 1793 on six counts of selling Paineite literature. They too were leading figures in the town's reform movement.

Prosecution for seditious libel was most common in the first half of the decade. Clive Emsley has recorded some fourteen provincial prosecutions in 1793, the highest annual figure and about half the total for the decade.[23] Gayle Pendleton estimates that of 1,022 radical and reformist pamphlets 18 titles were indicted as seditious libels during the 1790s.[24] The most prosecuted individuals were the London journalists Eaton, arrested six times between 1792 and 1795 for political libels, and Spence, arrested four times. The latter was again in prison in 1798 and 1801. The figures may seem modest but compared to the liberal decades of the 1770s and 1780s they represent a significant tightening of the application of the law. Moreover, because provincial magistrates were also encouraged to prosecute, repression appeared universal to nervous reformers. In February 1793 the Liverpool reformer James Currie wrote:

> I allow that liberty of speech, as well as the press, is completely over in France now; and in England itself, the land of freedom, it is greatly impaired. . . . The prosecutions that are commenced by government all over England against printers, publishers, etc., would astonish you. . . . For my part, I foresee troubles, and conceive the nation was never in such a dangerous crisis.[25]

Prosecution was, of course, only one end of a spectrum of legal persecution which shaded into many unrecorded instances of threatening and intimidating action. Seditious libel was a very loosely defined offence. Any criticism of the monarch or government was within its scope and it could be deployed against anyone involved in publication: even bill-stickers, as the unfortunate Thomas Carter discovered in 1792.[26] Arrest was often traumatic: house- and body-searches, the rifling through private papers, the threat or humiliation of being dragged through the streets to jail. Francis Place summed up the frustrations of reformers in his memoir of the much indicted Thomas Spence:

> No ceremony, no regard to the form of law was deemed necessary – any thing was a libell which any one in power chose to dislike, any man might . . . be seized by a thief taker, sent by a magistrate or by a political association, or of his own account, and all complaint of such outrages was useless.[27]

Once in prison, solitary confinement and rough handling were common. Bail could be set prohibitively high, and by proceeding ex officio, the government could dispense with the usual preliminary hearing before a grand jury. The use of special juries composed of government employees or wealthy tradesmen, vetted for their 'loyalty' was an additional weapon. At the Leicester trial of Richard Phillips in April 1793 for selling the *Rights of Man*, the jury was nominated by John Heyrick, father of the town clerk who had instituted the prosecution. In addition to sentences of up to four years and the penalty of being unable personally to supervise businesses, considerable fines and legal costs had to be paid. Public humiliation and loss of reputation were the final insults. John Hooton of Warrington, convicted of seditious libel in 1793, was sentenced to a year's imprisonment plus one hour in the pillory under a sign inscribed 'A Seditious and Ungrateful Man'.[28] It is hardly surprising that some 'offenders' fled before trial and that one or two committed suicide.

However intimidating, the law had its limitations. At both central and local levels there were insufficient personnel to staunch the flow of radical publications. The commitment of some radical journalists exacerbated the problem. Eaton, with the help of his family, continued to print whilst in prison and republished extracts of banned texts not named in his indictments. Prosecution was also expensive, and local magistrates were often left to foot the bill; making it difficult to obtain intelligence and witnesses to ensure the sort of watertight case which the Home Office demanded. Even then errors could occur. Faults in the indictments were more common than might be imagined and juries were unpredictable. In London the difficulty of securing convictions was well known, but juries in Sheffield, Nottingham, Newcastle and Derby also showed a marked reluctance to convict. A Derby magistrate, outraged at the acquittal of one Bowers for a seditious libel, wrote to the Treasury Solicitor: 'Although every necessary proof was made, the Jury, after being locked up three hours, brought him in Not Guilty: because they say it did not appear it was done with a view to raise commotion or disturbance in the county.'[29] Fox's Libel Act of May 1792 encouraged such verdicts by allowing the jury to decide the issue of intention and not just the fact of publication, as had previously been the case.[30]

The inadequacies of prosecution were dramatically demonstrated by the acquittals in the Treason Trials of 1794, and re-emphasised the following year when mounting political unrest produced a peak in radical pamphleteering. In October, the King's coach was attacked as he rode to open a parliamentary session. The blame was placed on the open-air protest meetings held in London over the previous months and the inflammatory publications said to have been on sale there. In the face of considerable opposition, the government introduced the first entirely new repressive legislation of the decade, the so-called Two Acts, which Gwyn Williams has described as 'the most serious invasion of traditional liberties since the Stuarts'.[31] In the

Commons debate on the Treasonable Practices Bill, the Attorney General referred to the impossibility of taking legal action against the flood of radical publications since 1792. Despite a legal campaign which had seen more prosecutions in the last two years than in the previous twenty, he argued, the libels on government 'were so numerous, so intricate and so dexterous, that no individual prosecution was sufficient to answer the wholesome purposes to be derived from such a proceeding'.[32] The Treasonable Practices Bill, passed in December 1795, was a particular blow to publishing. It extended the definition of treason to include those who

> shall maliciously and advisedly, by writing, printing, preaching, or other speaking, express, publish, utter or declare, any words or sentences to excite or stir up the people to hatred or contempt of the person of his Majesty, his heirs or successors, or the government and constitution of this realm.[33]

A more legislative phase in the repression of radical writing had begun.

The 'gagging acts' merely drove radicalism underground. Pamphleteering may have slowed, but the radical writing that remained became more subversive than ever – and more difficult to track down.[34] In 1797, amidst fears of invasion, the stamp duty – a longstanding means of government control of the press – was raised from twopence per sheet to threepence-halfpenny, raising the price of a newspaper to sixpence. The intention was to price newspapers beyond the pockets of the lower classes, at a time when ministers increasingly recognised that 'the great mass of the readers of newspapers were not the most discerning class of society' but rather 'chiefly the lower orders of the community . . . those who were least of all accustomed to reflection, to any great mental efforts'.[35] In June 1798, a Newspaper Regulation Bill compelled newspapers to register the names and addresses of the printers, publishers and proprietors with the Stamp Office and print the names and addresses of printer and publisher on every copy. A copy of each paper was to be filed at the Stamp Office within six days of publication. The law also required the keeping of strict accounts of the sale of presses and types. At about the same time a parliamentary Committee of Secrecy began to assemble information which was to culminate in a final legislative attempt to silence the voice of radical opposition. The Corresponding Societies Act of 1799 constituted what one historian of the book trade has called 'the most draconian legislation in the eighteenth century'.[36] It banned all corresponding societies and united societies and imposed a registration scheme on all printers, publishers, pressmakers and typefounders. All printed material was to include the name and address of the printer, who was to keep a copy of everything printed, except catalogues and trade cards, and produce it upon request from a magistrate.[37] The century which had seen such a flowering of press freedoms ended with the greatest legislative restrictions since the Stuarts. It was a mark of how important print had become in the battle for men's minds.

The most direct action against radical writing, however, was conducted on the streets of towns and villages across the country. In local arenas a wide array of weapons could be deployed to create an atmosphere of suffocating intensity. From 1792, loyalists set about isolating their opponents within their own communities. Rumour abounded: of greater arrests than for many years past, of men handcuffed and chained to bare boards in prison merely for selling Paine's work. It is difficult to unravel the truth, but everywhere the fears of reformers were tangible. The most common tactic was to seal off all avenues of political communication. This was a battle of the streets as much as of the courts; a fluctuating war of intimidation most overt at times when the perception of radical threat was most intense. War against France after 1793 made the task of the suppression easier against opponents who had identified with the French Revolution. In towns throughout the country the streets were carefully watched by local loyalists, though at night most streets were so badly lit as to make their task a thankless one. In Ipswich, Birmingham and many larger towns, loyal associations kept an eye on hawkers, ballad sellers, news carriers, handbill deliverers and anyone chalking slogans on walls, doors and shutters – a common means of political expression.[38] In London the constables were ordered to arrest anyone seen writing seditious words on the capital's walls.[39] Everywhere, radical posters were pasted over with loyalist ones. Even shop windows, particularly those of printers and booksellers, were placed under surveillance in the effort to close off public space.

All social institutions were regarded with suspicion. Libraries were purged, particularly in the dangerous northern districts. At Wakefield and Bolton any reformist literature was consigned to the flames. A Failsworth librarian was confronted by a mob demanding the surrender of any copies of the *Rights of Man*.[40] The Manchester Reading Society and the town's Broom Street circulating library were forced publicly to disclaim rumours that they were circulating reformist publications. A book society in Preston was closed down; the Liverpool Literary Society closed its doors due to public hostility.[41] Debating societies experienced similar treatment, and theatres were carefully patrolled.[42] Public houses were, not unnaturally, particular targets. In late 1792 thirty Bury publicans determined 'to prevent within our dwellings the reading of any treasonable or seditious books, pamphlets or newspapers, political disputes, or any treasonable songs, toasts, or sentiments, which only tend to mislead the unwary, and poison the mind of the honest labourers'.[43] One hundred and twenty Birmingham innkeepers signed a similar pledge, as did over a hundred in Bath. It was the same across the country. Many of Manchester's publicans went so far as to nail gilt boards above the entrances to their premises with the legend 'No Jacobins Admitted Here'. Others had little choice. As Thomas Hardy, secretary of the LCS, put it

> The poor publicans were obliged to submit. There was no appeal, for the Magistrates on Licencing day have it in their power to stop their Licence without giving a reason why. They succeeded so far in their alarm and threats that not one publick house, tavern nor Coffee House would receive a branch of the society that professed a reform in parliament.[44]

The Manchester reformer Thomas Walker bitterly remarked that in public houses throughout the kingdom, 'you see none but such contemptible papers as the *Sun* and the *True Briton*'.[45]

Loyalists also promised to police their own families' and servants' reading habits.[46] Some interfered with the correspondence of suspected radicals, with the Post Office as a key means of surveillance. John Thelwall, radical lecturer, writer and leading member of the LCS, was one of many activists to have their mail systematically opened.[47] As early as December 1792, Thomas Walker wrote to his friend James Watt:

> I have great reason to believe that some of your letters are stopped; a meanness which I understand is now generally practised, and which prevents me from writing to you so fully as I could wish; not that I have anything to say that I care if all the world knew; but I do not chuse that a set of impudent and unprincipled scoundrels shall pry into the correspondence of warm and unreserved friendship.[48]

It was to be a common complaint throughout the decade, made more irritating as the authorities built up a considerable network of spies and informers in the later 1790s. Newspapers were particularly vulnerable to interference. The *Manchester Gazette*, *Sheffield Iris* and *Cambridge Intelligencer* were frequently delayed in the post and occasionally arrived torn or partially burned. When the readers of the *Sheffield Iris* went to pick up their newspapers from their local post offices in Leeds, Halifax and Wakefield, they received such a barrage of abuse as to deter many of them from collecting one of 'Tom Paine's papers'.[49]

Surveillance could easily lead to more direct personal harassment. Writers, printers, publishers and booksellers depended upon the patronage of the public and were particularly vulnerable to the withdrawal of custom. The threat of loss of business undoubtedly forced many publicans and booksellers to remove reformist material from their premises; to do otherwise was to invite economic retribution. When Edward Rushton, a Liverpool bookseller and reformer, became a marked man, all who entered his shop were watched and his business declined. Thomas Spence, after being arrested in 1793, returned to his bookstall to find the shutters had been plastered-up with notices warning that the occupier was a vendor of seditious books. As a result, several of his landlord's customers threatened to stop dealing with him unless he turned Spence out, which he duly did.[50] Almost all radical newspapers were similarly victimised by advertisement boycotts, intended to ruin their greatest source of income. The 'jacobin' playwright William Holcroft was forced to present his work anonymously and died penniless in 1809.[51] Holcroft, like other radical authors such as John Thelwall and the poet Samuel Coleridge, found that his reputation was enough to damn his writing.

Economic pressures, however strongly urged by MPs, Anglican clergy or local worthies, could only work with the co-operation of ordinary townspeople. Eliza Gould, for instance, a Devon schoolmistress who regularly took the *Cambridge Intelligencer*, met with nothing but 'insult and persecution' from her neighbours as a result of her allegiance to the paper.[52] Rejection by the very people they sought to emancipate was, perhaps, the most dispiriting aspect of repression for reformers, and the threat of violence hung heavy in the air, particularly in the years 1792–4 when every public gathering seemed fraught with the possibility of personal attack. During the winter of 1792–3, waves of loyalist demonstrations saw copies of the *Rights of Man* symbolically burned alongside its author's effigy sometimes wrapped in radical newspapers. Public hostility was demonstrated most violently in the 'Church and King' riots of the period. Sometimes hundreds strong, 'Church and King' mobs broke windows and, on occasion, tore to pieces reformist petitions awaiting signature, as at Liverpool in December 1792, and Manchester three years later. The most notable attack was that on the premises of the *Manchester Herald* in December 1792, when a mob of several hundred 'attacked the shop and house with stones and brick bats, till the windows were almost entirely destroyed'.[53] There were similar attacks on booksellers and newspaper staff in Bath and Sheffield, and in Preston the strength of public hostility took the *Preston Review* to its grave within a year of its birth.[54] The constant fear of violence was extremely wearing. The radical Thelwall was profoundly depressed by his treatment during a lecturing tour in 1796–7 and the physical threats of mobs composed of the very men he wished to reach. His friend Coleridge felt much the same sense of isolation from the public during 1797. Both men retreated to the country: Thelwall to Wales, Coleridge to Somerset. But even in rural surroundings it was impossible to escape the watchful eyes of informers and the threats of the locals. It was a bitter pill for men whose object had been education and enlightenment.

Radicals blamed their rejection upon the ignorance of the masses, duped by a loyalist propaganda of feverish intensity.[55] Whatever the truth, there is no doubt that the repression of radical writing involved a skilful manipulation of all aspects of the information process, from subsidising and creating loyal newspapers to the publishing loyal sermons and judicial utterances. In this campaign the most notable tactic was that of disinformation. Tens of thousands of pamphlets, broadsides and ballads were distributed: carried free by the Post Office, sold for a penny, given away, pushed under doors, pasted on walls and left lying around in public places. From the vantage point of 1819, Francis Place recalled how

> The Association against Republicans and Levellers . . . printed a large number of what they called Loyal songs and gave them to the ballad singers; if any one was carried before a magistrate who admonished him or her, they were then told they might have loyal songs for nothing, and they would not be molested while singing them.[56]

Such material was deliberately constructed to prevent radical ideas reaching the masses without raising their political awareness. The language of radicalism was deliberately scrambled and all distinctions between radical and moderate reformers erased. A key word in the radical vocabulary was equality. What radical writers stressed was equality of rights; all men were born equal, and equality of opportunity was a natural right. In loyalist terminology this became 'levelling', an attempt to reduce all to the same state. There was often no argument as such. 'Thomas Bull' tells his 'Brother John': 'They begin by telling us all mankind are equal; but that's a lie John; for the children are not equal to the mother, nor the mother to the father; unless there is petticoat government and such families never get on well.'[57] In this way, the issues separating radicals and loyalists are collapsed, and prejudice is presented as common sense. The lower-class audience is simultaneously flattered, and discouraged from thought. None the less, if like much radical propoganda addressing a new public its mode of address was a little clumsy, it was a skilful attempt to obstruct the flow of radical ideas by disrupting the language of radicalism in an attempt to confuse the lower-class reader.

Censorship is predicated upon fear, and in the 1790s the existence of a mass reading-public had to be addressed as a serious political problem for the first time. War magnified the sensitivity of a government surprised by the success of Paine and his followers. The attack on radical writing was multi-faceted, involving official and unofficial action, legal and extra-legal pressures and both direct and indirect forms of repression. Censorship, however, is not in the final analysis about this or that form of repression, but about the total environment within which writing occurs. In the 1790s loyalty became the litmus test of writing, and those found wanting were branded 'jacobins' even by the mass public they wished to emancipate. They found themselves intimidated in a hundred small ways in their everyday lives, and denied membership of their own communities. Surprisingly large numbers refused to submit, but they recognised that a dense and suffocating fog of political censorship had descended. It was little wonder that by the end of the century, 'The memory of the liberty of the press' seemed the only appropriate political toast.[58]

NOTES

1 J. Boswell, *The Life of Samuel Johnson*, ed. G. B. Hill, Oxford, Clarendon Press, 1934, pp. 115–16.
2 On the crucial role of the Wilkes affair, see J. Brewer, *Party Ideology and Popular Politics at the Accession of George III*, Cambridge, Cambridge University Press, 1976, ch. 9; A. Aspinall, 'The reporting and publishing of House of Commons' debates 1771–1834', in R. Pares and A. J. P. Taylor (eds), *Essays Presented to Sir Lewis Namier*, London, Macmillan, 1956; P. D. Thomas, 'John Wilkes and the liberty of the press', *Bulletin of the Institute of Historical Research*, vol. 33, 1960, pp. 86–98.
3 I. Watt, *The Rise of the Novel*, Harmondsworth, Penguin, 1963, p. 302. On the growth of the press, see J. Black, *The English Press in the Eighteenth Century*, Beckenham, Croom Helm, 1987; on the literary world, M. Butler, *Romantics, Rebels and Reactionaries: English Literature and its Background 1760–1830*, Oxford, Oxford University Press, 1981.
4 See J. H. Plumb, 'The commercialisation of leisure in eighteenth-century England', in N. McKendrick (ed.), *The Birth of a Consumer Society*, London, Europa, 1982.
5 The historical debate on literacy levels at this time is summed up in M. Sanderson, *Education, Economic Change and Society in England 1780–1870*, London, Macmillan, 1983, pp. 9–16.
6 Anon, *Strictures on benefit or friendly societies; comprising observations on their defects, and proposing various improvements*, Stockport, 1798.
7 M. Thale (ed.), *The Autobiography of Francis Place 1771–1854*, Cambridge, Cambridge University Press, 1971, p. 47.
8 *Gore's Liverpool Advertiser*, 9 June 1791.
9 See J. Goody, 'Literacy, criticism and the growth of knowledge', in J. Ben-David and T. N. Clark (eds), *Culture and Its Creators*, Chicago, University of Chicago Press, 1975; J. Goody and I. Watt, 'The consequences of literacy', in J. Goody (ed.), *Literacy in Traditional Societies*, Cambridge, Cambridge University Press, 1968.
10 On the appeal and impact of the *Rights of Man*, see E. P. Thompson, *The Making of the English Working Class*, Harmondsworth, Penguin, 1969,

pp. 97–110; O. Smith, *The Politics of Language 1791–1819*, Oxford, Clarendon Press, 1984, ch. 1; J. T. Boulton, *The Language of Politics in the Age of Wilkes and Burke*, London, Routledge & Kegan Paul, 1963, ch. 8; A. J. Ayer, *Thomas Paine*, London, Secker & Warburg, 1988, chs 5, 6.

11 Quoted in R. R. Rea, 'The liberty of the press as an issue in English politics 1792–93', *The Historian*, vol. 24, 1961, p. 28.

12 It is worth noting that the formal organisation of popular radicalism in the 1790s seems to have been almost exclusively a male preserve. There are very few hints in the sources of female involvement in the movement, unlike the post-war period where the rise of the 'mass platform' offered greater opportunities for public involvement by women.

13 The best published collection of LCS records is M. Thale (ed.), *Selections from the Papers of the London Corresponding Society 1792–99*, Cambridge, Cambridge University Press, 1983.

14 See G. T. Pendleton, 'Radicalism and the English "Reign of Terror": the evidence of the pamphlet literature', *Proceedings of the Conference on Revolutionary Europe*, vol. 9, 1979, pp. 195–205.

15 See, for example, Windham's remarks in the House of Commons debate on the King's Proclamation against Seditious Writings, 25 May 1792, in W. Cobbett (ed.), *Parliamentary History of England*, 36 vols, London, 1806–20, vol. XXIX, col. 1502.

16 D. Read, *Press and People 1790–1850*, London, Arnold, 1961, p. 68.

17 *Parliamentary History*, vol. XXIX, cols 1476–7.

18 See R. R. Dozier, *For King, Constitution and Country: the English Loyalists and the French Revolution*, Lexington, University of Kentucky Press, 1983, ch. 2; C. Emsley, 'The London "Insurrection" of December 1792: fact, fiction or fantasy?', *Journal of British Studies*, vol. 17, 1978, pp. 66–86.

19 'At a meeting of the inhabitants of the town of Brigg', 29 December 1792: British Library, Reeves MSS Add. MSS. 16929.

20 *Morning Chronicle*, 10 December 1792, quoted in Rea, 'The liberty of the press', p. 31.

21 See Public Record Office (PRO), Treasury Solicitor (T.S.) 11/954/3498, T.S. 24/1–23.

22 F. Knight, *The Strange Case of Thomas Walker*, London, Lawrence & Wishart, 1957, pp. 116–17. On this case and others, see A. Goodwin, *The Friends of Liberty*, London, Hutchinson, 1979, pp. 271–2.

23 C. Emsley, 'An aspect of Pitt's Terror: prosecutions for sedition during the 1790s', *Social History*, vol. 6, 1981, Appendices a, b. In addition, a few writers and publishers were prosecuted for sedition and seditious expression.

24 Pendleton, 'Radicalism and the "English Reign of Terror" ', p. 199.

25 W. W. Currie (ed.), *Memoir of the Life, Writings and Correspondence of James Currie*, 2 vols, London, Longman, 1831, vol. 2, pp. 185–6.

26 On the flexibility of the law of seditious libel, see J. Feather, 'The English book trade and the law 1695–1799', *Publishing History*, vol. 12, 1982, pp. 62–3; J. F. Stephen, *A History of the Criminal Law of England*, 3 vols, London, Macmillan, 1883, vol. 2, pp. 348–53. On the Carter case, see C. Emsley, 'Repression, "Terror" and the Rule of Law in England during the decade of the French Revolution', *English Historical Review*, vol. 100, 1985, p. 818.

27 British Library, Place Papers, Add. MSS 27808.

28 'To the Worshipful the Mayor and Inhabitants of the town of Lancaster',

1793: Manchester Record Office, 'Politics from Nov. 1792 to Aug. 1793', MS 942.073 All.

29 Quoted in Knight, *Thomas Walker*, pp. 117–18. On errors in the preparation of indictments, see Emsley, 'An aspect of Pitt's Terror', p. 169.

30 See, for instance, *Proceedings on the Trial of Daniel Isaac Eaton . . . for selling a Supposed Libel . . . by Thomas Paine*, 1793, p. 42. This type of verdict had been a source of increasing irritation to judges in the later eighteenth century. See D. Thomas, *A Long Time Burning*, London, Routledge & Kegan Paul, 1969, pp. 99–100, 105, 109.

31 G. A. Williams, *Artisans and Sans-culottes*, London, Arnold, 1968, p. 100.

32 *Parliamentary History*, vol. XXXII, col. 488.

33 ibid., cols 243–4.

34 See A. Booth, 'Irish exiles, revolution and writing in England in the 1790s', in P. Hyland and N. Sammells (eds), *Irish Writing: Exile and Subversion*, London, Macmillan, 1991. The most detailed account of radicalism in this period is R. Wells, *Insurrection: the British Experience 1795–1803*, Gloucester, Alan Sutton, 1983.

35 *Parliamentary History*, vol. XXXIV, 1798–1800, cols 161–2. On the legislation of this period, see Emsley, 'Repression, Terror and the Rule of Law', pp. 816–18.

36 Feather, 'The English book trade and the law', p. 58.

37 See *Parliamentary History*, vol. XXXIV, col. 988, for Pitt's justification of such harsh measures.

38 James Bisset, self-styled Birmingham poet, recorded the battle over the town's walls in verse: Bisset, *Reminiscences*, c. 1805, unpublished MSS in Birmingham Central Reference Library, 184534.

39 R. R. Nelson, *The Home Office 1782–1801*, Durham, N.C., Duke University Press, 1969, p. 119. For similar concerns in Norwich in 1793, see PRO, Home Office, 42/27.

40 J. Scholes, *History of Bolton*, Bolton, 1892, p. 440; P. Percival, *Failsworth Folk and Failsworth Memories*, Manchester, 1901, p. 18.

41 *Manchester Chronicle*, 5 January and 16 February 1793; H. Roscoe, *The Life of William Roscoe*, 2 vols, London, 1833, vol. 2, p. 127; E. Baines, *Life of Edward Baines*, London, Longman, 1859.

42 See L. W. Conolly, *The Censorship of English Drama 1737–1824*, San Marino, Calif., Huntington Library, 1976, ch. 3; M. Thale, 'London Debating Societies in the 1790s', *Historical Journal*, vol. 32, 1989, pp. 61–5.

43 *Manchester Mercury*, 25 December 1792.

44 In Thale (ed.), *Papers of the London Corresponding Society*, p. 30.

45 T. Walker, *A Review of some of the Political Events which have occurred in Manchester during the last five Years*, 1794, p. 25. The *Sun* and *True Briton* were the two newspapers begun by the government in October 1792 to counter the growing influence of reformism in the press.

46 *Chester Chronicle*, 20 July 1792; *Manchester Chronicle*, 27 December 1792.

47 J. Thelwall, *Poems, Chiefly Written in Retirement: with Memoirs of the Life of the Author*, Hereford, 1801, p. xl. See also the circular letter from the LCS in August 1793: PRO, T.S. 11/956.

48 T. Walker to J. Watt, 20 December 1792, Birmingham Central Reference Library, Boulton-Watt Correspondence, M. Box 4W.

49 See M. J. Smith, 'English radical newspapers in the French Revolutionary era 1790–1803', unpublished Ph.D. dissertation, University of London, 1979, pp. 187–8, 199–205.

50 E. A. Rushton, *Poems and other Writings*, 1824, p. xx; O. Rudkin, *Thomas Spence and his Connections*, New York, Augustus Kelley, 1966, p. 85.
51 T. Holcroft, *The Life of Thomas Holcroft*, 2 vols, 1925; repr., New York, Benjamin Blom, 1968, vol. 2, pp. 247–8.
52 The Gould case is quoted in Smith, 'English radical newspapers', p. 187.
53 Walker, *A Review*, p. 55. On these disturbances, see A. Booth, 'Popular loyalism and public violence in the north-west of England 1790–1800', *Social History*, vol. 8, 1983, pp. 295–313.
54 Baines, *Life of Edward Baines*, p. 20.
55 See especially A. Booth, 'English popular loyalism and the French Revolution', *Bulletin of the Society for the Study of Labour History*, vol. 54, 1989, pp. 26–31; H. T. Dickinson, 'Popular conservatism and militant loyalism 1789–1815', in H. T. Dickinson (ed.), *Britain and the French Revolution 1789–1815*, London, Macmillan, 1989; R. Hole, 'British counter-revolutionary propaganda in the 1790s', in C. Jones (ed.), *Conflict, Subversion and Propaganda*, Exeter, Exeter University Press, 1983.
56 British Library, Place Papers, Add. MSS 27825, 'Songs'.
57 'One pennyworth of truth from Thomas Bull to his Brother John', in *Liberty and Property preserved against Republicans and Levellers: a Collection of Tracts*: British Library, 1141.d.6. See O. Smith, *The Politics of Language*, ch. 3.
58 The toast at a meeting of radicals and Whigs in October 1800 to celebrate the anniversary of C. J. Fox's first election as MP for Westminster. Quoted in A. Prochaska, 'English state trials in the 1790s', *Journal of British Studies*, vol. 13, 1973, p. 63.

Part III

The Victorian period: responsibility and repression

Chapter 9

A land of relative freedom: censorship of the press and the arts in the nineteenth century (1815–1914)

Robert Justin Goldstein

The recent deterioration of civil liberties in Britain has provoked many adverse comparisons with other western democracies. Thus, according to a 1990 scholarly survey of British civil liberties, although 'it was not so long ago that British democracy was synonymous with liberty and freedom', recent years have witnessed 'a marked decline in the level of political freedom'.[1] Lately, the United Kingdom has suffered more adverse decisions from the European Court on Human Rights than has any other European government, on issues ranging from the rights of women, homosexuals and mental-health patients, to telephone tapping and freedom of association. The British criminal justice system has been scarred by repeated scandals, of which the Guildford Four and Birmingham Six cases are only the most spectacular examples. *Index on Censorship*, a periodical which normally concentrates on abuses in the developing world and in eastern Europe, devoted its entire September 1988 issue to threats to British liberty, since 'if freedom is diminished in the United Kingdom, where historically it has deep roots, it is potentially diminished everywhere'.[2]

With specific regard to censorship policy, the 1989 report of the widely respected International Press Institute declared, 'The British government remains determined to stifle free discussion in the press and on the electronic media, to the extent that the country could be said to have a less than half-free press', while the 1988 report of Article 19, an international human-rights organisation which monitors global censorship, stated that, 'As far as freedom of expression and information is concerned, Britain is going through a very stormy period'.[3] The contemporary censorship crisis has become so notorious that Britain has frequently been held up as a pariah among democratic nations. Thus, the most influential United States newspaper, *The New York Times*, ran a lengthy article on 5 March 1989, entitled 'Censorship in Britain: Thatcher puts a lid on'. Perhaps the crowning blow to Britain's reputation was inadvertently delivered in 1988 by South African President Botha, who warned his country's journalists to 'exercise self-discipline and smother the views of people advocating violence', as otherwise 'they mustn't complain when we adopt measures similar to those used by the British government'.[4]

The contemporary situation is a dramatic change from that of the nineteenth century. Britain then was almost universally regarded as Europe's beacon of political freedom and as the land which set the democratic example for virtually all other countries, especially with regard to censorship and civil liberties. Britain's position as the centre of nineteenth-century European political freedom was clearly established and reflected by her willingness to welcome political refugees of all stripes from all countries, ranging from Marx to Metternich and from Louis Kossuth to Louis Napoleon and Louis-Philippe. Britain took great pride in its role as the refuge of Europe's politically oppressed. Thus, *The Times* declared in February 1853, 'Every civilized people on the face of the earth must be fully aware that this country is the asylum of nations, and that it will defend the asylum to the last ounce of its treasure and last drop of its blood.'[5]

The asylum policy, along with the comparatively unmatched level of general political freedom in Britain, evoked appreciation and often amazement among political exiles. Thus, the Russian revolutionary propagandist Prince Peter Kropotkin recounted that, when he sought passage on a ship from Sweden to England in 1876, having escaped from a Russian jail:

> As I went to the steamer, I asked myself with anxiety, 'Under which flag does she sail – Norwegian, German, English?' Then I saw floating about the stern the union jack – the flag under which so many refugees, Russian, Italian, French, Hungarian and of all nations, have found an asylum. I greeted that flag from the depth of my heart.[6]

Another famous Russian exile, Alexander Herzen, noted that

> Until I came to England the appearance of a police officer in a house where I was living always produced an indefinable disagreeable feeling, and I was at once morally on guard against an enemy. In England a policeman at your door merely adds to your sense of security.[7]

Johanna Kinkel, wife of the noted German exile Professor Gottfried Kinkel, termed Britain 'the only piece of Europe where you can freely think and speak as you like'.[8] Similarly, anarchist Emma Goldman, whose rights to free speech were repeatedly trampled upon by American police, declared upon visiting London in 1895 that 'By comparison with the United States the political freedom in Great Britain seemed like the millennium come'.[9]

Britain was viewed by European liberals and radicals not only as a model of political freedom but, more specifically, as a model of freedom for the press. Alone among the major European countries, Britain had eliminated prior censorship of the written and illustrated press before 1820, with the lapsing of the Licensing Act in 1695. In contrast, such censorship remained in force almost everywhere else in Europe until the middle of the nineteenth century or beyond. In France (where censorship of the written press was terminated in 1822, but the illustrated press remained subject to such prior approval until 1881), Britain was repeatedly pointed to by advocates of 'freedom of the crayon'. For example, when censorship of drawings was debated by the French legislature in 1820, Count Stanislaw de Girardin declared that the British example demonstrated that the 'mischief' created by 'piquant' caricatures would not worry 'true men of state':

> How many times have I not seen William Pitt and Charles Fox, in going to the House of Commons, stop before the print merchants, in order to attentatively examine the satiric caricatures which malignity has come to compose against them. How many times have I not seen them join their smiles to the bursting eruptions of laughter of John Bull! These great men don't attach much importance to little things. . . . There are men who see things from on high and others with less broad horizons [such as] those who class among the great dangers which they claim menace France the daily publication of more or less witty caricatures.[10]

Similarly, Charles Philipon, the founder of France's leading caricature journals in the 1830s (who was jailed for his efforts) lamented that he had been prosecuted for 'drawings 100 times less biting than those which are made in England without causing concern'.[11] The differential treatment accorded caricature in Britain and France was particularly highlighted when issues of *Punch* were banned from sale in France. The French caricature journal *Le Pétard*, commenting on one such episode in 1878, depicted 'Punch' as assertive and smiling, while French caricature, as represented in a self-portrait by artist Alfred Le Petit, was shown tearing its hair over the harassment by the censors, represented by an ugly old woman wielding huge scissors.

Although, in comparison to the other major European powers, Britain was a paragon of freedom during the nineteenth century, judged by any modern democratic standard this was certainly not the case. As Friedrich Engels aptly pointed out in 1844, 'England is undeniably the freest, in other words, the least unfree, country in the world.'[12] The so-called 'Reform Act' of 1832, while symbolically representing a significant democratic advance, only expanded the suffrage in the United Kingdom from about 2 per cent to about 3 per cent of the total population, and a slim majority of adult males was enfranchised only after 1884 (in this respect Britain was ahead of Austria, Hungary, Italy, the Low Countries and Russia, but it lagged behind France, Germany and Switzerland). While trade unions and strikes were formally legalised in 1824, far earlier than in any other major European country, in practice trade-union activity and workers' freedoms were severely limited until after about 1875, with thousands of workers prosecuted and often jailed simply for striking or even quitting their jobs. If freedom of speech, assembly and association were unquestionably better protected in Britain (although by no means in Ireland), during periods of tension before 1850, such as the industrial and political unrest of 1817–19 and the Chartist agitations of 1838–40, 1842 and 1848, severe limits were quite regularly placed on such freedoms. After 1850 these freedoms were very rarely infringed upon, in considerable contrast to much of Europe, but even then there were occasional exceptions, such as the 1887 'Bloody Sunday' police dispersal of crowds which defied a ban on rallies at Trafalgar Square.

The transitional nature of British democracy in the nineteenth century was fully reflected in policies of regulating the press and the politically sensitive arts, such as caricature, the theatre and the emerging cinema. While prior censorship of the press had ended in 1695, until about 1850 newspapers frequently endured post-publication prosecutions for 'seditious libel' and suffered from onerous taxes intended to raise their prices above levels the poor could afford. Throughout the nineteenth century (and indeed until 1968), 'legitimate' stage presentations such as dramas and operas remained subject to prior censorship, and after the cinema emerged in the late nineteenth century a quasi-legal but highly effective censorship was soon imposed. However, the nineteenth-century British stage and film censorships were generally far more lenient, at least in political areas, than their continental counterparts.

Although on the surface there seems to be a contradiction between the abolition of press censorship on the one hand, and the maintenance of stage censorship and the introduction of film censorship on the other, examination of the various regulatory policies reveals a basic consistency. The comparatively early début of party politics in Britain, coupled with the rapid emergence of a powerful and articulate middle class and a vocal urban, industrialised working class, and an early sanctification of the basic principle (if not always the implementation) of freedom of expression (as reflected in the refugee policy) effectively made a policy of harsh political censorship unsustainable in nineteenth-century Britain. However, the authorities still genuinely feared the spread of radical political ideas among the working class, and restrictions on the press were broadly maintained until mid-century. Further, since the theatre and the cinema were viewed as far more powerful than the press, and could even reach that small, but highly feared sector of the population that was illiterate, normal principles of free expression were simply waived. In practice, the censorship was restrained and largely, if not entirely, targeted at material which might arouse the dark masses.

Throughout at least the first third of the nineteenth century, many conservative Britons still feared the concept of a completely free press. Viscount Henry Sidmouth, Home Secretary under the reactionary ministry of Lord Liverpool (1812–22), termed the press the 'most malignant and formidable enemy to the constitution to which it owed its freedom'.[13] And yet the ingrained support for press freedom on the part of many well-respected and 'establishment' Britons placed limits on the implementation of repressive press policies after the defeat of Napoleon. Thus the *Edinburgh Review* in 1821 hailed the 'genuine freedom of the press as the fountain of all intellectual light, and the source of all that is great among mankind', and Whigs, during the early nineteenth century, frequently drank to the toast, 'The liberty of the press – 'tis like the air we breathe – while we have it we cannot die.'[14]

In practice, post-publication press prosecutions after 1695 were frequent only during periods of intense tension and perceived threats of revolution, such as the alleged 'Jacobin threat' of the 1790s, the unrest of 1817–20 in the wake of the French Revolutionary Wars and the Chartist upsurge of 1838–40. During the 1817–20 unrest, at least 175 politically inspired seditious and blasphemous libel prosecutions were initiated.[15] Although well over half of these efforts appear to have led to acquittals, among the convictions was the notorious three-year prison term given to printer Richard Carlile for publishing the works of Thomas Paine. After the unrest died down, libel prosecutions declined rapidly to eighty-one over the next fifteen years. In one extraordinary case, Humphrey Price was sent to jail for a year in 1829 for publishing two poems during a strike of carpet weavers at Kidderminster, in which he argued for the moral superiority of the strikers over their employers. The last real wave of press prosecutions in nineteenth-century Britain came during the 1838–40 Chartist agitation. Among the most notorious outcomes were the eighteen-month jail term given to Feargus O'Connor for a speech printed in the *Northern Star*, the most important Chartist newspaper, which urged a 'warm reception' in response to governmental force; and a shorter term of imprisonment for the drafter of the Charter, William Lovett, who was sentenced for signing a document urging similar resistance.[16]

Just as seditious-libel prosecutions could be carefully calibrated to meet especially threatening conditions, so they could be surgically aimed at those targets which were viewed as truly threatening. After

1815 the targets became almost exclusively those agitators who sought to stir the still-feared working class. By 1850, the fundamentally entrenched nature of political stability became increasingly apparent, and the last gasp of Chartism in 1848 made clear that the working class had been largely tamed by, among other things, growing prosperity and the increasing legitimisation of peaceful organisation and protest. Under these changed circumstances, post-publication prosecutions virtually disappeared. The handful of prosecutions after 1850 were generally under the 1867 Offences Against the Person Act and usually aimed at fringe elements, such as revolutionary exiles who applauded assassinations. Among these were, in 1881–2, the German anarchist Johann Most and two of his associates, jailed for publishing articles applauding the assassination of Tsar Alexander II and the Phoenix Park murders in Ireland; and in 1898 the Russian revolutionary Vladimir Burtsev and an associate were imprisoned for urging the assassination of Tsar Nicholas II.[17]

In comparison with the tribulations suffered by journalists in other major European countries, prosecution of nineteenth-century British journalists pales considerably. In the Habsburg lands and most of the German and Italian states, for example, prior censorship continued until mid-century or beyond, and in Russia until 1905. Furthermore, prosecutions in these lands and in France, were so pervasive that journalists were often only marginally more free than before censorship was abolished. For example, in France there were 530 press prosecutions in Paris alone between 1830 and 1834, far more than in the whole of Britain throughout the 1815–1914 period. In Austria there were over 2,000 prosecutions and confiscations of newspapers between 1877 and 1880; in Russia 175 journalists were jailed and 413 periodicals banned in 1907 alone; and in Germany over one hundred socialist journalists were convicted in the first six months of 1913, suffering combined sentences of forty years.[18]

If censorship and post-publication prosecutions were relatively insignificant as forms of press restrictions in nineteenth-century Britain, it must be added that the British perfected another form of less brutal and less visible, but quite effective, means of restricting the circulation of newspapers specifically among the poor, the notorious 'taxes on knowledge'. While several other countries, including Austria and France, also imposed special taxes on the press, Britain appears to have been unique in taxing not only each newspaper sold, but also in taxing newspaper advertisements and newsprint. These taxes were clearly directed at forcing newspapers to raise their cover prices so that the 'dark masses' most feared by the authorities would be unable to afford them. The most burdensome of these levies, the stamp tax, had been introduced at a halfpenny per newspaper in 1712, but as a result of steady increases it had reached fourpence in 1815, with the result that newspapers had to charge two to four times what they otherwise would have cost.

The authorities never sought to keep it secret that the purpose of the press taxes was to reduce newspaper circulation among the poor. Thus, when the stamp tax was extended in 1819 to cover those periodicals which circulated among the working classes and which had managed to avoid the tax by falling outside the technical definition of newspaper, the preamble explained that its purpose was to restrain publications printed 'in great numbers and at very small price' which tended to 'excite hatred and contempt of the Government'.[19] Lord Ellenborough told the House of Lords that the Act was not directed 'against the respectable press' but rather 'against a pauper press, which, administering to the prejudices and the passions of a mob', threatened to arouse 'mischief' from the 'lowest classes' against the 'best interests of the country'.[20]

The poor were, of course, well aware of the purpose of the taxes. As a newspaper vendor, charged with participating in a widespread and highly successful campaign to resist the stamp tax, by selling unstamped newspapers, told a court in 1831:

> I stands here, your worships, upon right and principle, on behalf of the poor working unedicated [sic] classes of the country. They are called ignorant, but what is the cause of their ignorance? Why the tax which prevents them from getting information. Your worships pretty well knows the reason them in power puts on the tax; it is to keep the poor from knowing their rights; for if poor working people knowed their rights, they would soon annihilate the corrupt institutions that oppress them.[21]

The battle to abolish the 'taxes on knowledge' raged for decades and was described by William Gladstone as the 'severest parliamentary struggle in which I have ever been engaged'.[22] As a result of these struggles, which were greatly aided by the 1830–6 so-called 'war of the unstamped' (at its height an estimated 500 unstamped periodicals sold 200,000 copies each week, despite the jailing of over 800 newspaper vendors and publishers), the stamp tax was reduced to one penny in 1836. It was not completely abolished until 1855; a fate which also befell the advertising tax in 1853, and the newsprint tax in 1861. The effect of lowering and, ultimately, abolishing the taxes was astounding. Between 1815 and 1836, when the stamp tax was four pence per newspaper, total newspaper sales increased by only 20 per cent, but during the two years following the 1836 reduction, total annual sales more than doubled, from 25.5 million to over 53 million. Until the final abolition of the stamp tax in June 1855, only a handful of daily newspapers were able to establish themselves outside London; after 1855 they developed in a flood, with six provincial dailies begun on a single day in July 1855, leading to about ninety publishing by 1870.

With regard to the illustrated press, and especially political caricature, for all practical purposes cartoonists were free of both prior- and post-publication censorship after 1815. Some conservatives still feared the power of hostile cartoonists. For example, in 1831 the *Athenaeum* characterised the work of the caricaturist as that of someone who 'insults inferiority of mind and exposes defect of body – and who aggravates what is already hideous and blackens what was sufficiently dark'. However, by 1820, prosecution of caricaturists had fallen into such disuse that the Prince Regent (later George IV), was reduced to buying up plates and unsold prints depicting him and his various peccadilloes. He even paid one hundred pounds to George Cruikshank in return for the latter's pledge 'not to caricature His Majesty in any immoral situation', but Cruikshank quickly evaded the agreement by depicting the new king atoning for his behaviour by doing penance in church for his numerous adulteries. Another caricaturist, Lewis Marks, took advantage of the king's vulnerability by extorting money from him on at least ten separate occasions in 1820.[23]

After 1841, political caricature was further insured against persecution by the near-monopoly of the genre maintained by *Punch*, which poked, at most, a gentle humour at the ruling class. Thus historians Ralph Shikes and Steven Heller have noted that *Punch*'s comedy was 'housebroken' as it 'never – well hardly ever – made its audience wince', and a contemporary English observer remarked, with reference to the bitter caricatures common in France: 'The Parisians say of our Victorian caricatures that they smile rather than laugh.'[24] To some extent French caricature was far more bitter precisely because it was either censored or hounded, and this remained the case in France and in other powers for much or all of the 1815–1914 period. On the other hand, on several occasions French harassment of caricature resulted either from British pressure, or at least from French perceptions of English sensibilities. For example, French authorities banned street sales of *L'Assiette au Beurre* in 1909, after it had published, as part of a special issue bitterly critical of British policy in the Boer War, a cartoon entitled 'Impudent Albion', which depicted a woman baring her bottom and revealing the features of Edward VII on her buttocks. This issue prompted a personal complaint from Edward to the French Ambassador, who privately termed the design 'scandalous' but conceded that it was 'very well done' and bore an 'exact resemblance' to the king. The magazine was forced to cover up Edward's features in subsequent printings, but the original ban apparently only stimulated sales, which reached an unprecedented 250,000.[25]

If British censorship and regulation with regard to the press were relatively liberal, this was not quite so true with regard to censorship of the stage and cinema. Although the British stage and cinema censorship was clearly less sensitive to political issues than were its counterparts in Germany, France and Russia, the British censors not only blue-pencilled many political scripts but kept many dramatists and directors from even writing or submitting politically contentious material. This contributed to what Matthew Arnold described in 1879 as an English stage which featured 'no modern drama at all'.[26] Furthermore, while British stage censorship continued throughout the 1815–1914 period (and likewise in Russia and Germany), France abolished theatre censorship in 1906; and while decisions of the British drama and film censors were beyond any judicial review (as in Italy, France and Russia), in Germany appeals could be taken to the courts – where they frequently succeeded.[27]

The apparent British contradiction of abolishing press censorship in 1695 yet maintaining drama censorship throughout the nineteenth century and introducing, in the early twentieth, a censorship for the new medium of film, appears to be due largely to the fact that the theatre and the cinema were seen by British elites as more powerful and more threatening than the press. First, the live appearance of human beings on stage and their vivid portrayal on film were perceived as far more likely to sway people than the printed word or even the relatively 'lifeless' printed illustration. Second, drama and film (like caricature) were accessible to the especially feared 'dark masses' who could not read. Third, theatre and cinema were viewed collectively by large numbers of people, who were seen as more susceptible to incitement to immediate disorder than the solitary newspaper reader. While mere inaction by Parliament allowed theatre censorship to continue, active enforcement by local authorities of the 'recommendations' of the film industry's British Board of Film Censors (BBFC) was required in order to implement the new film censorship. This reflected the fact that cinema was seen as even more threatening than the stage, since, compared to the theatre, the cheaper admission prices and less elegant surroundings of the 'movie palaces' attracted a younger and lower class of audience.

Concerns over the impact of stage and screen were reflected in the comments of a stage-censorship supporter who told a parliamentary committee in 1832 that the theatre needed to be restrained because 'it is presented to the eyes and ears in the most attractive manner'. Moreover, the BBFC rejected the concept that 'because a story has been published in literary form it is necessarily suitable for the screen' since such an idea ignored the 'fundamentally different psychological impression made by the printed word in the book and the photographic representation on the film, a principle which is understood by those with only a rudimentary knowledge of human psychology'.[28] Fears of 'mob mentality' surfaced in warnings to the 1832 and 1909 parliamentary inquiries into theatre censorship: on the stage, material, 'instead of being offered to one reader, as is the case of a book, is presented to hundreds or perhaps thousands at once' and 'the intellectual pitch of the crowd is lowered and its emotional pitch is raised', thus making theatre audiences likely to be 'irrational, excitable, lacking in self-control'.[29] This fear of lower-class audiences was reflected in a comment by *The Times* in 1907 in support of banning a play dealing with abortion, on the grounds that although the forbidden drama was 'probably the most authentic presentation we have yet had on the English stage of great social and political questions', its subject matter and the 'sincere realism with which it is treated makes it in our judgement wholly unfit for performance, under ordinary conditions, before a miscellaneous public of various ages, moods and standards of intelligence'.[30] Movies were particularly feared as having a damaging impact on the young, as was conveyed in 1916 by the Home Secretary's report that police chiefs in many towns had declared that the 'recent increase in juvenile delinquency is, to a considerable extent, due to demoralizing cinematograph films'.[31]

Although the origin and mechanisms of the British stage and film censorships varied somewhat, both were essentially alike in their arbitrariness, since they lacked any clear standards and were effectively insulated from judicial challenge. The Licensing Act of 1737, which was renewed by the Theatre Regulation Act of 1843, banned the presentation of dramas from any theatre not licensed for that purpose and required that all new plays presented for commercial purposes should be approved in advance by the Lord Chamberlain. Under the 1843 law, all theatre scripts, including operas and pantomimes, had to be submitted to the Lord Chamberlain seven days prior to production. The Lord Chamberlain had the unreviewable power of banning any production, whenever he felt it would be 'fitting for the preservation of good manners, decorum or of the public peace'.[32]

While theatre censorship was based on parliamentary authority and was standardised throughout Britain, the film censorship which grew up after 1910 was based on the 'recommendations' of the BBFC, which established itself as a form of 'voluntary' self-regulation to avoid the perceived alternative of official censorship. The BBFC's 'recommendations' were legally enforced by local authorities under colour of a 1909 law which empowered them to ensure that cinema owners avoided fire hazards before they could obtain licences to operate. The result,

as one film historian has noted, was 'censorship by a completely
unofficial body [the BBFC], enforced by the local authorities by means
of an Act of Parliament which was originally intended to secure the
public's safety'.[33] Although most local authorities simply rubber-
stamped the BBFC's recommendations, film producers and exhibitors
could ask local officials to act independently of the Board, which they
sometimes did, at the cost of a standard censorship.

The criteria of the drama and film censors were extremely vague.
Aside from the 'preservation of good manners', the Lord Chamberlain
was given no guidance by Parliament and, in turn, could give little to
the public, apart from a few flat prohibitions. Thus the depiction of
any living individuals and the presentation of any biblical dramas were
strictly forbidden, leading to the modification of the setting and title
of many operas such as Rossini's *Moses*. Otherwise, explanations of
censorship criteria offered by the Lord Chamberlain's Examiners of
Plays included those by George Colman (1824–36), who said he tried
to strike anything which 'may make a bad impression on the public
at large'; the statement by William Donne (1857–64) that he deleted
'anything in the shape of an oath, anything which turns religion into
ridicule and any political joke'; and the explanation given by G. A.
Redford (1895–1911) before the 1909 parliamentary inquiry: 'There are
no principles that can be defined. I follow precedent.'[34]

Inevitably, the result was that the personality of individual examiners came to the fore. Colman was notorious for his odd decisions,
which included striking the word 'thighs' as indecent and banning a
reference to members of the royal family as 'all stout gentlemen'.[35]
Donne banned Dumas's *La Dame aux camélias* but allowed the production of *La Traviata* (Verdi's opera based on Dumas's play), since,
'If there is a musical version of a piece it makes a difference, for the
story is then subsidiary to the music and singing.'[36] E. F. Smyth Pigott
(1874–95), who banned Ibsen's *Ghosts*, declared: 'I have studied Ibsen's
plays pretty carefully and all the characters in Ibsen's plays appear to
me morally deranged.' When Pigott died in 1895, George Bernard
Shaw termed his reign

> one long folly and panic, in which the only thing definitely discern-
> ible in a welter of intellectual confusion was his conception of the
> English people rushing toward an abyss of national degradation in
> morals and manners, and only held back on the edge of the preci-
> pice by the grasp of his strong hand.[37]

Although the BBFC periodically published censorship guidelines, they
were generally so vague as to be incomprehensible. Among the subjects listed by the BBFC as forbidden was any material

'repulsive and objectionable to the good taste and better feelings of English audiences' or 'calculated and possibly intended to foment social unrest and discontent'; scenes 'which bring into contempt public characters acting in their capacity as such'; 'stories showing any antagonistic or strained relations between white men and the coloured population of the British empire'; and 'themes calculated to give an air of romance and heroism to criminal characters, the story being told in such a way as to enlist the sympathies of the audience with the criminals, while the constituted Authorities and Administrators of the Law are held up to contempt as being either unjust or harsh, incompetent or ridiculous'.[38]

One factor which clearly affected drama and film censorship was the political climate of the day. Thus, during the unsettled political period between 1825 and 1852 (marked by the 1832 Reform Act crisis and the Chartist upsurges) virtually all presentations dealing with Charles I's execution two hundred years earlier were forbidden as 'insulting to monarchy'; and, amidst the labour turmoil of 1874, a play entitled *Lords and Labourers* was forbidden on the grounds that industrial relations was a subject 'not fit for representation on the stage at any time, still less now when there has been considerable agitation on the subject among the inflammable part of the population'.[39] Perhaps the clearest example of the impact of political considerations upon stage censorship came in 1907 when Gilbert and Sullivan's *Mikado* was temporarily banned after twenty years of unmolested performance, because officials feared it would give offence to a visiting Japanese prince.[40]

Although the vast discretion exercised by the authorities theoretically could have led to draconian limitations on political themes, overall, political censorship of stage and screen seems to have been relatively relaxed in comparison with France, Germany and Russia. Between 1852 and 1912 only 103 out of 19,304 plays submitted in Britain were completely refused a licence, and in the vast majority of cases the refusals appear to have been on the grounds of religion or morality rather than overtly political considerations. Similarly, the vast majority of the 35 films banned outright and the 314 movies censored in part by the BBFC in 1913–14 (of 14,119 films submitted) were found objectionable on grounds such as 'indecent dancing', 'cruelty to animals', 'gruesome murders', 'medical operations' and 'scenes suggestive of immorality'.[41] By contrast, in France between 1835 and 1847, 219 out of 8,330 plays were completely forbidden and a further 488 were censored in part, and 48 per cent of all material censored out of plays which were eventually allowed was apparently excised due to political considerations. In Russia in 1866–7 about 10 per cent of all plays were completely rejected and another 13 per cent were censored in part, for reasons which are not recorded.[42]

If British political censorship of stage and film in the 1815–1914 period was considerably less stringent than elsewhere in Europe, the political diet of the British citizen was none the less still severely constricted by the censorship of these media. The very existence of the censorship acted as a deterrent to writers, directors and theatre and cinema owners, who had no wish to expend time, energy and money on projects which would probably be rejected. It is likely that the main impact of the censorship was to deter the submission of potentially objectionable material rather than actually to forbid submitted scripts and films. As Lord Chamberlain Viscount Sydney told a parliamentary committee in 1866, dramatists knew 'pretty well what will be allowed'.[43] And when authors exceeded these bounds, producers and managers sometimes censored materials before submitting them to the authorities. Thus, when the producer of Byron's *Marino Faliero* at Drury Lane sent the manuscript to the censor in 1821, he included a note stating that the play had been 'so curtailed that I believe not a single objectionable line can be said to ['remain' deleted] exist'.[44] The play was a failure, at least partly because it had been 'curtailed' by 45 per cent of its original length before the censors even saw it.

Unquestionably, some highly talented writers simply did not write for the stage due to censorship. For, as playwright Elizabeth Inchbald noted, the novelist 'lives in a land of liberty, whilst the dramatic writer exists but under despotic government'.[45] H. G. Wells told the 1909 inquiry that censorship 'has always been one of the reasons I have not ventured into play writing'. Joseph Conrad termed the censorship 'intolerable, a disgrace to the tone, to the character of this country's civilization', while Arnold Bennett declared it 'monstrous and grotesque and profoundly insulting, and to condescend to reason against a thing so obviously vicious humiliates me'.[46] In remarks whose obvious sincerity compensates for some exaggerations in his comparison of the British censorship with that in other countries, Henry James declared:

> The situation made by the Englishman of letters ambitious of writing for the stage has less dignity, thanks to the censor's arbitrary rights upon his work, than that of any other man of letters in Europe. . . . It is difficult to express the depth of dismay and disgust with which an author of books in this country finds is impressed upon him in passing into the province of the theatre . . . that he has to reckon anxiously with an obscure and irresponsible Mr. So-and-So, who may by law peremptorily demand of him that he shall make his

work square, at vital points, with Mr. So-and-So's personal and, intellectually and critically speaking, wholly unauthoritative preferences, prejudices and ignorances, and that the less original, the less important and the less interesting it is . . . the more it is likely so to square. He thus encounters an arrogation of critical authority and the critical veto, with the power to enforce its decisions, that is without a parallel in any other civilized country. . . . We rub our eyes, we writers accustomed to freedoms in all other walks, to think that this cause has still to be argued in England.[47]

NOTES

1 K. D. Ewing and C. A. Gearty, *Freedom Under Thatcher: Civil Liberties in Modern Britain*, Oxford, Clarendon Press, 1990, pp. v, 1.
2 Quoted in ibid., pp. 3–4.
3 'United Kingdom', *IPI Report*, December 1989, p. 27; K. Boyle (ed.), *Article 19. Information, Freedom and Censorship: World Report 1988*, New York, Times Books, 1988, p. 239.
4 'United Kingdom', p. 31. For details of some of the recent censorship controversies, such as the 1987 Zircon affair, the 1986–9 *Spycatcher* affair and the 1988 ban on broadcasting statements made by spokesmen for alleged terrorist groups and their supporters, see Ewing and Gearty, *Freedom Under Thatcher*.
5 B. Porter, *The Refugee Question in mid-Victorian Politics*, Cambridge, Cambridge University Press, 1979, p. 7.
6 J. W. Hulse, *Revolutionists in London: a Study of Five Unorthodox Socialists*, Oxford, Clarendon Press, 1970, p. 1.
7 E. H. Carr, *The Romantic Exiles*, Boston, Mass., Beacon Press, 1961, p. 136.
8 R. Ashton, *Little Germany: Exile and Asylum in Victorian England*, Oxford, Oxford University Press, 1986, p. 201.
9 B. Porter, 'The British government and political refugees, c. 1880–1914', in J. Slatter (ed.), *From the Other Shore: Russian Political Emigrants in Britain, 1880–1917*, London, Frank Cass, 1984, p. 38.
10 *Archives Parlementaires de 1787 à 1860*, Paris, Paul Dupont, 1874, vol. 27, p. 7. See the discussion in R. J. Goldstein, *Censorship of Political Caricature in Nineteenth-Century France*, Ohio, Kent State University Press, 1989, pp. 40–1.
11 *La Caricature*, 2 February 1832.
12 Ashton, *Little Germany*, p. xii. For a general discussion of this topic, see R. J. Goldstein, *Political Repression in 19th-century Europe*, London, Croom Helm, 1983.
13 A. Aspinall, *Politics and the Press c. 1780–1850*, London, Home & Van Thal, 1949, p. 42.
14 A. Lee, *The Origins of the Popular Press in England, 1885–1914*, London, Croom Helm, 1976, p. 21; E. Halevy, *England in 1815*, New York, Barnes & Noble, 1961, p. 159.
15 These data are from W. H. Wickwar, *The Struggle for the Freedom of the Press, 1819–1832*, London, Allen & Unwin, 1928, p. 315.
16 D. Thomas, *A Long Time Burning: the History of Literary Censorship in England*, London, Routledge & Kegan Paul, 1969, p. 224.

17 See B. Porter, 'The *Freiheit* prosecutions, 1881–1882', *Historical Journal*, vol. 23, 1980, pp. 833–56; A. Kimball, 'The harassment of Russian revolutionaries abroad: the London trial of Vladimir Burtsev in 1898', *Oxford Slavonic Studies*, new series, vol. 6, 1973, pp. 48–65.

18 See R. J. Goldstein, *Political Censorship of the Arts and the Press in Nineteenth-century Europe*, London, Macmillan, 1989, p. 85.

19 G. A. Cranfield, *The Press and Society: from Caxton to Northcliffe*, London, Longman, 1978, p. 107.

20 ibid.

21 J. H. Wiener, *The War of the Unstamped: the Movement to Repeal the British Newspaper Tax, 1830–1836*, Ithaca, NY, Cornell University Press, 1969, p. 117.

22 A. Smith, *The Newspaper: an International History*, London, Thames & Hudson, 1979, p. 122.

23 B. Hillier, *Cartoons and Caricatures*, New York, Dutton, 1970, p. 7; H. T. Dickinson, *Caricatures and the Constitution, 1793–1832*, Cambridge, Chadwyck-Healey, 1986, p. 16.

24 R. Shikes and S. Heller, *The Art of Satire*, New York, Horizon Press, 1984, p. 10; R. Searle, C. Roy and B. Bornemann, *La Caricature: art et manifeste*, Geneva, Skira, 1974, p. 157.

25 R. Bachollet, 'Satire, censure et propagande, ou le destin de l'impudique Albion', two-part article in *Le Collectionneur français*, December 1980, pp. 14–15, February 1981, pp. 15–16.

26 K. Macgowan, W. Melnitz and G. Armstrong, *Golden Ages of the Theater*, Englewood Cliffs, NJ, Prentice-Hall, 1979, p. 172.

27 For a general discussion, see Goldstein, *Political Censorship*, pp. 113–92.

28 L. W. Conolly, *The Censorship of English Drama 1737–1834*, San Marino, Calif., Huntington Library, 1976, p. 180; I. Montagu, *The Political Censorship of Films*, London, Victor Gollancz, 1929, p. 33.

29 Conolly, *The Censorship of English Drama*, p. 180; J. Palmer, *The Censor and the Theatre*, New York, Mitchell Kennerly, 1913, p. 189.

30 R. Findlater, *Banned! A Review of Theatrical Censorship in Britain*, London, Macgibbon & Kee, 1967, p. 99. Until recently, Findlater's book was the only volume which surveyed the entire history of the British drama censorship. It has now been joined by J. Johnston, *The Lord Chamberlain's Blue Pencil*, London, Hodder & Stoughton, 1990, which is, however, far sketchier for the nineteenth century.

31 J. Trevelyan, *What the Censor Saw*, London, Michael Joseph, 1973, p. 26.

32 The 1843 and 1737 laws are quoted, along with other documents useful for the history of British theatre censorship, in F. Fowell and F. Palmer, *Censorship in England*, New York, Burt Franklin, 1970, pp. 353–79.

33 R. Low, *The History of the British Film, 1906–1914*, London, Allen & Unwin, 1949, p. 85. Basic information about the BBFC can be found in J. C. Robertson, *The British Board of Film Censors: Film Censorship in Britain, 1896–1950*, London, Croom Helm, 1985; J. C. Robertson, *The Hidden Cinema: British Film Censorship in Action, 1913–72*, London, Routledge, 1989; D. Knowles, *The Censor, the Drama and the Film, 1900–1934*, London, Allen & Unwin, 1934; and N. M. Hunnings, *Film Censors and the Law*, London, Allen & Unwin, 1967, a source especially strong for comparative information on various European governments.

34 Findlater, *Banned!*, pp. 54, 66; J. R. Stephens, *The Censorship of English*

Drama, 1824–1901, Cambridge, Cambridge University Press, 1980, pp. 168–9.

35 Stephens, *The Censorship of English Drama*, p. 80.
36 ibid., p. 83.
37 Findlater, *Banned!*, pp. 74, 75.
38 Montagu, *The Political Censorship of Films*, pp. 30–2; Low, *The History of British Film*, p. 91.
39 Stephens, *The Censorship of English Drama*, pp. 42, 127.
40 E. P. Lawrence, 'The banned *Mikado*: a topsy-turvy incident', *The Centennial Review*, vol. 18, 1974, pp. 151–69.
41 The British data are from Fowell and Palmer, *Censorship in England*, p. 353; and from Low, *The History of British Film*, pp. 90–1.
42 French data are from O. Krakovitch, *Hugo censuré: la liberté au théâtre au XIXe siècle*, Paris, Calmann-Levy, 1985, p. 286. Russian data are from D. Balmuth, *Censorship in Russia*, Washington, University Press of America, 1979, p. 42.
43 Findlater, *Banned!*, p. 72.
44 T. L. Ashton, 'The censorship of Byron's *Marino Faliero*', *Huntington Library Quarterly*, vol. 36, 1972–3, p. 28.
45 Conolly, *The Censorship of English Drama*, p. 11.
46 This testimony from the 1909 parliamentary inquiry has been reprinted in L. T. Beman (ed.), *Selected Articles on Censorship of the Theater and Moving Pictures*, New York, H. W. Wilson, 1931, pp. 334–5.
47 ibid., pp. 333–4.

Chapter 10

Blasphemy, obscenity and the courts: contours of tolerance in nineteenth-century England

M. J. D. Roberts

> During a hundred and sixty years the liberty of our press has been constantly becoming more and more entire; and during those hundred and sixty years the restraint imposed on writers by the general feeling of readers has been constantly becoming more and more strict.
>
> (T. B. Macaulay, *History of England* (1848–61), vol. IV, ch. 21)

Censorship is something which most English people since at least the mid-eighteenth century have liked to think foreign to their cultural traditions – censorship, that is, defined as a system of direct official constraints on publication. As Macaulay noted in mid-Victorian times, self-censorship – indirect pressure to social conformity – has its own tradition. Yet the belief that the English were free to express themselves subject only to the legitimate (post-publication) constraints of the law was a Victorian commonplace. It summed up the way the nation liked to believe it had regulated its affairs since the lapse of the licensing laws in 1695 under William and Mary. The purpose of this chapter is to explore the reality behind this view – to investigate the nature and extent of these post-publication legal constraints – and, in particular, to trace the changing patterns of usage of the common-law criminal charges of blasphemous and obscene libel over the course of the nineteenth century.[1]

QUESTIONS OF DEFINITION

What was regarded as blasphemous, or obscene, by the criminal law and what was the rationale for punishing it? These are tangled questions – tangled in large part because of the highly procedural way in which lawyers and judges protected themselves against, or allowed themselves to be exposed to, extra-legal pressures. English law was, on the face of it, remarkably sensitive to community values and moods. Since Fox's Libel Act of 1792 the question of not simply the fact of publication but of its criminal nature had been turned over to juries for decision. In a sense the only definition of the offence was a descriptive list of the items which had, over time, failed to jump the hurdle of jury acceptance. This is an important point, and one which we will come back to in due course. The fact remains, though, that juries reached their decisions on the basis of legal guidance given to them by judges and lawyers who in turn relied on legal precedent. It is precedent, indeed, which explains why, in the eyes of the law, blasphemy and obscenity are yoked together.

The law of criminal libel (which included seditious as well as blasphemous and obscene variants) was an extension of the common (i.e., judge-declared) law which gradually came into recognition in the course of the late seventeenth and early eighteenth centuries. The opportunity to which common lawyers responded was one created by the collapse of the ecclesiastical and royal prerogative courts and the lapsing of their jurisdiction over 'morals' in the years which followed the English Civil War. Because of this jurisdictional switch, all criminal libels were thereafter conceptualised, basically, as expressions which threatened social rather than spiritual well-being. As the judgement in Curl's case (1727) put it, publication of such matter was a common-law offence if it 'tends to corrupt the morals of the King's subjects and is against the peace of the King'.[2] In other words, publications were to be judged on the basis of their assumed social consequences. As assumptions among judges and lawyers changed, so might their guidance to juries about the key elements of the offence. To pick and choose in this socially conditioned way was, of course, a form of deviance in its own right to well-trained common lawyers of the nineteenth century: judges of a theoretical cast, when they detected a case of it (even in a Lord Chief Justice) felt professionally bound to denounce the tactic as a usurpation of the law-maker's role.[3] None the less, such changes did take place.

In blasphemy the chief adjustment was a downgrading of the emphasis on 'moral corruption' and a reinterpretation of the 'King's peace' aspect of the offence. Judges and prosecutors of the French Revolutionary era and its aftermath had insisted, as the otherwise libertarian Lord Erskine put it, that it was an assault on the consolations of the poor, and on the foundations of social trust in general, to promote uncertainty in the minds of the ignorant about the Christian doctrines of ultimate reward and punishment in an afterlife. By the 1880s, when professional policing and compulsory schooling had taken up much of the burden of moral instruction from religious agencies, less was heard of the offence as a threat to social stability but a great deal more was heard of it as a threat to the feelings (individual or collective) of religious believers. The test of blasphemous libel, as laid down by Lord Chief Justice Coleridge in 1883, became one based not on *what* was said but on *how* it was said: religious controversy was beyond the law's interest unless it was expressed in a way 'calculated and intended to insult the feelings and the deepest religious convictions of the great majority of the persons amongst whom we live'.[4]

A similar drift in definition can be detected in the case of obscene libels. Obscenity, perhaps even more obviously than blasphemy, is a term covering a bundle of meanings, all of which are culture-specific. For an understanding of nineteenth-century usage it is helpful to distinguish between at least two of these meanings. There is, on one hand, that type of obscenity which serves (and is intended to serve) a public purpose – the shocking of an audience or the ridiculing and shaming of a public figure by deployment of sexual or scatological imagery. On the other hand, there is the type which serves the private purpose of sexual arousal.

By the mid-nineteenth century the presumption in favour of a 'private' definition was already established. (The term 'pornography' to encapsulate this meaning was apparently a coinage of the period.[5]) Yet the persistence of a populist tradition of the bawdy exposure of vice among public figures claiming political, social or moral authority was one which kept alive the reflex responses of judges and politicians throughout the period. As we shall see, the concern of these groups to defend authority against ridicule ensured that the public-order aspect of the offence was never entirely forgotten.

However, it must be admitted that the most significant development in defining the offence was clearly the refining of the tests for judging not 'breach of the peace' – but 'tendency to corrupt' individual character. As the market for printed publications expanded and diversified, it became a matter of urgency to reconcile the liberties of the culturally trustworthy with the perceived needs of the culturally vulnerable. The dilemma was resolved in 1868 in the precedent-setting case of *Regina* v. *Hicklin*. In this case public decency was upheld, rather unexpectedly, at the expense of freedom to engage in religious controversy: *The Confessional Unmasked*, a publication of the Protestant Electoral Union, was held, on appeal, to be an obscene libel because of its 'tendency . . . to deprave and corrupt those whose minds are open to such immoral influences and into whose hands a publication of this sort may fall'.[6] This was not an explicit switch in the socio-legal underpinning of the offence (as had taken place in cases of blasphemous libel). By drawing attention to the varied possibilities of audience-response as a material element in proof of the offence, it did, however, help to update the offence in its own way.

PATTERNS OF PROSECUTION

If this was the law, how extensive were the efforts made to enforce it? Standard surveys sometimes give the impression that 'the Victorian era' was one of steady legal repression of intellectual and social diversity only gradually modified by the sacrificial efforts of individual martyrs to the cause. Modern standards of freedom of inquiry and rights to self-expression, it is implied, were won in a series of symbolic victories cumulatively won through courtroom confrontation.[7] The cast-list of this moral drama is a relatively short and well-agreed one. It usually includes, in the pre-Victorian period, radical free-thinking publicists such as William Hone (acquitted of blasphemous libel in 1817 after conducting his own defence), and the publishers of Tom Paine's deistic attack on religious superstition, *The Age of Reason* (Thomas Williams, 1797; Daniel Isaac Eaton, 1812; Richard Carlile, 1819: all convicted). In the Victorian period the mantle of 'infidel' martyrdom passes to victims such as Henry Hetherington (1840), G. J. Holyoake (1842) and G. W. Foote (1883). Among these, Foote is particularly remembered for his response from the dock on hearing sentence passed: 'Thank you, my Lord. The sentence is worthy of your creed.' In the final decades of the century the cast diversifies to include Charles Bradlaugh and Annie Besant (convicted in 1878 for publishing a birth-control manual), Henry Vizetelly (convicted in 1889 for publishing Zola in English translation) and George Bedborough (convicted as publisher of Havelock Ellis's *Studies in the Psychology of Sex* in 1898).

All these cases are, of course, exceptionally well documented, each being a *cause célèbre*. The question needs to be asked, all the same: to what extent is it safe to accept a series of show-trials as representative of trends overall? In some instances, it seems reasonable to suspect, for the selection of 'show-case' illustrations gives a distorted view of the law's operation. While the statistics of obscene-libel prosecutions, for example, are both incomplete and difficult to compare over time, they do indicate that the bulk of cases dealt with by the courts did involve, to quote Lord Campbell, the control of material of 'no artistic merit or aspiration at all . . . purely manufactured for purposes of trade'.[8] Overall, however, the fragmentary statistical sources suggest that show-trials can be accepted as representative on most occasions – recognised as the crests of large waves of social anxiety. The crest-and-trough pattern of legal activity is, indeed, one of the most notable features of prosecutions for the criminal-libel group of offences. This holds true in spite of the fact that opportunities for law enforcement were substantially increased in the course of the century: urban Police Acts, Post Office Acts and Customs Acts all came to contain clauses which made it a great deal easier and cheaper to prosecute traders of blasphemous or obscene publications in the 1880s than it had been in the 1820s.[9] From this uneven pattern of activity it can be deduced that those setting out to enforce laws against blasphemy and obscenity were apparently as eager to engage in symbolic confrontation as the more famous of those they prosecuted. The aim was to use the shaming methods of selective publicity to set limits to public tolerance – a strategy which, it was hoped, would make the costly and liberty-infringing alternative of blanket law-enforcement unnecessary. A few brief periods aside, it is rare to find sustained attempts by either public or private agencies to prosecute every known offence. The most professional private agency in the field between 1802 and 1886, the Society for the Suppression of Vice, calculated in 1857 that it had prosecuted only 159 cases of obscene libel in fifty-five years, and that this figure represented somewhere between one in six and one in ten of cases brought to its attention. Blasphemous libel cases were even rarer (and more tightly clustered when they came). The number and rate of prosecutions rose in the final twenty years of the century as police forces added their efforts more consistently to those of private prosecutors. Even so, the peak year for London Metropolitan Police obscene publication apprehensions, 1886, brought in no more than fifty-four cases, nine of which were summarily dismissed. Later years showed a gradual falling-back. All in all, prosecutions for matters of opinion, decency and taste over the century were seldom wide-spread.[10] Indeed, legal intervention, when it was attempted, was notably responsive to fluctuations in public mood – to changing perceptions of social threat.

CONTEXTS OF ANXIETY

How did waves of public anxiety build up? Which sections of the public did the worrying? Which groups gave special cause for concern? The most straightforward situations are ones in which publication of controversial material might plausibly be interpreted as an incitement to disorder and disrespect. It is no surprise, therefore, to find that prosecutions for blasphemous libel were normally instituted only at times when the propertied classes had particular reason to fear the spread of general disaffection for public institutions among the unpropertied lower orders. 'What . . . I saw amongst the papers of the Secret Committee [of the House of Commons, 1817], gave me but too much reason to fear that the enemies of our political constitution were also enemies to our religion', wrote William Wilberforce, one of the leading supporters of early-century blasphemy prosecutions.[11] The provocation which, in practice, usually ensured official support for legal action in the earlier part of the century was the aggressively anti-clerical, and specifically anti-established church, tone of popular radicals – rather than doctrinal unorthodoxy as such. Obscene scandal, as previously noted, also triggered action when its purpose was deemed to be the undermining of respect for rank. Direct legal onslaughts on incitements to civil disaffection reached their peak in the period of popular unrest which followed the Napoleonic Wars: lesser waves of anxiety broke through during the years of constitutional crisis (1828–31), and of Chartist agitation (1838–42).

After mid-century, the direct link between libel prosecutions and periods of political tension fades away in large part. The lower orders themselves are judged to be less alienated, and therefore more capable of defending themselves against moral subversion. The 'respectable' among them are increasingly recognised as allies. The most infamous blasphemer of the 1820s, Richard Carlile, had, from the start, given hint of this development by endorsing the Vice Society's work against obscene publications even as it prosecuted him for publishing Tom Paine. Yet, the vision of a subversive anti-culture, blending political, social and sexual deviances into one, was a vision of which the more stable Victorian period was never entirely able to rid itself. It was no accident that Bradlaugh and Besant in the 1870s and 1880s, and Bedborough in the 1890s, were picked out as legal targets: each was believed to pose a threat to political and social institutions as well as to standards of sexual propriety.[12]

A second shaping influence on the contours of legal tolerance was the long-running debate about the impact of mass literacy. Again, the focus of anxiety was the labouring population – but the problem was defined in less directly political terms. That is, the point of concern was the supposed power of the printed word to corrupt individual character and capacity for right judgement. The concern can be traced back to later Hanoverian times. Anxieties were especially easy to arouse during the 1820s, as social conservatives and progressives alike took stock of the contrast between the purposes for which religious and social activists had been promoting mass literacy since the 1780s, and the socially destabilising purposes which the ability to read had apparently come to serve. What if 'the boon which we warranted as a blessing, perverted [sic] into a calamity and a curse'? (as one MP asked in the course of rowdy debate over the blasphemy laws in 1823).[13] In fact, the parliamentary classes were overrating the part they had played in creating an appetite for literacy among the masses. Yet the vision of a Frankenstein escaping the control of his creator had a powerful impact at the time, and the literacy debate (unlike the public-order debate) remained an open one throughout the century. It resurfaced in the post-mortems of the Chartist era, and it helped to shape reactions to the arrival of the mass-circulation, sensation-retailing, Sunday newspapers in the 1840s and 1850s. Qualms were temporarily set aside in the following decades as liberal, progressive opinion convinced law-makers of the need to encourage universal literacy as a training for entry to the new age of political democracy. However, by the 1880s, the old ambivalence had re-emerged: disillusion among educated and religious elites plumbed depths not reached since the 1820s.[14]

What had thwarted the liberal vision of a society educated to civic virtue through its ability to read? Partly, of course, it could be explained as a 'demand-side' failure. The 'depraved' reading tastes of the mass public could be interpreted as yet more evidence of human gullibility and sinfulness. Partly, too, it could be seen as a problem of unregulated supply, and it is the recurrent concern of middle-class opinion-formers with the commercialisation of nineteenth-century culture which must be recognised as a third major influence shaping patterns of anxiety about moral subversion. This is a point of significance because of the way in which it helps to make clear the origins of anxiety about the reading habits of the upper and middle ranks in society, as well as those of the labouring masses.

In a self-consciously hierarchical society undergoing a drawn-out process of political, economic and cultural negotiation, it was vital to the collective self-esteem of the more sensitive of the socially privileged that they be able to present themselves as something more than merely holders of political and economic power. They also needed to feel confident of their moral fitness for leadership. One strategy by which moral fitness could be demonstrated was to take up the role of cultural consumer-protection on behalf of the 'victims' of the commercialised leisure industry. The temperance movement was, among other things, a major agency for the expression of this type of thinking.

Critics of popular literature never formed such a coherent public pressure-group as temperance did, but their crusades against 'artificially stimulated' trade in addictive literary 'poisons' were a recurring feature of most decades between the 1820s and the 1890s. So too were their attempts to swing market demand in the direction of their own purified product. From time to time, however, the more authoritarian either lost patience – or lost their nerve in the face of new evidence of market penetration. The targeting of new markets by commercial publishers caused particular anxiety when it drew in younger readers. The first major scare occurred in the early 1850s as magistrates, educators and philanthropists moved to condemn the glamorisation of crime, violence and 'horror' in cheap literature aimed at working-class juveniles. In the decades which followed, more than one 'penny dreadful' met its fate in a magistrate's court, seized under the 1857 Obscene Publications Act.[15]

The Act of 1857 had been passed, however, with an eye on the reading habits of a wider range of society than the youth of the urban working class. As I have explained elsewhere, the debate that Act aroused gives evidence of an increase in anxiety about the vulnerability to market temptation of middle- and upper-class adolescents as well. In later Victorian times that anxiety spread and flourished. Middle-class feminists, provincial nonconformists, churchmen and supporters of the national imperial mission all had reason to develop arguments for the stricter policing of elite and 'respectable' culture. The climax of moral-reform politics came in 1885–6 with W. T. Stead's 'Maiden Tribute of Modern Babylon' press campaign against child prostitution, and the foundation of a countrywide network of citizen pressure-groups to campaign for public decency across the board.[16] By the end of the 1880s the campaign to avert moral contagion by market forces was a well-established social fact, and its leaders took special pride in advertising their determination to pursue vice at whatever level of society it might be found.

THE LEGAL PROCESS IN ACTION

Having sketched some reasons for the changing intensity and focus of campaigns to protect public morals, we are left with the task of working out precisely who was charged with the responsibility for taking legal action, and with what degree of community encouragement. The first point to stress here is one already indirectly acknowledged – the general disinclination of governments to make prosecution of criminal libels (other than seditious libels) a continuing state responsibility. This reluctance was more marked in the case of obscene than of blasphemous libel but, even in the second case, governments preferred to leave the running to private prosecutors unless the threat to public order seemed (as in 1817–23) a sustained and immediate one. Reliance on private prosecutors was, of course, a standard feature of the English legal system until the general overhaul of urban police forces in mid-century. By the 1880s, though, with Home Secretaries still being asked to take over prosecution duties and expenses for offences against public morals, the situation was becoming distinctly anomalous.[17]

The resulting gap was chiefly filled by volunteer associations formed by moral activists themselves – the Vice Society until 1886, the National Vigilance Association (NVA) thereafter. What effect did this have on public acceptance of moral regulation by law? The theory was that a system directly responsive to community feeling was one likely to be more respected than one activated by public officials: 'If the general moral sense of the community did not compel individuals to prosecute, no good would be done by trying to create an artificial sense by the action of the Public Prosecutor', as one Home Secretary put it.[18] This was a convenient rationalisation. Governments often benefited from being able to distance themselves from awkward issues involving the arbitration of clashing moral imperatives. There was no shortage of critics, either, willing to attack volunteer societies as 'conspiracies against the liberties of the subject' – busybody associations of sectarian tendencies, representative of no-one but themselves.[19]

These accusations also had their effect in conditioning the responses of legal officers to cases brought before the courts. Significantly, the public agencies from which the private societies felt they drew most consistent support were the reformed urban police forces. Once a case reached court, however, hazards multiplied. Certain judges and magistrates, at times, became notorious among volunteer prosecutors for their 'trimming' behaviour when faced with demands for the enforcement of controversial laws. Even cases for the prosecution of 'consensus offences' might break down if they failed to meet the exacting standards of proof imposed by the higher courts. Moreover, witness-credibility was a recurrent stumbling block, with the animus against paid or over-zealous 'spies' a legacy of the eighteenth century which faded only gradually.[20]

In the face of these uncertainties it is understandable that volunteer prosecuting societies should have been fairly regular lobbyists for law reform. The Vice Society, for example, claimed a key role in the passing of Lord Campbell's Obscene Publications Act of 1857: this Act of procedural reforms certainly simplified the Society's task of evidence-gathering. The renamed NVA took lobbying tactics even further by endorsing candidates in local-government elections and bringing 'democratic' pressures to bear on police and magistrates.[21] In cases such as these, activists were successful only in so far as they could claim to speak on behalf of a wider constituency. They failed as often as they won. Yet their role as agenda-setters is not to be under-estimated; and their conversion, through experience, to a belief in the need for streamlined judicial procedures also helped a general trend towards summary trial before magistrates which often served them well.

When prosecutors came up against ideologically committed opponents, however, the normal way of resolving conflict remained the traditional one of trial before jury – a fact leading us to pose the final question: what role did juries play in shaping the contours of tolerance? In theory, of course, juries were the last bastion of the liberties of the subject. Their decisions gave the criminal law a strengthened claim to social legitimacy. (Trial before jury also offered wonderful publicity opportunities to both sides, especially the side which won.) In practice, jury decisions articulated community values in a rather specialised way. Jurors were drawn from the ranks of property-owning males. In early nineteenth-century London they were usually drawn from an even more restricted group of social reliables. This had its effect: the learned and gentlemanly radical William Hone was triumphantly acquitted of blasphemy in 1817; but self-taught, chip-on-shoulder artisan 'infidels' such as Carlile and Holyoake were readily convicted by bored and angry panels of businessmen and tenant farmers who saw public order more at risk than liberty. The redefinition of the offence, in the later part of the century, as one of outrage on public feelings seems to have softened the attitudes of juries, though the total number of cases tried before jury is too small to be certain.[22]

What of obscene libels? Here, too, juries reserved the benefit of the doubt for those who impressed them as reliable in cultural manner and intention. The most famous verdict was that of the Bradlaugh–Besant jury in 1878 – 'calculated to deprave . . . but . . . we entirely exonerate the defendants from any corrupt motives in publishing'. This was apparently intended to acquit but the judge ruled it a conviction. In cases presented as tainted with motives of commercial gain, any concern to protect 'freedom of expression' seems hardly to have emerged once juries were exposed collectively to the materials at issue and instructed that the test of obscenity was the likely effect of those materials on the most susceptible group 'into whose hands' the materials might 'fall'. The Vizetelly jurors in 1888 specifically begged to be spared extended readings from Zola.[23] The collective suspicion among early-century jurors of the motives and methods of operation of prosecutors also faded. On the evidence it is difficult to believe that juries were fiercer defenders of the right to publish morally controversial material than were magistrates or judges.

INTO THE TWENTIETH CENTURY: WRITERS, PUBLISHERS AND THE CRIMINAL LAW

When, in 1910, G. W. Foote, the secularist martyr of the 1880s, looked back on trends over his lifetime he summed up as follows:

> The censorship does not become more difficult under democracy. It becomes easier. What right have cranks and freaks to quarrel with the people's representatives acting for the people's good? Must not the rule of the majority prevail? . . . The result is that a censorship is developing against new ideas in every direction. Government by the mob, or its agents, is extending over the whole field of

intellectual and moral activity; and the friends of liberty and progress will have to make a desperate effort to free themselves if they wish to escape being smothered to death.[24]

Foote's view was a highly personal interpretation of his times, but his conclusion was one which more famous names than his – Tocqueville and J. S. Mill, for example – had already reached. The greater the degree of public participation in law-enforcement, they reflected, the less tolerable the deviant would become. Not everyone agreed. However, an increasing number of late-century literary intellectuals did. The evidence, it must be admitted, did pile up during the later Victorian years. In the 1820s it had been writers and publishers for plebeian audiences who faced the criminal law: the Shelleys and Byrons had been disciplined, so far as they were, by public opinion and the denial of civil law copyright. In the 1850s the tightened policing of the trade in 'low literature' had been conceded to Lord Campbell by a sceptical legislature only after he had given it assurances that control of literary and artistic expression fell beyond the intention of his bill. Yet, from the late 1860s onward, this class-conditioned goodwill towards the culture of elites came increasingly under pressure. By the 1890s it was possible for the chairman of the NVA to declare: 'If a great artist thinks fit to transgress the laws of decency, so much the worse for him. And the jury know what is obscene even if they do not know what is literature.'[25]

Seen from this angle, the future looked grim for libertarian intellectuals. What Tocqueville, Mill and Foote tended to underestimate, however, was the extent to which the forces of cultural democratisation would, over time, encourage a process of counter-mobilisation. The medical and scientific community, for example, had its immunities against obscenity confirmed by the judgement in *Hicklin*, so long as it distributed its publications with discretion. As science spread to include social science so the area of contestable territory expanded. The defence of 'literary merit', certified by experts, took longer to sell to politicians – until the Obscene Publications Act of 1959, in fact – though it needs to be recognised that the campaign to achieve it began in later Victorian times as a direct response to those court judgements which had called elite cultural immunities into question.[26] The moral protection of mass audiences remained (and remains) more contentious. Here, the pressure to 'liberalise' community standards of decency has been applied most consistently, and with eventual success, not by cultural elites but by commercial promoters of mass consumption.

The most curious fate of all has been reserved for the law of blasphemous libel. Late Victorian political elites had themselves been of two minds whether to abolish it or to extend it to the protection of all main types of religious sensibility.[27] The decline of that evangelical religious fervour which had helped to sustain the law seemed thereafter to make the concept of blasphemy socially redundant. Recent events have now given it a new lease of life; but those events reflect a very different world from the one explored in this chapter – a world which even the most incisive Victorian secularist would have been at a loss to predict.

NOTES

1 For continuing civil-law constraints on authors and publishers, see E. Royle, *Radicals, Secularists and Republicans*, Manchester, Manchester University Press, 1980, p. 17; D. Saunders, 'Copyright, obscenity and literary history', *English Literary History*, vol. LVII, 1990, pp. 431–44; D. Thomas, *A Long Time Burning. The History of Literary Censorship in England*, London, Routledge & Kegan Paul, 1969, p. 207.

2 P. R. MacMillan, *Censorship and Public Morality*, Aldershot, Gower, 1983, pp. 2–4.

3 J. F. Stephen, 'Blasphemy and blasphemous libel', *Fortnightly Review*, vol. XXXV, 1884, p. 315.

4 *Parliamentary Debates* (PD), 1st series, vol. XLI, col. 707, 6 November 1819; Royle, *Radicals, Secularists and Republicans*, p. 274; P. Jones, 'Blasphemy, offensiveness and law', *British Journal of Political Science*, vol. X, 1980, p. 134.

5 I. McCalman, *Radical Underworld. Prophets, Revolutionaries and Pornographers in London, 1795–1840*, Cambridge, Cambridge University Press, 1988, p. 286.

6 *Reg.* v. *Hicklin*, 1868, LR 3QB 360 at 371.

7 A. Calder-Marshall, *Lewd, Blasphemous and Obscene*, London, Hutchinson, 1972; Thomas, *A Long Time Burning*.

8 PD, 3rd ser., vol. CXLVI, col. 337, 25 June 1857. For early nineteenth-century statistics of prosecutions for criminal libel see *Parliamentary Papers* (PP) 1823 (562), vol. XV, pp. 239–71. Some glimpse of later trends in the London area may be gained through the Annual Reports of the Metropolitan Police Commissioners for 1869 and following years.

9 C. Manchester, 'Obscenity law enforcement in the nineteenth century', *Journal of Legal History*, vol. II, 1981, pp. 45–61.

10 ibid., pp. 50, 54–5; Royle, *Radicals, Secularists and Republicans*, pp. 272, 275; PP 1887, col. 5216, vol. XL, p. 340.

11 R. and S. Wilberforce, *The Life of William Wilberforce*, 5 vols, John Murray, 1838, vol. V, p. 40. Cf. R. Hole, *Pulpits, Politics & Public Order in England 1760–1832*, Cambridge, Cambridge University Press, 1989, pp. 207–13; McCalman, *Radical Underworld*, pp. 139–47.

12 Royle, *Radicals, Secularists and Republicans*, pp. 32, 256–77.

13 PD, 2nd ser., vol. IX, col. 1398, 1 July 1823.

14 D. Vincent, *Literacy and Popular Culture: England 1750–1914*, Cambridge, Cambridge University Press, 1989, pp. 178–9, 210–11, 233–4; V. Berridge, 'Popular Sunday papers and mid-Victorian society', in G. Boyce, J. Curran and P. Wingate (eds), *Newspaper History*, London, Constable, 1978, pp. 247–64; A. J. Lee, *The Origins of the Popular Press in England 1855–1914*, London, Croom Helm, 1976, pp. 29–40.

15 J. Springhall, ' "A life story for the people"? Edwin J. Brett and the London "low life" penny dreadfuls of the 1860s', *Victorian Studies*, vol. XXXII, 1990, pp. 223–46, esp. 231–40; P. Dunae, 'Penny dreadfuls: later 19th-century boys' literature and crime', *Victorian Studies*, vol. XXII, 1979, pp. 135–50.

16 M. Roberts, 'Morals, art and the law: the passing of the Obscene Publications Act, 1857', *Victorian Studies*, vol. XXVIII, 1985, pp. 612–15; E. J. Bristow, *Vice and Vigilance. Purity Movements in Britain since 1700*, Dublin, Gill & Macmillan, 1977, pp. 117–21.

17 *PD*, 3rd ser., vol. CCCXXV, col. 1719, 8 May 1888.

18 ibid., cols 1719–20. Cf. *PD*, 2nd ser., vol. VIII, col. 720, 26 March 1823; Royle, *Radicals, Secularists and Republicans*, pp. 271 ff.

19 M. Roberts, 'Making Victorian morals? The society for the suppression of vice and its critics, 1802–1886', *Historical Studies*, vol. XXI, 1984, pp. 157–73.

20 W. A. Coote, *A Romance of Philanthropy*, London, National Vigilance Association, 1916, pp. 113–14; E. Royle, *Victorian Infidels*, Manchester, Manchester University Press, 1974, p. 80.

21 *Society for the Suppression of Vice. Occasional Report*, London, 1868, pp. 4–5; *National Vigilance Association. Report for 1886*, London, 1887, pp. 24–5, and *Report for 1888*, p. 5.

22 Royle, *Radicals, Secularists and Republicans*, pp. 33–4, 273–4.

23 C. Manchester, 'Lord Campbell's Act: England's first obscenity statute', *Journal of Legal History*, vol. IX, 1988, p. 236. For the way in which Dickens envisaged the restraining effects of jury trial operating on the literary imagination, see L. Hutton (ed.), *Letters of Charles Dickens to Wilkie Collins*, New York, Kraus, 1969, p. 138.

24 Royle, *Radicals, Secularists and Republicans*, p. 288.

25 Coote, *Romance of Philanthropy*, p. 47.

26 The 1908 Joint Parliamentary Select Committee on Lotteries and Indecent Advertisements was the first official body to recommend the exemption of 'works of art and literature' from the law of obscene libel.

27 Royle, *Radicals, Secularists and Republicans*, p. 274.

Chapter 11

Victorian obscenity law: negative censorship or positive administration?[1]

David Saunders

THE CENSORSHIP APPROACH TO OBSCENITY LAW

In *Regina* v. *Hicklin*, in 1868, the Court of Queen's Bench defined obscenity. It had not been asked to do so. In the United Kingdom, the United States and other common-law jurisdictions, Lord Chief Justice Cockburn's dictum became the test for criminal obscenity:

> I think the test of obscenity is this, whether the tendency of the matter charged as obscenity is to deprave and corrupt those whose minds are open to such immoral influences, and into whose hands a publication of this sort may fall.[2]

In question was a pamphlet distributed by the Protestant Electoral Union, *The Confessional Unmasked: Showing the Depravity of the Romish Priesthood, the Iniquity of the Confessional, and the Questions put to Females in Confession*. The pamphlet's *obscenity* was not in doubt. The issue before the High Court – a Quarter Sessions' request for clarification concerning an appeal against a magistrate's order for the destruction of this publication – was whether an honest purpose justified the criminal act of publishing an obscene libel.

The dictum has been termed 'one passing judicial comment which has survived the passage of time and which returns regularly to plague the courts and parliaments of England, America and the common-law world'.[3] I shall argue, however, that *Hicklin* is consonant with a sophisticated administration of a social problem – street pornography. It will be a matter of asking when, how, and for whom pornography surfaced *as a social problem*; and to answer these questions Victorian obscenity law is not usefully described in terms of censorship.

A notion has arisen that after *Hicklin* the law started to be used indiscriminately: we are thus told that 'armed at last with a definition of obscenity, Victorian prosecutors proceeded to destroy many examples of fine literature'.[4] This comment by the arch-liberal jurist Geoffrey Robertson invites our indignation at the literary depradations caused by nineteenth-century obscenity law. But there are two problems. First, there is no evidence of this destruction of 'fine litera- ture'. Like the literary historians whose word he follows, Robertson cites the 1888 prosecution of Henry Vizetelly, a London-based pub- lisher of translations of Gautier, Flaubert, Daudet, Maupassant and Zola. In addition, commentators dredge up the 1877 prosecution of Charles Bradlaugh and Annie Besant for publishing Charles Knowl- ton's *The Fruits of Philosophy* and George Bedborough's prosecution in 1898 for selling Havelock Ellis's *Sexual Inversion*, the first volume of *Studies in the Psychology of Sex*. Had there been more such actions in the thirty years following *Hicklin*, or the forty years following the Obscene Publications Act of 1857, the 'censorship historians' would have said so. Their *claim* of a mass destruction of serious literature is the interesting phenomenon. There is in fact an entirely practical reason for this *lack* of legal action against serious literature, as we shall see. The second problem concerns Robertson's reference to 'fine literature'. The phrase contains an aesthetic and ethical assumption; but this too is ill founded, as I hope to show.

A deficiency of supporting evidence or a misplaced conviction that 'fine literature' is an unproblematic cultural entity will not eliminate a major obstacle to analysis of nineteenth-century obscenity law: the universal knowingness of later commentators – liberal jurists, literary historians, aesthetic psychoanalysts – who *assume* the failure of the Victorians to differentiate art from pornography and the immoral from the harmful. Such knowingness has its problems. It assumes that these distinctions – which lie at the heart of twentieth-century concerns with pornography – also governed nineteenth-century arrangements. This is an anachronism. However, it has perpetuated the image of ignor- ance and philistine moralism that we prize so highly in Victorianism.

The censorship approach to the history of obscenity law requires revision. We cannot explain how pornography surfaced *as a social problem* if we follow the liberal-psycho-aesthetic framework in which nearly all discussion of pornography and obscenity law proceeds.[5] The censorship approach shares with this framework an emancipatory (for literary critics) and deregulatory (for lawyers) demand to free sexual expression from the heavy hand of the law. Looking back it sees only a repressive Victorian society that silences sex, perverting it into pornography rather than achieving its balanced expression in erotic art.[6] Not everyone agrees. Feminist campaigns have re-established the linkage between (male) pornography and conduct that is socially harm- ful (to women).[7] This linkage, made by the Victorians, is an object of derision by (complacent) censorship historians. Moreover, Michel Foucault challenges the received idea that western sexuality has been repressed. His *History of Sexuality* (1979) undoes the 'fable' that our sexuality has been silenced by a long repression which reached a peak in Victorian times.[8] For Foucault, the 'repressive hypothesis' is not sustained by the facts. On the contrary, his Victorians multiplied inducements to speak of sex, to watch for it at every turn. Yet, defining the relationship of sex – and literary writing about sex – and law in terms of repression and censorship has become our special habit.

This habit of mind sees as the cornerstone of nineteenth-century obscenity law a generalised repression to which that law gave social form and legal sanction. However, I want to explore the different picture that might emerge if we abandon this 'repressive hypothesis' and view the history of nineteenth-century obscenity law independently of the concept of censorship. The law's instruments might then appear not as negative and censorial but as regulatory devices in a cultural milieu characterised by an 'explosion of discourse' about sex.

VARIABLE OBSCENITY

Let us start from the fact that those nineteenth-century authorities responsible for the legal regulation of pornography recognised that the meaning and effect of a publication varied with the circumstances of its consumption and the cultural capacities of its users. Printed pornography, after all, concerned not humans in general, but only the literate. For the purposes of policing pornography, the law confronted demographically and culturally differentiated audiences. Criteria were elaborated to define those categories of person at risk from involuntary exposure to pornography and thus entitled to the protection afforded by obscenity law. In other words, nineteenth-century obscenity law is inseparable from a specific cultural demography.

The Obscene Publications Act of 1857 and the *Hicklin* judgement must also be seen against the triple configuration of the contemporary literate field. On one side there was street pornography. This comprised ancient bawdy broadsheets, French and Egyptian postcards, salacious cullings from the classics sold in penny part-editions – the whole pile moving along a sub-booktrade network of pedlars and hawkers. This was called 'Holywell Street' literature, after the central location of the London pornography trade. On the other side there was the tolerated specialist esoteric and 'curious' pornography. Circulating privately, often published by subscription and in costly editions, this circuit linked pursuit of rare perversity and bibliophile enthusiasm for the rare edition. That this might be in French, German or Latin was no obstacle to 'private case' collectors such as Henry Spencer Ashbee who, under the pseudonym Pisanus Fraxi, had privately printed an *Index librorum prohibitorum* (1877), a *Centuria librorum absconditorum* (1879) and a *Catena librorum tacendorum* (1885). Their common subtitle, *being notes bio-biblio-iconographical and critical, on curious and uncommon books*, says it all. Third, in the central space, were the 'educative' novels of Dickens, Eliot, Thackeray, Trollope, the Brontës, Collins, the poetic and historical works of Macaulay, and so on. Sometimes serialised in literary and improving journals and issued in parts, these publications were directed at the expanding middle class and the literate working household. They display few references to sex, except in forms requiring skill to disinter. Of course, at their margins these three circulations overlapped; but obscenity law was concerned only with the first of them.

The Obscene Publications Act of 1857 (also known as Lord Campbell's Act) was the British Parliament's first statutory move with regard to obscene publications. Its rationale derived from its delimited purpose: regulation of conduct in certain vulnerable places and populations. To this end, the Act established a summary seize-and-destroy procedure administered by police and magistrates as part of the routine policing of the streets. No new offences were created. The mid-century legislature did not acclaim the bill as the censorship approach might have us expect. Nor did the legal profession offer unqualified endorsement; opinions in *The Justice of the Peace* and the *Law Times* expressed concern at the extension of police powers.[9]

As a police measure dependent on the emergence of an urban police force, the 1857 Act was regulatory, not extirpative. The target was a specific traffic; the means made available by the legislation were limited in scope. As to enforcement of the new Act, this too was far from massive. By 1868 – that is, by the year of the *Hicklin* judgement – the *Saturday Review* of 5 December could write of Holywell Street that 'the dunghill is in full heat and steaming with all of its old pestilence'.

At the heart of nineteenth-century obscenity law lies the recognition that because cultural abilities are unevenly distributed, obscenity is variable or circumstantial. It thus required a flexible not a uniform mode of regulation. A modern myth makes variable obscenity a sophisticated twentieth-century reform of crude Victorian jurisprudence, but this is not so.[10] Among the *obiter dicta* in *Regina* v. *Hicklin* Lord Cockburn thus confirmed that under the 1857 Act the mere possession or sale of a work 'in a certain sense obscene' is not in itself sufficient for an indictment. A *circumstantial* disposition to commit the offence must be proved: 'the question is therefore quo animo was the publication'.[11] For the judges of the Queen's Bench, a publication was definable as criminally obscene not by an inherent quality but by its mode of dissemination and by its demographic target:

> This work [*The Confessional Unmasked*] . . . is sold at the corners of streets and in all directions, and of course it falls into the hands of

persons in all classes, young and old, and the minds of those hitherto pure are exposed to the danger of contamination and pollution from the impurity it contains.[12]

The danger of individual and social harm from pornography is a function of the places where the traffic flows and the cultural equipment of those whom it targets: the streets of the city where the vulnerable are exposed to harm.

There is no question of a general censorship of sexual publications, driven by what Thomas and Tribe, Robertson and MacMillan take to be the Victorians' determination to silence sex everywhere.[13] The court was much too sophisticated for that:

> A medical treatise, with illustrations necessary for the information of those for whose education or information the work is intended, may, in a certain sense, be obscene, and yet not the subject for indictment; but it can never be that these prints may be exhibited for anyone, boys and girls, to see as they pass. The immunity must depend upon the circumstances of the publication.[14]

Could there be clearer evidence of the law's intention and capacity to distinguish one circumstance from another, or a clearer statement of the notion that serious works could fall within the scope of the obscenity statute if distributed to those whose judgement is not yet fully formed (boys and girls), or in locations unregulated by the requisite ethical competence (the corners of the streets)? A decade later, variable obscenity is installed in the textbooks:

> The publication of an edition of Juvenal, Aristophanes, Swift, Defoe, Bayle's Dictionary, Rabelais, Brantôme, Boccaccio, Chaucer, etc. cannot be regarded as a crime. . . . On the other hand, a collection of indecencies might be formed from any one of the authors I have mentioned, the separate publication of which would deserve severe punishment.[15]

Hicklin should not be thought exceptionally discriminating because it was a High Court judgement. In 1900, a London bookseller was charged in the Central Criminal Court with having offered for sale a 'certain lewd, wicked, bawdy and obscene libel in the form of a book entitled *The Heptameron of Margaret, Queen of Navarre*'. Even to cite this charge seems to promise proof conclusive of Victorian ignorance which mistakes moral offence for harm, and classic works of art for pornography. Yet listen, in the mundane setting of *Regina* v. *Thomson*, to the Common Sergeant advising the jury that it must deal with the 'circumstances under which the book was put forth': 'If it had been in a library to which students had access, no one would deny that the book was properly there and properly kept for a proper use.'[16] Testimony by the Head Constable of Liverpool to a 1908 Joint Select Committee on lotteries and indecent advertisements reiterates the point:

> I think you must consider the circumstances of the case – the circumstances of how the thing is advertised, how it is distributed, and so on; for instance, we had a case before His Majesty's Judge of Assize last year, a case of some indecent photographs, and the learned counsel who was defending the prisoner drew rather a red-herring across the scent by alluding to the fact that he kept classical books like the *Contes Drolatiques* of Balzac, but the judge said: 'Balzac's works are classic, and they would not be regarded as indecent.' I do not think he would have used that expression if he had known that the particular edition of the *Contes Drolatiques*, which was found there, were penny editions of certain of those stories, mostly sold to dirty-minded little boys. In the same way, there is the *Decameron* of Boccaccio; I think it would be very undesirable if that were split up into penny editions, although regarded as classic, perhaps it may be all right.[17]

The Head Constable sees with practical clarity that no general distinction can be drawn between the classic and pornographic. The distinction will always depend on the effects of the publication relative to the cultural abilities of the audience.

The character of the work depends on the use to which the work is put by a particular category of person. As the Head Constable of Liverpool demonstrated in 1908, the Common Sergeant in 1900 and the Court of Queen's Bench in 1868, a publication circulating in one form to one audience in the streets is obscene and indictable; not so, however, circulating in another form in another place to specifically competent or qualified readers. This point is made by many feminists: it is fatuous to claim an inherent distinction between pornography and authentic erotica. Moreover, the policeman's practical truth has now become a 'breakthrough' in literary reader-response theory. Better late than never.

Notions of literature that is inherently 'fine' are too crude to do justice to the flexibility of nineteenth-century obscenity law and its regime of variable treatment. To give a positive historical description of such a regime we must shift down a gear, from the global notions of expression and repression that organise the standard history of censorship to the practical sphere in which pornography emerged and was policed as a definite social problem.[18]

PUBLIC CRITERIA AND CATEGORIES OF PERSON

In the last two centuries an array of governmental institutions, professions and specialist knowledge – administrative, medical, psychiatric, pedagogical, ethical and, latterly, aesthetic – has variously defined distinct categories of person and differentially equipped them. In some cases these categories were buttressed by legal provisions; this was so with regard to thresholds of personal vulnerability to obscenity. Again, this seems grist for the censorship historians' mill – a censorial order imposed on individuals by power. However, a description of the cultural circumstances of the emergence of the 1857 Act and the *Hicklin* judgement does not confirm the censorship approach.

These legal initiatives are more properly seen as phenomena in the field of 'police'. In early modern absolutist states, 'police' was cognate with 'policy' and referred to programmes for the administration of all spheres of life – economic, political, military, medical, legal and cultural.[19] In the English context, Colquhoun's 1796 *Treatise on the Police of the Metropolis* displays this administrative disposition. Policing in England saw the elaboration of social programmes in public health and sanitation, domestic economy, education (in literacy and morality) and penality. Nineteenth-century obscenity law takes its place alongside programmes for improving individual and public health, and for forming capacities of taste. In this respect it is inappropriately classified as censorship.

Here Foucault is again of help, with his distinction between 'governmentality' and sovereign rule.[20] While the latter had been indifferent to the well-being of the populace, governmentality viewed individuals as members of a potentially productive population and to this end sought to model interests and abilities on specific norms of conduct – social, medical, moral, mental, cultural – not absolute ideals. Those who fell below the norm were assisted and corrected, rather than punished. The 1857 Act and the *Hicklin* judgement show legal regulation and medical policing of vulnerable populations combining in a manner at once pragmatic and novel. Lord Campbell's reference to obscene publications as a poison might thus be other than Victorian confusion of moral offence and physical harm: 'From a trial which had taken place before him on Saturday, [Lord Campbell said] he had learned with horror and alarm that a sale of poison more deadly than prussic acid, strychnine or arsenic – the sale of obscene publications and indecent books – was openly going on.'[21] The metaphorics of a contagion aimed at the poor joins the medical specification of a social pathology. These were 'the years that saw the correlative appearance of a medicine, an "orthopedics", specific to sex: in a word, the opening up of the great medico-psychological domain of the "perversions", which was destined to take over from the old moral categories of debauchery and excess'.[22] William Acton acknowledges the public orientation of the new medicine of sex, writing that his object in *The Functions and Disorders of the Reproductive Organs in Childhood, Youth, Adult Age and Advanced Life* (1865) is to exercise 'some good and practical influence on public health and public morals'.[23]

Representative of these concerns is Elizabeth Blackwell's manual, *Counsel to Parents: On the Moral Education of their Children in Relation to Sex* (1864). Bringing to bear medical guidance, sanitary and moral reconstruction of lives, women's rights and Christian socialism, Dr Blackwell treats sex as the determinant of individual and social improvement and degeneration, its dangers directly connected to the consumption by the vulnerable of 'vicious literature of any kind':

> Whether sensuality be taught by police reports, or by Greek or Latin literature, by novels, plays, songs, penny papers, or any species of the corrupt literature now sent forth broadcast, and which finds its way into the hands of the young of all classes and both sexes, the danger is equally real. It is storing the susceptible mind of youth with words, images, and suggestions of vice, which remain permanently in the mind, springing up day and night in unguarded moments, weakening the power of resistance, and accustoming the thoughts to an atmosphere of vice.[24]

In this milieu, permeated by pathogenic sex, individuals became hypersensitised about their own or their children's contacts with 'vicious literature', especially when the doctor's warning is backed by 'all that we know about the structure and methods of growth [and, of course, decay] of the human mind'.[25] Thus the 'deprave and corrupt' test was a rational legal buttress of a medical policing extended to those who lacked the capacities to protect themselves, one element in a complex of measures regulating the conditions of 'those whose health is depressed by disease, mental anxiety or the want of comforts and conveniences of life'.[26]

The circumstances which nineteenth-century obscenity law confronted were novel. Defined by the criteria of sexual medicine, street pornography became a specified social problem falling squarely within the purview of governmental responsibility. On the other hand, as the great anti-masturbation campaign demonstrated, concern with sex was increasingly generalised. Yet, in the mainstream educative literature, sex remained conspicuous – to our eye – by its absence. However, this was a matter of chronology, not of censorship.

CULTURAL HISTORY LESSONS

The Obscene Publications Act of 1857 and the *Hicklin* judgement were not specifically directed either for or against the cause of serious literature. No literary *cause célèbre* is associated with them. They generated none of the public proclamations of literary rights that accompanied the Obscene Publications Act of 1959 and twentieth-century literary show-trials before judge and jury, such as *Regina* v. *Penguin Books Ltd* in 1960 (the case of Lady Chatterley) or *Roth* v. *United States* where, in 1957, the constitutionality of American obscenity law was tested against First Amendment freedom of speech and press.[27] True, in debate on Lord Campbell's bill, Lord Broughham was concerned that 'works of some of [our] most eminent poets' risked prosecution, but Lord Campbell, brandishing Dumas's *La Dame aux camélias*, confirmed that the new law did not seek to ban such publications. This intention was carried into practice: 'invoking the Act against literary or artistic works . . . proved to be the exception rather than the rule, and for the most part such works suffered no disability before the law.'[28] In *Hicklin*, Justice Blackburn recalls *Regina* v. *Moxon* – a libel suit some half a century earlier, involving Shelley's *Queen Mab* – as a 'prosecution instituted merely for the purpose of vexation and annoyance'. He proffers this comment to support his reading of the 1857 legislation as intended 'to guard against the vexatious prosecution of publishers of old and recognised standard works, in which there may be some obscene or mischievous matter. . . . So whether the publication of the whole works of Dryden is or is not a misdemeanour, it would not be a case in which a prosecution would be proper.'[29]

In 1857 the law's concern was not with serious literature, and serious literature's concern was not with the law. It was not authors and literary intellectuals who questioned Lord Campbell's Act, but members of the legal profession concerned at an extension of police powers. If the legislators and jurists of the 1850s and 1860s specified obscene publications as a social and criminal harm, this was of no consequence to the educative literary mainstream. On the contrary, regulation of this printed social toxin had the approval of a reformer such as Charles Dickens. Writing in 1867 to Wilkie Collins, Dickens imagines himself under cross-examination as editor of a 'large circulation' journal in which questionable material might be published:

> asked whether, as Editor, I would have passed these passages, whether written by the Plaintiff or anybody else, I should be obliged to reply No. Asked why? I should say that what was pure to an artist might be impurely suggestive to inferior minds (of which there must necessarily be many among a large mass of readers), and that

I should have called the writer's attention to the likelihood of those passages being perverted in such quarters.[30]

The absence of literary interest in the 1857 Act, and Dickens's apparent concurrence with the police approach to the circulation of publications 'in such quarters' are not signs of repression or Victorian hypocrisy. Rather, they are a reminder that before embarking on histories of censorship, we should at least establish who actually read what.

Such responses to the 1857 Act signal that what was to be a crucial but unforeseen mutation in literary culture had not yet taken place. Sex had not yet *become* the founding theme of literary writings and the key to literary authorial personality. On the other hand, where the type of printed matter directed at the vulnerable sectors of the population was concerned, a newly pathogenic sex had been positioned at the centre of individual and social existence. The 1857 Act and the *Hicklin* definition registered the extension of this normative domain of sexual medicine into the governmental sphere. The condition of those touched by the traffic in street pornography was appropriately regulated by an obscenity law grounded on a medical norm. However, serious literary authors had not yet taken up the thematics of sex. Until a circle of highly specialised literary intellectuals embraced what doctors had installed in medically regulated conducts of living – the centrality of sex – and transposed it into the sphere of serious literature, there was no confusing pornography and 'fine literature'. What for the Victorians was a problematic social conduct – the use of pornography – underwent mutation to become the object of a discipline whereby sex was aestheticised and aesthetics sexualised.

The sexual personae elaborated by the Victorian doctors provided the avenue to what literary intellectuals thus came to envisage as a pristine sexual subjectivity long subjugated by repression and censorship. As Foucault shows in closing his *History of Sexuality*, Lawrence's is the exemplary formulation: 'Now our business is to realise sex. Today the full conscious realisation of sex is even more important than the act itself.'[31] Lawrence was among the band of advanced sex reformers.[32] The same commitment to confront sex (which for literary intellectuals also meant confronting pornography) was made by James Joyce 'experimenting with the grossly masturbatory prose of "dirty" books'.[33] By 1920 E. M. Forster was convinced that 'nothing is more obdurate to artistic treatment than the carnal, but it has to be got in, I'm sure: everything has to be got in.'[34] By the time of the Obscene Publications Act of 1959, sexuality had become the *sine qua non* of serious literary self-interrogation.

In the nineteenth century, aesthetic value and the criminal harms attributed to obscenity did not come into conflict. The threshold

between 'pornography' and literature was not yet the crucial but problematic marker it became once serious literary works were published
that were both pornographic and of literary merit – or, most importantly, once their circulation grew beyond the tolerated 'private case'
dimensions to become a public cultural phenomenon. In this new
circumstance, obscenity law continued to guard a boundary drawn to
protect a less specialised population from what was still counted as a
social harm.

Three tendencies of the censorship approach to the history of
obscenity law obscure the historical particularity and contingency of
this development. First, that approach collapses quite different issues
into the one synthetic theme of censorship. Donald Thomas's *A Long
Time Burning* (1969) conflates the legal regulation of obscenity with
that of blasphemy and sedition.[35] Yet blasphemy and sedition were
never medicalised into a social problem, as was obscenity; as cultural
phenomena they were quite separate from that of pornography. A
recent instance of this approach refers in a single sweep, the better
to anathematise 'censorship', to homosexuality, abortion, freedom of
expression, the British Board of Film and Video Classification, the
Broadcasting Standards Commission and – inevitably – Salman Rushdie's 'victimisation' by the Ayatollah Khomeini's charge of blasphemy
against Islam.[36] Second, if such different issues are run together the
historical variation in specifications of pornography – medico-legal in
the nineteenth century, aesthetico-legal in the twentieth – will not
receive due attention. Third, the demographic and distributional differences on which the category of variable obscenity rests will scarcely
register in a censorship approach which envisages not audiences of
variable cultural competence but a general human subject – the individual, or the authorial personality said to embody human subjectivity
– threatened by a censorial state.

BEYOND CENSORSHIP

The censorship approach to obscenity law rests on a particular
antinomy. On the one hand, the individual subject is assumed to have
a natural capacity for sexual self-expression of which literature is the
most developed form. On the other hand, the law is assumed to play
a repressive role in relation to the circulation of literary works, operating as the vehicle of puritanism or Victorian moral prejudice. This
antinomy might make for sweeping assertions, but it also makes for
an impoverished history of obscenity law. Different phenomena are
flattened into a single series of 'anti-censorship' struggles 'as old as
history',[37] and the history of obscenity law is forced into a 'before',
where sexual desire and expressive capacities are suppressed and

distorted into 'pornography', and an 'after', where the same desire and capacities find full expression in an erotic literature untrammelled by legal or other social norms. Hence the familiar periodisation: obscenity law, it is said, emerges as a Puritan reaction to healthy Elizabethan and Restoration bawdy.[38] Or again, the repressive urge and the pornography it is alleged to generate is a Victorian reprise of puritanism, this repressive phase being followed by turn-of-the-century liberalisation assisted, in some accounts, by Freudian psychoanalysis.[39] The same discursive formula does service too for more local histories, as when the years 1960 to 1982 mark a sexual decensorship and emancipation followed by a (feminist) reprise of censorship and repression.[40]

Nineteenth-century obscenity law deserves better. To this end, I have registered what that law actually was and did: street policing. The censorship approach does not operate at street level because that is no site for grand statements on the fate of (aesthetic) literature and sexuality. On the street corner the great Romantic antinomy which organises the work of censorship historians – repression and expression – is useless. The censorship approach is further disabled by the belief that in attacking obscenity law one is on the side of history and the human subject. This conviction suggests a Kantian ability to see beyond mere circumstances and particular purposes. The temptation, of course, is to believe that in the matter of sexuality we have got it right, in contrast to the Victorians' repressive disposition and their obscenity law which gave it social form. Here, surely, beyond circumstance and imposed norms, we have come to grips with the source of our personal truth.

This conviction – which impedes discussion of obscenity law other than as censorship – is Foucault's target. He shows this sexuality as our recent invention, a rich cultural acquisition but also a dependent conduct of life. It is not the register of human subjectivity. In this sense, the shift from no sex in Dickens to little else in Lawrence signals not a victory against repression but a new manner of personal identity among literary intellectuals (and one which they never guessed would later be disseminated as an educative and ethical norm, a 'prevailing form of training'). The unified narrative of the censorship approach makes human sexuality an unchanging 'given', the constant measure of the outrage of obscenity law. But, rhetoric apart, what is the use of invoking Ezekiel, Aristophanes and Ovid in a single series with the Puritans' 'legacy of shame and guilt about sexual pleasure which was never quite eradicated from the national conscience and which created consumer demand for the new pornography'?[41] In an American version, the great chain runs from Ancient Greece to the First Amendment and Arthur Schlesinger Jr.[42] Robertson claims that 'the only lesson we learn from the legal history of censorship is that the more the law changes, the more the social reality remains the same'.[43]

In fact obscenity law has been anything but a unified historical or theoretical project. It is flagrantly discontinuous in its shift from a medically backed policing of a social problem to an aesthetically grounded procedure whereby works can be obscene yet also of literary merit and thus legally publishable for the public good. We travesty this law when we attribute to it a single general function: prohibition.

Like Al Capone, the censorship approach needs Prohibition. It needs to speak endlessly of that which has been 'repressed' or 'silenced'. However, noting that ours is a society that 'takes great pains to relate in detail the things it does not say . . . and promises to liberate itself from the very laws that have made it function', Foucault continues:

> The question I would like to pose is not, Why are we repressed? but rather, Why do we say, with so much passion and so much resentment against our most recent past, against our present, and against ourselves, that we are repressed? By what spiral did we come to affirm that sex is negated? What led us to show, ostentatiously, that sex is something we hide, to say it is something we silence?[44]

The censorship approach needs Prohibition because without it the grand antinomy of censorship and literary emancipation cannot be sustained. Prohibition, in this context, overrules the fact that nineteenth-century obscenity law was not purely prohibitional but a variegated regulatory channelling of pornography.

At the outset I noted how the pressure of the censorship approach leads a lawyer to invent a destruction of 'many examples of fine literature'. Other inventions – it is not clear in what sense they purport to be factual – crowd the field. Marcus invents a psychic structure of repression and failed sublimation so autonomous he treats Victorian pornography as a state of mind, not a commodity whose distribution was inseparable from legal arrangements which codified and stabilised a defined pattern of audiences. For Marcus's psycho-aesthetic approach, positive law would be either part-cause of the problem or redundant (once the psychic balance of desire and norm is achieved).

More recently, the banner of transgression and emancipation has passed from sexuality and broken-marriage vows to 'language' and broken syntax. Psychoanalytically inflected accounts have been eclipsed by a post-structuralist or deconstructionist approach to literary censorship, still working, however, through notions of repression and constraint. It is language, not sexuality or the Romantic author's expressive intention, that is censored; writing, not sexuality, is what eludes the censor. In Annabel Patterson's *Censorship and Interpretation:*

the Conditions of Writing and Reading in Early Modern England (1984) this familiar scenography is played through once again, but with literary writing – from Sidney to Dryden – as the target for a censorial state. Of course, it is good to know that censorship is again resisted and outwitted, this time by 'the slipperiness of language', the 'indeterminacy inveterate to language' and 'the resistance of language itself to any codification'.[45] Yet linguistic accounts of this sort continue to subordinate law to an explanation from some sphere beyond legal and cultural circumstances.

In positing language as the fundamental reality, post-structuralist or deconstructionist theories of discourse point away from positive historical description to ethical gestures. Such theories imagine 'language' or 'writing' as producing elusive meanings and subjects in profusion, except when weighed down by arbitrary crudities such as law and censorship. Yet do the new 'discursive' histories of censorship recognise that the object of nineteenth-century obscenity law was not language as a universal and self-realising generator of all possible meanings and forms of subjectivity but a toxin in print-form, trafficked in places deemed dangerous to categories of persons deemed vulnerable to this particular social harm? Have historians of censorship begun to digest the fact that obscenity prosecutions have mostly been of printers and publishers, booksellers, hawkers and pedlars, not of the human subject, nor of authors, nor – even less – of 'language'? Or is it that these historians are less concerned with the particularity of historical facts than with demonstrating their own ethical, aesthetic and theoretical sensitivity?

NOTES

1 I am indebted to my co-authors, Ian Hunter and Dugald Williamson, in *On Pornography: Literature, Sexuality and Obscenity Law*, London, Macmillan, 1992, for insights and formulations through which I have questioned the adequacy of the concept of censorship to the historical description of a major episode in the emergence of Anglo-American obscenity law.

2 *Reg.* v. *Hicklin*, p. 371. *Law Reports*, Queen's Bench, 3, 1868.

3 G. Robertson, *Obscenity. An Account of Censorship Laws and their Enforcement in England and Wales*, London, Weidenfeld & Nicolson, 1979, p. 30.

4 ibid.

5 A powerful psychological account conceptualises pornography as the outcome of a breakdown in a fundamental human dialectic of sexual drives and social mores. This breakdown is occasioned by an overly strong impo-sition of social norms – in the form of literary censorship backed by obscenity law – said to have driven the sex drives underground, whence they return as socially undesirable pornography. See E. and P. Kronhausen, *Pornography and the Law: the Psychology of Erotic Realism and Pornography*, New York, Ballantine Books, 1959. 'Erotic realism' – fantasy maturely balanced against experience and aesthetic judgement – offers 'a basically

healthy and therapeutic attitude towards life', p. 23. This seems to mean: take D. H. Lawrence at face value.

6 S. Marcus, *The Other Victorians*, New York, Basic Books, 1974.

7 See, for instance, the Ordinance passed in Indianapolis on 1 May 1984 which gave legal form to the anti-pornography project of Andrea Dworkin and Catharine MacKinnon. The Ordinance defines pornography as a 'practice of exploitation and subordination based on sex which differentially harms women. The bigotry and contempt it promotes, with the acts of aggression it fosters, harm women's opportunities for equality of rights in employment, education, access to and use of public accommodations, and acquisition of real property; promote rape, battery, child abuse, kidnapping and prostitution and inhibit just enforcement of laws against such acts; and contribute significantly to restricting women in particular from full exercise of citizenship and participation in public life, including in neighbourhoods' (598 F. Supp., p. 1320). Two years later this controversial law was found to be unconstitutional.

8 M. Foucault, *The History of Sexuality, vol. 1: an Introduction*, trans. R. Hurley, London, Allen Lane, 1979, pp. 8–9.

9 See C. Manchester, 'Lord Campbell's Act: England's first obscenity statute', *The Journal of Legal History*, vol. 9, 1988, pp. 230, 235.

10 See, for instance, Robertson, *Obscenity*, p. 214.

11 *Reg.* v. *Hicklin*, pp. 367–8.

12 ibid., p. 372.

13 D. Thomas, *A Long Time Burning. The History of Literary Censorship in England*, London, Routledge & Kegan Paul, 1969; D. Tribe, *Questions of Censorship*, London, Allen & Unwin, 1973; Robertson, *Obscenity*; P. R. MacMillan, *Censorship and Public Morality*, Aldershot, Gower, 1983.

14 *Reg.* v. *Hicklin*, p. 367.

15 J. F. Stephen, *A Digest of the Criminal Law (Crimes and Punishments)*, London, Macmillan, 1877, article 228.

16 *Reg.* v. *Thomson. The Justice of the Peace*, 'Reports', London, 1900, pp. 456–7.

17 *Report from the Joint Select Committee on Lotteries and Indecent Advertisements*, London, 1908, p. 652.

18 The variable character of obscenity remains central to twentieth-century jurisprudence. Thus William Lockhart and Robert McClure recommend that in deciding the matter of obscenity American courts take account of the character of the audience to whom the work is addressed and the channels through which it reaches them. In some circumstances the work of an acclaimed author might be obscene. See W. B. Lockhart and R. C. McClure, 'Literature, the law of obscenity, and the constitution', *Minnesota Law Review*, vol. 38, 1954, pp. 295–395.

19 See, for instance, G. Oestreich, *Neostoicism and the Early Modern State*, Cambridge, Cambridge University Press, 1982.

20 M. Foucault, 'On governmentality', *Ideology and Consciousness*, vol. 6, 1979, pp. 5–23. See also the same author's *Discipline and Punish: the Birth of the Prison*, trans. A. Sheridan Smith, London, Allen Lane, 1977, and 'Omnes et singulatim: towards a critique of political reason', in S. McMurrin (ed.), *The Tanner Lectures on Human Values*, vol. II, Salt Lake City, University of Utah Press, 1981.

21 *Parliamentary Debates*, 1857, p. 103.

22 Foucault, *The History of Sexuality*, p. 118.

23 W. Acton, 'Preface', in *The Functions and Disorders of the Reproductive Organs*

in Childhood, Youth, Adult Age and Advanced Life, 4th edn, London, John Churchill & Sons, 1865, not paginated.

24 E. Blackwell, *Counsel to Parents: On the Moral Education of their Children in Relation to Sex*, London, Hatchards, 1884, p. 89.

25 On the impact of sexual medicine, see J. S. and R. M. Haller, *The Physician and Sexuality in Victorian America*, Urbana, University of Illinois Press, 1974.

26 J. Kay-Shuttleworth, 'The moral and physical condition of the working classes in Manchester in 1832', in *Four Periods of Public Education*, first published 1862, Brighton, Harvester, 1973, pp. 3–4.

27 See *Roth* v. *United States*, 354, US 476 1 L ed 2d 1488, 1957. In *Roth* a majority of the Supreme Court agreed on a standard determining what constitutes obscenity. *Roth* furnished an exemplary statement of the doctrine of variable obscenity: 'It is manifest that the same object may have a different impact varying according to the part of the community it reached', p. 495.

28 Manchester, 'Lord Campbell's Act', p. 237.

29 *Reg.* v. *Hicklin*, p. 374.

30 The 'Plaintiff' in question was Charles Reade, whose novel *Griffith Gaunt, or Jealousy* touched on adultery, bigamy and seduction. The litigious Reade had initiated suits against critics who had attacked the work. See D. Paroissien (ed.), *Selected Letters of Charles Dickens*, London, Macmillan, 1985, p. 358. Dickens's knowledge of 'large circulation' publishing ventures was second to none. As part of a practical sense of one's audiences, the theme of variable obscenity appears a working assumption of the times.

31 See Foucault, *The History of Sexuality*, p. 157. The historian comments:

> Perhaps one day people will wonder at this. They will not be able to understand how a civilization so intent on developing enormous instruments of production and destruction found the time and the infinite patience to inquire so anxiously concerning the actual state of sex.
>
> (pp. 157–8)

This sense of the contingency of the modern western arrangement of sexuality must be maintained if we are to describe nineteenth-century obscenity law in its own terms.

32 For a withering account of sex reform in the early twentieth century, see S. Jeffrys, 'Sex reform and anti-feminism in the 1920s', in London Feminist History Group (ed.), *The Sexual Dynamics of History*, London, Pluto Press, 1983.

33 M. Charney, *Sexual Fiction*, London, Methuen, 1981, p. 5.

34 See P. N. Furbank, 'Preface', in E. M. Forster, *Maurice*, London, Edward Arnold, 1971, p. 9.

35 On this problem, see D. Saunders, 'Copyright, obscenity and literary history, *English Literary History*, vol. 57, 1990, pp. 431–44.

36 G. Robertson, 'Foreword', in C. H. Rolph (ed.), *The Trial of Lady Chatterley, Regina v Penguin Books Limited*, Harmondsworth, Penguin Books, 1990.

37 This is the title of chapter 2 in Tribe, *Questions of Censorship*.

38 See, for instance, D. G. Loth, *The Erotic in Literature: a Historical Survey of Pornography as Delightful as it is Indiscreet*, London, Secker & Warburg, 1962.

39 See, for instance, Marcus, *The Other Victorians*.

40 See J. Sutherland, *Offensive Literature: Decensorship in Britain 1960–1982*, London, Junction Books, 1982.

41 Robertson, *Obscenity*, p. 20.

42 E. Widmer (ed.), *Freedom and Culture: Literary Censorship in the 70s*, Belmont, Calif., Wadsworth, 1970.
43 Robertson, *Obscenity*, p. 16.
44 Foucault, *The History of Sexuality*, pp. 8–9.
45 A. Patterson, *Censorship and Interpretation: the Conditions of Writing and Reading in Early Modern England*, Madison, University of Wisconsin Press, 1984, pp. 10–18.

Chapter 12

'The physiological facts': Thomas Hardy, censorship and narrative breakdown

Richard Kerridge

In current debate about censorship, a customary charge against liberal humanism is that it separates freedom of expression from other questions of freedom. The liberal tradition has tended to see censorship as an external threat, and to defend art and literature as protected space, where inequalities of power are suspended and people can meet equally. Some feminist criticism, in particular, has seen the idealism of this tradition as hopelessly indifferent to the dispositions of power which cannot be arbitrarily suspended, and which actually condition what is said and heard. In the context of recent debate about pornography, for example, Susanne Kappeler has argued, in *The Pornography of Representation* (1986)[1], that there is a basic structure of representation, common to art, literature and pornography, which reproduces the unequal power-relations of class and gender. Censorship of a deeper kind occurs at this structural level, which liberal accounts of freedom of expression ignore. The structure concerned is that of subject–object relationships; in novels this means the relationships between readers and characters. To explore the implications of this for the novel, it is instructive to go back to an earlier point at which liberal representation was felt to be in crisis: at the end of the nineteenth century. Particularly, it is revealing to look at the later novels of Thomas Hardy, who faced extensive censorship at a time when he was reaching his own sense, surprisingly comparable to Kappeler's, of the limitations of liberal artistic practice.

Hardy's writings were subject to censorship from his earliest attempts to publish. His first manuscript, 'The Poor Man and the Lady', was rejected as politically inflammatory, and his first published novel, *Desperate Remedies* (1871), was accepted only on condition that a scene involving a 'violation' was removed.[2] It is likely that such pressures were behind his decision, beginning with his next novel, *Under the Greenwood Tree* (1872), to move his work further into the superficially more charming and innocuous territory of rural romance. But as his preoccupations resurfaced, the work again began to get into trouble, always from a combination of Grundyish objection to sexual immorality, and more tacit disapproval of Hardy's treatment of social class. Between 1889 and 1895, this culminated in what he called the 'dismemberment' of the serial versions of *Tess of the d'Urbervilles* and *Jude the Obscure*. After *Tess* had been rejected by Tillotson & Son, *Murray's Magazine* and *Macmillan's Magazine*, on grounds of 'its improper explicitness',[3] Hardy made cuts and alterations before sending the novel to the more populist *Graphic*, which would not accept it without further changes – including the famous introduction of a wheelbarrow when Angel Clare carries the milkmaids across the flooded path.[4] *Jude* also was altered, with less ingenuity, before its serialisation in *Harper's New Monthly Magazine*.

Hardy declared his anger at these impositions, and in the essay 'Candour in English Fiction' (1890), written while negotiations over *Tess* were taking place, he argued that such restrictions would compromise the seriousness of any work of fiction. Specifically, the influence of Grundyism was preventing the English novel from achieving the tragic forms demanded by the most characteristic experiences of the age.[5] As a tactic, this invocation of tragedy is similar to the earlier movement of his work into pastoral forms: he conciliates, by suggesting that art is concerned to translate particular, politically dangerous cases into timeless and inevitable classical forms. Moreover, he takes up high ground by aligning 'candour' with classicism, against the implied vulgarity of Grundyism.

Snobbery enlisted in this way was valuable to Hardy, for by this time the most severe censorship he encountered was over serial publication in magazines. This was the most profitable form of publication, and the form assumed to reach a wider, more socially diverse readership. Hardy was thus exposed to the accusation that he was writing sensationally out of vulgarly commercial motives, a charge full of class-condescension towards him, to which he was always sensitive. Involved in his response to censorship, therefore, is the same uneasy sense of class-identity which made him deny that his novels had autobiographical content, and declare his real vocation to be poetry rather than the commercial business of novel-writing. Passages in *The Life of Thomas Hardy* – the 'biography' published after his death under his second wife's name, Florence, but actually prepared by Hardy himself – suggest that his sensitivity generally took the form of denial that condescension towards him ever occurred, or could occur: hence the lists of aristocrats he knew socially, and the glossing over of the humbler facts about his family.[6] The Hardy who protested about the censorship of his novels was constantly censoring himself. Peter Widdowson, in particular, has noted the extent of Hardy's suppression of his social origins, and sees the novels as formed, in large part, by the pressure exerted by those origins – the pressure of what Hardy wanted to say but also to be dissociated from.[7]

This defensiveness complicates his response to another argument employed by the magazine editors – one used repeatedly in the history of censorship: that what is instructive or harmless for a responsible elite would be devastating if released to the masses. Several comments in *The Life* seem to show that Hardy was not free from this attitude himself,[8] but his adoption of it can be read in terms of the anxieties of an *arriviste* class-position. By placing his work in the classical tradition, he was able to appropriate the Arnoldian language of culture as resistance to philistinism, anarchy and provincialism (he goes on to suggest that Shakespeare, Aeschylus, Sophocles, Goethe and Milton would have had their work rejected by the magazine editors of his day).[9] *The Life* describes Hardy as undertaking the revisions to *Tess* 'with cynical amusement, knowing the novel was moral enough and to spare'.[10] Here too, his response is to outflank: a key term, 'moral', from the vocabulary of censorship, is reclaimed in defence of the censored work – with cynical amusement, possibly.

So what was Hardy asking for, apart from freedom from clumsy interference with his work? What sort of explicitness did he really envisage for literature? The contradictions are clear. His self-censorship has already been noted. He wanted to pre-empt other biographies with his secret preparation of *The Life*. He destroyed most of his papers. Recent commentators have often seen the energy of his work in terms of distance, absence, disjunction, concealment, elision and deferment: that is the characteristic terrain of Hardy criticism. Some of the changes forced on Hardy seem, if anything, to intensify the effects he was producing. If he is asking for the freedom to be explicit, it is a freedom he means to use sparingly, at moments of intensity heightened by delay. Otherwise, he is demanding a change not merely in the rules applying to literature, but in the whole social condition which has imposed secrecy and inexplicitness upon him.

One thing he asks for is the freedom to state physiological facts. In 'Candour in English Fiction' he wrote: 'Life being a physiological fact, its honest portrayal must be largely concerned with, for one thing, the relations of the sexes'.[11] Like the idea of classical tradition, 'physiological fact' has a special function in Hardy: it is one side of a recurring opposition between nature and social convention. 'Physiological fact' is objective, while convention may be arbitrary and false. As the word 'physiological' suggests, this objectivity is a property of scientific discourse. Moreover, a view which is free of conventional assumptions is an external view, with a kind of omniscience, in contrast to the views of characters caught in the action of the novel. A narrative aspiring to state the physiological facts is, therefore, in the Victorian tradition of realist narrative: a secular form attempting to continue the offices of religion. Hardy's argument invokes a familiar Victorian debate: one ideal version of the uncensored view is God's; another is pure scientific objectivity. With different measures of irony, Hardy appeals to both for his authority.

Most importantly, 'physiological facts' are significant because they do not change from social class to social class. This point is directly stated in *The Woodlanders* (1887), when Marty South is introduced. The gaze drops quickly to her hand:

> The palm was red and blistering, as if her present occupation were as yet too recent to have subdued it to what it worked in. As with so many right hands born to manual labour, there was nothing in its fundamental shape to bear out the physiological conventionalism that gradations of birth show themselves primarily in the form of this member. Nothing but a cast of the die of destiny had decided that the girl should handle the tool; and the fingers which clasped the heavy ash haft might have skilfully guided the pencil or swept the string, had they only been set to do it in good time.[12]

Here, scientific observation challenges the received ideologies which naturalise class difference. To view human beings as a species, to see the physical features they have in common, is to see the injustice of a system that treats them so unequally. Physiological fact gives the lie to 'physiological conventionalism'. But physiological fact quickly means the 'fundamental shape' rather than the marks inflicted by labour. Seeing Marty South in general terms means turning away from her particular presence, towards a general model of humanity and a different life 'she' might have had. When Hardy's narrative comes to the physical surface of the woman's body, it veers away, avoiding the whole person by focusing intensely on a small area, then moving rapidly between this and a highly generalised argument. The writing eroticises the woman as it pleads for her.

'Physiological' observation, then, does not simply mean a more explicit way of writing. Rather, it is accompanied by corresponding forms of inexplicitness, consequences of its tendency to generalisation. A disengagement is called for, like a doctor's impersonality, involving the suppression or holding off of personal exchange with the character described: a kind of defamiliarisation. In the passage quoted, a woman – not yet named – is being watched, without her knowledge, by a man, whose gaze the reader seems to follow. Immediately before this, the first pages of the novel have drawn the reader in by describing what would be seen by an unspecified 'rambler', arriving in that part of the country.[13] The generally familiar piece of country, described in close detail but also not named at first, slowly becomes Little Hintock, and the arriving rambler is gradually identified as Barber Percomb (the man who later watches Marty). Thus identified, he is rapidly distanced, especially in class terms, from the implied reader. He ceases to be the reader's proxy and becomes a character in the scene, an object. But this change, emphatic as it is, does not stabilise the relationship between character and reader. Like other characters in Hardy, major and minor, Percomb continues to become at moments a generalised watcher: a proxy, a rambler, someone free to move. 'Physiological' observation takes place in these novels at moments of hiatus, when the plot is suspended. In this passage, the moment is one of arrival, when an outsider pauses at a threshold. Elsewhere the effect occurs when someone is seen after a long interval, or when a crisis has abruptly changed the meaning of things. Such moments are points of interruption, when events cease to confirm a character's self in the accustomed way: the character has to renegotiate terms of entry, and in doing so becomes a kind of reader. So Percomb, gazing at Marty, seems to share the narrative viewpoint, and it is a jolt when his 'character' resumes as he moves into the space he has been watching. The observation of 'physiological facts' here is radically incompatible with action. Entering the scene entails relinquishing the perspective which sees the arbitrariness of Marty's class-position: that perspective is available only from outside. Marty herself is treated as an object not least because she is engaged in work she cannot interrupt. When she is seen as a specimen, a type to be found in the external world, the plot is held while she is contemplated. When she is a named person, caught up in particular events, the plot resumes.

This alternation – between pause and action, detachment and involvement, general and particular, present and past tense – is essential to the treatment of class in the novels, and to their eroticism. To concentrate on a small area is to make horizons disappear; paradoxically, it is a way of *not* looking, of finding detachment in the midst of action. 'Physiological' explicitness is often, therefore, an alternative to responding to particular characters, to meeting their gaze. Often erotically charged, it means looking closely but seeing the body as a specimen – as confirmation of a rumour, as an example of something happening elsewhere. The particular case is displaced by the generality, and the observer is left free, rather than committed to a time and a person. This is close to the pornographic structure identified by Susanne Kappeler, and Hardy finds it a source of excitement. Yet he is also prepared to have the reader feel that freedom as exclusion – and as a compromised class-position, or gender-position.

A critical example is the rape in *Tess of the d'Urbervilles*, and the inability of the narrator to be there describing. A comparison between the censored version which appeared in the *Graphic* in 1891, and the version in the novel,[14] is instructive here, because the censored text is not a departure so much as a cruder, in some ways more radical, version of the complete one. In the *Graphic*, the reader is kept at such a distance that the event becomes murkily general, even as the writing implies a precise, unspeakable knowledge held by that reader:

> Her first day's experiences were fairly typical of those which fol-lowed through many succeeding days. A familiarity with Alec d'Ur-berville's presence – which that young man carefully cultivated in her by playful dialogue, and by jestingly calling her cousin when they were alone – removed most of her original shyness of him, without, however, implanting any feeling which could engender shyness of a new and tenderer kind. But she was more pliable under his hands than a mere companionship would have made her, owing to her inevitable dependence upon his mother, and, through her comparative helplessness, upon him.
>
> But where was Tess's guardian-angel now? Perhaps, like the god of whom the ironical Tishbite spoke, he was talking, or he was pursuing, or he was on a journey; or peradventure he was sleeping and was not to be awaked. Why things should have been thus, why they should so often be thus, many thousand years of analytical philosophy have failed to explain to our sense of order. As Tess's own people down in these retreats are never tired of saying to each other in their fatalistic way, 'It was to be.' There lay the pity of it.[15]

With this the chapter ends. Even for a reader who does not know the uncensored text, this version is marked by an abrupt foreclosure, a leap to the end of the episode. For the reader who does, a whole sequence of events has fallen into the fissure – Tess's visit to the fair in Chaseborough, her refusal of a lift from Alec, the fight with Car Darch, Alec's 'rescue' of her, what happened in the Chase that night.[16] The censored text closes over these events. Lost in the elision is the specificity of what happens to Tess, the anecdotal detail which gives the event its place and time, the physiological fact of what happened to a particular body. Instead, the reader is presumed to know what is meant – and the reader can only know in general terms. Censorship has forced a change of emphasis, cutting the intensity of feeling for Tess as an individual, but opening up space for the reader to fill with a knowledge of cases *like* hers.

In the *Graphic*, Tess subsequently tells her mother what happened.[17] She was not caught, alone in a dark wood, sleeping. Rather, she agreed, reluctantly, to marry Alec, because of her mother's urging and her sense of her family's need. This version does not insist that Tess is 'pure' in the sense of being innocent of all desire for social mobility; it rather makes that desire a factor in her vulnerability, and further generalises her story. She explains that she later discovered that the marriage-ceremony had been a fraud. There is no baby. The account is calm and brief. Though the idea of marriages turning out to be invalid was always interesting to Hardy, this explanation seems little more than a token: the melodramatic possibilities, for example, are not explored. The effect remains one of foreclosure.

In the uncensored text, the foreclosure occurs much nearer the decisive moment. As the threshold approaches, the reader is teased, in thriller-fashion, with a succession of apparent escapes.[18] The danger recedes and then returns. A rescue turns out to be a capture. Even when Tess and Alec are alone in the Chase, it seems possible that all will be averted simply through Alec getting lost and not finding her again in the darkness.[19] Salvation could result from a slight adjustment that would scarcely register as intervention – and the idea of intervention haunts the narrative, which casts around for conceivable forms of it. Bitter, vestigial ideas of divine intervention are mixed with visions of the reader, or some proxy, some rambler, entering the frame, empowered to bring the help Tess has been placed in need of. Later in the novel it is said that people were nearby, and 'it mid ha' gone hard wi' a certain party if folks had come along'.[20] Earlier, even Alec parodies providence, when he arrives to rescue Tess from the brawl. Eventually, in its effort to gain a proxy witness, the narrative attempts, with labouring irony, to achieve a notion of presiding divinity compatible with the facts as they occur. The reader is offered a long historical perspective in which Tess's two class-identities, aristocrat and farm-labourer, are resolved:

> One may, indeed, admit the possibility of a retribution lurking in the present catastrophe. Doubtless some of Tess d'Urberville's mailed ancestors rollicking home from a fray had dealt the same measure even more ruthlessly towards peasant girls of their time. But though to visit the sins of the fathers upon the children may be a morality good enough for divinities, it is scorned by average human nature; and it therefore does not mend the matter.[21]

From such a viewpoint, events can be made to make moral sense in a way which justifies the non-intervention, the conservatism, of the watcher. But this reasoning contrasts brutally – as the narrator points out – with what the reader is likely to feel, so that the similarity between the divine impassiveness and the reader's inability to intervene becomes a challenge to the activity of reading.

What Hardy does, at the critical moment, is deny the reader that subject-to-object relationship described by Susanne Kappeler: that readerly combination of distance and unhindered scrutiny. He rejects the distinction between readers and characters. At this crisis, his narrative challenges the reader's right to watch without intervening; without making the fictional space into real space. Already, in the darkness, Tess has become 'a pale nebulousness'. D'Urberville locates her by touch and by the feel of her breath.[22] A point comes at which she is no longer available to a reader whose scrutiny is of no more use than her guardian-angel's. No detached, proxy witness is present to naturalise the reader's viewpoint, except for 'primaeval yews and oaks', and 'hopping rabbits and hares'. Finally, there can no longer be a narrative of events: only a generalised, argumentative address to the reader, a series of urgent rhetorical questions, with fading momentum.[23]

In both versions, narrative comes to a crisis here, in its relations with characters and readers. Censorship has brought about this crisis, by defining events that must not be described. But Hardy forces the issue rather than avoids it: the fissure that censorship creates, and which he chooses to leave open, reveals differences of class and gender that the freedom of reference sought by liberal narrative might actually obscure. In this respect censorship – by overt prohibition or by other forms of pressure – clarifies the issue for Hardy. At its most successful, censorship would make a seamless text, but here, in each version, the sudden divergence of the fictional world from the reader's throws responsibility for the production of meaning back to the reader, who is no longer a watcher. At that point narrative breaks down. In both texts, the chapter ends, and a period of Tess's life passes unrecorded before narrative can return.

In such a crisis, the dualism always insistent in Hardy's work becomes absolute. There are people as others construct them, and there are people as physical facts, trapped by those constructions, which, of course, include the narrative. A particularly direct example is the introduction of Gabriel Oak in *Far from the Madding Crowd* (1874):

> Or, to state his character as it stood in the scale of public opinion, when his friends and critics were in tantrums, he was considered rather a bad man; when they were pleased, he was rather a good man; when they were neither, he was a man whose moral colour was a kind of pepper-and-salt mixture.[24]

Exactly the same formula is used for William Dewy in *Under the Green-wood Tree*.[25] One very similar introduces Clym Yeobright in *The Return of the Native* (1878).[26] Oak's meaning, his 'character', is determined not by physiological fact but by the mood of whoever observes him. 'Oak' is a floating signifier: the physical body is defined by these meanings only in so far as they surround it, have consequences for it, indicate its presence, push it into certain spaces. So when Hardy invokes physiological fact, he invokes the physical world as something lying on the other side of meaning and interpretation: in texts something only to be sensed through fissures. The idea insists on the dialogic text and the frequent disruption of reading. When, at the end of *The Mayor of Casterbridge*, Henchard walks out of the novel, demanding 'that no man remember me',[27] he is asking that the reader's gaze should not follow him: that he should cease to be a signifier. A departure like this seeks to draw the reader into the space the character has left. Particularly, with Tess, a male fantasy of intervening to rescue is incited and then left stranded, exposed.

Critics as diverse as Penny Boumelha, Judith Wittenberg, Mary Childers, Howard Jacobson and James Kincaid[28] have identified this pattern as sadistic, with its positioning of the victim, its sorrowing concentration on marks on the body, its comparison of that marked body to an unmarked ideal. Kappeler's terms, in *The Pornography of Representation*, offer a way of acknowledging this and saying more.

Kappeler identifies the pornographic principle, in the literary novel and elsewhere, as 'a structure of representation': 'the systematic objectification of women in the interest of the exclusive subjectification of men'.[29] A key feature of this is the separation of the fictional space from the outside world, so that the (male) audience can be positioned as observers, rather than challenged to acknowledge themselves as participants. 'Fiction . . . wants no part *in* reality, it is the Other to the real'.[30] Hardy's writing is full of this impulse, but also arrives, repeatedly, at moments of breakdown, in which the stranded reader has to confront the idea of somehow crossing into the fictional space, or is thrown back into the external world. 'Tess', for example, is a working-class woman constructed erotically; constructed out of a tacit sense of shared class-experience, and so out of a dream of intimacy with her that would atone for class mobility and relieve the sense of class estrangement. The breakdown of narrative is the denial of this dream.

The absence of censorship would be unrestricted freedom of speech: the freedom to be candid about physical events, desires, fears. In insisting that this freedom cannot be had without others, Hardy's novels refuse to allow literature to be a separate, protected, liberal domain.

NOTES

1 See S. Kappeler, *The Pornography of Representation*, Cambridge, Polity Press, 1986.
2 See R. Gittings, *Young Thomas Hardy*, Harmondsworth, Penguin, 1978, pp. 205–7, and P. Widdowson, *Hardy in History*, London, Routledge, 1989, p. 135.
3 Florence Emily Hardy, *The Life of Thomas Hardy*, London, Macmillan, 1975,

p. 222. *The Life* was first published in two parts: *The Early Life of Thomas Hardy, 1840–1891*, London, Macmillan, 1928, and *The Later Years of Thomas Hardy, 1892–1928*, London, Macmillan, 1930.

4 Some details of the correspondence in each case can be found in M. Millgate, *Thomas Hardy: a Biography*, Oxford, Oxford University Press, 1982, pp. 300–1.

5 H. Orel (ed.), *Thomas Hardy's Personal Writings*, London, Macmillan, 1967, p. 127.

6 See, for example, F. E. Hardy, *The Life*, p. 266. A sustained analysis of the feelings about class expressed in *The Life* can be found in Widdowson, *Hardy in History*, ch. 4.

7 See Widdowson, *Hardy in History*.

8 See, for example, F. E. Hardy, *The Life*, p. 236.

9 Orel (ed.), *Thomas Hardy's Personal Writings*, pp. 130–1. This is another stock argument, of course.

10 F. E. Hardy, *The Life*, p. 222.

11 Orel (ed.), *Thomas Hardy's Personal Writings*, p. 127.

12 *The Woodlanders*, Harmondsworth, Penguin, 1986, p. 48.

13 ibid., pp. 41–4.

14 The New Wessex Edition of 1912 became the stable text, and was reproduced in the Penguin Classics edition of 1985, edited by David Skilton. Small variations in the editions between 1891 and 1912 do not concern this argument.

15 *Graphic*, 1 August 1891, p. 134.

16 *Tess of the d'Urbervilles*, Harmondsworth, Penguin, 1985, pp. 105–19.

17 *Graphic*, 1 August, 1891, p. 136.

18 *Tess of the d'Urbervilles*, pp. 106–18.

19 ibid., p. 118.

20 ibid., p. 140.

21 ibid., p. 119.

22 ibid., pp. 118–19.

23 ibid., p. 119.

24 *Far from the Madding Crowd*, Harmondsworth, Penguin, 1985, p. 51.

25 *Under the Greenwood Tree*, Harmondsworth, Penguin, 1985, p. 50.

26 *The Return of the Native*, Harmondsworth, Penguin, 1985, pp. 194–5.

27 *The Mayor of Casterbridge*, Harmondsworth, Penguin, 1985, pp. 408–9.

28 See P. Boumelha, *Thomas Hardy and Women: Sexual Ideology and Narrative Form*, Brighton, Harvester, 1984; J. Wittenberg, 'Thomas Hardy's first novel: women and the quest for autonomy', *Colby Library Quarterly*, vol. 18, 1982, pp. 47–54; M. Childers, 'Thomas Hardy, the man who "liked" women', *Criticism*, vol. 23, 1981, pp. 317–34. All of these are cited and discussed in P. Ingham, *Thomas Hardy*, Brighton, Harvester/Wheatsheaf Feminist Readings, 1989. See also H. Jacobson, *Peeping Tom*, London, Chatto & Windus, 1984, partially reproduced in L. St John Butler (ed.), *Alternative Hardy*, Macmillan, 1989, and J. Kincaid, ' "You did not come": absence, death and eroticism in *Tess*', in R. Barreca (ed.), *Sex and Death in Victorian Literature*, London, Macmillan, 1990.

Both Jacobson and Kincaid rewrite Hardy, substituting an aggressively comic plain-speaking for his circumlocution, thus: 'Tess slogs her way through Nature's vomit' (Kincaid, p. 21), and ' "So what, for fuck's sake, *did* you mean?" Hardy decided against letting him reply' (Jacobson, p. 141).

This is a comic alternative and, in terms of the argument here, another surface; it is not explicitness set against inexplicitness.

29 Kappeler, *The Pornography of Representation*, p. 103.
30 ibid., p. 9.

Part IV

The twentieth century: radicals and readers

Chapter 13

Censorship and the Great War: the first test of new statesmanship

Adrian Smith

Today's *New Statesman & Society* rightly proclaims a long and honourable tradition of cocking a snook at state censorship, formal or informal. Duncan Campbell is only the latest in a long line of inquisitive and investigative editorial staff who at one stage or another have come into conflict with the law. A political weekly's experience of being silenced can range from the casual – the off-the-record advice to 'back off' – to the judicial: court orders and confiscation. The *New Statesman* has, in its time, experienced just about every kind of censorship, whether voluntary or imposed. The usual assumption is that the paper's recruitment to the 'awkward squad' dates from Kingsley Martin's appointment as editor in 1931. However, while the early *New Statesman* could scarcely be labelled radical, in time of war its Fabian founders were not averse to challenging the power of the state over fundamental issues of press freedom. Although acquiescent and cooperative for the majority of the First World War, at the height of the conflict both chairman and editor took issue with a government enjoying unprecedented statutory powers of control over information and opinion. This willingness to take on the principal agency of censorship, the Press Bureau, in defence of pacifist papers with which the *New Statesman* was in almost total disagreement, enchanced the magazine's standing and influence within a previously sceptical Labour movement. By the time Lloyd George's coalition sought a fresh mandate in November 1918, the *New Statesman* had fulfilled an important role uniting pro- and anti-war factions inside a newly constituted Labour Party; with the Liberals divided, in the new Parliament Labour for the first time became the official Opposition. Under Martin in the 1930s the paper became the undisputed intellectual flagship of the left, and an earlier generation of reporters, commentators, critics and polemicists, was largely forgotten. Their record as campaigning journalists had been, to say the least, modest. The early *New Statesman* was never intended to be that sort of a paper anyway; its principal purpose was to educate, instruct and persuade. However, when confronted by a

powerful executive increasingly indifferent to civil liberties, both editorial staff and board readily took up the challenge.

When Sidney and Beatrice Webb launched the *New Statesman* in the
spring of 1913 few anticipated its survival until the end of the decade,
let alone the century. Not even the prospect of regular contributions
from the magazine's principal shareholder, George Bernard Shaw, dis-
suaded Fleet Street sceptics from the view that here was a project
well-intentioned but doomed. Given the Webbs' low standing in the
Labour movement at the time, what hope was there for a weekly
review which announced their distinctly didactic brand of collectivism
as the most suitable if not the speediest path to the New Jerusalem?

For years the first Fabians had diligently pursued their task of per-
meating both major parties, but with only scant success. The failure
of a nationwide campaign to generate popular support for Beatrice's
Minority Report of the Poor Law Commission had exposed the Webbs'
lack of any obvious power-base. Party leaders such as Lloyd George
and A. J. Balfour felt few qualms about dining at Sidney's expense,
and then all-too-often ignoring his advice. An unenthusiastic, but at
least unqualified, embrace of Labour only came as late as 1912. Thus
the Fabians' new weekly was, in part, a belated attempt to establish
status, credibility and influence within the mainstream Labour movement. The *New Statesman*, along with the London School of Economics
and the Fabian Research Department, made up a network of institutions which, while still embracing the now-tarnished strategies of
permeation and mass propaganda, were intended to assimilate, articulate
and disseminate the Webbs' distinctive interpretation of collectivism:
an enlightened and inevitably middle-class elite, expertly managing an
all-embracing state's no-nonsense assault on social deprivation and
proletarian 'ignorance'.

The *New Statesman* was never envisaged as a self-appointed champion of free speech. The Webbs were not interested in a campaigning
review, challenging the establishment of the day head-on. Such a
posture would, by definition, have been confrontational, and thus
wholly at odds with a strategy of influencing rather than alienating the
exercisers of power. Whitehall mandarins and their political masters in
the final years of peace were no less hostile to charges of conspiracies
of silence than their contemporary counterparts. On no known
occasion did the *New Statesman*'s directors and editorial staff address
the very topical issues of censorship, and the growing statutory power
of government – Unionist, or even Liberal – to control information
and/or suppress dissent. Freedom of information, although, with the
benefit of hindsight, clearly a major area of concern in Edwardian
England, was perhaps not surprisingly near the bottom of the Fabians'
ideological baggage. In a golden age of empiricism, guaranteed

dissemination of information was not a tangible, easily resolvable problem, on a par with pension provision or improved public utilities; and as such it did not attract the remorseless attention of social investigators and reformers. To be fair, it took the onset of 'total war' to make news management and the systematic suppression of information and dissent a visible political issue, and to jolt all but the most radical and sensitive journalists out of their complacency. Thus, the fact that the *New Statesman* was not in the vanguard of uninhibited free speech from its inception should not be a cause for serious censure. In any case, at least one director of the fledgling weekly regularly poured scorn upon the nation's moral guardians. The shadow of the Lord Chamberlain made Shaw as a playwright particularly sensitive to official complaint; but his journalism during the first two years of the war confirmed an earlier impression of characteristic indifference to the views of authority, censorious or otherwise.

Shaw's early influence was considerable, and his capital critical. Yet, after only three years, he resigned from the *New Statesman*'s board, having clashed repeatedly with the first editor, Clifford Sharp. Born into the late Victorian middle class, trained in both engineering and law, and cultivating political ambitions to match his evident skills as a journalist and propagandist, Sharp epitomised Shaw's and Sidney Webb's 'intellectual proletariat': those superior 'gravediggers of capitalism' who were to pioneer the new social order and signal the demise of a merely ameliorative Liberalism. Ironically, Sharp was also the man who, having created a firm base for the *New Statesman*'s later success under Kingsley Martin, entered a twilight world of whisky, women and the Wee Frees.[1] He had helped to found the 'Fabian Nursery' in the early 1900s but, unlike several other younger members had distanced himself from H. G. Wells's celebrated mauling of the Webbs, thereby establishing his credentials with the 'Old Gang'. Although he later published their work, he had little in common with the world of Rupert Brooke, 'Ben' Keeling and the Cambridge Fabians, described so vividly in Ben Pimlott's biography of Hugh Dalton.[2]

Sharp was even less attracted to the ideas and lifestyle of G. D. H. Cole, erstwhile Fabian and apostle of guild socialism. On the eve of the First World War, Cole was busy refining the ideas of other ex-Fabians, such as A. J. Penty and A. R. Orage. Orage, editor of the *New Age* (1907–22) and Sharp's first employer, had acquired a deep-rooted antipathy to the Webbs' brand of state socialism, arguing that, contrary to syndicalism's assumption of unavoidable class conflict, workers could peacefully organise themselves into democratic national guilds. Alienation would then give way to a genuine partnership with management. Dismissive of Orage's ideas, Sharp nevertheless learnt from him how to edit a political weekly.

The *New Age* drew on an impressive array of young writers, in addition to Cole. It boasted one of the century's finest cartoonists, Will Dyson, and even when it fell into decline during the First World War, displayed verve, flamboyance and a rare quality of writing. Comparing the two papers, Shaw judged *New Statesman* highmindedness as scarcely conducive to circulation and style. In short, no matter how vehemently the leader-pages denounced Ulster Unionism, the force-feeding of suffragettes, lock-outs or conscription, the paper lacked excitement and conviction. Although keen to share editorial anonymity, Shaw knew his value in terms of boosting sales. So did Sharp, but more and more he exercised his right to edit, alter and even reject Shaw's copy. Throughout his life Sharp rarely stood in awe of anyone – his contempt was indiscriminate. In the 1920s this penchant for wholesale abuse cost him his job on more than one occasion but, more immediately, in 1916 it cost him his most prestigious contributor. Shaw's highly original, if somewhat eccentric, views on the pursuance of the war caused the final rupture. Writing to an equally eccentric, but High Tory, correspondent eighteen months later, Shaw declared his delight upon learning that there existed an 'Anti-Socialist' magazine: 'If it does half as much to hinder its own course as most of the Socialist magazines and societies, the triumph of Socialism is assured.'[3]

Shaw's support had, of course, proved crucial in launching the paper. From the outset, the *New Statesman* was in direct competition for a very limited audience. A core of Fabian subscribers was vital for the magazine to realise its twin potentials as a collectivist response to the heresies of the *New Age*, and as a commercial challenge to the premier Liberal weekly, the *Nation* (1907–31). The bulk of the early readership was a relatively homogeneous middle-class intelligentsia, invariably of radical or socialist persuasion. Yet London and the other big industrial cities offered a genuinely socialist journal a mass of untapped readers; these were skilled, semi-skilled and clerical workers, whose radicalisation was largely a consequence of self-education, of trade unionism, and of the propagandist success of the Independent Labour Party (ILP). At the same time, in the capital itself there flourished a not inconsiderable number of privileged young 'new' men and women busily engaged in undermining their parents' moral code and social mores. Their enthusiastic embrace of 'the modern' revealed a self-confidence, an assertiveness and a political conviction rarely discernible among the preceding generation's speculative pioneers of self-improvement and social reconstruction. These ambitious and intellectually precocious young graduates guaranteed the literary pages a creative reservoir; their poems and reviews complementing – and often outshining – the contributions of more firmly established writers. Their champion was Jack Squire, the *New Statesman*'s literary editor and another veteran of the *New Age*. For a man whose name was synonymous in the 1920s with chauvinism, philistinism and censorship, the young Squire displayed a surprising degree of eclecticism, enterprise and enlightenment. A modish blend of the country man-of-letters and the urban Bohemian, the future Sir John was not the last literary editor to attract a sizeable body of readers solely to the back half of the paper.

As editor of the *London Mercury* (1919–34), Squire was later to become a notorious scourge of D. H. Lawrence. The winter of 1915 offered an early indication of what was to come, when the *New Statesman* failed to condemn the government's obscenity charge against *The Rainbow*. Clive Bell and Lytton Strachey, neither of whom actually liked the novel, urged Squire to take a stand, but he declined: the book was not only poor, it was 'perverse', and its prosecution was clearly not a veiled response to Ursula Brangwen's denunciation of war. Squire did eventually come around to the view that, for a writer 'of an earnestness . . . almost awe-inspiring', censorship was absurd. Even so, Lawrence never forgot; witness his posthumous poetic assault in *More Pansies* (1932). Bell could scarcely have expected the paper to demonstrate support for Lawrence, given his own experience a few months earlier. In September 1915 Bell's pamphlet, *Peace At Once* was destroyed by order of Salford magistrates. Its author wrote asking whether the *New Statesman* could justify an infringement of civil liberties that not even the Germans would tolerate. A terse reply, while acknowledging that such suppression was wrong, pointed to the folly of Bell's pacifism; similarly, to believe that England ranked second to any nation in respecting the freedom of its press was a delusion.[4] On this evidence the *New Statesman* could scarcely be considered a fearless wartime champion of free speech, and yet, as we shall see, within a few months of spurning Bell and Lawrence the paper was directly challenging the authorities over this very question.

However much they appreciated the freelance contributions, most young progressives on the eve of the war still viewed the *New Statesman* as far too sombre and utilitarian ever to rank beside the *New Age* in the vanguard of modernism and fundamental social change. Sharp and the Webbs shared a common assumption that their three or four thousand readers sought relentless edification, if necessary at the expense of entertainment. Sidney confessed to being constantly bemused by the literary pages, but left Squire to get on with it. Not surprisingly, the hard core of the *New Statesman*'s readership would remain among the more liberal members of the nation's professional classes. Was it not upon their technical and managerial expertise that Sidney and Beatrice's well-ordered collectivist oligarchy would so heavily depend?

Initially, directors and editorial staff were agreed on giving higher priority to securing a small but powerful audience within Westminster and Whitehall, than upon strengthening their relatively informal liaison with both the political and industrial wings of the Labour movement. Constantly reiterating to ILP and trade-union leaders the merits of Fabian policies was now judged necessary albeit wearisome, but not at the expense of promoting those same policies in the corridors of power. Despite Sharp's increasingly vituperative views on Lloyd George, he always insisted – ostensibly, in the national interest – on positive criticism of all three wartime administrations. The leader-writers never seriously questioned the official view that Belgium's invasion constituted a *casus belli*, and that the strategy of attrition must be pursued at all costs. Thus, despite Sharp and Lloyd George's personal feud, the *New Statesman* secured ministers' and civil servants' healthy respect for its coverage of, and commentary upon, a comprehensive range of domestic issues.

The final eighteen months of the war were especially important to the paper's consolidation of its position as the third major political weekly (after the *Nation*, which it would soon overtake and eventually absorb, and the *Spectator*). Although editors were technically exempt from national service, Downing Street ensured Sharp's conscription in 1917. Commissioned in the Royal Artillery, Sharp was later recruited by the Foreign Office for intelligence activities in Scandinavia.[5] As acting editor, Squire relied heavily on Arnold Bennett, a director since 1915. Bennett walked the wartime corridors of power and enjoyed the confidence of the government's opponents. As such, his knowledge and advice were invaluable. Sharp's absence meant that the *New Statesman* drew much closer to a reconstituted Labour Party (the founder of one, Sidney Webb, co-drafted the constitution of the other). In addition, the paper's credibility as an organ of 'loyal opposition' secured it a modicum of respect among the nation's political elite. So by the Armistice the paper could claim to represent a remarkably broad consensus of pro-war Labour and Independent Liberal opinion. Despite its low circulation and weak financial position, the *New Statesman* spoke with *gravitas*, justifying Beatrice Webb's boast that 'Fleet Street and Whitehall count it as a great success'.[6]

In August 1914 Robert Ensor, the *New Statesman*'s chief leader-writer on foreign affairs, assumed responsibility for military matters. He reported the progress of the war, or rather the lack of it, with all the fervour of the true convert. Prior to hostilities, Ensor, ILP candidate and freelance journalist, was best known as Secretary of the Foreign Policy Committee, an august body of Liberal-Radicals enthusiastic for open diplomacy and hostile to any continental commitment that entailed alliance with tsarist autocracy. While many of his former colleagues soon joined the anti-war Union of Democratic Control (UDC), Ensor now spoke for the pro-war faction within the Fabian Society. For the next four years, in the *New Statesman* and the *Daily Chronicle*, he urged the uncompromising defeat of the 'Prussian militarists' and the dismemberment of their empire. Although the editor invariably added his own equally ill-informed views on the fighting, after Sharp's call-up Ensor was left to get on with it. While Sidney Webb and Leonard Woolf drew up blueprints for national and international reconstruction, Ensor indulged in military punditry. Rarely able or willing to challenge orthodox strategic thinking, he became especially adept at manipulating news to ensure an almost permanent optimism. Sharp shared Ensor's enthusiasm for the Imperial General Staff and for a 'Western' strategy based on attrition because it conformed to the overall editorial policy of opposing Lloyd George. Even after Gallipoli the Welshman remained at heart an 'Easterner', seeking final victory away from the Western Front.

Until May 1915 the *New Statesman* shared the same problem as the dailies, upon whose sources it so often relied: irregular and unreliable information in the absence of recognised war correspondents. The government had tacitly encouraged a pre-war assumption that the army would welcome reporters, but Kitchener imposed a blanket ban upon his appointment as Secretary for War. In terms of Asquith's administration maintaining goodwill with the national press this was a public-relations disaster. However, as controls were relaxed following the establishment of the first Coalition, so contributors began visiting the Front. Touring the trenches in July 1915, Bennett was unhappy with what he saw, but a reluctance to risk controversy ensured a bland report in the *Illustrated London News*. At the same time, however, he passed his true feelings on to Sharp for unattributed use. Sharp's own tours seldom involved the front-line. All they generated were jingoistic accounts of high morale and dogged determination among the troops; no doubt to the disgust of subscribers such as Graves and Sassoon.

The irony is that Sidney Webb had predicted at the outset an enormous credibility-gap between the general public's preconceived, romantic notions of warfare, and the harsh reality of history's 'least actually observed, least contemporaneously reported, and most imaginatively lied, war'. Thus, the *New Statesman* would provide a weekly summary of the best-authenticated news, 'The progress of the war'.[7] The demise of Webb's initiative after only a month symbolised the ease with which the magazine unconsciously adapted to the style and content of those newspapers whose coverage of the war it so frequently criticised. By fulfilling its propagandist function just as smoothly as so many other non-pacifist publications, the *New Statesman*'s claim to independence and the high moral ground was scarcely justified. Sharp and Ensor rarely displayed any true understanding of what conditions were like in the trenches, and in this of course they were by no means unique – neither did the overwhelming majority of the civilian population. Nevertheless, there still remained this prevailing attitude that somehow *New Statesman* reportage was different from – and, by implication, superior to – the majority of newspaper coverage and commentary. Such an attitude rendered Ensor's propaganda even more insidious and unattractive. It is scarcely surprising that so few people at home were interested in the depressing and distressing news that soldiers brought home on leave. Ignorance was bliss, and civilian sources of information – professional writers such as Ensor, Sharp and Squire – conveniently lacked the imagination, the language and, above all, the motivation, to convince the public of the Western Front's real horrors. In such circumstances one may wonder how the *New Statesman* ever fell foul of the Press Bureau.

The final years of peace had seen a system of voluntary censorship and self-regulation work remarkably smoothly. The British Expeditionary Force, for example, only became public knowledge in August 1914, two years after its formation.[8] The Boer War and the subsequent creation of the Committee of Imperial Defence (CID) had generated an extensive and, at times, cantankerous, debate between newspaper proprietors and the guardians of the nation's secrets. The heat was only taken out of these negotiations when the 1911 Official Secrets Act was rushed through Parliament at the height of the Agadir crisis. Predictably, attention focused on the clauses concerned with espionage in Section 1. The indiscriminatory nature of Section 2 – with all that it implied regarding coverage of defence matters – was scarcely acknowledged. Such a vague and draconian measure necessitated urgent agreement between the military and the press on ground rules regarding what could or could not be published; in other words, a buffer needed to be established. In October 1912 a new liaison body, the Joint Standing Committee of Admiralty, War Office and Press Representatives, was empowered to issue 'D' (for Defence) Notices formally advising non-publication of material specifically related to national security. As today, editors would receive directives advising them on the treatment of a news item, and the parameters within which coverage of a particular story should operate.

The success of the voluntary system exacerbated Fleet Street's annoyance over the arbitrary imposition of direct controls following the outbreak of hostilities. Regulations 18, 27 and 51 of the 1914 Defence of the Realm Act (DORA), together with the 1911 Act and Lord Kitchener's ban on war correspondents, gave the government all the power it needed to underpin editorial self-censorship. Nevertheless, on 7 August 1914 the Press Bureau was set up, responsible both for the dissemination of official information and the censorship of all material voluntarily submitted by the press (cables were compulsory). Technically speaking, on a day-to-day basis non-statutory censorship still prevailed, and the majority of editors and proprietors were remarkably acquiescent when advised via 'D' Notices as to tone and content. Such acquiescence was often deemed irritating and inconvenient but, nevertheless, in the national interest. Whatever restraint Fleet Street exercised with regard to overtly military matters, it more than made up for in its coverage of domestic issues, especially the politicians' record in conducting the war. The pacifist press suffered the most hardship, but in an ostensibly liberal democracy the government was unwilling to use DORA to impose permanent and comprehensive suppression. Such an act would have offered invaluable ammunition for enemy propaganda, particularly when targeted at the United States.

Resentment towards the Press Bureau was based on the feeling that the pre-war system of self-censorship was both more efficient and more effective. Newspapers now submitted relevant copy, excepting editorials, to censors drawn from the Services. The latter – rarely former journalists – were responsible for the control of front-line and naval news, and the suppression of any information potentially useful to the enemy. However, the Press Bureau rapidly acquired a reputation for incompetence under its first Director, F. E. Smith. As a prominent barrister and uncompromising Unionist prior to the war, Smith had acquired many enemies at the height of the Home Rule crisis – particularly in the Liberal press. Fleet Street pressed Asquith's government for a replacement familiar with the mechanics of producing newspapers to a deadline. But, neither the sympathy expressed by Smith's equally inappropriate successor, the Solicitor-General, Sir Stanley Buckmaster, nor the wholesale reforms pioneered from June 1915 by Sir Edward Cook, offered adequate recompense for the inevitable delay in processing all-too-scarce news stories. Cook, a former editor and an unrepentant Liberal imperialist, was the first Director of the Press Bureau who genuinely appreciated the problems involved in going to press on time. Until his appointment, delays were a regular occurrence, with censors' decisions often arbitrary and confused. In November 1914 Lord Northcliffe had complained to Asquith that 'our people have nothing but the casualty lists and the mutilated scraps with which it is quite impossible to arouse interest or follow the war intelligently'.[9] In response, Downing Street eased cablegram censorship and sent Buckmaster to placate the Commons. Soothing words and a promise to do better clearly failed. Northcliffe's *Daily Mail* still insisted that the failings of the Press Bureau reflected the performance of the Liberal government as a whole.[10]

With the exception of Lloyd George, who throughout his career assiduously cultivated editors and proprietors, Asquith and his colleagues were notoriously indifferent towards the press. Both the Prime Minister, and the Foreign Secretary, Sir Edward Grey, would confide only in J. A. Spender, whose *Westminster Gazette* rarely sold a copy beyond the confines of St James's and Pall Mall. Before the war *The Times* correspondent at the Foreign Office received a daily briefing, and C. P. Scott would exercise the *Manchester Guardian*'s historic right to quiz Liberal grandees, but that was about as far as the Party's news management stretched. Antagonising Fleet Street by tolerating incompetence at the Press Bureau further provoked Unionist – and some Liberal – newspapers. The press destroyed Haldane, drafter of the Official Secrets Act, in the spring of 1915, and within eighteen months had hounded Asquith and Grey from office. There are many reasons why Asquith's wartime administrations collapsed, not least the Prime Minister's ineffectual handling of the war, but it is clear the press's relentless undermining of his authority had a corrosive effect.

Naturally the weeklies were far less dependent upon the Press Bureau than was the daily press, although early in the war St Loe Strachey was convinced that a Liberal bias caused the *Spectator* to be especially victimised.[11] Heavily dependent on secondary news-sources, the *New Statesman* submitted very little for censorship. But this did not stop Ensor and Sharp bitterly criticising the Press Bureau from the outset. After the first month's fighting they joined other journalists in petitioning the War Office to remove F. E. Smith. *The New Statesman*'s position was simple and consistent; all creditable information not of benefit to the enemy should be available for publication; the Press Bureau's work should be limited to preventing the leak of vital military information; maximum discussion should be encouraged; and there should be absolute frankness in the interests of public morale.[12] Prior to the Somme, Sharp was a great believer in the 'stimulating effect' that reverses would have on the British temperament; announcement of a defeat could be a great morale-booster. Indifferent to the lengthening casualty-lists, Ensor suffered from similar delusions.[13] Even so, the paper adhered to 'D' Notice requests for silence on the 1915 Zeppelin raids and the surrender of Kut-el-Amara to the Turks in April 1916. In September 1915 thirty-five socialist and pacifist papers were removed from the 'D' Notice list, either for ignoring the Press Bureau's directives or for not submitting contentious material. Pro-war and respectable, the *New Statesman* retained establishment approval.

Sharp explained to Wells in January 1917 that he respected the Press Bureau's wishes, 'unless I am pretty sure of my ground'. Thus, Cook's only contact had been a letter to 'warn' Sharp about publishing the Glasgow ILP's account of the stormy reception they gave Lloyd

George: 'In that case being quite sure of my ground I replied suitably and published a fuller account the following week. But of course military stuff is a much more tricky question.' Sharp would risk attacking the generals, but would never take issue with the censor over criticising soldiers in the field, 'because I don't think any such general right can reasonably be held in wartime'.[14] Sharp and Sidney Webb's unexpected assertion of anti-war ILP members' right to publish is explored fully in due course. It marked a rare occasion when discretion was abandoned. Such was not the case when dealing with Wells, a man who had never hidden his disdain for the paper. He offered the *New Statesman* copy already heavily censored by the Press Bureau when submitted by the *Daily News*. Wary of Lloyd George, Sharp rejected the offer, despite boasting that the *New Statesman* was 'the only paper in England that has made any serious attempt to criticise the military people'.[15] This was of course nonsense. H. W. Massingham, editor of the *Nation*, was a far more trenchant critic of the High Command. In April 1917 overseas sales of the *Nation* were banned on the grounds that enemy propaganda had quoted its criticism of Haig's tactics. This was less than three months after Sharp's warning to Wells that he could never risk the same penalty, 'just for the fun of having a row with the authorities'.[16]

By the time news of the *Nation*'s ban had caused uproar in the Commons, Sharp was in the army. At Massingham's request, Bennett and Squire campaigned for the order to be revoked. In October 1917 the restriction was lifted, by which time the War Office was busy filtering and sanitising news from the killing fields of Passchendaele.[17] In his weekly column Bennett castigated the Press Bureau as 'the most unsatisfactory, exasperating and inefficient war-organisation on the island'. The general public needed the positive, direct instruction and guidance which an official review of operations might periodically provide, but which the Services were clearly loath to initiate.[18] Bennett and Squire's patriotism was obvious to all. Above suspicion, and indifferent to prime ministerial threats, they felt little need to follow the same pragmatic path as Sharp. Nevertheless, in the following year the *New Statesman* did come under Foreign Office scrutiny when an article on deserters was taken up by German propaganda. As this was a solitary example, and any action against the magazine would surely have focused on Bennett – best-selling author, and, embarrassingly, Ministry of Information propagandist – the incident was quickly forgotten. Prosecuting a small-circulation weekly was one thing, but silencing the nation's most popular novelist was quite another.[19]

Administratively, it proved extremely difficult for the authorities to impose a rigorous censorship policy across a sophisticated pluralist society for over four years of war. Politically, it proved a major undertaking, albeit not impossible, to over-rule a combination of sectional interests within the British press. The government correctly perceived that among newspapers of all political persuasions there existed a certain bond. The *New Statesman* was no exception; for example, in attacking the April 1916 restriction on references to Cabinet proceedings. In November 1917 it was to join the rest of the Liberal and Labour press in endorsing backbench opposition to the compulsory censorship of pamphlets. Both incidents offer an interesting insight into Clifford Sharp and Jack Squire's contrasting views on free speech in time of war. In 1916 the former genuinely feared that the new DORA regulations would affect only the weakest papers, those with 'no special Cabinet friends'. By November 1917 the acting editor's only concern was a deepening conviction among the pacifist 'dissentient majority' that the right to free speech was theirs alone.[20] What Squire meant by such a remark is open to interpretation, but it clearly fails to place him in a very flattering light. In contrast, Sharp, the unashamed pragmatist, could stake a modest claim to defending the freedom of the press. In this respect, his finest hour was undoubtedly in the early months of 1916 when he found himself an unlikely hero of the ILP.

As an editor, Sharp demanded of his writers no more than sound intellect, technical expertise and journalistic competence. It was these criteria (note the absence of individual talent), as opposed to straightforward loyalties of party and class, that at first led to the *New Statesman* naively ignoring the Labour press, and most obviously the *Daily Herald*. Demoralised by the split in the Labour movement at the outbreak of war, and starved of trade-union backing, the *Herald* staggered on as a weekly newspaper. More resilient, with a circulation of between 1,500 and 2,000 readers, was the *Labour Leader*, the main organ of the ILP. Edited by Fenner Brockway, the *Labour Leader* was a vociferous opponent of the war. Sharp regularly challenged Brockway's views, but after January 1917 was prevented by DORA from mentioning any pacifist newspaper. This ban followed a German wireless broadcast quoting a *Labour Leader* call for civil disobedience in the face of conscription. Brockway felt honour-bound to resign as editor and, no longer enjoying exemption, was ultimately imprisoned as a conscientious objector.

Prior to 1917 the *Labour Leader* had already been prosecuted twice. Sharp's protests were characteristically ambivalent: why prosecute, given the government's forbearance of several equally damaging Unionist newspapers, and why enhance the prestige of the ILP among trade unionists?[21] So begrudging a protest was hardly heroic – no risk of martyrdom here. However, in January 1916 the *New Statesman* surprisingly sprang to the defence of the Glasgow ILP's *Forward*. The voice of 'Red Clydeside' had been silenced for mocking Lloyd George's unsuccessful efforts to appease striking shipbuilders. Sidney Webb paid tribute to the ILP newspapers and the *Herald* for publishing the truth about the Minister of Munitions' visit, as opposed to the 'official' version carried by the established press.[22] The following week Sharp revealed that the *New Statesman* had been contacted by the Press Bureau, no doubt on Lloyd George's orders. At issue, apparently, was not Webb's leader, but a previous issue's letter from 'A Glasgow Labour man', a pseudonym for P. J. Dollan. Dollan, a conscientious objector and later a well-known figure in the ILP, had given his version of Clydeside's welcome for the Minister.[23] So also had another comrade's letter, in a subsequent defiance of the Bureau's warning. With the skill of a trained lawyer, Sharp dissected and demolished Lloyd George's parliamentary defence of *Forward's* suppression. However much it differed from the *New Statesman* in its thinking, the paper had always scrupulously adhered to the principle of free speech and had provided its readers with a balanced and truthful account of the visit. This was certainly more than could be said for the government.[24]

Antipathy towards Lloyd George demanded that this unholy alliance with the Glasgow ILP be maintained. Tom Johnston, *Forward's* editor and a future Labour minister, wrote in appreciation of the *New Statesman's* stand, thus prompting yet another thundering leader.[25] Had Parliament ever been subjected to such 'a tissue of misrepresentation and calculated misquotation'?[26] By the following week the order suppressing Glasgow's Civic Press had been lifted following a visit by Johnston to the Ministry of Munitions. Sharp naively looked to Asquith for reassurance that any future action along similar lines would receive cabinet, and not simply departmental, clearance.[27] This was a distinctly peacetime understanding of wartime decision-making, at precisely the moment when the War Cabinet was consolidating its control of both military and domestic affairs. A more obvious irony was Lloyd George's subsequent protection of the *Herald* and the ILP newspapers once the retention of Labour support for the second Coalition became of paramount importance.[28]

The *New Statesman* was never again as uncompromising in its support of the pacifist and socialist press. Sharp eventually fired one too many barbs against Lloyd George, and friendly Liberals could no longer ensure his protection. Ironically, once the new Prime Minister had wreaked his vengeance, Sharp thoroughly enjoyed life in the mess, and resented being posted to civilian duties. Oddly for a Fabian paper, the *New Statesman* always insisted that, in agreeing to disagree over the war, the ILP had abdicated the intellectual leadership of the Labour movement. On this basis even Webb was reluctant to demonstrate overt sympathy when the *Labour Leader* and its sister papers were harassed. After Sharp's departure Webb was happy to hand over supervision of editorial matters to Bennett and Squire, both men sharing a good working relationship and similiar views on the conduct of the war. As a result the *New Statesman*'s views regarding the well-being or otherwise of the pacifist press noticeably hardened.

Nevertheless, at a crucial moment in the history of the Home Front, when faced with a clear threat to the freedom of the press, the paper had been prepared to stand up and be counted. Whatever Sharp's motives, the editor – secure in the support of his chairman, Sidney Webb – had stood his ground. Such a gesture, so clearly identifiable with a man who in the last year of the war was to play a crucial role in establishing the modern Labour Party, helps explain why the ILP and indeed the whole of the Labour movement were able to reunite in the autumn of 1918 to fight the 'Coupon Election'.[29] Unlike the Liberals, Labour's wartime divisions were not permanently damaging. Supporters and opponents of the war held fundamentally different views, although even here there was growing area of agreement in the final year and a half of fighting – particularly after Arthur Henderson was dismissed from the War Cabinet for attending the Stockholm Conference. What they were clearly in agreement on was resistance to a residual erosion of basic civil liberties, and here censorship was a key issue. The *New Statesman*'s record of resistance was, to say the least, patchy; at the same time, it was by no means dishonourable.

NOTES

1 The Wee Frees was the nickname for the Independent Liberals who followed Asquith into opposition after Lloyd George became Prime Minister in December 1916. For a fuller portrait of Clifford Sharp, see A. Smith, 'Heart to the right, brain to the left', *New Statesman*, 8 January 1988, and 'Sharp, Clifford Dyce (1883–1935)', in J. Bellamy and J. Saville (eds), *The Dictionary of Labour Biography*, vol. VII, London, Macmillan, 1984. For more detailed information on the *New Statesman* before and during the First World War, see A. Smith, 'The *New Statesman* 1913–31: a study of intellectual attitudes', unpublished Ph.D. dissertation, University of Kent, 1980.

2 B. Pimlott, *Hugh Dalton*, London, Jonathan Cape, 1988, pp. 38–57.

3 G. B. Shaw to J. B. Barnhill, 18 May 1918: Dartmouth College Library, USA.

4 'Books in general', *New Statesman*, 20 November 1915. M. Holroyd, *Lytton Strachey, a Critical Biography. Volume II, the Years of Achievement 1910–1932*, London, Heinemann, 1968, p. 160. C. Bell to the editor, *New Statesman*, 4 September 1915.

5 A. Smith, '*New Statesman* editor in pay of British security services', *New Statesman*, 22 and 29 December 1978.

6 Beatrice Webb, diary, (?) August 1918: British Library of Political and Economic Science, Passfield Papers.

7 'The progress of the war', *New Statesman*, 8 August 1914.

8 This account of official censorship during the First World War draws upon E. Cook, *The Press in War-time, with some account of the Official Press Bureau*, London, Macmillan, 1920; D. Hopkin, 'Domestic censorship in the First World War', *Journal of Contemporary History*, vol. 5, 1970, pp. 151–69; S. Inwood, 'The role of the press in English politics during the First World War, with special reference to the period 1914–16', unpublished D.Phil. dissertation, University of Oxford, 1971; and G. Lovelace, 'British press censorship during the First World War', in G. Boyce, J. Curran and P. Wingate (eds), *Newspaper History from the Seventeenth Century to the Present Day*, London, Constable, 1978, pp. 307–19.

9 Lord Northcliffe to H. H. Asquith, (?) November 1914, quoted in Earl of Oxford and H. H. Asquith, *Memories and Reflections 1852–1927*, London, Cassell, 1928, vol. 2, p. 234.

10 *Daily Mail*, 10 February 1915.

11 John St Loe Strachey to (?) Hutton, 18 February 1915, quoted in Inwood, 'The role of the press', p. 90. Yet the *Spectator* could regularly argue for suppression of the pacifist press.

12 'The censorship of the news', *New Statesman*, 22 August 1914; 'The Press Bureau', *New Statesman*, 22 August 1914.

13 'Our wonderful censorship again', *New Statesman*, 13 March 1915. The Press Bureau kept a list of fifty editors to whom confidential information could be relayed. The list is unobtainable but, given his views, it is unlikely that Sharp's name was on it. Public Record Office, H.O. 45–297549 fol. 52.

14 Sharp to H. G. Wells, 19 January 1917: H. G. Wells Archive, University of Illinois, Champain-Urbana.

15 ibid.

16 ibid.

17 'In our place "The Nation" would probably not do as much.' Arnold Bennett to J. C. Squire, 11 April 1917: Berg Collection, New York Public Library.

18 'Sardonyx' [Bennett], 'Observations', *New Statesman*, 20 October 1917.

19 Public Record Office, F.O. 281 81–5050.

20 'The new press law', *New Statesman*, 29 April 1916; 'Comments', *New Statesman*, 24 November 1917.

21 'Comments', *New Statesman*, 21 August 1915.

22 'Comments' and 'The seizure of *Forward*', *New Statesman*, 8 January 1916.

23 'The case of *Forward*', *New Statesman*, 15 January 1916; 'A Glasgow Labour man' to the editor, *New Statesman*, 1 January 1916.

24 'The case of *Forward*', *New Statesman*, 15 January 1916.

25 T. Johnston to the editor, *New Statesman*, 22 January 1916.

26 'Comments', *New Statesman*, 22 January 1916.

27 'Comments', *New Statesman*, 29 January 1916.

28 The unholy alliance between Sharp and the Glasgow ILP was confirmed by the late Lord Fenner Brockway in conversation with the author, 7 February 1979.

29 Asquith contemptuously referred to the public endorsement by Lloyd George and the Tory leader, Andrew Bonar Law, of the Coalition's parliamentary candidates as the 'coupon', thus associating his political enemies with wartime Britain's inefficient and unpopular system of rationing.

Chapter 14

D. H. Lawrence: a suitable case for censorship

Damian Grant

'But Bertie, you used to be such a good little boy.' Reflecting on the degree of mutual antagonism that characterised his relations with the world at large, Lawrence would recall the mildly reproachful words of his mother: even before he began to write. But Mrs Lawrence's good little boy was destined to become a declared enemy of the society within which he grew up, a formidable opponent of its institutions, values, patterns of behaviour and structures of belief; an exorcist of its consciousness. In his 'Introduction to these paintings' Lawrence asserted that Cézanne was a 'pure revolutionary' in that his art put us in touch once again with our intuitive selves; implying 'the collapse of our whole way of consciousness, and the substitution of another way'.[1] Lawrence likewise wanted to destroy the corrupt structures he saw around him and play his part in creating 'a new heaven and a new earth'.[2] It is hardly surprising, then, that Lawrence's writing eventually brought him into conflict with the authorities. The scandal surrounding the prosecution of *The Rainbow* in 1915 made Lawrence a marked man for the rest of his life; and his publishers, anxious to avoid any further trouble with the law, henceforth required him to be more circumspect.[3] But after an uneasy truce lasting twelve years, Lawrence reopened hostilities with the private publication of *Lady Chatterley's Lover* in July 1928; to be followed by the unrepentant *Pansies* (1929) and the uncompromising exhibition of his paintings in the same year.

Even so, an account of Lawrence's public engagement with the forces of law after 1915 would in itself give an inadequate picture of his experience of censorship. The very nature of Lawrence's writing meant that he offended the sensibilities of many different groups of people in different ways. What we need to imagine is a series of concentric circles of censorship, moving outwards from the inherited reflex of self-censorship (which Lawrence did learn to cope with – if only because others were keen to exercise that role on his behalf), to his family (first his parents and siblings, and later Frieda), his friends (with a special category for his former friends), his typists (who had their own say in what should and should not be written), his agents (who often played a double game), his publishers (more active than most in 'toning down' Lawrence's work), booksellers and libraries (especially the private circulating libraries like Boots and Mudies, who operated their own in-house system of censorship), reviewers (often eager to speak out on behalf of their readers' moral welfare), readers themselves (in so far as they made themselves heard) and, finally, the actual intervention of the law, in the shape of the police, the Postmaster General, or customs officials.

Only when we have grasped the density of the undergrowth through which Lawrence had to scramble in what he called 'the jungle of literature' (L1: p. 222) can we understand the force of Aldington's observation, that Lawrence's unstable temper 'was created in him by the spirit of persecution and hostility which met nearly everything he wrote'.[4] Nor, we should remember, was the operation of the law confined to Lawrence's writing. He was detained for speaking English in Germany early in 1914, and later that year incurred suspicion for speaking German in England. The situation became more grave when Lawrence and Frieda were ordered out of Cornwall in 1915, on suspicion (apparently) of signalling to German submarines, and forbidden to live in any restricted area. From this time until the end of the war the Lawrences were under some kind of surveillance. Even in France, in 1929, Lawrence and his party managed to attract the attention of the French police. So, in a sense, even his person was censored. It will therefore be necessary to maintain a multiple perspective, in order to reflect the diverse influences which sought to persuade, cajole, coerce and threaten Lawrence into compromising his vision, or silencing his 'demon', to use his own term.

There is something curiously appropriate in the fact that Lawrence worked furtively on the first version of *The White Peacock* while at Nottingham University College in 1906, at the back of the class during lectures. Reading the work in progress on holiday next summer, Mrs Lawrence was not impressed: 'To think that *my* son should have written such a story.' As Moore remarks on this episode, 'Lawrence was already having troubles with censorship' (PL: pp. 107–8). His mother disapproved generally of his writing fiction, which she saw as offering no basis for the kind of advancement she intended for her son; and this hostility would no doubt have been compounded by the fact of Jessie Chambers's encouragement. His father's attitude may be gauged from the well-known story of his reaction to learning that Lawrence had earned fifty pounds for *The White Peacock*. 'And tha's niver done a day's work in thy life!' (PL: p. 167). We might complete the portrait of family supervision by looking ahead. His brother

George, we are told, read only part of *Sons and Lovers*, but on that evidence 'would have thrashed Bert . . . for what he did to my mother and father in that book' (*PL*: p. 284). As for his sisters: when Emily and her daughter visited Lawrence in Switzerland in 1928, 'He had to hide *Lady Chatterley* like a skeleton in his cupboard'; and a later visit from Ada (bringing with her 'the spirit of the Midlands') so depressed him that he felt 'I want to put my pansies in the fire, and myself with them'.[5]

Back in Edwardian England, Lawrence was well aware of the dangers of writing honestly about sexual matters. The reviews of *The White Peacock* had been generally favourable, one specifically praising it as a 'really masterly study of passion' made with 'praiseworthy frankness'; and while another did find against the 'physicality', 'brutality' and 'sick thoughts' characteristic of the novel, Lawrence could still afford to be amused by having 'upset *that* man whoever he was'.[6] But he was wary too. Hueffer's judgement that *The Trespasser* was unguardedly erotic had evidently unnerved him; in this same letter to his sister Ada, he announces he will 'suppress the Sigmund book. It is better so' (*L1*: p. 231). He had written a week earlier to Frederick Atkinson (reader at Heinemann's) asking for the return of the manuscript of *The Trespasser*, not only because it was 'execrable bad art' but because 'it is, finally, pornographic. And for this last reason I would wish to suppress the book.' The self-censor is still active. Moreover, despite his publisher's encouragement, he wrote later to Martin Secker that he was reluctant to publish the novel 'because it is erotic', and therefore 'I am afraid for my tender reputation' (*L1*: pp. 229, 276). H. G. Wells's new novel was the current by-word for sexual licence, and Lawrence did not want, he wrote, 'to be talked about in an Ann Veronica fashion' (*L1*: p. 339). However, it was not to be *The Trespasser* that would earn Lawrence this doubtful celebrity.

Lawrence had similar anxieties when he returned to work on the novel that was to become *Sons and Lovers*. 'I have begun "Paul Morel" again,' he wrote to Helen Corke in March 1911, 'glory, you should see it. The British public will stone me if it ever catches sight' (*L1*: p. 239). Later that month, however, Lawrence met Frieda; and among the many changes this brought to his life was a sudden assumption of maturity, a new certainty about the rightness of his vision. The man who could say 'I *know* I can write bigger stuff than any man in England' (*L1*: p. 546) had at last brought the self-censor to heel. Lawrence completed his 'Heinemann novel' and sent it to the publisher from Italy; only to be reminded very shortly that the outer circles of censorship were still very much alive. Heinemann wrote:

I feel that the book is unsatisfactory from several points of view;

not only because it lacks unity, without which a reader's interest
cannot be held, but more so because its want of reticence makes it
unfit, I fear, altogether for publication in England as things are. The
tyranny of the Libraries is such that a book far less out-spoken
would certainly be damned (and there is practically no market for
fiction outside of them).

There was conspicuous 'want of reticence' in Lawrence's reaction to
this. 'Why, why, why was I born an Englishman! – my cursed, rotten-
boned, pappy-hearted countrymen, *why* was I sent to *them*. . . . God,
how I hate them. . . . They've got white of egg in their veins, and
their spunk is that watery its a marvel they can breed.' As for Heinemann himself, 'may his name be used as a curse and an eternal
infamy' (*L*1: pp. 421–2).

From this point, Lawrence entrusted the novel to Edward Garnett,
reader for Duckworth. 'Anything that wants altering I will do', he
wrote (*L*1: p. 423), and did, at Garnett's suggestion; seeking reassurance particularly on the erotic aspect: 'Have I made those naked scenes
in Paul Morel tame enough? You can cut them if you like. Yet they
are so clean' (*L*1: p. 478). Even when dismayed by Garnett's intimation
that the novel would have to be cut, Lawrence accepted almost
meekly. 'I sit in sadness and grief after your letter. I daren't say
anything. All right, take out what you think necessary' (*L*1: p. 481).
But it is important to notice that Garnett's celebrated editing of *Sons
and Lovers* – sometimes compared to Pound's work on Eliot's *The Waste
Land* – was not an act of censorship. Mark Schorer, who prepared the
edited manuscript of the novel for facsimile reproduction, remarks:

> This drastic trimming by Garnett was motivated, examination of the
> deleted passages makes clear, not at all on moralistic grounds, as
> has been suggested by a critic or two who base their judgement on
> Lawrence's letters, but probably in order to reduce the manuscript
> to a length that was regarded as the maximum for a one-volume
> publication, and to make it a better novel.[7]

Duckworth himself did make some small cuts at proof stage, and may
have suggested more; we find Lawrence in March 1913 – only weeks
before publication – writing to Garnett as if past caring: 'I don't mind
if Duckworth crosses out a hundred shady pages in *Sons and Lovers*.
It's got to sell, I've got to live' (*L*1: p. 526). The truth is he was already
into his next novel and didn't want to be troubled any more by the
last one.

Yet, the fight for expression had to be endured. There was a scare
when *Sons and Lovers* was published, in that 'the libraries refused it
at first – then consented' or, as Lawrence wrote more pungently to

Ernest Collings, 'The damned prigs in the libraries and bookshops daren't handle me because they pretend they are delicate skinned and I am hot. May they fry in Hell' (*L2*: pp. 22, 47). This is the combative, contemptuous tone of all Lawrence's future dealings with his censors, as they are defined in the poem dedicated to them in *Pansies*:

> Censors are dead men
> set up to judge between life and death . . .
> And when the execution is performed
> you hear the sterterous, self-righteous heavy
>   breathing of the dead men,
> the censors, breathing with relief.[8]

The volume of short stories *The Prussian Officer* (1914) fell foul of the libraries, on the personal instruction (it appears) of Sir Jesse Boot himself. Lawrence has a half-amused letter on the subject, remarking 'I am booted out of my place as a popular novelist' (*L2*: p. 258). Whatever the tone, this censorship was actually very damaging to his prospects for survival as a writer in the troubled year 1915.

Ironically, the first mention we have of *The Rainbow* in Lawrence's correspondence is where he promises Garnett a new novel which will be 'absolutely impeccable – as far as morals go', only to admit two months later (in May 1913) that 'already it has fallen from grace' in this respect; 'I can only write what I feel pretty strongly about: and that, at the present, is the relations between men and women' (*L1*: pp. 526, 546). This problematic subject-matter is, of course, central to the finished novel. Two years (and several versions) later, when Lawrence was preparing the final manuscript for Methuen, he wrote to his agent, Pinker: 'I hope you are willing to fight for this novel . . . I'm afraid there are parts of it Methuen wont want to publish. He must. I will take out sentences and phrases, but I won't take out paragraphs or pages' (*L2*: p. 327). Lawrence did, in fact, make various alterations at Methuen's request, within these limits:

> I have cut out, as I said I would, all the *phrases* objected to. The passages and paragraphs marked I cannot alter. . . . There is nothing offensive in them. . . . And I can't cut them out, because they are living parts of an organic whole.

'Tell Methuen, he need not be afraid,' Lawrence continues sanguinely; 'I am a safe speculation for a publisher' (*L2*: pp. 369–70). Unfortunately this was never to be the case during Lawrence's lifetime.

The story of the prosecution and suppression of *The Rainbow* has been told many times, with some different interpretations or emphases.[9] It was two hostile reviews, by James Douglas in the *Star* and Clement Shorter in *Sphere*, that most probably brought the police to

Methuen's offices a month after the novel was published; certainly, these two reviews were later read out in court. (Lawrence was assured by Donald Carswell that he had 'a clear and complete case of libel' against the two critics in question: (*L2*: p. 462.) There is no evidence for Lawrence's own assertion that the prosecution was 'instigated by the National Purity League' (*L2*: p. 477), nor any conclusive evidence for the plausible suggestion that it might have had a political motive.[10] After all, Lawrence was very active at this time, alongside Bertrand Russell, in the unpopular anti-war movement; even his friend Cynthia Asquith confided (to her diary) of one of his essays published at this time: 'I am not sure that technically it doesn't amount to treason.'[11] And his German wife made him even more conspicuous to the authorities. The key factor – and the real reason why the case remains obscure, in that there was no trial to clarify the issues – is that the publishers made no attempt to defend either the novel or its author. They surrendered all copies to the police, and apologised in open court for having published it. Pinker's letter to the Society of Authors (who considered intervening on Lawrence's behalf) makes it plain that Methuen not only did nothing themselves but positively discouraged anyone else from taking up Lawrence's case: the directors 'felt very strongly that the matter should be hushed up'.[12] They were not totally successful in this design, in that Philip Morrell asked questions in Parliament concerning Lawrence's rights in the case; only to be told, however, that since the publishers had pleaded guilty there was nothing Lawrence could do. Meyers reminds us that therefore *The Rainbow* was never banned, since there was no trial; and furthermore, if there had been, there are indications that Lawrence may well have won the case.[13] This is mere hypothesis. The fact was that Lawrence had no novel to live on, and no future in England. 'I am not very much moved,' he wrote to Pinker after the seizure; 'I only curse them all, body and soul, root, branch, and leaf, to eternal damnation' (*L2*: p. 429).

Although we are concerned principally with Lawrence here, the point should be made that although there was no effective support for, or defence of, the novel the episode sent shock-waves through the literary establishment. Meyers notes that Pound

> wrote to friends in May 1916 that the suppression of *The Rainbow* had led to a panic among printers and created an oppressive wave of censorship: 'the printers have gone quite mad since the Lawrence fuss. . . . Something has got to be done or we'll all of us be suppressed, à la counter-reformation, dead and done for.'[14]

War fever had a lot to do with this situation; but when his paintings were censored in 1929 there was a similar susurrus of support, even from those who otherwise had little time for Lawrence. Writers and artists could at least recognise in the censor a common enemy.

Kinkead-Weekes concludes his account of the suppression of *The Rainbow* with the remark: 'It is impossible to exaggerate the effect on Lawrence himself, on his conception of his audience and therefore on the nature of his work, of the destruction of *The Rainbow* in the England of 1915.'[15] This is confirmed by the autobiographical note Lawrence supplied for a French publisher in 1928. A dozen years distant from the events themselves and, moreover, in the third person, Lawrence recalls their long-term effect on him:

> *The Rainbow* was suppressed for immorality – and the sense of detachment from the bourgeois world, the world which controls press, publication and all, became almost complete. He had no interest in it, no desire to be at one with it. Anyhow the suppression of *The Rainbow* had proved it impossible. Henceforth he put away any idea of 'success', of succeeding with the British bourgeois public, and stayed apart.[16]

Lawrence goes on to refer to the eventual publication (in America) of *Women in Love*, 'which every publisher for four years had refused to accept, because of *The Rainbow* scandal'. It is not possible to provide a detailed account here of Lawrence's four-year ordeal with *Women in Love*: four years when the novel languished, as it were, in the authorial birth canal.[17] One or two instances will serve. When Lawrence sent the nearly complete manuscript to Pinker in October 1916, he wrote: 'It is a terrible and horrible and wonderful novel. You will hate it and nobody will publish it. But there, these things are beyond us' (*L2*: p. 669). The prediction proved nearly true. It is a measure of the intractability of the problems involved that his friend Koteliansky actually proposed – in 1917! – that Lawrence should publish the novel in Russia (*L3*: p. 54). And on the eve of the English publication, Lawrence received a letter in these terms from Martin Secker:

> It seems to me that the decision we have to come to – or rather the decision you have to come to – about *Women in Love*, is whether you will aim at a full circulation, necessitating two or three excisions or paraphrases in the text, or whether it is to be printed as it stands, and to be sold only in booksellers' shops.

The ghost of Jesse Boot then reappears to give another kick: 'if we have to cut out the libraries, I shall only print 1500 copies', and Lawrence's advance will be reduced from one hundred pounds to fifty (*L3*: p. 647).

It was not only the pre-emptive fears of his publishers that delayed the publication of *Women in Love*. This novel, more than any other, incurred the wrath of Lawrence's former friends, who were enraged to find themselves (as they believed) unfavourably presented in its pages. Philip Morrell had defended Lawrence in the House in 1915; six months later, he threatened legal proceedings against him for the supposed portrait of Ottoline in the character Hermione.[18] Later, Philip Heseltine likewise threatened action for the account of Halliday and his relationship with 'Pussum'. The model in question was known as 'Puma'; Lawrence was forced to change the name to Minette, and (much to Lawrence's annoyance) Secker paid Heseltine fifty pounds in out-of-court damages (L4: pp. 113, 129). Nor was *Women in Love* Lawrence's only worry at this time. His letters bear witness to his persistent efforts to republish *The Rainbow* in England, without capitulating to the compromises proposed by different publishers. One stratagem was to smuggle the novel in the back door as Volume 1 of *Women in Love*: 'The Rainbow must appear as a new book' (L3: p. 459). All these efforts were frustrated, and it was not until 1926 that Secker dared to reissue the novel; ironically, reprinting not the original Methuen text but the American text published by Huebsch in November 1915, which was itself significantly expurgated.[19] It was not until the Penguin English Library edition of 1981 that Lawrence's original text was restored.

Meanwhile Chatto, concerned about the 'continuously sexual tone' of the poems in *Look We Have Come Through!* (a bizarre reaction to poems dedicated to a sexual relationship), demanded excisions from the volume (L3: pp. 145–8); and Secker insisted on the bowdlerisation of *The Lost Girl*. The editors of the third volume of Lawrence's letters summarise:

> He warned Lawrence that the lending libraries had refused to handle the book unless the accounts of the sexual encounter between Ciccio and Alvina were rewritten. Since the sale of 2000 copies was at stake, Secker urged Lawrence to comply. He did so and substituted a mutual version.
>
> (L3: p. 14)

The curious phrase 'a mutual version' sounds like something from an insurance policy, which is effectively what this was. And even Lawrence's plan to earn an honest penny by writing a history textbook ran into trouble. Less ambitious than H. G. Wells with his *History of the World*, Lawrence wrote his modest *Movements in European History* for Oxford University Press, but the press required Lawrence to disguise his authorship, which he did under the name Lawrence H. Davison. Implausibly, in 1925 the press negotiated an Irish edition to be taught in Catholic schools in the Free State; but only on condition that Lawrence removed 'every word of praise of Martin Luther, and any suggestion that any Pope may have erred' (*L5*: p. 324). Lawrence fumed at the surgery performed by Patrick O'Daly of the Irish publishing house:

> I'm sending the mauled *History* by this mail. When I went through it, I was half infuriated, and half amused. But if I'd had to go through it, personally, and make the decision merely from myself, I'd have sent those Irish b – s seven times to hell, before I'd have removed a single iota at their pencil stroke.
>
> (L5: p. 336)

In the last phase of his career, from the first version of *Lady Chatterley's Lover* to the posthumous essay written in its defence, Lawrence decided at last to confront the issue of censorship direct instead of compromising with the various agencies involved. Despite failing health, he advanced on several fronts simultaneously. His work on what he called 'the English novel' was closely involved with his rediscovery of painting; and the poems in *Pansies* are a kind of commentary on the world (the little world, the England) to which both were addressed. The different media combine in one final assault on the degenerate consciousness of that time; to be supported by the four powerful essays on literature, painting and pornography which form an integral part of Lawrence's last testament.[20] It is true that while Lawrence was working on his last novel, he had little thought of publishing it. He wrote to Secker in March 1927 (after completing the second version): 'I've finished my novel *Lady Chatterley's Lover*. . . . It's verbally terribly improper, but I don't think I shall alter it. I'll send it to you one of these days – am not keen, somehow, on letting it go out. What's the good of publishing things!' (*L5*: p. 655). But this reluctance to publish is something we can observe throughout his career; it had to do with his trials at the hands of the publishers themselves, and with his mistrust of *le grand public*. So Lawrence decided in this instance to take matters into his own hands, publishing and distributing his 'tender, phallic novel' privately.

Even this stratagem did not protect Lawrence from the filaments of censorship. He wrote to Catherine Carswell in January 1928: 'A woman in Florence said she'd type it – and she's done 5 chapters – now turned me down. Says she can't go any further, too indecent. Dirty bitch!'[21] To the offended typist herself, Nellie Morrison, Lawrence was kinder but no less firm, rehearsing the argument he was to use a dozen times in defence of the novel in the year to come:

> And remember, although you are on the side of the angels and the vast majority, I consider mine is the truly moral and religious position. You think I have pandered to the pornographic taste: I think

not. Every man to his own taste: every woman to her own distaste. But don't try to ride a moral horse: it could be nothing but a sorry ass.[22]

Although Aldous and Maria Huxley were keen supporters of Lawrence's venture, the sister-in-law Juliette was another reminder of the majority view. It was she, in scandalised reaction, who sarcastically suggested that Lawrence should call the novel 'John Thomas and Lady Jane'; and Lawrence became so keen on this idea, that it was only with great difficulty that he was talked out of it.[23]

There was to have been an expurgated version for the regular publishers; Lawrence was aware that without this there was no copyright, which would leave him more vulnerable to pirates. He worked on this for Secker and Knopf during March 1928; but in the end, significantly, he gave up the attempt; 'I might as well try to clip my own nose into shape with scissors. The book bleeds' (*Phoenix II*: p. 489). It was left to the two publishers to bring out a doctored version for themselves, in 1932. One of the advantages of private publication was that it obviated the sending of review copies, 'which might initiate a scandal at an early stage of the distribution'.[24] A similar calculation of the relative effectiveness of the censorship laws in the two countries led him to mail copies to the USA before posting the British orders: 'In this way there was no danger of news from Britain of the indecent character of the novel reaching the ears of the censor before the arrival of the books.'[25] In fact, the British operation was predictably inefficient; it was only 'belatedly, in mid-January [1929], the police began to confiscate copies of *LadyC* entering England. This scarcely mattered, since they were the last few copies.'[26] Unfortunately, though, the dragnet caught the manuscript of *Pansies* in the post. The police then visited the homes of many of Lawrence's friends, looking for copies of the book. It was not for nothing that Lawrence remarked later that the novel had cost him his friends; though he adds, in a jaundiced moment, 'it didn't matter because I never had any' (Nehls 3: p. 325).

The police may have been slow to act but the reviewers had somehow got hold of copies; and the general reaction was just as Lawrence had feared. Aldington describes a sheaf of reviews sent to Lawrence in Port-Clos in October 1928: 'I have never seen such an exhibition of vulgarity, spite, filth, and hatred as was contained in those innumerable diatribes' (Nehls 3: p. 253). The predictable contribution from John Bull is reprinted by Draper as a sample. The magazine doesn't even dare to quote from the book: '*Lady Chatterley's Lover* defies reproduction in any manner whatsoever that would convey to our readers the abysm of filth into which Mr D H Lawrence has descended.'[27] However, Draper is also able to print half a dozen more sympathetic reviews, among them one from V. S. Pritchett which specifically takes up the theme of censorship:

> Because of its irrelevant issues censorship has not only made it difficult to see Lawrence whole and to put all these silly charges of pornography in their place, but it has artfully succeeded in making this question seem the most important one. His doctrine is not censored: it is his dramatization of it in his prophetic art which is made to suffer.[28]

And as we shall see, it was a further stage in the evolution of the 'issue of censorship' that brought *Lady Chatterley's Lover* into the dock in 1960.

It was the seizure of the *Pansies* manuscript that brought Lawrence again before the House.

> Aldous Huxley . . . wrote to his friend St John Hutchinson, a barrister and parliamentary candidate with contacts in the House of Commons, who already knew Lawrence from the war years. Hutchinson reported that he had several members willing to raise the matter in the House, and that they might even get Ramsay MacDonald . . . to do it. In the event a question to the Home Secretary was tabled by Ellen Wilkinson. Sir William Joynson-Hicks ['Jix'] said that he had ordered the MSS. to be kept for two months to give the author an opportunity to establish that they did not contain indecent matter. He assured the House that they did.[29]

Keith Sagar concludes his account of this episode by suggesting that 'rather than quarrel with Secker about proposed omissions and deletions, Lawrence would let Secker do as he liked and bring out his own unexpurgated edition with Charlie Lahr'. But this is not the spirit of Lawrence's letters to Secker in April 1929. 'Don't go and be so squeamish about the Pansies,' he tells him; 'I specially don't want you to make just a little bourgeois book of the Pansies. I want you to put in *all* the poems that won't expose you to Jix. . . . I want every poem included that is not open to legal attack'; and again,'

> My 'expurgation' was merely for the post. Do you think I would haul down my flag to such an extent in front of the public, for all the Jixes in Christendom? Not I. . . . That's outjixing Jix . . . make the Pansies into a good, 'innocuous', bourgeois little book I will not, and you shall not.[30]

Lawrence was more than prepared, then, to fight for the integrity of his poems, even in the official edition. Nevertheless, thirteen were omitted.

Not only do many of the poems themselves serve as commentary on the censor-culture Lawrence so despised, and the only-too-scrutable ways of the 'censor-moron', but Lawrence wrote in January 1929 an introduction to the uncensored private edition (published in August) which is the second of the four important essays composed in that year in response to his (or rather, our) cultural predicament. This essay contains a defence of the use of 'obscene words' that makes it directly relevant to *Lady Chatterley's Lover*. Lawrence's understanding of obscenity is distinctly practical: 'Obscene means today that the policeman thinks he has a right to arrest you, nothing else.' He argues, persuasively, that censoring words merely perpetuates our sickness: 'it is the mind which is the Augean stables, not language.' Because the mind 'hates certain parts of the body', it makes scapegoats of the words for them, and 'pelts them out of the consciousness with filth, and there they hover, never dying, never dead . . . haunting the margins of the consciousness like jackals or hyenas' (*Phoenix*: pp. 280–1).

The last act of the censor during Lawrence's lifetime was directed at his paintings, thirteen of which were seized while on exhibition at the Warren Gallery in July 1929.[31] The exhibition attracted some of the wrong kind of publicity because of Lawrence's reputation as a writer. On 17 June the *Daily Express* announced: 'D H Lawrence as Painter/ Censored Novelist's Intimate Nudes.' Also, there was one unfavourable review by Paul Konody, respected art critic of the Rothermere Press; whose neat formula for Lawrence's transgression proved only too quotable: 'This author-artist, weary, perhaps, of being subtly misbehaved in print, has elected to come straight to the point, and is frankly disgusting in paint' (*The Observer*, 16 June 1929). But the police raid on 5 July was in response to all the 1857 Obscene Publications Act required: one complaint brought by a 'common informer'. Extraordinarily, the informer in this case (whose identity was not revealed in court) was the publisher Grant Richards, founder of the World's Classics library. Richards wrote: 'Not as a joke but with a due sense of responsibility, I suggest that you should pay a visit to the Warren Gallery, 39A Maddox Street, and examine the paintings there exhibited.'[32] The police duly paid their visit, and adjudged thirteen of the paintings obscene by the rule of the thumb that pubic hair was represented in them. The law proved its asininity by impounding some pictures by Blake at the same time – providing an important line of defence (or at least, distraction) at the trial. This defence was to centre on the arbitrariness and inappropriateness of the exercise of the Obscene Publications Act in such a case. Geoffrey Scott wrote to Arnold Bennett to enlist support:

> The destruction or survival of the Lawrence pictures lies entirely at the discretion of Mr. Justice Mead. Quite apart from any particular

question as to the merit of Lawrence as an artist, this obviously raises a point of principle of the first importance. The lawyers say the action is entirely without precedent. The methods employed are those designed for the exculpation of the indecent postcard trade, and no such raid has previously been executed on the work of a serious man shown at a serious gallery.

(Nehls 3: p. 361)

The trial took place at Bow Street on 8 August, before the 80-year-old Justice Mead and with Harold Muskett as prosecutor – the man who had prosecuted *The Rainbow* fourteen years before. The obduracy of the magistrate looked dangerous, until Muskett unpredictably accepted the compromise solution worked out by Dorothy Warren's solicitors, whereby the gallery would give an undertaking that the paintings would not be exhibited again in England and they would then be restored to the owner. This solution was in accordance with Lawrence's instructions in a letter of 14 July:

> I want you to accept the compromise. I do not want my pictures to be burned, under any circumstances or for any cause. The law, of course, must be altered – it is blatantly obvious. Why burn my pictures to prove it? There is something sacred to me about my pictures, and I will not have them burnt, for all the liberty of England.

(Nehls 3: p. 358)

When the decision of the court was communicated to him, by telegram, Lawrence wrote to Orioli: 'I had a telegram to say: Pictures to be returned, books to be burned. Let them burn their own balls, the fools. This has given me a great sickness of England. I begin to loathe my "nice" fellow-countrymen.'[33] But it was nearer the end than the beginning of this antagonism.

The books to be burned were reproductions of the paintings published by the Mandrake Press (Lawrence saw the name as an ill omen). For this volume Lawrence had written his first essay on art and consciousness, accusing English painters of being out of touch with the body and hailing Cézanne as a revolutionary artist. The seizure of his paintings, on top of his earlier problems with the novel and the poems, provoked Lawrence to write the third of these remarkable analyses, 'Pornography and obscenity' (*Phoenix*: pp. 170–87). The reference to his own case only comes as an afterthought, at the end of the essay: one instance of the 'condition of idiocy' to which we as a nation are reduced by our 'morality' (p. 187). The present laws on pornography are the evident mechanisms of ignorance, fear and prejudice; 'and never was the pornographical appetite stronger than it is today. It is a sign of a diseased condition of the body politic.' The way to treat the disease 'is to come out into the open with sex and sex stimulus'; but our society has not the courage, preferring to degrade sex into a 'dirty little secret', and setting up 'the vicious circle of masturbation and self-consciousness' (p. 183). If we are happy with this state of affairs, says Lawrence, 'then the existing forms of censorship are justified' (p. 179); any other construction reveals them as either criminal or absurd. Lawrence's essay is a direct response not only to Jix's actions, but also to his arguments in the pamphlet *Do We Need a Censor?* (published, ironically, in the same Faber series as Lawrence's own). Lawrence actually quotes Viscount Brentford's arguments to prove that 'the law is a mere figment' (p. 186), and returns the charge of pornography to where it properly belongs, to dirty postcards, disgusting books, smoking-room stories, and to the all-licensed media: 'In the social world, in the press, in literature, film, theatre, wireless, everywhere purity and the dirty little secret reign supreme' (pp. 175, 182–3). Lawrence would not, however, be mistaken for a libertarian in such matters; as he is careful to insist, 'even I would censor real pornography, rigorously' (p. 175).

Another important statement on censorship occurs in the letter Lawrence wrote to Morris Ernst in November 1928, while engaged in the necessarily clandestine distribution of *Lady Chatterley's Lover*. Ernst had sent Lawrence a copy of his book on censorship, *To The Pure* (1928). Lawrence replied enthusiastically. Ernst's book, he wrote, suggested an image of social man like some primitive ape, 'fumbling gropingly and menacingly for something he is afraid of, but he doesn't know what it is'. This is the 'weird reactionary of the ageless censor-animal', which must be kept chained up; for 'censorship is one of the lower and debasing activities of social man'. Lawrence goes on to provide a succinct statement of his own views:

> Myself, I believe censorship helps nobody; and hurts many. . . . Our civilization cannot afford to let the censor-moron loose. The censor-moron does not really hate anything except the living and growing human consciousness. It is our developing and extending consciousness that he threatens – and our consciousness in its newest, most sensitive activity, its vital growth. To arrest and circumscribe the vital consciousness is to produce morons, and none but a moron would wish to do it.

'Print this letter if you like,' he tells Ernst, 'or any bit of it'; and as if recognising the opportunity, continues with his counter-credo:

> I believe in the living extending consciousness of man. I believe the consciousness of man has now to embrace the emotions and

passions of sex, and the deep effects of human physical contact. This is the glimmering edge of our awareness and the field of our understanding, in the endless business of knowing ourselves. And no censor must or shall or even really can interfere.[34]

Lawrence returns momentarily to the theme of obscenity in the first version of 'A Propos of Lady Chatterley's Lover', 'My skirmish with Jolly Roger', again rebuking the Home Secretary, who, 'himself growing elderly, is most loudly demanding and enforcing a mealy-mouthed silence about sexual matters' (Phoenix II: p. 491).

Exactly one week after Lawrence's death in March, a diligent servant of the Crown at the Home Office proposed reprosecuting The Rainbow (which had been republished in England – albeit expurgated – in 1926). He was overruled; and the stalemate with the censor persisted for another thirty years. In 1932, contradicting Lawrence's last instructions, Martin Secker published an expurgated version of Lady Chatterley's Lover. Allen Lane wanted to bring out an unexpurgated edition in 1950, alongside the other works by Lawrence published by Penguin that year; but, as he attested at the trial in 1960, he knew they were in no position to defend the novel from the prosecution which would inevitably have followed at that time. Everything changed with the introduction of the Obscene Publications Act in 1959. The new Act was the work of 'an action committee of publishers, writers, booksellers, and printers',[35] convened in the first instance by the Society of Authors (behaving more courageously than in 1915) in response to a series of arbitrary prosecutions. The express purpose of the Act was to provide a distinction sustainable in law between erotic literature and commercial pornography. Understandably, the lately knighted Allen Lane saw the adoption of the Act as offering him the opportunity, at long last, of publishing Lady Chatterley's Lover unexpurgated in Britain. He might also have taken encouragement from the fact that the full text of the novel had survived a court case in America the year before.

It came as a surprise to many that the Director of Public Prosecutions decided to prosecute the novel under the new Act. (One of its sponsors, Roy Jenkins, began to say as much while giving evidence, before being ruled out of order by the judge.) Moreover, there was a good deal of nervousness before the trial – set up as a 'test case'. A verdict against Penguin Books would have left things as they were under the 1857 Act: or worse, since the attempted reform would have failed. With hindsight, the prosecution (even with the judge on their side) clearly had an uphill case to persuade the jury of nine men and three women of both the propositions, that Lady Chatterley's Lover was obscene – that it tended to deprave and corrupt – and that it was not literature. The defence case was much better researched and presented than that of the prosecution; and Mervyn Griffith-Jones's celebrated own goals, concerning the reading habits of one's servants and the recollection of one's Greek, made any other verdict than acquittal difficult to conceive. The outcome might well have been different if the book on trial had been *Lolita* or *The Story of O*. With the snowball effect working, for once, in favour of freedom, it became increasingly difficult to obtain convictions of any work for obscenity: especially after the disreputable convictions (later quashed on appeal) of *IT*, *OZ* and *Nasty Tales* in the early 1970s, and the conviction in 1977 of twelve officers of the Obscene Publications Squad for accepting protection money.[36] From this point on, the role of censor came more and more to be assumed by individuals and pressure groups (invoking the law or other sanctions), rather than by the law itself. In his book *The Cost of Free Speech* (1990), Simon Lee has described this new situation in a chapter significantly entitled 'The privatization of censorship'.[37]

Is it ironic, therefore, as many maintain, that Lawrence's novel, cocooned for thirty years, became at last the butterfly that heralded the sexual liberation of Albion? Philip Larkin's poem 'Annus Mirabilis' has become proverbial: sexual intercourse began in 1963, between the end of the *Chatterley* ban and the Beatles' first LP,[38] and so we should perhaps let Larkin also speak for another point of view: as he did in an address at the University of Nottingham Library in 1980, opening an exhibition of Lawrence manuscripts. Larkin refers here to 'the postwar Penguin Lawrence explosion', and the trial of *Lady Chatterley's Lover*, 'which unwittingly installed Lawrence as something like the high priest of the permissive society, a canonization he would certainly have viewed with the utmost repugnance'.[39] Well, not so much repugnance as Larkin himself would have felt, I suspect. Though Lawrence did hate the trivialising of sex, sex as entertainment, I believe he hated the hypocritical legacy of the nineteenth century even more.

We cannot leave the story there, as if brought to a happy ending in the 1960s. Although now monumentally endorsed, beyond the powers of any censor, in the Cambridge edition, Lawrence's work inevitably retains its power to disturb, to challenge assumptions, to stimulate disagreement and resistance. *Lady Chatterley's Lover* actually featured in BBC Radio 4's 'Book at Bedtime' in 1990; but this novel in particular continues to be controversial. Simon Lee makes a point made by Lawrence himself in the 'Pornography and obscenity' essay, that our criteria of what is acceptable are always changing: but here Lawrence is presented as a victim of the shift in attitude:

Some liberals have remained caught in a 1950s time warp, still arguing as though the great crusade was to publish *Lady Chatterley's*

Lover. Life has moved on, to the point that D H Lawrence's novel is sometimes criticized as sexist exploitation by some of those who once championed its publication.[40]

An extreme of this revisionism is evident in a recent review of Lawrence by Tom Paulin in the *Times Literary Supplement.* Leaving Griffith-Jones a long way behind in the art of excoriation, Paulin describes *Lady Chatterley's Lover* as a 'racist tract which exults in male violence', a 'specimen of sadistic porn' containing 'many viciously obscene passages', and suggests there is 'good cause for prosecuting the novel under the Race Relations Act'.[41] Let us hope today's jury (however composed) would be no more impressed by such an intemperate and newly ignorant attack than were the nine men and three women on whose opinions the outcome of the original trial depended. Whether the charge was sex itself in 1930, adultery in 1960 or racism/sexism in 1990, the arguments for suppression are equally disreputable; and it is clear that literature, and Lawrence, still need our vigilance against the malice and imbecility of censors old and new.[42]

NOTES

1 *Phoenix: the Posthumous Papers of D. H. Lawrence,* ed. E. D. McDonald, London, Heinemann, 1936, p. 578. Further references to this and to *Phoenix II,* ed. W. R. and H. T. Moore, London, Heinemann, 1968, are included parenthetically in the text.

2 *The Letters of D. H. Lawrence,* ed. J. T. Boulton *et al.,* Cambridge, Cambridge University Press, 1979, vol. 2, p. 555. All references to Lawrence's letters (up to March 1927), are to the five volumes so far published in this edition, in the form (L2: p. 555).

3 See J. Worthen, *D. H. Lawrence: a Literary Life,* London, Macmillan, 1989; esp. chs 5, 6.

4 Cited by H. T. Moore, *The Priest of Love: a Life of D. H. Lawrence,* 1974, rev. edn 1976, Harmondsworth, Penguin, p. 567. All subsequent references to this work (abbreviated to *PL*) are included parenthetically in the text.

5 K. Sagar, *The Life of D. H. Lawrence,* London, Eyre Methuen, 1980, pp. 227, 231–2.

6 R. P. Draper (ed.), *D. H. Lawrence: the Critical Heritage,* London, Routledge, 1970, pp. 40–3.

7 M. Schorer (ed.), *D. H. Lawrence's 'Sons and Lovers': a facsimile of the manuscript,* Berkeley, University of California Press, 1977, p. 4.

8 V. de Sola Pinto and W. Roberts (eds), *The Complete Poems of D. H. Lawrence,* London, Heinemann, 1964, p. 528.

9 See Moore, *PL,* pp. 305–14; E. Nehls, *A Composite Biography of D. H. Lawrence,* 3 vols, Madison, University of Wisconsin Press, 1957–9, vol. 1, pp. 328–36; J. Carter, 'The Rainbow prosecution', *Times Literary Supplement,* 27 February 1969, p. 216; E. Delavenay, *D. H. Lawrence: the Man and his Work,* London, Heinemann, 1972, pp. 235–42; P. Delaney, *D. H. Lawrence's Nightmare,* Brighton, Harvester, 1978, pp. 155–67; and, more recently, M. Kinkead-Weekes (ed.), Introduction to *The Rainbow,* Cambridge, Cambridge

University Press, 1989, pp. xlv–li; Worthen, *D. H. Lawrence: a Literary Life*, pp. 41–9; J. Meyers, *D. H. Lawrence: a Biography*, London, Macmillan, 1990, pp. 182–96. Delaney records the 'legend . . . passed down in the Methuen office' that seized copies of *The Rainbow* 'were burned by the public hangman outside the Royal Exchange' (p. 162).

10 'May Sinclair . . . used to say that the suppression was partly political. As Aldington remembers it, the prosecution seems to have gone so far as to suggest that the novel's implied criticisms of imperialism and the Boer War had begun to hamper recruiting. . . . Another friend of Lawrence's, Gilbert Canaan, suggested in a New York newspaper in 1920 that war hysteria probably contributed to the suppression of *The Rainbow*', H. T. Moore, 'Introduction: D. H. Lawrence and the "Censor-Morons' "', *Sex, Literature, and Censorship* [a collection of Lawrence's essays on the subject], New York, Twayne, 1953, pp. 6–7. See also the examination of the available evidence in Delavenay, *D. H. Lawrence*, pp. 232–42; and the sceptical verdict in Delaney, *D. H. Lawrence's Nightmare*, p. 158.

11 A diary entry quoted in Meyers, *D. H. Lawrence*, p. 195.

12 Quoted by Carter, 'The Rainbow prosecution', p. 216.

13 Meyers, *D. H. Lawrence*, pp. 190–4.

14 ibid., p. 190.

15 *The Rainbow*, ed. Kinkead-Weekes, p. li.

16 Nehls, *A Composite Biography*, vol. 3, p. 234. Subsequent references to Nehls are included parenthetically in the text.

17 See the Introduction to the Cambridge edition of the novel, eds D. Farmer, L. Vasey and J. Worthen, 1987.

18 Delaney, *D. H. Lawrence's Nightmare*, pp. 272–7.

19 *The Rainbow*, ed. Kinkead-Weekes, pp. lviii–lx.

20 Typically for Lawrence, three of these essays exist in two versions. Brief details of the essays (all written between December 1928 and October 1929) are as follows:

  i (a) 'Introduction to pictures', *Phoenix*, pp. 765–71;
      (b) 'Introduction to these paintings', *Phoenix*, pp. 551–84;
  ii (a) 'Introduction to *Pansies*' [private edition], *Phoenix*, pp. 279–82;
      (b) 'Foreword to *Pansies*' [trade edition], *Collected Poems*, vol. I, pp. 423–4;
  iii 'Pornography and obscenity', *Phoenix*, pp. 170–87;
  iv (a) 'My skirmish with Jolly Roger' [being pages 487–92 of:]
      (b) 'A Propos of *Lady Chatterley's Lover*', *Phoenix II*, pp. 487–515.

21 *The Collected Letters of D. H. Lawrence*, ed. H. T. Moore, London, Heinemann, 1962, vol. 2, p. 1033.

22 ibid., p. 1032.

23 D. Britton, *'Lady Chatterley': the Making of the Novel*, London, Unwin Hyman, 1988, p. 259.

24 ibid., p. 262.

25 ibid.

26 Sagar, *The Life of D. H. Lawrence*, p. 231.

27 Draper (ed.), *D. H. Lawrence: the Critical Heritage*, p. 279.

28 ibid., p. 288.

29 Sagar, *The Life of D. H. Lawrence*, p. 231.

30 *Letters from D. H. Lawrence to Martin Secker*, privately printed, 1970, pp. 117–19.

31 The fullest account of this episode is the memoir by Philip Trotter (husband of the owner of the gallery, Dorothy Warren) which appears in Nehls, *A Composite Biography*, vol. 3, pp. 326–90. This includes details of the exhibition itself, criticism of the paintings (informed and uninformed), the story of the police raid (on 5 July), the court proceedings (on 8 August), and various newspaper reports; interspersed with letters from Lawrence, Frieda and others.
32 Meyers, *D. H. Lawrence*, p. 369.
33 Moore (ed.), *Letters*, vol. 2, p. 1176.
34 ibid., p. 1099.
35 C. H. Rolph (ed.), *The Trial of Lady Chatterley*, Harmondsworth, Penguin, reissued with a Foreword 1990, p. 3.
36 ibid., Foreword by G. Robertson QC, p. xx.
37 S. Lee, *The Cost of Free Speech*, London, Faber, 1990.
38 P. Larkin, *Collected Poems*, London, Faber, 1988, p. 167.
39 *Times Literary Supplement*, 13 June 1980, p. 671.
40 Lee, *The Cost of Free Speech*, p. 36.
41 *Times Literary Supplement*, 6 July 1990, p. 773.
42 It is worth recording the latest legal development. A programme on Lawrence's paintings, *Lost Lawrence*, produced and directed by Michael Jones, was broadcast by Channel 4 Television on 12 March 1991. The makers of the programme enquired of the government as to the status of the 1929 ban on the paintings, and were able to report that

> the Home Office minister John Patten has formally confirmed that the Government regards the ban as no longer having any legal force; and the Customs and Excise has given a written undertaking not to seize any of the paintings now in Taos if they are bought and imported into Britain.

Chapter 15

The treatment of homosexuality and *The Well of Loneliness*

Katrina Rolley

'Why am I as I am – and what am I?'[1] For decades men and women who experience homosexual desire have asked themselves this. Underlying the seemingly infinite number of questions concerning the aetiology of homosexuality is one fundamental opposition – that of nature versus nurture – and bound up with this opposition are the questions of responsibility and treatment. This issue lies at the centre of any rationalisation of censorship and homosexuality – as the debates around Section 28 of the Local Authorities Act (1988) demonstrated. In 1928 the publication of Radclyffe Hall's *The Well of Loneliness* caused the same questions to be asked. Radclyffe Hall was unequivocal about the propagandist nature of *The Well*; however, her stated aim was to promote an understanding of the 'true' nature of the homosexual, not homosexuality itself. Hall's understanding of homosexuality came, primarily, from the work of Havelock Ellis who defined 'inversion' as 'congenital', and who perceived the female invert as a male mind trapped within a female body. This description of the aetiology of homosexuality was integral to Hall's defence of her novel:

> I claim emphatically that the true invert is born and not made. . . .
> Only when this fact is fully grasped can we hope for the exercise
> of that charitable help and compassion that will assist inverts to
> give of their best and contribute to the good of the whole.[2]

As congenital inversion was a part of the body corporeal so congenital inverts were a part of the body politic; both conditions were 'natural', according to Hall, and needed to be recognised and accepted as such to ensure the health of the bodies they inhabited.

James Douglas, author of the initial article calling for suppression of *The Well*, was equally convinced that 'these moral derelicts . . . are damned because they choose to be damned, not because they are doomed from the beginning'. Hall's novel was, therefore, especially dangerous as 'a seductive and insidious piece of special pleading'.[3] If inversion was actually perversion, a suggestive illness propagated by publicity, it could best be prevented by silence. Lord Desart subscribed to this rationale when he opposed the 1921 attempt to legislate against lesbianism on the grounds that it would 'tell the whole world that there is such an offence'; whilst his colleague Lord Birkenhead added that 'of every thousand women . . . 999 have never even heard whisper of these practices. Among all these . . . the taint of this noxious and horrible suspicion is to be imparted?'[4] Once this 'suspicion' took hold of the mind and produced somatic symptoms, however, more drastic measures were required if the infection's progress through the body were to be checked. Douglas claimed:

> I have seen the plague stalking shamelessly through great social assemblies. I have heard it whispered about . . . [and] thrust upon healthy and innocent minds. The contagion cannot be escaped. It pervades our social life.
>
> What, then, is to be done? The book must at once be withdrawn. I hope the author and the publishers will realise that they have made a grave mistake, and will without delay do all in their power to repair it.
>
> If they hesitate to do so, the book must be suppressed by process of law.[5]

In response to this call for the suppression of *The Well* the publishers, Jonathan Cape, voluntarily submitted a copy to the Home Office for approval. The Home Secretary subsequently advised Cape to cease publication or face legal proceedings for obscenity; and Cape complied. However, the telegram instructing the printers to cancel the third edition of *The Well* also requested the moulds of the type be made. These were sent to Paris where the Pegasus Press commenced publication of 'a replica of the original London edition . . . without the alteration of so much as a comma'. So, in little over a month after the book's initial suppression, 'a steady flow of copies began crossing the Channel'.[6]

The ensuing trial of Jonathan Cape and the condemnation of *The Well* as an obscene libel further publicised the novel which, according to Una Troubridge (Hall's lover), 'had sold over 7,500 copies outside America by the end of 1928, 4,000 of these since James Douglas's attack on the book'.[7] As a correspondent to *Time and Tide* noted:

> Since the first announcement of the law-suit in the Press, the daily newspapers have been filled with nauseous details, discussions and suggestions far more harmful than anything in the well-written book itself. . . . After reading the final summing-up, I defy any young girl or boy to remain ignorant of certain facts which ordinarily would never have come to their notice.[8]

As James Douglas discovered, whatever the origin of homosexuality, any cure which addressed merely the symptoms of this condition was bound to failure. Symptoms thus suppressed inevitably return, in different guise and greater numbers, and the trial of *The Well* ensured inversion a prominent place within the public consciousness whilst the attempted repression of copies of the novel only caused them further to multiply within the public body.

Such paradoxical productivity of censorship has been identified by Michel Foucault, who writes:

> The seventeenth century was the beginning of an age of repression emblematic of what we call the bourgeois societies. . . . Calling sex by its name thereafter became more difficult and more costly. As if in order to gain mastery over it in reality, it had first been necessary to subjugate it at the level of language. . . . [Whilst] there was an expurgation . . . of the authorized vocabulary . . . at the level of discourses and their domains . . . the opposite phenomenon occurred. There was a steady proliferation of discourses concerned with sex . . . a discursive ferment that gathered momentum from the eighteenth century onward.[9]

According to Foucault, of course, this phenomenon was no chance consequence of censorship but the very means by which control was maintained. Hall, in her determination to 'smash the conspiracy of silence'[10] and call sexual inversion by its name, added her voice to this 'proliferation', whilst the subsequent censoring of this voice bred its own 'discursive ferment'.

Symptoms of repression were not merely grafted onto *The Well* as a part of its post-publication history. The novel was conceived in response to censorship, is structured around censorship, and its text and characters embody the consequences of censorship. Hall felt she had 'written the life of a woman [Stephen Gordon] who is a born invert' with 'sincerity and truth', refusing 'to camouflage in any way',[11] but her text rarely mentions inversion by name, and sex remains largely theory rather than practice: the physical consummation of Stephen and Mary's love is reduced to the now immortal line 'and that night they were not divided' (p. 316). Sex and inversion need not be named *within The Well*, however, because they *are The Well*; they are as integral to the body of the text as they are to the body of Stephen Gordon. Foucault writes, with regard to the evolution of the Catholic pastoral:

> According to the new pastoral, sex must not be named imprudently, but its aspects, its correlations, and its effects must be pursued down to their slenderest ramifications . . . everything had to be

told. A twofold evolution tended to make the flesh into the root of all evil, shifting the most important moment of transgression from the act itself to the stirrings . . . of desire. For this was an evil that afflicted the whole man, and in the most secret of forms.[12]

Hall catalogues the manifold indicators of Stephen Gordon's inversion – an affliction of 'the whole [wo]man' rooted in the flesh – and documents her heroine's 'stirrings of desire' with an attention to detail similar to that demanded by this pastoral:

'Examine diligently . . . all the faculties of your soul. . . . Examine with precision all your senses as well. . . . Examine . . . all your thoughts, every word you speak, and all your actions. . . . And do not think that in so sensitive and perilous a matter as this, there is anything trivial or insignificant.'[13]

Censorship results in proliferation, and whilst sex and inversion are expurgated from the 'authorised vocabulary' of *The Well*, 'at the level of discourses' they dominate the novel.

The text of *The Well*, which thus embodies unconscious censorship, was also subject to a more deliberate authorial expurgation. All writing is built on selective censorship: which thoughts, themes, impulses and explanations are to be pursued, which to be suppressed? Hall prioritised Ellis's understanding of inversion, thereby suppressing the suggestion that environment played a part in the invert's genesis. However, like a laboratory-tested drug which performs differently in the body, theory is difficult to sustain in practice and, in writing *The Well*, Hall was attempting to theorise two lives: Stephen Mary Olive Gordon's and Marguerite Radclyffe Hall's.

Whilst it is important to avoid conflating Hall and Gordon it was the former's 'absolute conviction' that *The Well* 'could only be written by a sexual invert, who alone could be qualified by personal knowledge and experience to speak on behalf of a misunderstood and misjudged minority',[14] and Hall demonstrably drew on her own life when writing Gordon's. Hall saw herself, her novel and her heroine as champions of the oppressed: examples to other inverts and society as a whole. To sustain her theorising of her own perceived congenital inversion Hall rewrote her past and censored her present. She had, for example, an early portrait of herself repainted so as to appear more boyish, and Una Troubridge's *The Life and Death of Radclyffe Hall* (1961) is clearly the 'authorised' version.[15]

Troubridge's biography contains many echoes from *The Well* and both books exhibit the ambiguities integral to life, if not theory. According to Hall, Stephen's birth is, like an earlier nativity, preordained: 'Man proposes – God disposes, and so it happened that on

Christmas Eve, Anna Gordon was delivered of a daughter' (p. 9). Sir Philip Gordon wanted a son. God gave him a congenital invert; but it is easy for the reader to perceive Stephen's temporal and spiritual fathers as equally responsible for her creation:

> Sir Philip never knew how much he longed for a son until . . . his wife conceived of a child. . . . It never seemed to cross his mind . . . that Anna might . . . give him a daughter; he saw her only as a mother of sons. . . . He christened the unborn infant Stephen.
>
> (p. 8)

'Stephen', named after the saint. Thus when 'Anna Gordon held her child to her breast . . . she grieved while it drank, because of her man who had longed so much for a son', whilst Sir Philip insisted on calling the infant Stephen, since 'We've called her Stephen so long . . . that I really can't see why we shouldn't go on' (p. 9).

Any girl named Stephen was likely to feel different from her peers, especially if she were also allowed to ride astride, to learn fencing and gymnastics and, at the onset of adolescence, she hears her father say:

> 'I've considered this matter of your education. I want you to have the same education, the same advantages as I'd give to my son. . . .'
>
> 'But I'm not your son, Father,' she said very slowly . . .
>
> 'You're all the son that I've got,' he told her . . . 'and in many respects you're like me. I've brought you up very differently from most girls . . . look at Violet Antrim. . . . But you've now got to prove that my judgement's been sound. . . . I love you so much that you can't disappoint me.'
>
> (pp. 58–9)

Violet Antrim, 'that small, flabby lump who squealed if you pinched her' (p. 38), is the mean against which Stephen's deviation is measured: ' "Dear me," remarked her hostess, "you are a great girl; why your feet must be double the size of Violet's!" ' (p. 47). Violet is the purely feminine girl/woman but, whilst rejecting the role of nurture in the development of the invert, Hall admits that Violet's femininity has as much to do with nurture as with nature:

> Violet was already full of feminine poses; she loved dolls, but not quite so much as she pretended. People said: 'Look at Violet, she's like a little mother; it's so touching to see that instinct in a child!' Then Violet would become still more touching.
>
> (p. 45)

In writing and life, Hall suppressed the suggestion that the 'true invert' might be made, not born. This interpretation of Hall's text makes Stephen's unusual education and identification with her father the *consequence* – not the *cause* – of her inversion and of Sir Philip's early perception and sympathetic treatment of his daughter's condition. It is, however, possible to reverse this argument and to see Stephen Gordon as the conjunction of her father's will for a boy and the 'natural' conception of a girl: a male mind within a female body. Hall may have amputated 'nurture' from the body of her text but pains from the phantom limb continue to be felt by the reader.

State- and self-censorship were integral to the conception, pre- and post-natal life of *The Well;* however, whilst censorship deforms the novel's body and biography, it is also the text's thematic skeleton. Hall's polemic identifies censorship as the cause, not the cure, of perversion: 'persecution was always a hideous thing,' she writes, 'breeding hideous thoughts – and such thoughts were dangerous' (p. 413).

The Well traces Stephen Gordon's life from conception to martyrdom (through the self-inflicted loss of her partner, Mary Llewellyn). The novel takes the form of a physical, mental and spiritual journey with Stephen as both pilgrim and saint, redeemed and redeemer. Hall's writing style is deliberately archaic. She continually refers to religious texts, especially the Bible, and the novel's form and content are reminiscent of the Sorrowful Mysteries of the Rosary: a series of significant episodes punctuated by moments of crisis and revelation. The impetus behind Stephen's pilgrimage is the search for enlightenment, articulacy and a unified identity. Her initial quest for self-knowledge takes place in the Eden of Morton Hall from which she is expelled after discovering the nature of her 'difference': she falls in love with Angela Crossby and reads Krafft-Ebing's work on sexual inversion. This enlightenment is central (literally) to the novel, after which Stephen seeks self- and social acceptance. The prime impediment to this pilgrim's progress in censorship.

As a congenital invert Stephen is 'as much a part of . . . nature as anyone else' (p. 153). She loves nature and her emotions are attuned to it: it is springtime when 'Stephen first became conscious of an urgent necessity to love', and her 'childish perceptions' subsequently 'quickened' with that season (pp. 13, 20). However, Stephen's incomprehension of her inversion divides her from nature:

> She tried to tread softly for she felt apologetic, she and her troubles were there [in the garden] as intruders; their presence disturbed this strange hush of communion. . . . A mysterious and wonderful thing this oneness, pregnant with comfort could she know its true meaning – she felt this somewhere deep down in herself, but try as she would her mind could not grasp it.
>
> (pp. 100–1)

It is society's censorship of knowledge which perverts Stephen's relationship with nature. As an 'intersex', however, her relationship with culture – which acknowledges only heterosexual men and women – is fundamentally problematic. As cultural discourses make evident, Stephen does not fit – as child or woman:

> Sometimes Anna would drive Stephen into Great Malvern. . . . Stephen loathed these excursions . . . but she bore it with them because of the honour . . . she felt . . . when escorting her mother. . . .
>   Stephen . . . would look right and left for imaginary traffic, slipping a hand under Anna's elbow.
>   'Come with me,' she would order, 'and take care of the puddles, 'cause you might get your feet wet – hold on by me, Mother!'
>   Anna would feel the small hand at her elbow, and would think that the fingers were curiously strong . . . like Sir Philip's and this always vaguely displeased her.
>
> (pp. 29–30)

Stephen's behaviour is inappropriate, as are her emotions: 'What was she, what manner of curious creature, to have been so repelled by a lover like Martin' (p. 98), but to take 'Angela into her arms' instead? 'Normal' beings, who have a place within culture, sense this difference, are confounded by it and in ignorance call it unnatural:

> Then Anna began to speak . . . 'All your life I've felt very strangely towards you. . . . I've felt a kind of physical repulsion. . . . I've often felt that I was being unjust, unnatural – but now I know that my instinct was right. . . .'
>   'It is you who are unnatural, not I. And this thing that you are is a sin against creation . . . against nature, against God who created nature.'
>
> (pp. 203–4)

Sir Philip's self-censorship perverts Anna and Stephen's relationship – 'In his infinite pity for Stephen's mother, [Sir Philip] sinned very deeply and gravely against Stephen, by withholding from that mother his own conviction that her child was not as other children' (p. 51) – and deprives Stephen of her birthright, Morton Hall. Similarly, a more culpable 'tyranny of silence evolved by . . . [the] world for its own well-being and comfort' (p. 121) allows society 'to persecute those who, through no fault of their own, have been set apart from the day of their birth' (p. 395). This censorship renders the invert 'more hopeless than the veriest dregs of creation. For since all that to many of them had seemed fine . . . had been covered with shame . . . so gradually they themselves had sunk down to the level upon which the world placed their emotions' (p. 393). The 'natural' invert is thus perverted by the censorship of an 'unnatural' culture.

The most articulate of the discourses which speak of Stephen's inversion is the discourse of the body. Even within the womb, the foetal Stephen 'stirred strongly' and, at birth, this 'narrow-hipped, wide-shouldered little tadpole of a baby' is visibly different. Stephen's body assures Sir Philip of his daughter's inversion. Moreover, Stephen's body prompts Anna's physical repulsion:

> there were times when the child's soft flesh would be almost distasteful to her; when she hated the way Stephen moved or stood still, hated a certain largeness about her, a certain crude lack of grace in her movements, a certain unconscious defiance.
>
> (p. 11)

This discourse underlines Hall's understanding of inversion: 'the outward stigmata of the abnormal' are borne on the body like the mark of Cain, rendering inverts both visibly different and visible to each other. Thus, Jonathan Brockett immediately recognises Stephen as a fellow 'abnormal' whilst she knows from his hands, 'white and soft as a woman's' that 'this man would never require of her more than she could give' (pp. 227–8). Both Anna and Sir Philip perceive Stephen's body as a sign of her difference; however, Anna, lacking Sir Philip's theorised understanding of inversion, is unable either to articulate her instinctive perception or to translate it into sympathy.

Stephen's 'grotesque and splendid' body could fascinate as well as alienate: Angela Crossby could not get Stephen out of her mind. This body invests Stephen with an 'animal magnetism':

> Angela moved a step nearer to Stephen, then another, until their hands were touching. And all that she was, and all that she had been and would be again . . . was fused at that moment into one mighty impulse, one imperative need, and that need was Stephen. Stephen's need was now hers, by sheer force of its blind uncomprehending will to appeasement.
>
> Then Stephen took Angela into her arms and kissed her full on the lips, as a lover.
>
> (p. 144)

When Martin's declaration of love paralyses Stephen's mind, rendering her inarticulate, her body continues to act, and speaks most eloquently:

> [Stephen] was staring at [Martin] in a kind of dumb horror, staring at his eyes that were clouded by desire, while gradually over her colourless face there was spreading an expression of the deepest repulsion. . . . He could not believe this thing that he saw . . . he

came a step nearer. . . . But at that she wheeled round and fled
from him wildly . . . without so much as a word she left him, nor
did she once pause in her flight to look back. Yet even in this
moment of headlong panic, the girl was conscious of . . . amazement at herself.

(pp. 96–7)

Stephen's animality heightens her instincts: her 'natural' body and/or
her subconscious mind instinctively understands its inversion,
although her 'cultural' and/or conscious mind's comprehension is frustrated by Sir Philip's censorship. Whether it is her body, her subconscious mind, or a combination of the two which drives Stephen to
action remains unclear: physical body, subconscious mind and metaphysical spirit are all referred to in Hall's analysis of the 'intuition of
those who stand mid-way between the sexes' (p. 81). This intuition
enables Stephen to 'discover that all was not well with her parents':

Their outward existence seemed calm and unruffled. . . . But their
child saw into their hearts with the eyes of the spirit; flesh of their
flesh, she had sprung from their hearts, and she knew that those
hearts were heavy. They said nothing, but she sensed that some
deep, secret trouble was afflicting them both; she could see it in
their eyes.

(pp. 81–2)

Hall's explicit demand in *The Well* is for the reception of the invert
into culture: for the move from a primitive state of nature dependent
upon a subconscious animal language of the body, to human civilisation and its conscious language of the mind. However, passages
within Hall's novel suggest that the former may sometimes be more
expressive than the latter: 'Language is surely too small to contain
those emotions of mind and body that have somehow awakened a
response in the spirit' (p. 320). Physical communication can possess a
directness lost in language, whilst spiritual communion transcends
language and is akin to prayer. Stephen's inversion allows her to
'write both men and women from a personal knowledge' (p. 208),
enhancing her ability to communicate within culture. It also enables
her to communicate directly with nature (in the form of her horse,
Raftery) using a 'quiet language having very few words but many
small sounds and many small movements, which . . . meant more
than words' (p. 56). The ambiguities evident in Hall's discussion of
the aetiology of homosexuality also complicate her call for the acceptance of the invert into culture: gaining the conscious language of the
mind may entail losing the language of the physical body.

Stephen attained a conscious, articulate understanding of her body's significance from reading her father's copies of Krafft-Ebing. However, this victory over external censorship is, like the mark of Cain, double-edged. Knowledge brings with it responsibility and self-censorship; that double burden which causes Sir Philip 'to stoop', perverts his relationship with his wife and, subsequently, reveals itself upon Stephen's body and perverts her mind's relationship with that body:

> All her life she must drag this body of hers like a monstrous fetter imposed on her spirit. . . . She longed to maim it, for it made her feel cruel; it was so white, so strong and so self-sufficient; yet withal so poor and unhappy a thing that her eyes filled with tears and her hate turned to pity. She began to grieve over it, touching her breasts with pitiful fingers, stroking her shoulders, letting her hands slip along her straight thighs – Oh, poor and most desolate body!
>
> (pp. 187–8)

Stephen's congenital inversion is a physical disability with which her mind has yet to come to terms; a lack of acceptance exhibited by the repression of physical desire. This self-censorship, in conjunction with society's censorship of inverts as a whole, perverts Stephen's body and mind. 'For an *external* frustration to become pathogenic,' Freud writes, with regard to the development of neuroses, 'an *internal* frustration must be added to it.'[16] Whilst not suggesting that Freud's theorising of neurosis can be applied to Stephen Gordon in its entirety, the latter does exhibit many of his perceived consequences of a repressive self-censorship. 'There are,' Freud says, 'many ways of tolerating deprivation of libidinal satisfaction . . . one [of] which has gained special cultural significance. It consists in the sexual trend abandoning its aim of obtaining . . . a reproductive pleasure and taking on another which is . . . no longer sexual . . . "sublimation".'[17] Thus Stephen's life in London, following her enlightenment and exile, is 'one long endeavour, for work to her had become a narcotic' (p. 210). Freud maintains, however, that there is 'a limit to the amount of unsatisfied libido that human beings . . . can put up with . . . and sublimation is never able to deal with more than a certain fraction'.[18] The repudiated libidinal trends succeed in getting their way by certain roundabout paths, i.e. the construction of symptoms. Stephen's 'symptoms' render her writing 'lifeless' and are visible on her face:

> The mouth was less ardent and much less gentle, and the lips now drooped at the corners. The strong rather massive line of the jaw looked aggressive these days by reason of its thinness. Faint furrows had come between the thick brows and faint shadows showed at times under the eyes. . . . Her complexion was paler than it had been in the past . . . and the fingers of the hand that slowly

emerged from her jacket pocket were heavily stained with nicotine – she was now a voracious smoker.

(p. 210)

Censorship of something which 'naturally' exists is, according to Freud and Hall, bound to failure, as Stephen Gordon discovers:

'Why have I been afflicted with a body that must never be indulged . . . that must always be repressed until it grows much stronger than my spirit because of this unnatural repression? And now it's attacking . . . my work – I shall never be a great writer because of my maimed and insufferable body.'

(p. 217)

Stephen's suffering eases once she makes contact with the invert community in Paris and is temporarily resolved when she and Mary give themselves up to 'Nature' and become lovers. In the 'primitive' Eden of Orotava (Tenerife) 'a happiness such as she had never conceived could be hers . . . possessed [Stephen] body and soul' (p. 318). The power inherent in this unification is apparent on the lovers' return to Paris, as Mary watches Stephen dress whilst, simultaneously, examining her lover's clothes and possessions. The latter are so integral to Stephen's identity, that:

they had drawn into themselves a species of life derived from their owner, until they seemed to be thinking of Stephen with a dumbness that made their thoughts more insistent, and their thoughts gathered strength and mingled with Mary's so that she heard herself cry out: 'Stephen!' . . .
    And Stephen answered her: 'Mary—'
    Then they stood very still, grown abruptly silent . . . they seemed at that moment . . . to be looking straight into the eyes of a love . . . made perfect, discarnate.

(p. 326)

Now that Stephen's soul is no longer in thrall to a body sickened by censorship, the trinity of body, mind and spirit facilitates a metaphysical union, as opposed to the instinctive physical union with Angela. Once Stephen and Mary return to culture, however, external censorship reasserts itself, urging the perversion of this relationship:

Oh but she knew . . . what it would mean should they be there [Morton Hall] together; the lies, the despicable subterfuges . . . the guard set upon eyes and lips; the feeling of guilt at so much as a handtouch . . .
    Intolerable quagmire of lies and deceit! The degrading . . . of love

and . . . of Mary, Mary . . . so loyal . . . so gallant, but so pitifully
untried in the war of existence.

(pp. 337–8)

Stephen is caught between nature and culture: if she accepts culture
she is alienated from her nature; if she accepts her nature she is
alienated from culture. To live within culture is to be subject to censorship: the 'normal' and the inverted both 'possess in their mental life
what . . . makes possible the formation . . . of symptoms'. Thus,
Freud writes, 'a healthy person, too, is virtually a neurotic'. This
reduces 'the distinction between nervous health and neurosis . . . to
[the] practical question . . . [of] whether the subject is left with a
sufficient amount of capacity for enjoyment and efficiency'.[19] The
extent of the censorship determines the severity of the sickness;
making it impossible according to Hall, for the invert, and the inverted
relationship, to remain healthy within heterosexual society.

This 'war of existence' gradually takes its toll on Mary, coarsening
her finer perceptions and hardening her mouth and eyes. To stop this
'spiritual murder' Stephen martyrs herself. She is elevated from sinner
to saviour, redeemer of all inverts:

The quick, the dead, and the yet unborn. . . .
    They possessed her. . . . They would turn first to God, and then
to the world, and then to her. They would cry out accusing. . . .
You, God, in Whom we, the outcast, believe; you, world, into
which we are pitilessly born; you, Stephen, who have drained our
cup to the dregs – we have asked for bread; will you give us a
stone?

(pp. 446–7)

Stephen's inversion – subjected to this final censoring of spiritual love
– multiplies, consumes and translates her. Her transcendent identity
and purpose are revealed: through Stephen Gordon – embodiment of
inversion – the afflicted would find a voice with which to overcome
the world's conspiracy of silence:

And now there was only one voice, one demand; her own voice
into which those millions had entered. . . . A terrifying voice that
made her ears throb, that made her brain throb, that shook her
very entrails, until she must stagger and all but fall beneath this
appalling burden of sound that strangled her in its will to be uttered.
    'God,' she gasped. . . . 'Acknowledge us, oh God, before the
whole world. Give us also the right to our existence!'

(p. 447)

Hall's impassioned plea for tolerance went unanswered. Censorship remains central to 'the homosexual experience', as censorship has remained central to the biography of *The Well*: current concerns around 'positive images' have resulted in Hall and her novel being censored as oppressive by the very community they sought to defend. However, for those who read the novel as Hall wrote it – from the heart – and who hear its emotional as well as its theoretical discourse, the book remains a resonant evocation of survival within a censoring, censorious culture.

NOTES

1 Radclyffe Hall, *The Well of Loneliness*, 1928, repr. London, Virago, 1982. All further references are to the modern edition, cited parenthetically in the text.
2 Cited in M. Baker, *Our Three Selves. A Life of Radclyffe Hall*, London, Gay Men's Press, 1985, p. 238.
3 *Sunday Express*, 19 August 1928, p. 10.
4 J. Weeks, *Sex, Politics and Society*, London, Longman, 1981, p. 105.
5 *Sunday Express*, 19 August 1928, p. 10.
6 Pegasus Press publicity circular, cited in Baker, *Our Three Selves*, p. 231.
7 ibid., p. 246.
8 V. Brittain, *Radclyffe Hall. A Case of Obscenity?*, London, Femina Books, 1968, p. 113.
9 M. Foucault, *The History of Sexuality*, vol. I, Harmondsworth, Penguin, 1981, pp. 17–18.
10 Baker, *Our Three Selves*, p. 222.
11 ibid., p. 202.
12 Foucault, *The History of Sexuality*, pp. 19–20.
13 ibid., p. 20.
14 U. Troubridge, *The Life and Death of Radclyffe Hall*, London, Hammond & Co., 1961, pp. 81–2.
15 For a more detailed discussion of Hall and Troubridge's self-censorship, see K. Rolley, 'Cutting a dash: the dress of Radclyffe Hall and Una Troubridge', *Feminist Review*, vol. 35, 1990, pp. 54–66.
16 S. Freud, *Introductory Lectures on Psychoanalysis*, Harmondsworth, Penguin, 1973, pp. 394–5.
17 ibid., pp. 389–90.
18 ibid., pp. 390–5.
19 ibid., p. 510.

Chapter 16

Censorship and children's literature: some post-war trends

Peter Barry

In recent years there has been a resurgence of what can broadly be called the censorship of children's books. I want to discuss why this has happened, and look at some of the issues and dilemmas it poses. I am using a very wide definition of censorship, taking it to include the withdrawal of books from print, or from schools, libraries and resource centres, because of pressure from outside bodies, and the alteration of passages before publication in anticipation of such pressures. I also include the publication of guidelines for authors, teachers, librarians and parents on writing or selecting books for children.

From 1900 to the 1960s there was really very little overt censorship of children's literature. Instead, according to Anne Scott MacLeod, children's books were characterised by an air of 'protective optimism', and the more painful aspects of life were muted in children's literature.[1] This decorum was maintained by 'consensus rather than coercion', for the writers, publishers, buyers and borrowers of children's books were people of similar tastes and background who had a wide degree of social and moral agreement. The classics of the 'golden age' of children's literature still dominated, and there was no strong tradition of contemporary realism, of the kind which would later throw contentious issues into stark relief. In the 1960s, however, the pace of social change accelerated dramatically, and this consensus, like so many others, was broken. The civil rights movement in America challenged social values in a radical way; the Vietnam war, the European upheavals of 1968, and the growing crisis in southern Africa polarised political opinion; and the feminist and gay rights movements challenged moral and social values generally, and the central notion of the 'nuclear' family in particular. By the 1970s, MacLeod concludes, children's books had become 'a battleground for the personal, social and political forces of a changing society'.[2] The issues and conflicts involved were, of course, heightened by the Sex Discrimination Act of 1975 and the Race Relations Act of 1976.

Censorship in children's books first became an issue with the growth of the 'new realism' of the 1960s, for when the veil of 'protective optimism' was lifted, and writers moved away from the mythological, historical or middle-class settings which had been traditional in children's fiction, then whole areas of life which had never featured before in children's books became important in the plotting and characterisation of stories. Thus, divorce, 'broken homes', unmarried parenthood, drug-taking, prostitution, violence, swearing, prejudice, truancy, bullying and gay relationships gradually found their way into children's fiction. An early (and very mild) example of the new realism was John Rowe Townsend's *Gumble's Yard* (1961) which, in his words, featured 'children from the poorest kind of home . . . four abandoned children [who] fight to keep the family together even though this means a moonlight flit to a derelict warehouse on the canal bank'.[3] Attempts to suppress the representation of these harsher aspects of life constitute what Jessica Yates calls sexual/moral censorship, a form of censorship which is illiberal and reactionary in intent, and is directed, in the main, towards the prevention of social change, or, more accurately, perhaps, towards bringing about its reversal.[4] It can be called, for short, 'conservative censorship'.

There was also, however, a strong desire to exert control over the content of children's fiction from a quite different quarter, for the changing outlook of the times resulted in a determination to prevent the representation in children's books of racist and sexist attitudes. This tendency aimed, from the 1970s onwards, to consolidate the changes in social attitudes brought about by the civil rights, gay rights and feminist movements of the 1960s. The kind of censorship which resulted is liberal and progressive in intent, says Yates, and aims to accelerate, rather than prevent, social change. Call it 'liberal censorship' for short.

Now, as Yates says, most of those who have views on what children should read strongly advocate one of these forms of censorship and strongly deplore the other, apparently without having any sense that there is something inconsistent in doing so. But there are further inconsistencies: both kinds of censorship are founded in the conviction that children are profoundly influenced, in forming their social attitudes, by the contents of the books they read. Though both sides fear the effects of children's reading, and wish to counteract them, they share what is essentially a very optimistic view of the continuing power of books (especially fiction) in an electronic age. Yet these convictions about the power of reading matter over young minds have never been systematically investigated, much less proven.

We might expect both sides to be equally concerned about the effects of other media, such as records, videos and television, but in practice campaigning about these has been almost exclusively the preserve of the conservative censors. They have argued fiercely, in both Britain and America, that children's speech and behaviour patterns are influenced by what they see on television or hear in the lyrics of pop songs. For this belief, too, there is no empirical evidence, though attempts are being made in the courts to establish legal liability on the part of entertainers for the supposed consequences (such as suicides or criminal acts) of young people's exposure to their work. All the same, there is a puzzling absence of any left-wing lobby arguing, for instance, that minorities ought to be equally represented in children's TV programmes and adventure stories, or that girls should be shown in active roles. This is just one of the anomalies in a field which has so many.

LIBERAL CENSORSHIP

What were some of the landmarks in the growth of liberal censorship during the 1970s? One key event took place in 1970 when Elaine Moss, compiler of the National Book League's list of children's Books of the Year, recommended Helen Bannerman's *Little Black Sambo* (1899) in a bibliography entitled *Reading for Enjoyment: with Two to Five Year Olds*. In the early 1970s Bannerman's book became the focus of a campaign by teachers and librarians against racial bias in children's books. Another target was Hugh Lofting's *The Story of Dr Dolittle* (1920), especially the scene where the black Prince Bumpo tries to wash his face white.[5]

Another important factor in the trend towards liberal censorship in the 1970s was the growth of the 'community bookshops', of which there were around six in 1970 and around a hundred in 1980.[6] These sometimes had local authority support, usually operated as collectives, and specialised in books on left-wing politics, 'alternative life-style' material and 'multicultural' books. They issued lists of non-racist and non-sexist children's books, and such lists have appeared regularly since the 1970s. In turn, this process of assessing children's books by essentially non-literary criteria resulted in a new kind of criticism: literary criticism proper became identified with conservative values, and an approach known as social criticism developed which was overwhelmingly directed towards issues of race, sex and class. It was featured prominently in a number of sympathetic journals, such as *Books for Keeps* (the magazine of the School Bookshop Association), *Dragons Teeth* (the journal of the National Committee on Racism in Children's Books), and the *Children's Book Bulletin* (the magazine of the Children's Rights Workshop). The social critics have been very influential on in-service training for teachers, and hence on book selection for schools and libraries.

Another landmark occurred in 1974 when the McGraw-Hill Book Company in America published its guidelines to editors and authors on non-sexist writing. This widely disseminated document proscribed terms such as 'man-made' (preferring 'synthetic') and 'fireman' ('fire-fighter'), and encouraged the use of 'inclusive language' and the non-stereotyped representation of women and girls. In Britain there was a feeling that America was ahead in the formulation of guidelines, and steps were taken to catch up. In 1976, for instance, the Writers and Readers Publishing Cooperative issued *Sexism in Children's Books: Facts, Figures and Guidelines*, a collection of mainly American essays (including the McGraw-Hill document). The issue remained high on the educational agenda throughout the 1970s. In 1978 the Education Institute of Scotland passed a resolution expressing concern at racism and sexism in children's books, and the National Union of Teachers (NUT), at their annual conference in the same year, called on members to 'examine critically the books and other learning materials used in schools and to guard against those which are racially biased'.[7] A set of guidelines for teachers on racial stereotyping in textbooks and learning materials was issued by the NUT in 1979 and reissued in 1982.

The churches, too, have been active in the production of guidelines. One document of great influence originated at a working party on racism in children's books which was part of the 1978 conference of the World Council of Churches (WCC) which met in Germany. This was printed in full in the first issue of the *Children's Book Bulletin* in June 1979. It has sections of advice and questions directed at various groups, such as buyers ('Does the publishing house . . . have a policy of hiring Third World people as editors and illustrators?'), and teachers ('Am I willing to participate in workshops designed to increase my ability to develop strategies to handle and counteract racist material?').

Another widely circulated list was that of the Council on Interracial Books for Children (CIBC), in New York, called 'Ten quick ways to analyse children's books for racism and sexism'. This avoids the over-elaboration of the WCC document, but item six gives an indication of its general tone:

> Are the persons identified as heroes or heroines only those who have served the interests of Europeans? Are these persons identified as heroes, persons who have been so identified by third world people?[8]

On sexism, under 'Consider the message in the story', we are asked: 'Are women shown as independent, active and capable of making decisions or are they dependent and passive?'[9]

Yet another set of guidelines was issued by the Inner London Education Authority's Centre for Urban Educational Studies, this time with the refinement that books which possess either the recommended or the undesirable qualities are mentioned by name:

> Avoid fiction such as Willard Price's *Cannibal Adventure* or the *Biggles* series where 'goodies' and 'baddies' are divided according to their race. . . . If a book is set in a multicultural city such as London, both text and illustrations should reflect the whole population, as in Methuen's *Terraced House* books.

This is a rather more relaxed and informal document than the previous two; it puts the onus on the judgement, common sense and sensitivity of the teacher, rather than on the formal adoption of a set of ready-made criteria. On the other hand, like the CIBC document, it ends with the suggestion that the date of publication, at a time when attitudes are changing so rapidly, may be important in considering the acceptability of a book. Finally, there is the NUT document already mentioned which is somewhat different in character from all previous examples. Its title is *In Black and White: Guidelines for Teachers on Racial Stereotyping in Textbooks and Learning Materials*. It ends with a checklist of ways of using books for multicultural education, rather than with specific criteria for finding them acceptable or unacceptable. The advice given is general and unexceptionable:

> Do not use books which would cause offence to ethnic minority group pupils by derogatory references which suggest the inferiority of minority groups. . . . Point out stereotypes: do not allow them to pass unchallenged. . . . Check whether there are people in the story with whom black or brown children could identify. . . . Assess whether the book is factually accurate and ensure that it does not perpetuate the myth of white superiority.[10]

The movement in favour of publishing sets of criteria or guidelines of the type just illustrated is distinctively American in origin and seems to typify the approach of the 1970s. This outlook was challenged in 1980 when the *New Statesman* published a symposium on the subject. Teachers, writers, publishers and librarians took part, and a number of problems were explored. For instance, the twinning of racism and sexism in the guidelines begs a number of questions, since books which rate highly on grounds of being anti-racist may well offend on grounds of sexism, and vice versa. In *Doctor Sean* (1975), for example, one of the highly acclaimed *Sean* series by the black writers and illustrators Petronella Breinburg and Errol Lloyd, the central characters are black. But in the game with his sister, which is the main focus of the book, Sean plays a doctor while she plays a nurse. This is pointed out by Jill Paton Walsh as part of her contribution to the *New Statesman* symposium.[11] Likewise, there have been many modern, anti-sexist fairy stories which feature active heroines: one such is *The Wrestling Princess* by Judy Corbalis (1986): but the princess on the cover is, of course, white and blonde.

Another problem is that the guidelines tend to gloss over the difficulties of making judgements about the nature of the literary effects of a piece of writing, trying instead to substitute criteria which operate automatically. Thus, Walsh complains that the guidelines place writers in a quandary. If their books have no black characters they are guilty of racism by omission; if they have just a few they are accused of tokenism, and, if they write directly about ethnic minorities, they will be seen as inadvertently patronising. We can use her own picture-story book *Babylon* (1982) as a case in point: it is about a young black girl and her friends who come across luxuriant vegetation on a disused railway-viaduct. She calls it a hanging garden, like Babylon, and the three black children walk along singing of the waters of Babylon and of remembering Zion. Zion is Africa, where they all come from, one of the boys tells her, while the other says that it is 'Back home in Jamaica', and they reminisce about the lush vegetation there. The boys agree they could weep about that, but Dulcie, born in England, is sad that she has no remembered past to weep for. She tells the mother of one of the boys 'I'm not going again. . . . Babylon aint no fun without you got Zion to weep for', but she cheers up when told 'You surely will have something to weep for, by and by'.[12]

All this is obviously well meant, but is it patronising? It is surely very difficult to say: if we follow the criteria suggested by a number of the guidelines and enquire into the author's social and educational background we will find no grounds for acquittal. But the question cannot be answered by the methods of social criticism, for it depends upon the literary treatment of the topic: the black speech, for instance, is rendered in a rather embarrassing equivalent of stage Irish, and the Zion and Babylon imagery is something of a cliché. If the book is to be found wanting, it might be on grounds such as these.

On the whole, however, the case against liberal censorship was more persuasively put than the case in favour. The left-wing identity of the *New Statesman* made it difficult to see this opposition to guidelines as merely reactionary. Whether in consequence or not, less emphasis now seems to be placed upon this approach. Perhaps it could be said that we now have a new consensus, a new decorum, which replaces the one which obtained until the 1960s. This new consensus on children's writing takes for granted a non-racist, non-sexist, pluralist view of society, offering a new kind of protective optimism which makes the guidelines less needed. Of course, advocates would argue that this consensus is not accidental, but is, rather, a consequence of the guidelines movement.

Although guidelines typified the liberal censorship of the 1970s, they were essentially negative in intent: their main aim was the removal of offending books from circulation. The 1980s, by contrast, were characterised by the publication of multicultural and non-sexist book-lists for teachers and parents; this shift had been foreshadowed in the 1970s when some of the guidelines began to mention or describe approved material in a specific way. Rather than trying to suppress bad material, the book-lists took the positive alternative and set out to promote the good. Examples are Judith Elkin and Pat Triggs's *Books for Keeps Guide to Children Books for a Multi-Cultural Society* (1985), and Susan Adler's *Equality Street: A Penguin Multi-Cultural Booklist* (1988) and *Ms Moffet Fights Back: A Penguin Non-Sexist Booklist* (1988).

CONSERVATIVE CENSORSHIP

Like liberal censorship, this kind has been strongly advocated in some quarters during recent years. Again, the rise of this form of censorship is related to shifts in social attitudes, especially the mood of renewed moral conviction fostered by the Reagan era in America, and the brief it gave to Christian fundamentalist attitudes. As British children's author Jean Ure puts it, American editors seem to 'live in permanent dread of the moral majority and will often not even permit one to say "My God!" or "Bloody Hell!" '.[13] Hamida Bosmajian, in a review of several books on the topic of censorship and children's literature, accuses the pro-censorship lobby of 'agnosis', a fear of knowing.[14] This fear, she says, and the tendency of courts to uphold parental objections to the contents of children's books, poses a major threat to the constitutional right to free speech enshrined in the First Amendment. The problem now for educators is to 'know how to confront the arguments of rigid incantatory iteration of biblical or political phrases that block all communication'.[15]

In Britain the Thatcher period tended to have the same effect, and there have been moves to embody these attitudes in legislation, particularly the new laws directed against the expression of gay sexuality. Indeed, conservative censorship is typically directed against the representation in children's books of most forms of sexuality, especially gay, unmarried, or teenage sex. The graphic portrayal of violence has also attracted demands for censorship, as has violent language, supernatural horror and the occult, and material which can be seen as constituting political propaganda. As an example of 'bad' language attracting censorship, Jessica Yates cites Robert Westall's *The Machine Gunners*, first published by Puffin in 1977, but reprinted in 1979 with certain changes, after complaints were received from parents. Thus, the 1977 version's 'Frigg off, Audrey Parton, we're busy' becomes 'Faff off' in 1979: 'Leave the poor bugger alone' becomes 'Leave the poor thing alone', and so on. The prissy, substitute phrases simply draw attention to what would really be said in the circumstances, so that the veil of censorship, as so often, turns out to be a spotlight.

In *The Great Divide: Second Thoughts on the American Dream* (1989) Studs Terkel reports an American case of pressure for censorship on linguistic grounds. The target was his book *Working* (1974), in which 'people talk about what they do all day and how they feel about what they do'.[16] It was prescribed reading in a high school course on American labour in Pennsylvania. Parents of two children objected because they had discovered that it contained four-letter words. A neighbourhood protest was organised. One girl told Terkel her mother had seen the words: he asked her 'Have you any idea what effort it would take to find those words in a six hundred page book?'[17] At the protest meeting, none of the parents had read the book, but all had read the offending words.

Another example of conservative censorship, also concerning language regarded as unacceptable, is described by Rosemary Sandberg.[18] She was publishing editor of a picture-story book, *Abigail on the Beach* by Felix Pirani which shows Abigail enjoying a day on the beach, but threatened by two boys who want to demolish her sandcastle. Her weapon against them is some vividly colourful counter-threats: she tells the boys, 'You touch one of my towers and I'll get Daddy to hang you upside down by the heels. He's in the Mafia.' On the next visit she tells them, 'I'll get my daddy to break both your arms and frazzle your bike. He's in the Secret Service.'[19] It all sounds harmless, but fifty-four MPs signed a motion to have the book withdrawn. The objections were that it incites children to violence (though there is none in the book), and condones alcoholism, as daddy takes three cans of beer to the beach. The furore over the book was a prominent news item for two or three days, with most papers supporting the banning. This kind of press support is, of course, a feature of conservative censorship. Liberal censorship is treated with hostility by the press: indeed, it is most frequently mentioned in the reductive form of urban myths about left-wing councils banning nursery rhymes like 'Baa Baa Blacksheep'. On such occasions the Tory papers take the opportunity of defending our national literary heritage.

Conservative censorship objects not just to language but also to the content of children's books. In 1986 a row erupted over the English translation (by Louis Mackay) of Susanne Bosche's picture-story book *Jenny Lives with Eric and Martin*, which had been published by the Gay Men's Press in 1983. The book shows 5-year-old Jenny at home with her father and his gay partner, mostly engaged in routine domestic tasks, but the photographic illustrations include scenes of Jenny having breakfast on the bed while Eric and Martin are in it. The book had been available for some years in ILEA resources centres, but the ILEA called for it to be withdrawn after a headteacher complained that the content was inappropriate for children. As reported in the *Times Educational Supplement* on 23 May 1986, the ILEA then set up a panel, chaired by the Chief Inspector of Schools, to look at material that might be contentious. Kenneth Baker, the Minister of Education, called for the withdrawal of this 'book on homosexual behaviour', and the Department of Education and Science sent a letter to the ILEA stressing Baker's objections. Richard Luce, the Arts Minister, also appealed to the ILEA, deploring its 'unashamed use of photographic portrayals'.[20]

This unprecedented government pressure was criticised by George Cunningham, Chief Executive of the Library Association, who said that the government should not try to dictate others' reading. This was an astute way of drawing attention to the double standards which always operate in matters of censorship. The government was being, he said, as bad as left-wing councils, like Lambeth, which it had criticised for wanting to dictate what other people read when the Council withdrew *Biggles* and Enid Blyton's books from the borough's libraries for alleged racism and sexism.[21] At Belmont Junior School in north London angry parents withdrew pupils from classes because of Haringey's 'gay lib' policy, and there was a similar protest at Devonshire Hill Junior School, where gay rights and Socialist Workers' Party demonstrators opposed parents who were demonstrating against Haringey's refusal to withdraw *Jenny*. The row was symptomatic of the wider antipathy between the ILEA and the Conservative government and, in spite of the ILEA's attempt at conciliation, the whole affair probably contributed to its determination to get rid of the ILEA, and to the eventual formulation of Section 28 of the Local Authorities Act of 1988.

In this case the forces attempting to impose censorship were external ones, but, more often, censorship is self-imposed by authors and publishers in anticipation of such problems. In a useful symposium in which authors talk about their own experience of censorship, Norma Klein assembles a body of testimony on what is 'a growing problem'.[22] The striking feature of this collection of interviews is the sense of shame to which many of the authors confess as they give accounts of concessions and changes they have made. Betty Miles, for instance, relates how, just before the signing of the contract for a school book-club reprint of *All It Takes Is Practice* (1976), her editor had been rereading it for 'possible words or sentences that might be "red flags" to parents, principals and teachers across the country'.[23] She discovered the sentence in which a character says 'I just finished this book about a white boy who falls in love with a black girl, but in the end they break up. I wanted them to get married. I don't see why they shouldn't, if they really love each other.' The editor felt that she could not defend 'a flat statement about sex mores to parents of fourth and fifth graders'.[24] The author had the option, therefore, of deleting the paragraph, and thereby diluting her liberal message, or insisting that it stay, and then losing the reprint deal and the vastly extended readership which it would give her.

Censorship very frequently operates in America at this stage of reprinting a book for adoption by schools. In an article called 'Censoring the sources' the American author Barbara Cohen writes about the problems which occurred when her book *Molly's Pilgrim* (1983) was to be adapted for use in a third-grade reader. One of the points of her children's story is that the American festival of Thanksgiving derives from the Jewish celebration of Sukkos. But the editors objected to specific religious references: 'If we mention God some atheist will object. If we mention the Bible, someone will want to know why we don't give equal time to the Koran. Every time that happens we lose sales.'[25] After a lengthy wrangle over several months a compromise was worked out, but she ends by saying 'Censorship in this country is widespread, subtle, and surprising. It is not inflicted on us by the government. It doesn't need to be. We inflict it on ourselves.'[26]

The publisher's point about the loss of sales indicates what might be seen as the bottom line on censorship. As Jean Ure says, 'virtually all censorship does seem to stem from economic forces'.[27] But this oversimplifies matters somewhat: the motives for censorship are often very mixed; there is an economic motive, for both publishers and authors, in seeking to produce acceptable material, and there is ego-gratification for authors in extending their readership, and promulgating passionately held views. Yet both conservative and liberal censors seek to benefit society, the former by removing the threat posed by what they see as corrupting material, the latter by improving the lot of disadvantaged groups. The liberal censors carry an additional burden, for to achieve a greater good they are willing to compromise their own liberal principles. What is essential is that we recognise that there is a compromise of principle involved in liberal censorship, and that there are always dangers when we accept restrictions on the printed word. It is a matter of all-too-frequent observation that the realm of the impermissible has an inbuilt urge for territorial expansion.

NOTES

1 A. S. MacLeod, 'Censorship and children's literature', *Library Quarterly*, vol. 53, 1983, pp. 26–38.
2 ibid., p. 34.

3 J. R. Townsend, *Written for Children*, 2nd rev. edn, Harmondsworth, Penguin, 1983, p. 268.
4 J. Yates, 'Censorship in children's paperbacks', *Children's Literature in Education*, vol. 11, 1980, pp. 180–91.
5 This scene is discussed by D. Milner in *Children and Race*, Harmondsworth, Penguin, 1975.
6 *New Statesman*, 21 November 1980, p. 17.
7 Foreword to *In Black and White: Guidelines for Teachers on Racial Stereotyping in Textbooks and Learning Materials*, London, National Union of Teachers, 1979.
8 *Children's Book Bulletin*, No. 1, June 1979, p. 8.
9 ibid., p. 7.
10 *In Black and White*, p. 9.
11 *New Statesman*, 28 November 1980, p. 28.
12 J. P. Walsh, *Babylon*, London, André Deutsch, 1982, no pag.
13 J. Ure, in 'Who censors?', *Books for Keeps*, September 1989, p. 19.
14 H. Bosmajian, 'Fear of knowing', *Children's Literature in Education*, vol. 20, 1989, pp. 191–200.
15 ibid., p. 199.
16 The quotation is the book's subtitle.
17 Studs Terkel, *The Great Divide: Second Thoughts on the American Dream*, London, Headline, 1989, p. 47.
18 R. Sandberg, in 'Who censors?', *Books for Keeps*, September 1989, p. 23.
19 ibid., p. 23.
20 *The Times*, 16 and 17 September 1986.
21 *The Times*, 3 October 1986.
22 N. Klein, 'Some thoughts on censorship: an author symposium', *Top of the News*, Winter 1983, pp. 137–53.
23 ibid., p. 145.
24 ibid.
25 B. Cohen, 'Censoring the sources', *School Library Journal*, March 1986, p. 98.
26 ibid., p. 99.
27 Ure, in 'Who censors?' p. 19.

Chapter 17

Joyce, postculture and censorship

Richard Brown

More than half of modern culture depends on what one shouldn't read.

Oscar Wilde, The Importance of Being Earnest

A CURIOUS HISTORY

Joyce's battle with literary censorship, along with that of Lawrence, survives as a structuring myth for our modern cultural situation. As the narrative has been handed down in biography and, still more, in the everyday currency of half-mythologised literary opinion, Joyce represents the type of the avant-garde artist who stuck heroically to his vision despite the attempts of the narrow-minded and the hypo-critical to silence him.[1] Such was the narrative that Joyce himself disseminated when in 1911 he sent a letter about the publication of *Dubliners* to the British and Irish press complaining about his treatment at the hands of the London publisher Grant Richards and Dublin's George Roberts, of Maunsel & Co. Pound reprinted it as part of a longer account by Joyce under the title 'A Curious History' in *The Egoist* in January 1914: a prelude to the serialisation of *A Portrait* in February, and to the publication of *Dubliners* by Grant Richards that was finally to take place in June.[2] Joyce's prose fictions were first published in the context of this narrative of his life and work, and the chronology of his publications was thus curiously inverted by censorship.

The next instalment of the narrative came in 1918 when the serialis-ation of the thirteenth episode of *Ulysses* (where Bloom is shown masturbating on the beach) was seized in the United States under a law that prevented the circulation of 'obscene' material in the mail, and was then brought to the Court of Special Sessions at which the editors of the *Little Review* were fined. By the time the full text of *Ulysses* was published in Paris in 1922, the rights and wrongs of censoring or publishing Joyce's work had become a *cause célèbre* of the

1920s and, much as with Salman Rushdie, most literary papers came out with something for or against publication. The debate lasted until well into the 1930s when the American (1934) and British (1936–7) trade editions finally appeared. The British edition carried appendices which documented the American trials and judgements in full, and presented the book in the context of its triumph over the forces that had attempted to censor it.[3]

By then, instalments from Joyce's *Work in Progress* had been coming out for ten years or more, and the chronological sequence of Joyce's publication was inverted for a second time. In 1932 he published another curious history, a Wakean defence of the tenor John Sullivan entitled 'From a banned writer to a banned singer', in which he characterises himself once again as a victim of censorship.[4] Since this sketch serves as a convenient moment from which we can date Joyce's new experimental style as having developed into a language of its own – a 'Wakese' – we might ponder the extent to which that language itself should be understood not merely as an autonomous stylistic experiment but as a language made necessary by, and intrinsically related to, his experience of censorship – though it may need to be understood more widely and deeply than simply in terms of the explicit practices of state control. If *Finnegans Wake* (1939), as Joyce and many subsequent critics have claimed, is a dream (and a Freudian dream at that), then we should also register the traces in it of the dream mechanisms of condensation and displacement that were themselves defined by Freud precisely as a result of an impersonal force of 'censorship' (what he called *Die Zensür*). From *Stephen Hero* (with its satire on the prudish literary values of Stephen and Joyce's own education) to *The Wake*, writing and censorship were inextricably bound together for Joyce.

In the 1960s, when the paperback publication of works like Cleland's *Fanny Hill* and Lawrence's *Lady Chatterley*, as well as stage nudity, became the censorship issues of the day, Joyce's example was a powerful justification for derestriction. By the 1970s the serious literary author had less to fear from censorship. The love letters that Joyce had written to Nora in 1909 were freely published. They were crammed with Joyce's uninhibited and passionate declarations of his 'beast-like craving for every inch of your body, for every secret and shameful part of it, for every odour and act of it' (*SL*: p. 181) and with carnivalesque expressions of his polymorphous desires to be 'flogged', to 'fuck a farting woman', to be fucked by her 'grunting like a young sow doing her dung' and so on (letters which, it could be argued, had been 'censored' from previous volumes of his correspondence, and had only been described in general terms in Ellmann's biography).

The narrative took an unexpected turn in the 1980s when a reassessment of many liberal assumptions was on the agenda. The well-considered Williams Report of 1979 recognised the different impli-cations of censoring sexual obscenity for different media. It found that 'almost any printed book now seems likely to secure acquittal' and, whilst attempting to define what should be restricted in the cinema, it recommended that 'no publication shall be liable to either sup-pression or restriction in virtue of matter that it contains which consists solely of the written word'.[5] That did not, however, prevent a reaction across all the media in the next decade. In Britain the tabloid news-papers came to be seen as exploitative and intrusive on personal privacy. The 'clean-up-television' lobby became more vocal and better organised, and (in the midst of so much routine sleaze) quite oddly selective in its opposition to some of the most original and most literary work, like that of Ian McEwan and Dennis Potter. Women's groups campaigned against representations that they felt were exploit-ative and degrading. Explicit political pressures on freedom of opinion in all the media were tightened. Sinn Féin and the IRA were banned from direct expression in the British media. The Falklands and Gulf wars seemed to legitimise restrictions of militarily sensitive infor-mation. The freedom of expression of such an evidently serious and literary writer as Salman Rushdie was questioned, even in some west-ern liberal circles, in as much as it was supposed to offend the sensibili-ties of minority groups. Typically of our postmodern culture – our *postculture* – these issues came to be debated so often in the media, we might even have begun to feel in some way 'censored' by the very quantity of – and the limited terms of reference within – discussion of censorship itself.

The presentation of *Ulysses* to an English audience provided one symptom of changing times. The first English Bodley Head editions of the book in 1936 bore lengthy appendices. The first appendix docu-mented the bootlegging of the book in America by Samuel Roth who took advantage of censorship for private profit. The New York District Court judgement by John Woolsey which lifted the ban was printed in full, as was that of the Circuit Court of Appeals which confirmed the lifting. A letter from Morris Ernst, the lawyer for the American publishers, which was printed as the foreword to the first American edition, followed. This praised Woolsey's judgement and reminds us that it took place on 6 December 1933, the day after the repeal of Prohibition. The readers of these first legally available editions in America or England may have been forgiven for conceiving of *Ulysses* as the literature of the 'speak-easy'.

The next familiar edition introducing *Ulysses* to the English reader was the Penguin paperback of 1968. Paperback Joyce for the 1960s no longer required such elaborate juridical justification or apology. *Ulysses* apparently remained a book which required some special form of presentation in that it was published with a 'Short history' by Richard Ellmann, contextualising it in terms of biography and publishing history. By 1968, parts of the debate over *Ulysses* had begun to read 'like some ancient controversy of Church Fathers'. Some aspects of Joyce himself, however, may still perhaps have been 'censored' in this presentation through the lens of such eminence and respectability. The 1975 *Selected Letters* might be thought of as restoring that partly censored self in some of its Whitmanesque complexity and contradictoriness.

The current Penguin edition, first published in 1986 (though itself soon to be replaced), tells a third story. In his preface, Ellmann re-read the text in terms of the material that the new editors identified as having previously been left out, most notably the famous 'love' passage from the library episode, chapter 9. No longer was this *Ulysses* the dangerous prohibited text of the speak-easy; nor was the text so radical in its representation of sexuality that it had been 'censored' by a repressive or conformist orthodoxy. *Ulysses* was now the central text of an academic liberal humanist morality and, if something had been consciously or unconsciously omitted or obscured, it was not the dangerous physicality or obscenity of sex but the great redeeming myth of human love. The humanistic rhetoric of this piece of Ellmann's late criticism was powerful and convincing. But it seemed to make a dogma out of something that was essentially paradoxical, and it obviously sat rather awkwardly with the Joyce who, in his twenties, had set out to redefine romantic assumptions, declaring himself 'nauseated by their lying drivel about pure men and pure women and spiritual love and love for ever: blatant lying in the face of the truth' (*SL*: p. 129). The Afterword by Hans Gabler seemed to confirm what Joyce's denigrators had often claimed: that *Ulysses* was a vast scholarly crossword puzzle. Moreover, in describing his own editorial practice as 'endeavouring to attack the corruption at the roots', Gabler seemed to wish to adopt the rhetoric of the zealous censor of the text: a tone that caught on as some began to assume that the true 'scandal' of *Ulysses* was a matter of textual editing or typographic errors.[6] In the anxious and ambivalent 1980s it was even suggested that Joyce's 1909 letters should not have been published or should retrospectively be suppressed and should no longer figure in the still-burgeoning postmodern literary-critical debate about Joyce. Lawrentian idealism about natural sexual purity might not quite have fitted the bill, but it still sounded odd to hear even some of Joyce's supporters lapsing into an agreement to refer to the Keatsian 1909 letters as 'dirty letters'.

It is, perhaps, central to the kinds of thought that have emerged from Freudian psychology to propose that the thing that is censored

or excluded from a system is precisely that in whose terms the exclud-
ing or censoring system should be best understood. But such a model
of thought may have an inevitable tendency to turn itself into its own
opposite. The Social Freudians of the 1960s may have imagined a linear
narrative, progressing effortlessly by means of further revelations, each
one a revelation of more truth. But in the changing presentation of
Joyce we apparently have a more curious narrative history of reversal
and self-contradiction, or else a double history in which one version
of the text has necessarily excluded or 'censored' some aspects of
another. Formerly, the 'truths' of sexual passion were said to have
been 'censored' by narrow-mindedness, by shallow romantic idealism
or by authority. Then, the chaos of unrestrained passions (whether
they be the uncompromising intellectual passions of Stephen repress-
ing his mother's love, or the nationalistic passions of the Citizen in
'Cyclops' silencing Bloom, or even the human errors of the publishing
process) was said to be censoring the unobtrusive altruistic message
of love. Joyce may have been rescued from the censorship which
restricted his works only to become the victim of a classic case of
recuperation which had neglected, and might even proceed deliberately to obscure their discomfiting aspects and to draw their radical
sting.

Instead of transforming Joyce, it might have made more sense to
have transformed the social myth or commonsensical view of Freud.
The assumption that 'censorship' can be removed and some inner
truth revealed is, after all, only superficially or mythically Freudian.
It might be a more accurate version of the model of mental process
offered in *The Interpretation of Dreams* (1900) (where the role of *Die
Zensür* in the dream work is frequently discussed) to say that it is a
model in which censorship plays an intrinsic and ineradicable part.
The 'will to censor' may be a psychic drive as strongly ingrained in
us as are the more familiar positive and negative Freudian drives and
therefore should itself perhaps be subject to our analysis and control.[7]

THE ANGRY YOUNG JOYCE

The belief that there is such a thing as a simple, single truth, which
has been censored but which can easily be restored once that censorship has been removed, will probably not get us very far with Joyce;
though it may be a central paradox of our cultural discourses about
censorship that they please us precisely because they allow us to
retain such a reassuringly unitary conception of truth. Much post-war
American fiction has sought this thin truth-telling line on the edge of
moral legitimacy which may be seen as a cultural legacy of its Puritan
past. The tradition continues: 'get in touch with your child . . . the

raw, uncensored part of yourself' is the advice from her drama teacher that sex-and-drug-crazed 20-year-old Alison Poole has apparently taken in full in Jay McInerney's *Story of My Life* (1989).[8] Joyce's fictions may occupy a place both on and across this line, and his disruptions of the traditional reassurance of narrative forms may put us on our guard against even such complex oversimplifications as these. From a contemporary perspective the relationship between Joyce's authorship and forms of censoring social authority may be seen as close, almost symbiotic, dating from his first attempts at publication: from the opaque 1904 version of *A Portrait* that he believed, according to his brother Stanislaus, had been rejected by the magazine to which he submitted it because of the 'sexual experiences narrated in it'.[9] In Joyce's narrative of Stephen Dedalus as it appeared some ten years later, the 'sexual experiences' are much more prominent, and so also is the sense that Stephen's experience of being 'censored' can be traced back to the supposed 'heresy' in his school essays, to bullying, to the punitive nursery, perhaps even – a Kleinian or Lacanian psychoanalytic perspective may deduce – to the origins of his linguisticity in his first expulsions from the maternal breasts and womb. Recent post-Deleuzian theory about the psychodynamics of masochism invites us to see ways in which, in Joyce, the censorious punishment may produce the outrageous writing as much as the outrageous writing produce the censorious punishment.[10]

The twelve *Dubliners* stories (without 'Two Gallants', 'A Little Cloud' and 'The Dead') which he submitted to Grant Richards in 1905 were at first accepted, but by the following April a series of objections were made by Richards's printers to the thirteenth story 'Two Gallants' and to words and passages in some of the other twelve. At first defiant, Joyce's desperate position left him no choice but to agree to certain changes. That there was no logic in the printer's intermittent objections to the word 'bloody', to the inconsequential chat about Edward VII in 'Ivy day', or to the girl with her 'Cockney accent' who 'changed the position of her legs often' in Mulligan's bar in 'Counterparts' was no defence. Joyce pointed out other examples of 'bloody' and that 'An Encounter' told a far more sordid story and Richards promptly objected to those too.[11]

It was neither legal authority nor the protest of offended groups that prompted this act of censorship but the more insidious self-censorship of a cautious printer and publisher. Joyce was left in a powerless situation of the kind definitively described by Kafka. Despite the fact that – as Joyce exasperatedly pointed out – the printer's response to his text was 'plain' and 'blunt', the precise logic of the censoring mentality was almost impossible to predict. Perhaps – as the television reporter John Simpson said of the Iraqi military censorship that vetted his coverage from Baghdad – it was based on certain 'trigger words', in this case words like 'bloody' and references to British royalty. Since the 'obscenity' of the sexual perversion in 'An Encounter' had been communicated by silence and innuendo it had been overlooked.

It would be possible for an editor to reconstruct the 1905–6 *Dubliners* and thereby present an authentic kind of angry young Joyce untainted by 'censorship'. Joyce's own objection to 'operations which I dislike from the bottom of my heart' should be authority enough.[12] In that form the volume would have had a neater twelve-story structure, ending with the hollow sermon delivered by Father Purdon in 'Grace' rather than the lyrical coda of 'The Dead'. The tone would be more bitter and more extreme, the authorial stance more pointedly detached. The qualities in 'The Dead' that were praised by several reviewers would be absent but those noted by the *Times Literary Supplement* reviewer who found Joyce 'more successful with his shorter stories' would be brought to the fore.[13]

The argument that may come nearest to justifying the text of *Dubliners* that we currently read would be the apparent paradox that the version we have (which includes the suggestions of Richards and his printer as well as Joyce's own afterthoughts) tells an equally-if-not-more authentically Joycean story of the self-censorship or self-punishment implied in Joyce's endless writerly self-revision. This may give us an insight into what increasingly became Joyce's attack not only on the 'authorities' but on the traditional assumptions of writerly 'authority'. The early stage of *A Portrait*, dating from 1904–6, which was published as *Stephen Hero* in 1944, may represent another version of the authentic angry young Joyce. This Joyce was also obscured by revisions partly forced on him from outside by lack of recognition but which themselves became characteristic of his writing practice, so that the narrative becomes further detached from the manageable articulations of a single speaking voice in a stable subject position. The fact that the final version of *A Portrait* is so much more literary, more written and overwritten than *Stephen Hero*, may paradoxically also make it as or more authentically Joyce than the authentic Joyce it effaced.

The role of rewriting in Joyce's compositional practice became most marked in his composition of *Ulysses*, which was extensively expanded, restructured and rewritten over the full period of its composition from 1906 to 1922. After Joyce's move to Paris in 1920 especially, he set about revising and rewriting the book on successive stages of proof to bring it up to the high pitch of experimental energy that was increasingly characteristic of the later episodes as he completed them.[14]

The rewriting of *Ulysses* was driven by a desire to make the book increasingly encyclopedic: the opposite of the usual censorious desire to select or exclude. It includes plenty of the 'trigger words' excluded from *Dubliners*. It is even, on one level, an act of literary revenge on Richards's London printers (as well as on Joyce's English theatrical adversary in Zürich, Henry Carr) that Private Carr in 'Circe' comes out with his surrealistically patriotic English sentiment: 'I'll wring the neck of any fucking bastard says a word against my bleeding fucking king'.[15] Along with such increasing 'obscenity', Joyce's self-revision (in the headlines of 'Aeolus', in the phantasmagoric recapitulations of 'Circe', as well as in the more obvious divergences of style and point of view in the later episodes) also increases the doublenesses and multiplicities of perspective that are characteristic of the text.

Much of this rewriting was not done until Joyce had found himself in trouble with the censors once again, not only in America (where the serialisation of the early episodes in the *Little Review* went ahead – thanks to Pound's having cut Bloom's visit to the lavatory in 'Calypso' and to a tolerant Serbian printer – until the censorious Post Office made its objection) but also in England where Pound and Harriet Shaw Weaver hoped to serialise the book in *The Egoist*.

THE CENSOR IN THE MIRROR

Part of the correspondence from the printer of *The Egoist*, W. Lewis, has recently come to light and it may give us some indication of the archaic Edwardian perspective from which *Ulysses* may have been thought 'filthy'.[16] His objections to the opening chapter led him in March 1918 – despite Harriet Weaver's offer to make decorous deletions – to tell her that if monthly publication were to continue she would have to find another printer for *The Egoist*.

To see the opening chapter of *Ulysses* as 'filthy' is presumably to scan humourlessly through it for offensive 'triggers': the jokey irreverance to Catholic Mass; Mulligan's off-hand attack on his friend Haines and the 'bloody English! Bursting with money and indigestion'; the 'scrotum' in Mulligan's mock-Homeric 'scrotumtightening sea'; the image of Stephen's mother's vomiting ghost; the libel on Haines's father's supposed 'bloody swindle'; Mulligan's joke about Mother Grogan and the teapot, and his obscene verses on Mary Ann; references to 'prepuces', especially in relation to God; mention of the milkwoman's 'paps' or the cattle's 'squirting dugs' or 'horsedung and consumptives' spits'; Stephen's 'snotrag'; the pastiche Stations of the Cross; the blasphemous rhyme about Joking Jesus; Stephen's thoughts about 'A crazy queen, old and jealous'; Haines's anti-semitism; the elderly bather's 'sagging loincloth'; Mulligan's reference to 'Redheaded women'. Any or all of these things, perhaps almost everything about Buck Mulligan, might be thought to give some kind of 'offence'.

To start from the premise that literature is to be scoured for things that might possibly offend is absurd, implying a merely passive or reflective literary ideal. That much of literature may come into the category of the 'offensive' and that anyway to be 'offensive' in literature is not necessarily a fault are among the implications of John Sutherland's study *Offensive Literature* (1982) with its class-based model of the inner logic of literary censorship in Britain.[17] If we cannot even imagine laughing with Mulligan's humour as well as grumbling with Stephen's bitterness, and if we cannot see brilliance rather than dirtiness in Joyce's use of language, then there would be little point in us ever reading, except perhaps a literature of escapist consolation, nostalgia, sentiment or flattery. The printer's offended response may even itself be confirmation of the effectiveness of the language of the chapter which works to represent Stephen – from whose implied perspective we may read the episode – as himself the recipient of certain kinds of 'offence'. The exponential growth of offence from 'trigger word' to totality is suggested in the printer's accusation that Joyce's 'filthiness' is 'absolute'.

At a subtler level, the lack of an authorial narrative voice to direct and structure our response – central to Joyce's modernist experiment – may further destabilise the reader, making him or her feel anxious and imagine any amount of 'offence'. Freud made an interestingly analogous connection between anxiety and psychological censorship in *The Interpretation of Dreams*. Readers of *Ulysses* have a new responsibility for the terms of reference in which they read and any reading of such a de-authorialised text must ultimately rebound as a reflection on the reader him or herself. On the one hand this may be a commonplace of the reader-response school of literary criticism, but it also has implications for the issue of censorship. As Joyce pointed out in his 1909 essay on Oscar Wilde, the censor falls into a logical trap of 'sinfully' knowing precisely what it is he or she declares it a 'sin' to know: 'What Dorian Gray's sin was no one says and no one knows. Anyone who recognises it has committed it.'[18] The censor is Claudius seeing his own guilt in the working of the play and calling out for it to be stopped. The silences and ellipses of *Dubliners*, the multiple perspectives of *Ulysses*, and the polysemy of *Finnegans Wake* may all be seen to exploit such instabilities in the logic of censorship. It is no accident that, in the context of such punishing censorship, Joyce's works became more ambivalent, more opaque, undermining the position of the censor in ever more sophisticated ways.

Paradoxically, the logic of the censor's position implies a wish to deny not only to others but also to him or herself the freedom of interpretation necessitated by the modernist text. The author is denied the possibility of being an objective Flaubertian ironist and is forced into that impossible corner constructed by what critics call the 'intentionalist fallacy'. The current English law on obscenity may not be explicitly based on this theoretically fallacious 'intentionalist' premise since it declares that a work be defined as culpable whose 'tendency' is to 'deprave and corrupt'. Yet part of its oddity can be demonstrated in terms of intentionalism. Even were a novelist explicitly to avow the 'intention' to create such a 'tendency', the inevitable workings of literary ambiguity would make the intentional element in the statement subject to comic instability. Such is the effect when the narrator of Samuel Beckett's *Murphy* (1938), after a delightfully absurd description of a kiss, writes: 'The above passage is carefully calculated to deprave the cultivated reader.'[19]

The modern and postmodern displacement of authorial intention as the ultimate guarantor of meaning, and the ambiguities essential to the written text may both be things that the censorious mentality finds threatening and implicitly seeks to constrain. Equally, the concept of the obscene in art (which seems etymologically to suggest something 'off' the 'scene', something previously unavailable to representation) may itself be coterminous with the idea of originality (or with the quality of having not previously been seen) that is fundamental to our recognition of art. Though, in case we fall into some high-minded complacency, we should note that the relationship between the new and the obscene may be just as close in the cynically exploitative cultural product, were we ever able clearly to state where art ended and that began.

There are obviously patronising and self-censoring social implications, of the kind described by Sutherland, in the printer's judgement. There may perhaps be subtly anti-Irish (or defensively pro-English) implications too. There are surely anti-feminist ones. One of the oddest and most absurd Joycean censorship stories concerns the *Little Review*'s Margaret Anderson who was to be excluded from her own trial in case the passages she herself had published be read out and offend her. She was then instructed to refrain from publishing further 'obscenities' of the kind that she was presumed as an 'innocent' woman not to be able to recognise or to understand.[20] A similar set of assumptions may have coloured her printer's relationship with Harriet Shaw Weaver.

We should not ignore the anti-literary implications of the kind that dogged Wilde, Joyce and Beckett, not just because they were Irish, or because they may have held outrageous views on moral questions, but because they shared a similar kind of radically comic or carnivalesque intelligence which called into question any set of beliefs except a radical commitment to exploring and expanding the boundaries of thought and writing. In these cases the distinction between the heterodoxical and the paradoxical is no longer clear. Perhaps the suggestion made in one of Wilde's 'Phrases and Philosophies' that 'Wickedness is a myth invented by good people to account for the curious attractiveness of others' is close to the truth about the 'will to censor', or closer than we would like to believe.[21]

Ultimately prevailed upon to print parts of 'Nestor', 'Proteus', 'Hades' and 'Wandering Rocks', the printer finally refused to go any further. In a letter of 17 April 1919 Lewis described Joyce's writings as blasphemous and vulgar and complained to Harriet Weaver of the time wasted by his press reader in looking through *Ulysses*. He declared that he could not undertake the printing of any further numbers of *The Egoist*. That a recognised literary expert rather than a self-appointed (and thereby intrinsically self-censoring) layman should always be consulted in such matters and that the printer should not be legally liable in such cases as this, are among the obvious practical conclusions to be drawn.

It may be pointless to comment on the likely attitudes of all those subsequent printers who have made their living out of printings of *Ulysses* or of writings about it, or to plead the case of all those readers, printers, press readers and others, who have found reading *Ulysses* anything but a 'waste of time'. It may still turn out to be the case, as print becomes an old technology, increasingly overtaken by the electronic media, that works like *Ulysses* will be the last and best saviours of print itself.

Readers may see in texts only what they have the time, the inclination, the energy, the imaginative resource, the educational opportunity, the enlightened tolerance and/or guilty conscience to see. By any standards of intelligent critical reading, the censor would appear the very worst reader of a text as well as the most patronising or restrictively authoritarian in his or her attitudes to other readers. Should not any offence to the censor's sensibilities be assessed alongside other critical readings and weighed in the balance against its offence to readerly imaginative potential? That we need to educate readers rather than censor texts is clear. Amongst other things, in finding *Ulysses* merely 'blasphemous and vulgar' the printer denies himself what, in the 'Aeolus' episode of the book, might be one of the best-informed, most accurately detailed and most sympathetic portraits of the skills of the printer's trade in our literature.

In imagining that readers see themselves in the 'mirror' of artistic representation and that even the censorious may be consciously or unconsciously reacting to that potentially traumatic self-recognition, Joyce's text, as it does in so many other things, pre-empts us. In the very first episode of *Ulysses* Stephen, the self-idealising poet, is made to take a look at himself in Mulligan's over-protective aunt's stolen and broken shaving mirror in which he must seem to himself to be a 'dreadful bard' indeed. Mulligan, the 'usurper', quicker to the witty literary quip than the morbid Stephen, immediately quotes Wilde's Preface to *The Picture of Dorian Gray* (1891) in which nineteenth-century cultural 'Philistinism' is mocked for its dislike of Realism ('the rage of Caliban seeing his own face in a glass') and Romanticism ('the rage of Caliban not seeing his own face in a glass') alike.[22]

THE 'HETEROPARADOXICAL'

Relevant as Wilde's attacks on Victorianism may seem to Joyce and to the present situation, we should try to make explicit their relevance in terms of more contemporary literary theory. There are of course those who, like the George Steiner of the early 1970s, worked to imagine, label and define a 'post-culture' in which the critic may express fundamental scepticisms about the role accorded to culture in the Arnoldian–Eliotic tradition whilst still retaining and reinforcing many of the ideals and assumptions of that tradition and remaining fundamentally resistant to – or even sometimes disdainful of – many aspects of the new.[23] In such Steinerian ambivalences there are many valuable and productive paradoxes, but also a resistance to the heterodox that may contribute to, rather than disrupt, the museuming of high culture, the proliferation of the postliterate media and the peripheralisation of literature into genre.

Quasi-Saussurean notions – that, since the linguistic sign is in some sense non-referential, literature too should be read as non-referential, as operating at the level of the signifier not at that of the signified – have also contributed influentially to arguments for literary culture and against censorship. Such may be seen as the basis of the approach of a critic like David Lodge to a writer like William Burroughs, and of more recent defences of Kathy Acker as producing a literature of 'pure signifier'.[24] Derridean deconstruction provides a far more wide-reaching account, whose relevance in essays like 'The theatre of cruelty and the closure of representation' (1966) should not be overlooked. Here, and elsewhere, Derrida uses the cases of Artaud and Bataille in the context of his complete unravelling of the theory of good and bad representations on which Plato's arguments for censorship in Book Two of *The Republic* – and much subsequent western theory of art and truth – are based.[25]

These are arguments, aside from their undoubted importance as heuristic positions across the whole cultural sphere, to which we must also attend here, since without some concession to them we would have to find many texts – and certainly most of the literary experiment or fantasy of our or probably any other time – unreadable. Such arguments have frequently figured in defences of Joyce's published works. Even his 1909 letters, the argument might run, were written in (and are to some extent defined by) the absence of their referents and more particularly of their addressee. Yet in too simplistic an adherence to anti-representational positions we may again run the risk of diluting the heterodoxical impact of those parts of language whose power and interest derive from the very possibility that they may be said, or at least imagined, to refer.

Roland Barthes took up an anti-consensual position whose resonances for both Wilde and Joyce may be still more clear. 'The real instrument of censorship is not the police,' he wrote in *Sade, Fourier, Loyola* (1976), 'it is the *endoxa*' and the ultimate anti-censorship a paradoxical discourse. A sense of why censorship so often objects to the best and most original, as well as to the most tawdrily exploitative of work, emerges here – as does a sense that censorship and originality are closely related as opposites, and an indication of why the duty of the artist must be to continue to offend. For Barthes

> true censorship . . . does not consist in banning (in abridgement, in suppression, in deprivation) but in unduly fostering, in maintaining, retaining, stifling, getting bogged down in (intellectual, novelistic, erotic) stereotypes, in taking for nourishment only the received word of others, the repetitious matter of common opinion.[26]

The passage, conceived as a justification of reading De Sade, should not of course imply that if Barthes were law (as in this sphere of art perhaps he should be) any writing, however influentially ugly, evil, violent or malicious, could be justified as a potentially valuable subversion. Nor does it especially confirm those parts of Barthes's writing which have been so influential in justifying an explicit political *prise de position* in order to escape the fallacies or dishonesties of claiming an objective stance. It is the definition of originality as a co-presence of the paradoxical with the heterodoxical – surely analogous to the development in Joyce's writing, both towards more radical, discomfiting attitudes and positions and towards greater indirection, inexplicitness and polyvalence of expression – that stands out. Barthes turns the spotlight of attention away from the text (whether or not any given text should be designated a 'good' or 'bad' text) and focuses instead on the working of censorship and its submersion in the '*endoxa*', thereby confirming both the need to educate readers and implicitly suggesting the vitally important role of the heteroparadoxical text in opening that *endoxa* to question.

It would be nice to think that there was a simple, rational logic to censoring which we could happily endorse or else completely reject without further analysis, but it is more likely that there isn't or isn't always so. Freudian theory may not imply – as some 1960s Freudians may have supposed – that censorship could be easily eradicated and the truth thereby revealed once and for all. On the contrary, it may imply that the will to censorship is as intrinsic or 'natural' to our mental functions as other thanatopsic or power-seeking urges and therefore probably to our social functions also, and that our primary duty must be to guard against the false reassurances it may offer us. Partly arbitrary mixtures of personal and public issues and anxieties, justifiable and unjustifiable, and even – the cynic would say of aspects of censorship in the contemporary cultural scene – a degree of self-publicising on the part of the censored must all play a part.

In reassessing the 'curious history' of Joyce's relationship with his printer/censors in the light of the postcultural, we may no longer be able to rely on inverted Puritan myths of the single truth that lies beneath censorious obscuration, nor on quasi-Saussurean or Derridean anti-representationalist theories of art. We can no longer see censorship as easily eradicable from the social or psychological circumstances that govern our production of knowledge and truth, nor believe that such eradication would either be a popular or even always necessarily a good thing. Many British viewers and listeners were reassured (not only of the efficient workings of state security but also, paradoxically, of the validity of the information they were actually receiving) by being told repeatedly that the vast quantities of media-reporting of the Gulf War were being censored, whether by Iraqi or Allied military censors. The claims of the uncensored 'angry young Joyce' and those of the more variously and deeply, if more evasively subversive, later Joyce vie against each other for our attention. We need to liberate ourselves from our tendencies to censor both clear critical accuracies and also inherently heteroparadoxical aspects of truth. Above all, we may need to articulate the reticences implicit in the self-censorship to which Joyce's writings were subjected by certain of his printers in the interests of conformity and to define the differences between it and the self-revisions to which he subjected his own work in the more arduous interests of the heteroparadoxical. The development of Joyce's writing towards the creation of the increasingly anti-authorial, reader-oriented semantics of the later works may be understood both as an evasive reaction to, and as an increasingly well-defined engagement with, the internal and external forces that censored him.

The censorship of Joycean narrative inevitably reveals a Joycean narrative of censorship that is still both a part of, and a point of reference for, the contemporary postcultural scene. That we should return to the 'curious history' of Joyce's publication may be explained by the extent to which that history was in part a product of his own deliberately destabilising narrative art; but it is also because of the very curious history that it was, and is, and probably will continue to be.

NOTES

1 R. Ellmann, *James Joyce*, Oxford, Oxford University Press, 1959, rev. edn, 1982.
2 J. Joyce, 'A curious history', in *Selected Letters of James Joyce*, ed. R. Ellmann, London, Faber, 1975, pp. 208–9. All subsequent references in the text are to this edition, cited as *SL* in parentheses.
3 *James Joyce: The Critical Heritage*, ed. R. H. Deming, London, Routledge & Kegan Paul, 1970, vol. 1, pp. 184–370, gives many examples of this kind of criticism.
4 R. Ellmann and E. Mason (eds), *The Critical Writings of James Joyce*, London, Faber, 1959.
5 *Report of the Committee on Obscenity and Film Censorship* (Williams Report), London, HMSO, 1979, pp. 97, 102.
6 The phrase used by John Kidd has now been taken up by Bruce Arnold in 'The *Ulysses* scandal' in *The Independent on Sunday*, 24 June 1990, and subsequent correspondence.
7 S. Freud, *The Interpretation of Dreams*, Harmondsworth, Pelican, 1976.
8 J. McInerney, *Story of My Life*, Harmondsworth, Penguin, 1989, p. 8.
9 R. Brown, *James Joyce and Sexuality*, Cambridge, Cambridge University Press, 1985, pp. 145–53.
10 F. Restuccia, *Joyce and the Law of the Father*, Princeton, Princeton University Press, 1989.
11 I summarise and discuss some of these changes in 'Shifting sexual centres: Joyce and Flaubert', in *La Revue des lettres modernes*: 'Scribble' 2, Paris, Minard, 1990, pp. 63–84. The relevant drafts are reproduced in *James Joyce Archive*, New York, Garland, 1978, vol. 4, and the correspondence with Richards in *Selected Letters*, pp. 81–90.
12 J. Joyce, *Dubliners*, London, Cape, 1967.
13 Deming (ed.), *The Critical Heritage*, vol. 1, p. 60.
14 The sense of *Ulysses* as a text in progress characterised by Joyce's rewriting of it has become commonplace in Joyce criticism thanks to Litz, Groden, Lawrence and others. Its implications are perhaps most clearly developed in J. J. McGann, "*Ulysses* as postmodern text", *Criticism*, 1985, vol. 27, pp. 283–305.
15 *Ulysses*, Harmondsworth, Penguin, 1986, p. 488.
16 These letters are presently in private hands.
17 J. Sutherland, *Offensive Literature*, London, Junction Books, 1982.
18 Ellmann and Mason (eds), *Critical Writings*, p. 204.
19 S. Beckett, *Murphy*, London, Picador, 1973, p. 69.
20 Ellmann, *James Joyce*, p. 503.
21 O. Wilde, 'Phrases and philosophies for the use of the young', in *Complete Works*, London, Collins, 1966, pp. 1205–6.
22 O. Wilde, Preface to 'The picture of Dorian Gray', in *Complete Works*, p. 17.
23 G. Steiner, 'In a post-culture', in *Extraterritorial*, London, Faber, 1972, pp. 155–71, and *In Bluebeard's Castle*, London, Faber, 1971. In 'Eros and

idiom', in *On Difficulty*, London, Faber, 1975, pp. 95–136, Steiner further argues that a supposed 'code of sexual explicitness may be related to the general malaise of the novel'.

24 D. Lodge, *The Modes of Modern Writing*, London, Edward Arnold, 1977, pp. 35–41.

25 J. Derrida, 'The theatre of cruelty and the closure of representation' (1966), in *Writing and Difference*, trans. A. Bass, London, Routledge & Kegan Paul, 1981, pp. 232–50.

26 R. Barthes, *Sade, Fourier, Loyola*, New York, Hill & Wang, 1976, p. 126.

Select bibliography

Appignanesi, L. and Maitland, S. (eds), *The Rushdie File*, London, Fourth Estate, 1989.

Arnstein, W. L., *The Bradlaugh Case. A Study in Late Victorian Opinion and Politics*, Oxford, Clarendon Press, 1965.

Aspinall, A., *Politics and the Press c. 1780–1850*, London, Horne & Van Thal, 1949.

Beman, L. T. (ed.), *Selected Articles on Censorship of the Theater and Moving Pictures*, New York, H. W. Wilson, 1931.

Bond, D. H. and McLeod, W. R. (eds), *Newsletters to Newspapers: Eighteenth Century Journalism*, Morgantown, Va, School of Journalism, West Virginia University, 1977.

Boyle, K. (ed.), *Article 19. Information, Freedom and Censorship: World Report 1988*, New York, Times Books, 1988.

Bristow, E. J., *Vice and Vigilance. Purity Movements in Britain since 1700*, Dublin, Gill & Macmillan, 1977.

Brittain, V., *Radclyffe Hall. A Case of Obscenity?*, London, Femina Books, 1968.

Buchan, N. and Sumner, T. (eds), *Glasnost in Britain?*, London, Macmillan, 1989.

Calder-Marshall, A., *Lewd, Blasphemous and Obscene*, London, Hutchinson, 1972.

Chandos, J. (ed.), *To Deprave and Corrupt, Original Studies in the Nature and Definition of Obscenity*, London, Souvenir Press, 1962.

Clare, J., *'Art Made Tongue-tied by Authority': Elizabethan and Jacobean Dramatic Censorship*, Manchester, Manchester University Press, 1990.

Clyde, W. M., *The Struggle for the Freedom of the Press from Caxton to Cromwell*, London, Oxford University Press, 1934.

Cobbett, W. and Howell, T. C. (eds), *A Complete Collection of State Trials to 1783*, 33 vols, London, Longman, 1809–26.

Conolly, L. W., *The Censorship of English Drama, 1737–1824*, San Marino, Calif., The Huntington Library, 1976.

Copp, D. and Wendell, S. (eds), *Pornography and Censorship*, London, Prometheus Books, 1982.

Craig, A., *The Banned Books of England and other Countries*, London, Allen & Unwin, 1962.

Cranfield, G. A., *The Press and Society: from Caxton to Northcliffe*, London, Longman, 1978.

Curtis, L., *Ireland: the Propaganda War*, London, Pluto Press, 1984.

Davenport-Hines, R., *Sex, Death and Punishment: Attitudes to Sex and Sexuality in Britain since the Renaissance*, London, Fontana, 1991.

Dawes, C. R., *A Study of Erotic Literature in England*, Cheltenham, typescript, 1943.

Duke, A. C. and Tamse, C. A. (eds), *Too Mighty to be Free: Censorship and the Press in Britain and the Netherlands*, Zutphen, Netherlands, De Walburg Pers, 1987.

Dworkin, A., *Pornography: Men Possessing Women*, London, Women's Press, 1981.

Ernst, M. L. and Schwartz, A. U., *Censorship: the Search for the Obscene*, New York, Macmillan, 1964.

Ewing, K. D. and Gearty, C. A., *Freedom under Thatcher: Civil Liberties in Modern Britain*, Oxford, Clarendon Press, 1990.

Findlater, R., *Banned! A Review of Theatrical Censorship in Britain*, London, Macgibbon & Kee, 1967.

Foucault, M., *The History of Sexuality, vol. 1: an Introduction*, trans. R. Hurley, London, Allen Lane, 1979.

Fowell, F. and Palmer, F., *Censorship in England*, New York, Burt Franklin, 1970.

Foxon, D., *Libertine Literature in England, 1660–1745*, New York, University Books, 1965.

Goldstein, R. J., *Political Censorship of the Arts and the Press in Nineteenth-Century Europe*, London, Macmillan, 1989.

Green, J., *The Encyclopedia of Censorship*, New York, Facts on File Inc., 1990.

Haight, A. L., *Banned Books*, New York, R. R. Bowker Co., 1955.

Hanson, L., *Government and the Press, 1695–1763*, Oxford, Oxford University Press, 1936.

Helmholz, R. H., *Juries, Libels & Justice: the Role of English Juries in Seventeenth- and Eighteenth-Century Trials for Libel and Slander*, Los Angeles, William Andrews Clark Memorial Library, 1984.

Herman, E. S. and Chomsky, N., *Manufacturing Consent: the Political Economics of Mass Media*, New York, Pantheon, 1988.

Holmes, G. S., *The Trial of Doctor Sacheverell*, London, Methuen, 1973.

Hooper, D., *Official Secrets: the Use and Abuse of the Act*, London, Coronet, 1988.

Hunnings, N. M., *Film Censors and the Law*, London, Allen & Unwin, 1967.

Hyde, H. Montgomery, *A History of Pornography*, London, Heinemann, 1964.

Jackson, H., *The Fear of Books*, London, Soncino Press, 1932.

Jansen, S. Curry, *Censorship: the Knot that Binds Power and Knowledge*, Oxford, Oxford University Press, 1988.

Johnston, J., *The Lord Chamberlain's Blue Pencil*, London, Hodder & Stoughton, 1990.

Jones, D. and Platt, S. (eds), *Banned*, London, Channel 4 Television, 1991.

Joynson-Hicks, W., *Do We Need a Censor?*, London, Faber, 1929.

Kappeler, S., *The Pornography of Representation*, Cambridge, Polity Press, 1986.

Knightley, P., *The First Casualty*, London, Pan, 1989.

Kronhausen, E. and P., *Pornography and the Law: the Psychology of Erotic Realism and Pornography*, New York, Ballantine Books, 1959.

Lawrence, D. H., *Pornography and Obscenity*, London, Faber, 1929.

—— *A Propos of Lady Chatterley's Lover*, London, Mandrake Press, 1930.

Lee, S., *The Cost of Free Speech*, London, Faber, 1990.

Levy, L. W., *Emergence of a Free Press*, Oxford, Oxford University Press, 1985.

Liesenfeld, V. J., *The Licensing Act of 1737*, Madison, University of Wisconsin Press, 1984.

Loth, D. G., *The Erotic in Literature: a Historical Survey of Pornography as Delightful as it is Indiscreet*, London, Secker & Warburg, 1962.

McCalman, I., *Radical Underworld. Prophets, Revolutionaries and Pornographers in London, 1795–1840*, Cambridge, Cambridge University Press, 1988.

MacMillan, P. R., *Censorship and Public Morality*, Aldershot, Gower, 1983.

Montagu, I., *The Political Censorship of Films*, London, Victor Gollancz, 1929.

Negrine, R., *Politics and the Mass Media in Britain*, London, Routledge, 1989.

Nokes, G. D., *A History of the Crime of Blasphemy*, London, Sweet & Maxwell, 1928.

Ould, H. (ed.), *Freedom of Expression. A Symposium . . . to Commemorate the Tercentenary of the Publication of Milton's 'Areopagitica'*, London, Hutchinson International Authors, 1944.

Palmer, J., *The Censor and the Theatre*, New York, Mitchell Kennerly, 1913.

Patterson, A., *Censorship and Interpretation: the Conditions of Writing and Reading in Early Modern England*, Madison, University of Wisconsin Press, 1984.

Phelps, G., *Film Censorship*, London, Victor Gollancz, 1975.

Radcliffe, C. J., *Censors. The Rede Lecture*, Cambridge, Cambridge University Press, 1961.

Robertson, G., *Obscenity: an Account of Censorship Laws and their Enforcement in England and Wales*, London, Weidenfeld & Nicolson, 1979.

_____ *Freedom, the Individual and the Law*, Harmondsworth, Penguin, 1989.

Robertson, J. C., *The British Board of Film Censors: Film Censorship in Britain, 1896–1950*, London, Croom Helm, 1985.

_____ *The Hidden Cinema: British Film Censorship in Action, 1913–72*, London, Routledge, 1989.

Rolph, C. H. (ed.), *The Trial of Lady Chatterley*, Harmondsworth, Penguin, 1961 [reissued with a Foreword by G. Robertson, 1990].

Rude, G., *Wilkes and Liberty: a Social Study of 1763–1774*, Oxford, Clarendon Press, 1962.

Siebert, F. S., *Freedom of the Press in England, 1476–1776*, Urbana, University of Illinois Press, 1952.

Stephens, J. R., *The Censorship of English Drama, 1824–1901*, Cambridge, Cambridge University Press, 1980.

Stevas, N. St John, *Obscenity and the Law*, London, Secker & Warburg, 1956.

Sutherland, J., *Offensive Literature: Decensorship in Britain, 1960–1982*, London, Junction Books, 1982.

Theiner, G. (ed.), *They Shoot Writers, Don't They?*, London, Faber, 1984.

Thomas, D., *A Long Time Burning: the History of Literary Censorship in Britain*, London, Routledge & Kegan Paul, 1969.

Thompson, A. H., *Censorship in Public Libraries in the United Kingdom during the Twentieth Century*, Epping, Bowker, 1975.

Thornton, P., *Decade of Decline: Civil Liberties in the Thatcher Years*, London, National Council for Civil Liberties, 1989.

Trevelyan, J., *What the Censor Saw*, London, Michael Joseph, 1973.

Tribe, D., *Questions of Censorship*, London, Allen & Unwin, 1973.

Vincent, D., *Literacy and Popular Culture: England 1750–1914*, Cambridge, Cambridge University Press, 1989.

Wickwar, W. H., *The Struggle for the Freedom of the Press, 1819–1832*, London, Allen & Unwin, 1928.

Widmer, E. (ed.), *Freedom and Culture: Literary Censorship in the 70s*, Belmont, Calif., Wadsworth, 1970.

Wilson, D. (ed.), *The Secrets File*, London, Heinemann, 1984.

Index

Acker, Kathy 254
Acton, William 161; *The Functions and Disorders of the Reproductive Organs in Childhood, Youth, Adult Age and Advanced Life* 161
Addison, Joseph 71
Adler, Susan 238; *Equality Street* 238; *Ms Moffet Fights Back* 238
advertising tax 131
Aeschylus 173
Aesop 30–2; *The Frogs desiring a King* 31–2; *The Sheep and the Butcher* 30, 32
AIDS 2, 9
Ailesbury, Thomas Bruce, Earl of 40
Aldington, Richard 201, 209
Alexander II, Tsar 130
Anderson, Margaret 252
Anglesey, Arthur Annesley, Earl of 65
Anne, Queen 41, 59–77
Ariosti, Attilio 88; *Coriolanus* 88
Aristophanes 158, 165
Aristotle 49
Arlington, Henry Bennet, Earl of 49
Arnold, Matthew 133, 173, 254
Artaud, Antonin 254
Article 19, 125
Ashbee, Henry Spencer 156; *Catena librorum tacendorum* 156; *Centuria librorum absconditorum* 156; *Index librorum prohibitorum* 156
Association for the Preservation of Liberty and Property 110
Association against Republicans and Levellers 118
Asquith, Cynthia 205
Asquith, H. H. 191, 193–4, 197

Atkinson, Frederick 202

Babington, Anthony 25, 28–33
Bacon, Francis 7
Baker, David Erskine 98; *Biographica Dramatica* 98–9
Baker, Kenneth 240
Bakhtin, Mikhail 12, 26
Balfour, A. J. 186
Balzac, Honoré de 159; *Contes Drolatiques* 159
Bannerman, Helen 234; *Little Black Sambo* 234
Barber, John 67–8
Barry, Peter 3
Barthes, Roland 255; *Sade, Fourier, Loyola* 255
Bataille, Georges 254
Baudelaire, Charles 11
Baxter, Walter 18; *The Image and the Search* 18
Beauclerk, Diana, Lady 100–2
Beckett, Samuel 252; *Murphy* 252
Bedborough, George 18, 144, 146
Bedford, Hilkiah 74–7
Bell, Clive 189; *Peace at Once* 189
Bennett, Arnold 137, 190–1, 195, 198, 211
Bernard, Jonathan 38
Berry, Mary 103
Besant, Annie 17, 144, 146, 150, 155
Biggles 236, 240
Birch, Samuel 111–12
Birkenhead, Lord (F. E. Smith) 193–4, 220
Blackburn, Justice 162
Blackwell, Elizabeth 161; *Counsel to Parents* 161

Blake, William 211
Bland, Margot 18; *Julia* 18
Blasphemy Act (1698) 16
Blount, Sir William Kirkham 38
Blyton, Enid 240
Bogdanov, Michael 7, 19
Bolde, Samuel 37, 41
Bolingbroke, Henry St John, Viscount 65, 69, 77
Bond, Edward 19; *Saved* 19
Bonner, Bishop Edmund 27
Boot, Sir Jesse 204, 206
Booth, Stephen 23–5
Borewell, Pego 17; *Essay on Woman* 17
Bosche, Susanne 239; *Jenny Lives with Eric and Martin* 239–40
Bosmajian, Hamida 238
Boswell, James 107–8; *Life of Samuel Johnson* 107
Boteville, Francis 24–5
Botha, P. W. 125–6
Boumelha, Penny 179
Bradlaugh, Charles 17, 144, 146, 150, 155
Bradley, Thomas 42
Branson, Richard 19
Breinburg, Petronella and Lloyd, Errol 236; *Doctor Sean* 236
Brenton, Howard 7, 19; *The Romans in Britain* 7, 19
Bridges, Harry 42
British Board of Film Censors 133–6
British Board of Film and Video Classification 164
Broadcasting Standards Council 1, 20
Brockway, Fenner 196
Bromley, George 75
Brontë, sisters 157
Brooke, Rupert 187
Brougham, Lord 162
Brownmiller, Susan 3
Brydges, Sir Samuel Egerton 99; *Censura Literaria* 99
Buckle, H. T. 1
Buckmaster, Sir Stanley 193
Bull, Richard 100
Bull, Robert 41–2
Burgess, Anthony 3
Burghley, Lord (William Cecil) 29
Burney, Frances 95
Burrell, William 38
Burroughs, William 254

Burtsev, Vladimir 130
Byron, George Gordon, Lord 137, 151; *Marino Faliero* 137

Caesar, Charles 73
Cambridge Intelligencer 110, 116–17
Campbell, Duncan 185
Campbell, John, Lord 144, 151, 160; *see also* Obscene Publications Act (1857)
Cape, Jonathan 220
Capone, Al 166
Carlile, Richard 129, 144, 146, 150
Carr, Henry 250
Carswell, Catherine 208
Carswell, Donald 205
Carter, Thomas 112
Caute, David 13n
Caxton, William 30
Cézanne, Paul 200, 212
Chamber, Alan 40–1
Chamberlain, Lord 1, 16–17, 19, 83, 88, 93, 103–4, 134–5, 187
Chambers, Jessie 201
Charlemont, James Caulfield, Earl of 100, 102
Charles I 16, 136
Charles II 16, 46–54
Charlotte, Queen 95
Chartism 129–30, 136, 146
Chaucer, Geoffrey 158
Cheap, Henry 63
Childers, Mary 179
Children's Rights Workshop 234; *Children's Book Bulletin* 234–5
Churchill, Winston 19
Cibber, Colley 88
Cleland, John 8, 17–18, 244; *Fanny Hill* 8, 17–18, 244
Clive, Kitty 92
Cockburn, Lord Chief Justice 154; *see also Hicklin* judgement
Cohen, Barbara 241; *Molly's Pilgrim* 241
'Censoring the sources' 241
Coke, Lady Mary 94, 101
Cole, G. D. H. 187–8
Coleridge, Lord Chief Justice, 142–3
Coleridge, Samuel Taylor 117–18
Collings, Ernest 204
Collins, Henry 38
Collins, Wilkie 157, 162

Colman, George, the Elder 88, 93
Colman, George, the Younger 135
Committee on Examinations 16
Committee of Imperial Defence 192
Conrad, Joseph 137
Constantine, Henry 41
Conway, Henry Seymour 97
Cook, Sir Edward 193–4
Corbalis, Judy 237; *The Wrestling Princess* 237
Corke, Helen 202
Corresponding Societies Act (1799) 114
Council on Interracial Books for Children (CIBC) 235–6
Court of High Commission 16
Craftsman, The 82–5
Craggs, James 69–70
Crisp, Quentin 6–7, 11
Crowne, John 47, 51–2; *The English Friar* 52; *Henry the Sixth, the First Part* 47, 52; *The Miseries of the Civil War* 52
Cruikshank, George 137
Cunningham, George 240
Curl, Edmund 17, 142; *Venus in the Cloister, or the Nun in her Smock* 17
Currie, James 112

'D' Notices 192–4
Daily Chronicle 191
Daily Express 211
Daily Herald 196–7
Daily Mail 193
Daily News 195
Dalton, Hugh 187
Dalton, James 32
Daudet, Alphonse 155
Davenant, William 46
Davenport-Hines, Richard 1–2, 8, 9; *Sex, Death and Punishment* 9
Defence of the Realm Act (DORA, 1914) 192–3, 196
Deffand, Madame du 93–4
Defoe, Daniel 60–1, 65, 68–9, 73–7, 158
Deleuze, Gilles 248
Derrida, Jacques 254, 256
Desart, Lord (H. J. Cuffe) 220
Dickens, Charles 153n, 157, 162–3, 165
Dilhorne, Viscount 19

Dodsley, James 96, 100, 102
Dollan, P. J. 197
Donne, William 135
Donno, Elizabeth Story 24
Douglas, James 204–5, 219–21
Draper, R. P. 209–10
Dryden, John 46, 51, 162, 167; *Absalom and Achitophel* 51
Duckworth, Gerald 203
Dumas, Alexandre 135, 162; *La Dame aux camélias* 135, 162
Dworkin, Andrea 3, 168; *Pornography: Men Possessing Women* 3
Dyson, Will 188

Eaton, Daniel Isaac 110, 112–13, 144; *Politics for the People* 110
Echard, Laurence 39
Education Institute of Scotland 235
Edward VII 132–3, 248
Egoist, The 244, 250, 253
Eliot, George 157
Eliot, T. S. 203, 254; *The Wasteland* 203
Elizabeth I 15, 23–4, 26–8, 34, 46
Elkin, Judith and Triggs, Pat 238; *Books for Keeps Guide to Children's Books* 238
Ellenborough, Edward Law, Lord 131
Ellis, Havelock 18, 144, 155, 219, 222; *Sexual Inversion* 155; *Studies in the Psychology of Sex* 18, 144, 155
Ellmann, Richard 244, 246
Emsley, Clive 112
Engels, Friedrich 127
Ensor, Robert 190–2, 194
Ernst, Morris 213–14, 245; *To The Pure* 213
Erskine, Thomas, Lord 142
Essex, Earl of 51
Etherege, Sir George 42
European Court of Human Rights 125
Exclusion crisis 16, 46–54
Ezekiel 165

Fabian Society 185–8, 191, 197
Farington, Joseph 101
Faulkner, Matthew 111–12
Fielding, Henry 17
Fiske, Roger 88
Flaubert, Gustave 155, 251
Fleming, Abraham 24–7, 31, 34

Foley, Thomas, 69–72
Foot, Michael 3
Foote, G. W. 144, 150–1
Ford, Charles, 69
Forster, E. M. 163
Foucault, Michel 5–10, 155, 160, 163, 165–6, 221–2; *The History of Sexuality* 5–6, 155, 163
Fox, Charles James 17, 113, 127, 141
Foxe, John 26–7; *Actes and Monumentes* 26–7
Freud, Sigmund 8–10, 104, 165, 228, 230, 244, 246–7, 251, 256; *The Interpretation of Dreams* 8, 247, 251; *Three Essays on the Theory of Sexuality* 8
Frost, Robert 81; 'Mending Wall' 81
Fuentes, Carlos 12

Gabler, Hans 246
Garnett, Edward 203–4
Garrick, David 92–3
Gautier, Théophile 155
Gay, John 12, 81–9; *The Beggar's Opera* 12, 82, 85–6, 88; *Dione* 82; *The Mohocks* 81; *Polly* 81, 83, 85–8; *Three Hours after Marriage* 81–2
Gay News 19
George I 77
George II 82, 85–6
George IV 132
Gide, André 15
Gilbert, W. S. and Sullivan, Arthur 136; *Mikado* 136
Gildon, Charles 49; *The Patriot* 49
Girardin, Count Stanislaw de 127
Gladstone, William 131
Godwin, William 8; *Enquiry Concerning Political Justice* 8
Goethe, Johann Wolfgang von 173
Goldberg, S. L. 29
Goldgar, Bertrand 83, 87–8
Goldman, Emma 126
Gould, Eliza 117
Grafton, Charles Fitzroy, Duke of 83–4
Grant, Bernie 4
Grant, Damian 10
Graphic 172, 175–8
Graves, Robert 191
Greer, Germaine 9
Grey, Sir Edward 194

Griffith-Jones, Mervyn 8, 215–16
Grundyism 171–2
Guernsey, Heneage Finch, Lord 68
Guiffardière, Charles de 95

Haig, General Sir Douglas 195
Haldane, R. B. 194
Hall, Radclyffe 12, 18, 219–31; *The Well of Loneliness* 12, 18, 219–31
Halifax, Lord (Charles Montague) 69
Hamilton, Mary 95, 101
Hamilton, Sir William 99
Handel, Georg Friedrich 88; *Scipione* 88; *The Water Music* 88
Hanmer, Sir Thomas 66, 73, 75
Harcourt, Elizabeth, Lady 100
Harcourt, Sir Simon 75, 95, 100
Hardy, Florence 172
Hardy, Thomas 12, 171–9; 'Candour in English Fiction' 172–3; *Desperate Remedies* 171; *Far from the Madding Crowd* 178; *Jude the Obscure* 172; *The Life of Thomas Hardy* 172–3; *The Mayor of Casterbridge* 179; 'The Poor Man and the Lady' 171; *The Return of the Native* 178; *Tess of the d'Urbervilles* 172, 175–8; *Under the Greenwood Tree* 171, 178
Hardy, Thomas (Secretary of London Corresponding Society) 116
Harley, Edward 69–70, 72–3
Harley, Robert 60–2, 65–7, 69, 74, 77
Harrington, James 49
Harrison, William 24
Hattersley, Roy 8
Hawkins, John 93
Hawkins, Laetitia-Matilda 93; *Anecdotes, Biographical Sketches and Memoirs* 93
Hayward, Sir John 24, 29; *History of Henry IV* 24, 29
Hazen, A. T. 93
Hearne, Thomas 42
Heinemann, William 202–3
Heller, Steven 132
Henderson, Arthur 198
Henderson, John 98
Henry VIII 15, 74
Herald 111
Herbert Committee 18
Hereditary Right, The 62, 65, 73–5
Hertford, Lord 93

Hervey, John, Lord 84–5; *Memoirs* 84
Herzen, Alexander 126
Heseltine, Philip 207
Hetherington, Henry 144
Heyrick, John 112–13
Hickes, George 74
Hicklin judgement (definition of
    obscenity, 1868) 143, 151, 154–60,
    162–3
Hill, Christopher 4
Hoadly, Benjamin 37, 43
Hobbes, Thomas 16; *Leviathan* 16
Holcroft, William 117
Holinshed, Raphael 23–35; *Chronicles*
    23–35; 'Tichborne's Elegie' 28–9, 32
Holt, Lord Chief Justice 60
Holyoake, G. J. 144, 149
Hone, William 144, 150
Hooker, John 24
Hooton, John 113
Howard, Sir Robert 46
Huebsch, Benjamin 207
Hueffer, Ford Madox 202
Hume, David 15
Hungerford, John 69
Hutchinson, St John 210
Huxley, Aldous 209–10
Huxley, Maria 209

Ibsen, Henrik 135; *Ghosts* 135
Illustrated London News 191
Inchbald, Elizabeth 137
Independent Labour Party (ILP) 188,
    190, 195–8; *Forward* 196–7; *Labour
    Leader* 196–7
Index on Censorship 125
Index Librorum Prohibitorum 14–15
Inner London Education Authority
    (ILEA) 235–6, 240
Inside Linda Lovelace 7, 19
Inskip, Thomas 18
Intelligencer, The 82
International Press Institute 125
Irish Republican Army (IRA) 245
IT 19, 215

Jacobson, Howard 179
James II 39, 46–54
James, Henry 137–8
Jarman, Derek 19; *Sebastiane* 19
Jeffries, George, Judge 40
Jenkins, Jolyon 1, 7

Jenkins, Roy 214
Jephson, Robert 98; *The Court of
    Narbonne* 98
Johnston, Tom 197
Jones, Charles 42
Jones, Stephen 99
Joyce, James 12, 163, 244–57;
    Dubliners 244, 248–51; *Finnegans
    Wake* 244, 251; 'From a banned
    writer to a banned singer' 244; *A
    Portrait of the Artist as a Young Man*
    244, 248; *Selected Letters* 246; *Stephen
    Hero* 249; *Ulysses* 244–6, 249–53
Joyce, Nora 244
Joynson-Hicks, Sir William ('Jix') 10,
    210, 213–14; *Do We Need a Censor?*
    213
Juvenal 158

Kafka, Franz 248
Kallich, Martin 104
Kant, Immanuel 165
Kappeler, Susanne 171, 175, 177–9;
    The Pornography of Representation
    171, 179
Kaufman, Stanley 18; *The Philanderer*
    18
Keats, John 246
Keeling, 'Ben' 187
Kenrick, Daniel 38–9
Khomeini, Ayatollah 2, 20, 164
Killigrew, Charles 46, 48–9, 51–2
Killigrew, Thomas 46
Kincaid, James 179
Kinkead-Weekes, Mark 206
Kinkel, Gottfried 126
Kinkel, Johanna 126
Kirkup, James 19; 'The Love that
    dares to speak its name' 19
Kitchener, Horatio Herbert, Lord 191
Klein, Melanie 248
Klein, Norma 240
Knopf, Alfred 209
Knowlton, Charles 17, 155; *The Fruits
    of Philosophy* 17, 155
Konody, Paul 211
Kossuth, Louis 126
Koteliansky, S. S. 206
Krafft-Ebing, Richard von 224, 228
Kropotkin, Prince Peter 126

Labour Party 190, 196, 198

Lacan, Jacques 248
Lahr, Charlie 210
Lane, Allen 214
Larkin, Philip 215; 'Annus Mirabilis' 215
Lawrence, Ada 202
Lawrence, D. H. 7, 9, 12, 18, 163, 165, 189, 200–16, 244, 246; 'Introduction to these paintings' 200; *Lady Chatterley's Lover* 7–8, 18, 162, 200, 202, 208–11, 214–16, 244; *Look We have Come Through!* 207; *The Lost Girl* 207; *More Pansies* 189; *Movements in European History* 207; *Pansies* 200, 208–11; *Phoenix* 211–12; 'Pornography and obscenity' 212–13; *The Prussian Officer* 204; *The Rainbow* 200, 204–7, 212–14; *Sons and Lovers* 202–3; *The Trespasser* 202; *The White Peacock* 201–2; *Women in Love* 206–7
Lawrence, Frieda 200–2
Lawrence, George 202
Law Times 157
Lee, Nathaniel 48–9; *Caesar Borgia* 48; *Lucius Junius Brutus* 48–9, 51
Lee, Simon 215–16; *The Cost of Free Speech* 215
Leicester, Robert, Earl of 23, 25
Le Petit, Alfred 127
Lesley, Charles 63
Lewis, W. 250, 253
Lewis, Wilmarth 104
Libel Act (1792) 17, 113, 141–2
Liberal Party 196–8
Library Association 240
Licensing Acts 1, 53, 59, 127, 141
Little Red Schoolbook 19
Little Review 244, 250, 252
Liverpool, Robert Jenkinson, Lord 129
Livy 48–9; *Ab Urbe Condita* 48
Llewelin, David 39
Lloyd, Errol *see* Breinburg, Petronella
Lloyd George, David 185, 190–1, 194–7
Local Authorities Act (1988) 20, 219, 240
Locke, John 4, 16; *Letters Concerning Toleration* 4
Lodge, David 254

Lofting, Hugh 234; *The Story of Dr Dolittle* 234
Lolita 215
London Corresponding Society (LCS) 109–10, 116
London Mercury 189
Lords and Labourers 136
Louisa, Princess 82
Louis-Philippe 126
Lovett, William 129
Lowndes, William 74
Lowth, Robert 93
Lowther, James 40
Luce, Richard 240
Lumley, Richard 70
Luther, Martin 207

Macaulay, T. B., Lord 142, 157
MacDonald, Ramsay 210
McEwan, Ian 245
MacGraw, Hugh 18; *The Man in Control* 18
Machiavelli 49
McInerney, Jay 248; *Story of My Life* 248
MacKinnon, Catharine 168
MacLeod, Anne Scott 232
Macmillan's Magazine 172
MacMillan, P. R. 158
Manchester Gazette 116
Manchester Guardian 194
Manchester Herald 110–11, 117
Manley, Mary 68
Mann, Horace 99–101
Mapplethorpe, Robert 11
Mar, Earl of (John Erskine) 67
Marcus, S. 166
Marcuse, H. 4–5, 11–12; 'Repressive tolerance' 4–5
Marks, Lewis 132
Marlborough, Henrietta, Duchess of 85
Marlborough, John Churchill, Duke of 72, 74–5
Martin, Kingsley 185, 187
Marx, Karl 4–5, 33, 126
Mary I 24–8
Mary, Queen 141
Mason, William 93, 95–8
Massingham, H. W. 195
Master of the Revels 15, 46, 48, 49, 51, 53–4

Matthews, John 17; *Vox Populi, Vox Dei* 17
Maupassant, Guy de 155
Mead, Justice 212
Mein Kampf 8
Methuen & Co. 204–5, 207
Metternich, Prince Klemens von 126
Meyers, J. 205
Miles, Betty 240–1; *All it Takes is Practice* 240
Mill, John Stuart 4, 17, 151; *On Liberty* 4, 17
Millett, Kate 20
Milton, John 4, 7, 16, 173; *Areopagitica* 4, 7, 16; *Mirror for Magistrates* 24
Molineux, Edmund 25
Montagu, George 92, 94
Montaigne, Michel de 3
Montalk, Count Geoffrey de 18; *Here Lies John Penis* 18
Moore, Arthur 69
Moore, H. T. 201
Moravia, Alberto 15
Morphew, John 67
Morrel, Ottoline 207
Morrel, Philip 205, 207
Morrison, Nellie 208–9
Moss, Elaine 234; *Reading for Enjoyment* 234
Most, Johann 130
Mouth, The 19
Murray's Magazine 172
Muskett, Harold 212
My Secret Life 6

Napoleon 129
Napoleon, Louis 126
Nasty Tales 215
Nation 188, 190, 195
National Book League 234
National Committee on Racism in Children's Books 234; *Dragons Teeth* 234
National Purity League 205
National Union of Teachers (NUT) 235–6; *In Black and White: Guidelines for Teachers* 236
National Vigilance Association (NVA) 148–9, 151
Nepean, Even 110
Neville, Henry 49
New Age 187–9

Newcastle, Duke of (Thomas Pelham-Holles) 82
Newspaper Regulation Bill (1798) 114
New Statesman 4–5, 185–98, 236–7
New York Times 125
Nicholas II, Tsar 130
Nicol, George 103
Northcliffe, Alfred Harmsworth, Lord 193
Northern Star 129
Northey, Edward 68
Nottingham, Daniel Finch, Earl of 68

Oates, Titus 46
Obscene Publications Act (1857, 'Lord Campbell's Act') 1–2, 17, 147–9, 155–7, 160, 162–3, 211
Obscene Publications Act (1959) 1–2, 7, 11, 18, 151, 162–3, 214
Observer 211
O'Connor, Feargus 129
O'Daly, Patrick 208
Official Secrets Acts: (1889) 17; (1911) 192; (1988) 20
Orage, A. R. 187
Orioli, Giuseppe 212
Ossory, Anne Liddell, Lady 99, 101–2
OZ 3, 9, 215

Paine, Tom 8, 17, 109–12, 115–19, 129, 144, 146; *The Age of Reason* 144; *The Rights of Man* 8, 17, 109–12, 115, 117
Parker, Thomas, Lord Chief Justice 60–1, 64, 74–5, 77
Parsons, William 102
Patterson, Annabel 10–11, 37, 46, 166–7; *Censorship and Interpretation* 10, 166–7
Paulin, Tom 216
Pendleton, Gayle 112
Penty, A. J. 187
Peploe, Samuel 39
Percival, Sir John 70–1, 73–4
Philip II of Spain 27
Phillips, Richard 111, 112–13
Pigott, Charles 111; *The Jockey Club* 111
Pigott, E. F. Smyth 135
Pigott, Henry 43
Piggott, John 42
Pimlott, Ben 187
Pinker, James Brand 204–6

Pinter, Harold 12; *One for the Road* 12
Pirani, Felix 239; *Abigail on the Beach* 239
Pitt, William 8, 108, 127
Place, Francis 108, 112, 118
Plato 4, 254; *The Republic* 4, 254
Pole, Sir Courtenay 38
Pomfrett, Thomas 40
Ponting, Clive 19
Pope, Alexander 82, 83, 88; *The Dunciad* 83
Potter, Dennis 245
Pound, Ezra 203, 205, 244, 250
Press Bureau 185, 192–5, 197
Preston Review 117
Pretender (James Edward Stuart) 59, 62, 66, 70–2
Price, Humphrey 129
Price, Willard 236; *Cannibal Adventure* 236
Pritchard, Hannah 92
Pritchett, V. S. 210
Protestant Electoral Union 143, 154; *The Confessional Unmasked* 143, 154, 157–8
Prynne, William 15; *Histriomastix* 15
Punch 127, 132

Queensbury, Catherine Hyde, Duchess of 85, 88–9

Rabelais, François 158
Race Relations Acts: (1965) 19; (1976) 216, 232
Raynsford, George 49
Reagan, Ronald 238
Reed, Isaac 98–9
Redford, G. A. 135
Rees-Mogg, William, Lord 1
Reeves, John 110–11
Regency Act (1706) 17
Rich, John 83–4
Richards, Grant 211, 244, 248–50
Richardson, Samuel 15; *Pamela* 15
Ridpath, George 60–1, 77
Roberts, George 244
Robertson, Geoffrey 14n, 154–5, 158, 165–6
Rossini, Gioacchino (Antonio) 135; *Moses* 135
Roth, Samuel 245
Royal Proclamation (1792) 110–11

Rushdie, Salman 2–3, 12, 20, 164, 244–5; *The Satanic Verses* 2–3, 8–9, 12, 20
Rushton, Edward 117
Russell, Bertrand 7, 205

Sabor, Peter 7
Sacheverell, George 43
Sacheverell, Henry 37, 43, 65, 75
Sade, Marquis de 255
St John Stevas, Norman 7
Sandberg, Rosemary 239
Sartre, Jean-Paul 15
Sassoon, Siegfried 191
Saunders, David 8
Saussure, Ferdinand de 254, 256
Scandalum Magnatum 15
Schlesinger, Arthur 165
School Bookshop Association 234; *Books for Keeps* 234
Schorer, Mark 203
Schütz, Georg Wilhem Sinold, Baron 70–1
Scott, C. P. 194
Scott, Geoffrey 211–12
Seasonable Queries 62, 75
Secker, Martin 202, 206–10
Sedgemoor, Brian 4
Sedition Act (1661) 49
Sedley, Sir Charles 16–17, 46, 52
Selby, Hugh 19; *Last Exit to Brooklyn* 19
Settle, Elkanah 47–8, 52; *The Female Prelate* 47–8, 52
Sex Discrimination Act (1975) 232
Sexual Offences Act (1956) 7, 19
Shadwell, Thomas 47, 51–3; *Bury Fair* 53; *The Lancashire Witches* 47, 52–4
Shaftesbury, Earl of (Anthony Ashley Cooper) 47–8, 51
Shakespeare, William 12, 23–4, 47, 49–52, 94, 101, 104, 173; *Henry VI* 47, 51–2; *Richard II* 12, 24, 49–51
Sharp, Clifford 187–8, 190–2, 194–8
Shaw, George Bernard 135, 186–8
Sheffield Iris 116
Sheffield Register 110
Shelley, Percy Bysshe 151, 162; *Queen Mab* 162
Shikes, Ralph 132
Shorter, Clement 204–5
Sidmouth, Henry, Viscount 129

Sidney, Sir Henry 25
Sidney, Sir Philip 23, 25, 167; *Arcadia* 25; *Four Foster Children of Desire* 23
Siebert, F. S. 1–2
Simpson, John 248–9
Sinn Féin 245
Sir Thomas More 24
Skerret, Ralph 39
Skingle, Richard 39
Smelt, Leonard 95
Smith, F. E. *see* Birkenhead, Lord
Smith, Richard 74
Society for the Suppression of Vice 145–6, 148–9
Society of Authors 18, 205, 214
Sophia, Electress of Hanover 62–3
Sophocles 173
Spectator 19, 190
Spence, Thomas 110, 112, 117; *Pig's Meat* 110
Spender, J. A. 194
Spenser, Edmund 35n; *Faerie Queene* 35n; *Shepheardes Calender* 35n
Sphere 204–5
Squire, Jack 188–9, 192, 196, 198
Stage Licensing Act (1737) 17, 134
Stamp Act (1712) 16, 60, 130–1
Stanhope, James 69–71
Star 204–5
Star Chamber, Court of 15–16, 26
Stationers' Company 29
Stead, W. T. 148
Steele, Sir Richard 59–77, 81–2; *The Crisis* 62–5, 69, 72–5; *Englishman* 62, 66, 69, 73; *Guardian* 62; *The Importance of Dunkirk Consider'd* 62; *Lover* 76; *Mr Steele's Apology* 66; *Reader* 76
Steevens, George 92–3, 98–9
Steiner, George 254
Stoppard, Tom 12; *Every Good Boy Deserves Favour* 12; *Professional Foul* 12; *The Real Thing* 12; *Squaring the Circle* 12
Story of O, The 215
Stow, John 24–5, 27
Strachey, John St Loe 194
Strachey, Lytton 189
Strafford, Thomas Wentworth, Earl of 63
Sullivan, Arthur *see* Gilbert, W. S.
Sullivan, John 244

Sunday Sport 20
Sutherland, John 1–4, 11–12, 251–2; *Offensive Literature* 251
Swift, Jonathan 3, 61–2, 66–9, 72, 75, 82–5, 88, 158; *The Drapier's Letters* 83; *Examiner* 62, 66, 70; *Gulliver's Travels* 108; *Project for the Advancement of Learning* 72; *Publick Spirit of the Whigs* 66–7, 69; *Some Free Thoughts upon the Present State of Affairs* 69
Sydney, Viscount 137

Tanner, Thomas 38
Tate, Nahum 49–52, 54; *The History of King Richard the Second* 49–51; *The Sicilian Usurper* 50
Taylor, William 103
Terkel, Studs 239; *The Great Divide* 239; *Working* 239
Thackeray, William Makepeace 157
Thatcher, Margaret 125, 238
Theatre Regulation Act (1843) 134
Thelwall, John 116–18
Thomas, Donald 1–2, 8, 158, 164; *A Long Time Burning* 164
Throckmorton, Sir Nicholas 26–7, 28, 33
Thynne, Francis *see* Boteville, Francis
Tighe, Edward 95
Time and Tide 220
Times, The 126, 134, 194
Times Educational Supplement 240
Times Literary Supplement 249
Tocqueville, Alexis de 151
Toland, John 64, 77
Townsend, John Rowe 233; *Gumble's Yard* 233
Treasonable Practices Bill (1795) 113–14
Tribe, David 1, 9, 158
Triggs, Pat *see* Elkin, Judith
Trollope, Anthony 157
Troubridge, Una 222; *The Life and Death of Radclyffe Hall* 222
True Briton 116
Two Acts (1795) 113
Tynan, Kenneth 19

Union of Democratic Control (UDC) 191
Ure, Jean 238, 241

Venereal Diseases Act (1918) 19
Verdi, Giuseppe 135; *La Traviata* 135
Vice Society *see* Society for the
    Suppression of Vice
Vizetelly, Henry 18, 144, 150, 154

Walker, Joseph 102
Walker, Thomas 116
Walpole, Horace 7, 91–104; *The Castle
    of Otranto* 91, 98, 104; *Description of
    Strawberry-Hill* 101; *Hieroglyphic
    Tales* 91; *The Mysterious Mother* 7,
    91–104; *Nature Will Prevail* 91–2;
    *Postscript to the Royal and Noble
    Authors* 91
Walpole, Sir Robert 17, 71–5, 82–4,
    86–7
Walsh, Jill Paton 236; *Babylon* 237
Walsingham, Sir Thomas 28
Warren, Dorothy 212
Weaver, Harriet Shaw 250–1, 253
Webb, Beatrice 186–7, 189–90
Webb, Sydney 186–7, 189–91, 194,
    197–8
Webster, Richard 9–10
Wells, H. G. 137, 187, 194–5, 202, 207;
    History of the World 207
Westall, Robert 238; *The Machine
    Gunners* 238–9
Wharton, Thomas, Earl of 67
Whitehouse, Mary 7, 10, 19
Whitgift, John, Archbishop 24

Widdowson, Peter 172
Wilberforce, William 145
Wilde, Oscar 18, 20, 243, 251–5;
    'Phrases and Philosophies for the
    Use of the Young' 253; *The Picture
    of Dorian Gray* 254; *Salome* 18
Wilkes, John 17, 119n; *North Briton* 17
Wilkinson, Ellen 210
William III 141
Williams, Gwyn 113
Williams, Thomas 144
Williams Report (1979) 245
Willis, Thomas 41
Wittenberg, Judith 179
Woodfall, Henry 99
Wolfe, John 28–9
Woolf, Leonard 191
Woolsey, John 245
World Council of Churches (WCC)
    235
Wright, Peter 20; *Spycatcher* 7, 20
Writers and Readers Publishing
    Cooperative 235; *Sexism in
    Children's Books* 235
Wyatt, Sir Thomas 26–7
Wycherley, William 46
Wyndham, William 69

Yates, Jessica, 233, 238
Yates, Mary Ann 93

Zola, Emile 15, 18, 144, 150, 155